D1523084

Burning for the Buddha

STUDIES IN EAST ASIAN BUDDHISM 19

Burning for the Buddha

SELF-IMMOLATION IN CHINESE BUDDHISM

James A. Benn

A KURODA INSTITUTE BOOK
University of Hawai'i Press
Honolulu

Library of Congress Cataloging-in-Publication Data

Benn, James A.
Burning for the Buddha : self-immolation in Chinese Buddhism
/ James A. Benn.
p. cm. — (Kuroda Institute studies in East Asian Buddhism ; 19)
"A Kuroda Institute book"
Includes bibliographical references and index.
ISBN 978-0-8248-2992-6 (hardcover : alk. paper)
1. Self-immolation—Religious aspects—Buddhism. 2. Self-immolation—China. 3.
Buddhism—China—Customs and practices. I. Title.
BQ5680.S45B46 2007
294.3'43420951—dc22
                                        2006035361

The Kuroda Institute for the Study of Buddhism and Human Values is a nonprofit,
educational corporation founded in 1976. One of its primary objectives is to
promote scholarship on the historical, philosophical, and cultural ramifications
of Buddhism. In association with the University of Hawai'i Press, the Institute
also publishes Classics in East Asian Buddhism, a series devoted to the
translation of significant texts in the East Asian Buddhist tradition.

Designed by University of Hawai'i Press production staff

Printed by The Maple-Vail Book Manufacturing Group

For Pema

Sedulo curavi humanas actiones non ridere non lugere neque detestari, sed intelligere.
—BARUCH SPINOZA (1632–1677)

Contents

Acknowledgments

To acknowledge fully the debt I owe to friends and colleagues who have helped me along the way would be to risk turning what is already a hefty tome into a multivolume work. For now, I can only offer these few lines.

None of my work would have been possible without the foundation (knowing what and how to read) and inspiration (knowing what and how to write) provided by my great teacher, T. H. Barrett. I really hope he likes this book.

I should like to thank the members of my doctoral committee at the University of California, Los Angeles (Robert Buswell, William Bodiford, Benjamin Elman, David Schaberg, and Richard von Glahn), for their careful reading of my dissertation (on which this work is based) and for their many suggestions for its improvement. I am particularly grateful to my adviser, Robert Buswell, for his encouragement and support over the last ten years. I may not have always taken his advice, but I have always appreciated having it.

The story of how Chen Jinhua and I met at the Italian School of East Asian Studies in Kyoto is well documented in the opening pages of both my dissertation and his book on Tanqian and need not be repeated here. For the last six years he has been my closest and most critical reader, my most trusted guide through the textual labyrinth of medieval China, and, above all, my friend. He has read drafts of this book not just once but several times, has offered sage advice, and has shared his own research with me in the most selfless manner. His enthusiasm and high standards of scholarship forced me to write a much better book than I could have managed otherwise.

The time I spent in Kyoto was particularly crucial for my research, and I look back with fondness on those days and on my friends and colleagues there (Hubert Durt, the late Antonino Forte, Aramaki Noritoshi, Robert Duquenne, Catherine Ludvik, Shayne Clarke). Although I did not meet him in Kyoto, Chen Jinhua put me in touch with Funayama Tōru of the Institute for Research in Humanities at Kyoto University, who generously shared with me his then-unpublished article on self-immolation, and whom I later had the pleasure of meeting in person at the University of British Columbia.

I benefited greatly from the wisdom of those who read my manuscript with an experienced eye. Koichi Shinohara, Robert Campany, John Strong, and two anonymous readers for the Kuroda Institute offered indispensable advice and encouraged me to think and write with greater clarity. I should like to thank everyone who invited me to give talks and conference presentations on self-immolation and related matters over the last few years. I am most grateful for those opportunities to share and test my ideas.

Although I cannot name them all here, I should like to thank my students at Lewis and Clark College and Arizona State University, especially participants in seminars relating to the topic of "Religion and the Body." They raised questions and problems that would otherwise never have occurred to me. I'm not sure whether Stuart Young is my student in any formal sense, but he has certainly been one of my most insightful readers and has offered many useful suggestions.

I have been the fortunate recipient of the kindness and wisdom of Raoul Birnbaum, who has always urged me to think harder about the nature of Buddhist practice in China and to never lose sight of the human element. I am particularly grateful to the following people for their assistance and advice: Robert Sharf, Buzzy Teiser, Eugene Wang, James Robson, John Kieschnick, Gregory Schopen, and Daniel Stevenson. I also spent many happy hours discussing the ins and outs of Buddhist studies with my comrades-in-arms George Keyworth and Rick McBride. If there are any good ideas in this book, they undoubtedly have their origin in the minds of others—all I can claim are the errors and omissions.

The Faculty of Social Sciences at McMaster University provided generous financial support for this publication. I should like to thank Peter N. Gregory of the Kuroda Institute and Patricia Crosby, Ann Ludeman, and Stephanie Chun of the University of Hawai'i Press for taking this book seriously.

Ever since we met, my wife, Emi, has had to share me with a host of dead monks. I'm sure she looks forward to waving them goodbye. I thank her for her patience, and so much else.

Abbreviations and Conventions

DZ	*Daozang* [*Zhengtong daozang* 正統道藏, 1445]. Includes the *Wanli xu daozang* 萬曆續道藏, 1607.
GSZ	*Gaoseng zhuan* 高僧傳 (Biographies of Eminent Monks). T 50.2059.
SGSZ	*Song gaoseng zhuan* 宋高僧傳 (Biographies of Eminent Monks Compiled under the Song). T 50.2061.
T	*Taishō shinshū daizōkyō* 大正新脩大藏經.
XGSZ	*Xu gaoseng zhuan* 續高僧傳 (Continued Biographies of Eminent Monks). T 50.2060.
XZJ	*Xuzang jing* 續藏經 (Continued [Buddhist] Canon).

Full citations from the *Taishō* canon include title and fascicle number (where relevant); T; *Taishō* volume number; text number; page, register (a, b, or c), and line number: for example, *Pusa dichi jing* 菩薩地持經 (**Bodhi-sattvabhūmisūtra*), T 30.1581.916b1–11. Citations from the *Xuzang jing* and the *Dazang jing bubian* give references to volume, page, and register. Citations from the *Daozang* provide references to fascicle, page, and register and follow the sequential numbers given in K. M. Schipper, *Concordance du Tao-tsang: Titres des ouvrages,* Publications de l'École Française d'Extrême-Orient, vol. 102 (Paris: École Française d'Extrême-Orient, 1975).

Introduction

For a few weeks in late December 526 and early January 527, a monastery on Mount Ruona 若那山 in Eastern Yangzhou 東楊州 played host to a series of remarkable and anomalous events.[1] The monastery and its environs echoed with mysterious sounds and were bathed in multicolored rays of light. Crowds of pilgrims in unprecedented numbers were drawn to the mountain, where they enthusiastically participated in ceremonies affirming their commitment to the Buddhist path. Flocks of birds were observed behaving in an unusual yet portentous manner. At the center of this web of activity that extended into both the natural realm and human society was the death of a single monk.

The events began on the third day of the eleventh lunar month of the seventh year of the Putong 普通 reign period (December 22, 526) when the monastery bell started ringing of its own accord. Five days later it rang again. On the twenty-third day (January 11, 527) a monk by the name of Daodu 道度 (462–527) invited a hundred of his fellows to his nearby mountain retreat to join him in religious practices. More than 300 people, both monks and laity, answered the call and 170 formally marked their affiliation to Mahāyāna Buddhism by receiving from him the bodhisattva precepts.

Having made these conversions and thereby formed karmic connections with those he would leave behind him, Daodu ceased eating. Each day he drank no more than a pint of water that he drew from the well with a bucket that was normally reserved for the monks' bathing water. On the morning of January 13th, Daodu's fellow monks were astonished to discover five-colored rays of light and multicolored vapor emanating from this humble vessel. Four days later the abbot and several other monks entered Daodu's meditation chamber and found a purple glow radiating from a niche within it. Towards evening on the same day, January 17th, a vast flock of birds, some five or six hundred strong, suddenly descended on the monastery. The birds perched together on a single tree before simultaneously taking off and flying together towards the west.

In the early hours of that night the whole monastery complex was illuminated by vivid displays of light that lit up the buildings for several hours.

Around midnight, from the summit of the mountain came the sound of a stone chime being struck and someone reciting verses on impermanence. The monks heard the crackling sound of wood starting to burn. Scrambling up the mountain to investigate, they discovered their comrade Daodu seated calmly with his palms together facing the west. His whole body was engulfed in flames.

Some time later, the local governor, the prince of Wuling 武陵王, ordered what remained of Daodu's incinerated body to be gathered up, cleaned, and interred beneath a pagoda.[2] By taking such extraordinary care with the remains, the prince was honoring Daodu with a funeral appropriate for an eminent monk. (Most ordinary monks in medieval China probably had their remains disposed of rather unceremoniously in unmarked graves.)[3] Even after Daodu's death, anomalies continued to be reported in the area. The clear and penetrating sound of a stone chime was frequently heard on the mountain. A large, old withered tree under which Daodu had practiced meditation suddenly flourished again, although it had been dead for ten years.

So much we can glean from Daodu's epitaph and the accounts of his life and death that appear in medieval Chinese sources, but can we say what *really* happened on Mount Ruona fifteen hundred years ago? Given the fact that our materials were composed by medieval authors with a strong interest and belief in the miraculous, it would now be impossible to discover any meaningful "objective" viewpoint or to reconstruct events in a way that could satisfy the sensibilities of the twenty-first-century reader. We can, however, try to understand the ways in which Daodu's contemporaries and later medieval Buddhists thought about what had happened, and how they made sense of these events. Daodu's death certainly did make sense to those who wrote and read about it: This was not the random act of a disturbed individual, but rather a single manifestation of a deeply rooted set of ideas and ideals in Chinese Buddhism that blossomed again and again in the history of premodern China.

Let us begin by pulling back the focus from Daodu's last days and contemplating his life as a whole to appreciate his standing in medieval society. Although he is not known now, in his own day Daodu was by no means an obscure monk; he was a religious figure of distinguished lineage who maintained connections with the royal family of the Liang 梁 dynasty (502–556), a pro-Buddhist polity that ruled most of South China for the first half of the sixth century. Daodu's death at the age of sixty-six is presented in our sources not as a spontaneous act of folly but the culmination of a lifetime of practice. In these narratives his fiery exit from the world is marked as a moment of cosmic significance accompanied by a plethora of auspicious signs that cast the monastery and the mountain as numinous sites. Daodu's persona, or his cha-

risma, did not go up in flames with his flesh but continued after his cremation to be remembered and celebrated by both monks and laity.

The most detailed source that survives for Daodu's life is his funerary inscription, composed by (or at least in the name of) Xiao Gang 蕭綱 (503–
551), the Liang prince who became the emperor Jianwendi 簡文帝 (r. 549–
551). We are very fortunate to have this text—as we shall see, although many
self-immolators had such epitaphs composed for them, very few inscriptions
have survived. This rare document begins, as biographies of monks usually
do, with the native place and surname of its subject: Daodu was a native of
Pingyang平陽, and before he became a monk his surname was Liu 劉.[4] He was
credited with a famous ancestor in the shape of Liu Bo 劉勃 (d. 143 BCE),
Prince Jibei 濟北王 of the Han 漢 dynasty (202 BCE–220 CE).[5] Both Daodu's
grandfather and father had served under the Northern Wei 北魏 dynasty
(386–534), a non-Chinese and largely pro-Buddhist regime that ruled North
China for a century and a half. Daodu became a monk at twenty *sui* 歲 (in
481) and was trained at the monastery Fawang si 法王寺 under the meditation master Bhadra (Fotuo 佛陀, d.u.).[6] Daodu acquired a reputation for pur-
suing his vocation with constant and demanding practice as well as for
choosing to dwell high in the mountains. He first arrived in the state of Liang
in 502 and stayed close to the capital at Dinglin si 定林寺 on Zhong shan 鐘山,
where he practiced *dhyāna* (meditation).[7] It was at this monastery that he first
forged links with the imperial house: The emperor Liang Wudi's 梁武帝 (r.
502–549) stepbrother, Prince Anchengkang 安成康王, became his disciple.[8]

The inscription suggests that Daodu drew his inspiration for burning
himself to death from the *Lotus Sūtra*, a major Mahāyāna scripture that contains (among other celebrated and influential stories) the most famous literary example of a living cremation, that of the Bodhisattva Medicine King
(Yao Wang 藥王; Skt. Bhaiṣajyagururāja). Daodu first aspired to become a
monk because of this scripture and in 518 he copied out the lengthy *sūtra*
one hundred times.[9] Such concentrated and painstaking acts of physical devotion to the *Lotus* were by no means uncommon in medieval China; they
indicate how strenuously Chinese Buddhists tried to enact and make real
what they imagined to be the world of that particular scripture.

Daodu's dedication to his practice won the respect of Liang Wudi himself.
On January 11, 526, he was granted a personal audience with the emperor in
the palace chapel, where he explained what he planned to do and why:[10]

"The body is like a poisonous plant; it would really be right to burn it and
extinguish its life. I have been weary of this physical frame for many a long
day. I vow to worship the buddhas, just like Xijian 喜見 (Seen with Joy)."[11]

Although at first glance his statement may appear so allusive as to be almost completely opaque, Daodu was in fact making explicit reference to the *Lotus Sūtra*'s Bodhisattva Medicine King, who was known as "Seen with Joy by Sentient Beings" when he set fire to his own body as an act of homage to the buddhas. But Liang Wudi, who must have caught the allusion and understood all too well what Daodu intended to do, disapproved:

> If you really desire to create merit for beings, you ought to follow conditions in order to cultivate the Way. When your body and life become impermanent, then you should have your corpse cast into the forest. By donating it to the birds and beasts one completely perfects *dānapāramitā* and also makes good *karma*. Because of the eighty thousand worms it is not appropriate to burn yourself. It is not something to be encouraged.[12]

In other words, Wudi was offering Daodu an alternative mode in which to employ his body as an offering. Rather than burn oneself alive, would it not be better to donate one's dead body to sentient beings?

Before we analyze the content of this dialogue between eminent monk and pious emperor, it is worth pondering the nature of the exchange itself, which can be seen to function on a number of levels. First, it seems to echo a trope found in the Indian Buddhist literature particularly concerned with heroic self-sacrifice, or the "gift of the body." As Reiko Ohnuma's analysis of this literature has shown, there are many tales in which the bodhisattva announces his intention to make a gift *(dāna)* of his body or parts of it.[13] The selflessly generous bodhisattva is often opposed by someone who attempts to persuade him not to offer himself.[14] Ohnuma identifies four classes of people in particular who oppose the gift of the body, the first of which are the officials and ministers, whom she sees as representing worldly political interests.[15] In the Indian tales the bodhisattva does not surrender to such forces but selflessly and dramatically offers his own body for the benefit of beings. This particular tension between the worldly and the nonworldly could not be rendered in quite the same way in Chinese accounts of self-sacrifice. The bodhisattvas who made gifts of their bodies in the Indian literature were usually represented as kings rather than renunciant monastics, and thus they were possessed of temporal as well as spiritual power in a way that Chinese monks were not.

Second, the exchange between Wudi and Daodu provides a succinct example of a doctrinal problem in Chinese Buddhism that often came to the surface in the history of self-immolation. This problem was sometimes made explicit in the form of the question of whether or not self-immolation was an appropriate practice for monks in particular as opposed to laypeople. Daodu presented his intended auto-cremation in terms of an explicit imitation of a scriptural model—that of the Bodhisattva Medicine King, a lay bodhisattva whose fiery offering of his own body is extolled at length in the *Lotus Sūtra*. As we shall see, this model, located as it is in one of the most important scriptures of East Asian Buddhism, provided inspiration, justification, and a template for many self-immolators.

Liang Wudi denied Daodu permission to burn himself for two specific reasons: (1) it would be better for Daodu to make a gift of his body after dying a natural death than by killing himself, and (2) by burning his body he would actually harm the parasites ("eighty thousand worms") that live in it. The first reason is perhaps somewhat specific to Daodu's time and place and requires some explanation. It reflects a mortuary practice popular among early medieval Chinese Buddhists that consisted of exposing the corpse for wild animals to eat rather than burying or cremating it.[16] Wudi's second reason—that cremation of the living body necessarily entails the murder of many miniscule beings—was drawn from the codes that regulate the practice of monks *(Vinayas)*.[17] In other words, Wudi's objections to self-immolation are perhaps not what we might expect of an emperor. They were not grounded in secular authority or Confucian morality but rather were drawn from popular Buddhist practice and monastic regulations—aspects of religious life in which Wudi apparently took a strong interest.

In front of some of his subjects Liang Wudi may sometimes have played the role of a humble disciple of the Buddha, but he was still an emperor. In the encounter related above it is not difficult to detect an undercurrent of the tension between religious and secular authority.[18] In a hierarchical and structured society like that of medieval China, there was little acknowledgment that people were free to do as they chose with their own lives, and monks who made offerings of their bodies always posed a potential danger to state control. Quite apart from the fact that the state could hardly be seen to condone or encourage suicide, there was the danger that a heroic monk could become the center of a cult that might threaten political stability or at least draw attention and support away from the emperor.

As we know, Daodu disobeyed Liang Wudi's edict and burned himself, although his *lèse-majesté* does not seem to have posed a problem for the prince of Wuling and Xiao Gang, nor for the officials who supervised the interment of his relics and the composition of his funerary inscription. It seems that relations between state and *saṃgha* were by no means clear-cut in medieval times, and both sides often had to adapt to rapidly changing situations as they negotiated a balance of power that was often precarious.

But the tensions and accommodations of the relationship between the *saṃgha* and the state or between a monk and his ruler are not the only themes that can be drawn from this account. We can also discern some inconsistencies and fragments of evidence that offer tantalizing glimpses of the religious landscape of medieval China, and we shall pursue them at length in this study. For example, Daodu pointed to a glorious scriptural precedent for his act, but apparently he chose to burn himself in secret. Also, his self-immolation was the cause of miracles that appeared before, during, and after his final act. There is even some evidence that suggests a postmortem cult to Daodu: His relics were enshrined, the sound of his chime was heard on the mountain, and a dead tree was restored to life. Finally, Daodu had close links with the royal family that endured even after he apparently disobeyed an imperial edict.

In the *Lotus Sūtra,* the text to which Daodu was so devoted, and in which we must imagine he was thoroughly immersed after having copied it out so many times, the Medicine King burns his body not in secret on a mountain but as a public act of devotion to the buddhas. As we shall see, auto-cremation in China could often take the form of a well-advertised performance, ritually staged in front of an emotional audience. The fact that Daodu and others resorted to more furtive ways of offering their bodies suggests that self-immolators were sometimes faced with active opposition to their plans.

Self-Immolation and Sympathetic Resonance

The lack of interest in the moment of death (or transformation) especially in contrast to the attention devoted to recording auspicious signs in Daodu's epitaph and many other accounts of auto-cremation alerts us to a fundamental assumption about the nature and efficacy of self-immolation. Although we do not find this assumption clearly articulated in Daodu's biographies, it seems that self-immolation was understood to operate according to the mechanism of "stimulus-response" or "sympathetic resonance" (*ganying* 感應), a paradigm that was all-pervasive in every aspect of medieval thought.[19] As Robert Sharf writes, "The notion of sympathetic resonance is deceptively simple: objects belonging to the same class resonate with each other just as do two identically tuned strings on a pair of zithers."[20] The miracles that occurred before, after, and during Daodu's auto-cremation indicated that his actions were stimulating (*gan*) a response (*ying*) from the cosmos, thus proving that his auto-cremation was efficacious and hence "right." Self-immolation, far from being a disrupting force, was an act that was supremely in harmony with the universe in which medieval people lived.

As we shall see, the paradigm of *ganying* offers us a way to make sense of many of the cases of self-immolation we shall examine. But to apply this model we need to bear in mind that *ganying* can operate at several levels simultaneously. First, within human society, interactions between inferior and superior (typically between rulers and their subjects) are predicated on the rulers responding to the needs of the people. This aspect of *ganying* may help us understand why members of the royal family treated Daodu with such reverence in death: They could not afford to ignore or disparage the sincerity of his actions, lest they be seen to violate the cosmic and human order.

Second, *ganying* determines the relationship between the realm of humans (*ren* 人) and heaven (*tian* 天): It is understood that human actions and emotions can and do cause cosmic response and transformation. Acts that are the most sincere because they are selfless (for example, self-immolation) will cause the cosmos to respond in accordance with the petitioner's intention. We shall see many examples of this in accounts of self-immolators who burned themselves to bring rain or to end famine or other human disasters.

Third, the relationship between beings and the Buddha was conceived of in China as one determined by *ganying*. Chinese Buddhists found in Mahāyāna *sūtra*s such as the *Lotus* the idea that buddhas and bodhisattvas were capable of assuming different forms and manifesting among humans in response to their needs. In the material that we shall examine there are frequent hints, and sometimes overt declarations, that self-immolators were in fact advanced bodhisattvas who had manifested to teach the *dharma* in a way appropriate to the age. But also, self-immolation offered a way of becoming a buddha—a response to the stimulus of the selfless offering that was promised in the *Lotus* and other Mahāyāna texts.

A History of Self-Immolation

The story of Daodu is but a part of a longer history of the ideals and practices of "abandoning the body" that weaves its way through the Chinese Buddhist tradition from the late fourth century to the early years of the twentieth century. For that period of some sixteen hundred years, we have accounts of several hundred monks, nuns, and laypeople who made offerings of their bodies for a variety of reasons, and in different ways. They represent the full spectrum of the *saṃgha* in China. Chan masters, distinguished exegetes, proselytizers, wonder workers, and ascetics as well as otherwise undistinguished or unknown monastics and laypeople all participated in the practice. The deeds of self-immolators were usually witnessed by large audiences; government officials and sometimes even emperors themselves attended the final moments, interred the sacred remains, and composed eulogies that extolled their acts. The act of burning the body in particular was frequently a dramatically staged spectacle, and its performance and remembrance took a strong hold on the Chinese Buddhist imagination.

Examining the representations of self-immolators, their motivations, and the literary crafting of their stories will help us better to understand the larger issue of the role of the body in Buddhism. We shall discover that self-immolation, rather than being an aberrant practice that must be explained away, actually offers a bodily (or somatic) path—a way to attain awakening and, ultimately, buddhahood. This path looks rather different from those soteriologies that stress practices of the mind (such as meditation and learning), which have probably received the most attention from Western scholars in Buddhist studies. Nonetheless, as we shall see, it was a path to deliverance that was considered valid by many Chinese Buddhists.

The remarkable history of self-immolation in Chinese Buddhism is a subject that has not received a great deal of sustained scholarly attention. Although it was touched upon in surveys of topics such as "suicide" by the founding fathers of Buddhist studies, to date, only three short studies have appeared in Western languages: those of Jacques Gernet and Jan Yün-hua published in the early 1960s and more recently my own article.[21] The pioneering works of Jan and Gernet are rather narrowly focused in terms of the primary material upon which they draw, and both are now somewhat out of date given the advances made in the study of Chinese Buddhism in the last forty or so years. My own article is specifically concerned with the role of apocryphal *sūtra*s in auto-cremation and other body-burning practices. Prior to the recent appearance of a detailed article on self-immolation in the early medieval period by Funayama Tōru, Japanese studies tended to be brief and narrowly focused.[22] Chinese scholars began to show an interest in self-immolation only from the late 1990s.[23]

The Terminology of Self-Immolation

"Self-immolation" is the term most often used by scholars for the range of practices we are interested in, but it may be worth paying some attention to the meaning of the word. In its strictest sense, it means "self-sacrifice" and is derived from the Latin *molare,* "to make a sacrifice of grain." It does not mean suicide by fire, although the term is now commonly used in that sense.[24] With these usages in mind, I shall employ the term "auto-cremation" to refer to the practice of burning one's own body, and "self-immolation" for the broader range of practices that we shall discuss, such as drowning, death by starvation, feeding the body to animals or insects, and so forth.

Three Chinese terms are commonly encountered in our sources, and they are used more or less interchangeably: *wangshen* 亡身, meaning "to lose or abandon the body" or perhaps "to be oblivious (*wang* 忘) to the body"; *yishen* 遺身, meaning "to let go of, abandon, or be oblivious to the body"; and *sheshen* 捨身, "to relinquish or abandon the body." Here the word *shen* (body) also implies "self," or the person as a whole. These binomes are also used to translate terms found in Indian Buddhist sources such as *ātmabhāva-parityāga*, *ātma-parityāga* (abandoning the self), and *svadeha-parityāga* (abandoning one's own body).[25] Thus, at least at the doctrinal level, self-immolation may be considered a particular expression of the more generalized Buddhist ideal of being detached from the deluded notion of a self. Auto-cremation is usually marked with expressions such as *shaoshen* 燒身 (burning the body) and *zifen* 自焚 (self-burning), but these terms are deployed for the most part descriptively rather than conceptually. That is to say, in our sources auto-cremation is treated as a way of abandoning the self but is not usually discussed as a separate mode of practice or as an ideal in its own right.

To understand how the somatic path of self-immolation was conceived and enacted we shall be obliged to take seriously a great deal of material that has largely been untouched by scholarship. To make sense of how acts of self-immolation were intended and how they were remembered, we shall examine them first in the context of medieval Chinese society and religion and then against the background of the later development of Buddhism in China.

Abandoning the body, or letting go of the self, took a variety of forms in Chinese history and not all of them involved death or self-mutilation.[26] For example, in Buddhist and Taoist texts and inscriptions, *sheshen* was paired with the term *shoushen* 受身 (to receive a body) to indicate what happened at the end of one lifetime in the endless round of *saṃsāra*—as one relinquishes one body, one obtains another.[27] *Sheshen* can also stand as an equivalent for the common Buddhist term *chujia* 出家, literally, "to leave the household," which means to become a monk or a nun. In a more extreme case, the pious emperor Liang Wudi actually gave himself as a slave to the *saṃgha* on a number of occasions and his ministers were obliged to pay a hefty ransom to buy him back.[28] This kind of offering of the body, which was not uncommon, was also referred to as *sheshen*.

But "abandoning the body" also covers a broad range of more extreme acts (not all of which necessarily result in death): feeding one's body to insects; slicing off one's flesh; burning one's fingers or arms; burning incense on the skin; starving, slicing, or drowning oneself; leaping from cliffs or trees; feeding one's body to wild animals; self-mummification (preparing for death so that the resulting corpse is impervious to decay); and of course auto-cremation. Thus, although the title of this book is "Burning for the Buddha," it is a study not just of auto-cremation, but of a broader mode of religious practice that involved doing things to or with the body. As we shall see this mode was by no means static; it was constantly being shaped and reformulated by practitioners and those who told their stories. At times auto-cremation was cast as the dominant form of self-immolation, at other times it receded into the background.

Self-Immolation in China

The fluid nature of the concept of self-immolation was partly a historical accident: It was not consistently defined or explained in canonical sources available to medieval Chinese Buddhists. It was also a consequence of the ways in which Chinese Buddhist authors composed their works. Of the three types of historical actors we shall consider in this study—practitioners, biographers, and compilers of exemplary biographies—the compilers were the most important in the invention of self-immolation as a Chinese monastic practice. By grouping biographies of exemplary individuals under the rubric of self-immolation, they created the appearance of unity from a diversity of practices, but in their reflections on the category they were often reluctant to draw precise boundaries around the tradition they had created. The difficulties of determining what actions constituted self-immolation, what mental attitude was required, and what purpose self-immolation served are not just ones that we face as scholars now; they also plagued Buddhist authors who were much more closely involved with self-immolators.

Two related questions will recur throughout our inquiry. First, why did these compilers group together the biographies that they did? Second, how did they justify the transmission of biographies of self-immolators as records of eminent monks (that is to say, models of monastic behavior) if the monastic regulations condemned suicide? There is no simple or single answer to such questions. Buddhist authors always struggled with these problems and were often preoccupied with other concerns that shaped their view of exemplary practice. The attitude of the state towards the *saṃgha* as a whole or towards certain types of practice; orthodoxy as presented in scriptural materials; orthopraxy as reported by Chinese pilgrims to India: These and other factors colored the views of those who wrote about self-immolators.

In the following chapters I aim to give a historical account of the complex construct of self-immolation by examining both text and practice in some detail. By reintegrating a better understanding of self-immolation into our larger conception of Buddhist practices in China, we may allow a fuller picture to emerge of the Buddhist tradition as a whole. By looking in detail at some specific cases of how the body was used in Chinese Buddhism, we may gain an appreciation of the broader range of possibilities for the body in religion.

Of all the forms of self-immolation, auto-cremation in particular seems to have been a primarily Sinitic Buddhist creation that first appeared in late fourth-century China. Although there seem to have been some Indian practitioners who burned their bodies, Buddhist auto-cremation became a distinct mode of practice in China, as evidenced by the acts of particular monks and nuns recorded and celebrated in Chinese hagiography.[29] Rather than being a continuation or adaptation of an Indian practice, as far as we can tell, it was constructed on Chinese soil and drew on a range of ideas, such as a particular interpretation of an Indian text (the *Saddharmapuṇḍarīka*, or *Lotus Sūtra*) and indigenous traditions, such as burning the body to bring rain, a practice that long predated the arrival of Buddhism in China.[30] The practice of auto-cremation was reinforced, vindicated, and embellished by the production of Chinese apocryphal *sūtras*, by the composition of biographies of auto-cremators, and by the inclusion of these texts in the Buddhist canon as exemplars of heroic practice. As time went on, more biographies were composed and collected. The increasing number and variety of precedents provided further legitimation for the practice. Although acts of extreme asceticism by non-Buddhist practitioners are well attested in Indian Buddhist sources and visible in contemporary Indian religious life, in China auto-cremation became a mode of practice that was accessible to Buddhists of all kinds.[31]

Self-immolation can thus be considered part of the larger process of the Sinification of Buddhism. In recent years the doctrinal side of this process has been explored at some length and is now better understood and appreciated.[32] A study of self-immolation affords us an opportunity to examine not just the ways in which elite monks made sense of the complex soteriologies they found in Buddhist literature, but also some of the modes in which Buddhist ideas and ideals were put into practice. In the following chapters we shall encounter a wide variety of bodily practices as performed in life and death by Chinese Buddhists, and we shall attempt to understand how and why these men and women aspired to embed and enact the teaching of the Buddha in China with their bodies. It will become apparent that their somatic devotions were not aberrant, heterodox, or anomalous, but part of a serious attempt to make bodhisattvas on Chinese soil.

What can a study of self-immolation tell us about the greater shape of Buddhism in premodern China? More than twenty years ago Erik Zürcher made some important remarks about the state of the field, which he cast in the form of three paradoxes:

First, that our view of Chinese Buddhism as a historical phenomenon is greatly *obscured* by the abundance of our source materials. Second, that if we want to define what was the normal state of medieval Chinese Buddhism, we should concentrate on what seems to be *abnormal*. Third, if we want to complete our picture of what this Buddhism really was, we have to look outside Chinese Buddhism itself.[33]

I have tried to keep Zürcher's advice in mind throughout this study. By concentrating on the practice of self-immolation we may cut through much of the mass of material produced by Buddhists that obscures our view of the overall shape of the religion. Self-immolation as an apparently "abnormal" practice throws into relief the normal (or normative) state of Chinese Buddhism. Finally, to understand the political and social contexts of self-immolation in this study, I have striven to include official historiographical sources as well as Buddhist materials.

Self-immolation resists a single simple explanation or interpretation. Cases of self-immolation were not simply recorded and filed away but continued to inspire and inform readers and listeners. Monks and nuns, emperors and officials, thought about the practice in different ways at different times. On the whole Buddhists tended to support their co-religionists who used their bodies as instruments of devotion, whereas the literati (at least in public) often regarded such acts with disdain or disapproval. But conversely, we shall see many literati who participated in the cults of self-immolators, and some Buddhist monks who were bitterly opposed to the practice. Self-immolation brought out tensions within the religion—and in society at large. Each case, in a sense, had to be negotiated separately, and there were clearly regional variations. The cults of self-immolators were both local—celebrated in particular places by shrines, *stūpas*, images, and steles—and made universal through accounts in collections of monastic biographies and in more popular works that celebrated acts of devotion to particular texts such as the *Lotus Sūtra*. Thus a study of self-immolation requires us to contemplate Buddhism in China from multiple perspectives.

Sources

Much of the material studied here is preserved in collections of the genre known as *Gaoseng zhuan* 高僧傳 (Biographies of Eminent Monks). Biographies of self-immolators in these collections were, for the most part, based on the funerary inscriptions composed for their subjects rather than on sources such as miracle tales and anecdotes. Some of these funerary inscriptions are preserved in other collections or in the form of the actual stelae, although in most cases this type of material evidence is sadly lost. Biographies of eminent monks, especially in the first *Gaoseng zhuan* collection, were largely based on epitaphs written by prominent men of letters (usually aristocrats in the medieval period) and so, not unnaturally, they stress the monks' contacts with the court.[34] Thus it is difficult to recover data on the everyday practice of ordinary people in medieval China; unfortunately most of our sources remain silent on such matters. This study, then, does not pretend to offer an account of "popular" Buddhist practice (however we wish to define that term); for the most part, its focus is on members of the monastic elite such as Daodu.

The scholarship to date on self-immolation has concentrated largely on materials contained within one early twentieth-century Japanese edition of the Buddhist canon with some occasional references to supporting evidence drawn from the mass of data preserved in Chinese secular sources.[35] This particular edition of the Chinese canon does, of course, contain much useful data that can be employed to reconstruct the history of Buddhist practice in China, but the texts chosen by the *Taishō* editors may give a somewhat lopsided picture of Chinese Buddhist history as seen from the perspective of the later Japanese sects. The immediate problem lies in the fact that the biographies of self-immolators in the *Taishō* canon are only collected in an easily accessible form for roughly the years 350 to 988. In particular, the absence of a specific category for self-immolators in the *Da Ming gaoseng zhuan* 大明高僧傳 (Great Ming Biographies of Eminent Monks, compiled by Ruxing 如惺 [fl. 1617], T 50.2062), such as is found in the first three *Gaoseng zhuan,* has led to the mistaken impression that self-immolation either occurred less frequently from the tenth century onward or that it was less frequently recorded in Buddhist sources.[36] In fact, when we consult materials in other editions of the Chinese canon, it is immediately evident that self-immolation continued to be practiced and recorded well beyond the end of the Five Dynasties 五代 (907–960) through the Song 宋 (960–1279), Yuan 元 (1279–1368), Ming 明 (1368–1644), and Qing 清 (1644–1912). Self-immolation was not just a medieval form of piety that was supplanted by other forms of devotion; it has remained significant until today. Although auto-cremation in China is now very rare, monks and laypeople continue to make offerings by burning their fingers in both China and Korea.[37]

No matter how diligent we are in gathering materials, we cannot assume that self-immolation lies waiting to be uncovered in these "primary sources"; rather, it was their compilers who created and perpetuated self-immolation as an object of knowledge when they placed the biographies of various individuals under that rubric. For example, the same biography could be assigned to different categories in different collections, as is the case with Jing'ai 靜藹 (534–575), who is classified as a self-immolator in the *Fayuan zhulin* 法苑珠林 (A Grove of Pearls in a Dharma Garden, compiled by Daoshi 道世 [596?–683], preface dated 668), but as a protector of the dharma (*hufa* 護法) in Daoxuan's 道宣 (596–667) *Xu gaoseng zhuan* 續高僧傳 (Continued Biographies of Eminent Monks).[38] These collections themselves do not claim to be exhaustive, and it is not hard to find brief notices of other self-immolators who are not accorded biographies in the *Gaoseng zhuan* collections.[39]

As we shall see, self-immolation remains a somewhat elastic category that is usually not very well articulated in the individual biographies of self-immolators. The compilers of biographical collections also took rather a circumspect approach to the topic in the critical evaluations (*lun* 論) in which they discussed the practice. Therefore, rather than beginning with any a priori assumption of what self-immolation is and picking out textual material that confirms this assumption, we ought to allow the contours of the practice to emerge from the material. What follows then may be regarded as a kind of textual ethnography that is sensitive to setting, time, place, and detail. Any attempt at defining the meaning (or meanings) of self-immolation must be contingent on a thorough investigation of what at first appears to be a mass of incidental detail.

Self-Immolation in the Literature of the Mahāyāna

Biographers often represented individual acts of self-immolation like that of Daodu as if they were predicated on a literal reading of certain texts, particularly *jātaka* tales (accounts of the former lives and deeds of Śākyamuni) and the *Lotus Sūtra*. But, one might ask, how else should Chinese of the early medieval period have taken these heroic tales, other than literally? In the Mahāyāna literature especially, the Chinese were presented with the blueprints for making bodhisattvas, and those blueprints said repeatedly and explicitly that such acts of extreme generosity were a necessary part of the process. For example, one of the most influential Mahāyāna texts known to the medieval Chinese, the *Da zhidu lun* 大智度論 (Great Perfection of Wisdom Treatise), which was attributed to the great Indian thinker Nāgārjuna (ca. 150–250 CE), says:

> What is to be understood by the fulfilment of the perfection of generosity appertaining to the body which is born from the bonds and *karma*? Without gaining the *dharmakāya* (dharma body) and without destroying the fetters

the bodhisattva is able to give away without reservation all his precious possessions, his head, his eyes, his marrow, his skin, his kingdom, his wealth, his wife, his children and his possessions both inner and outer; all this without experiencing any emotions.[40]

In other words, according to a text that was often referred to by medieval Chinese Buddhists, the bodhisattva has to surrender dispassionately his own body and even his loved ones long before he reaches awakening (gaining the *dharmakāya*). The text continues by recounting the stories of Prince Viśvantara, who famously gave away his wife and children; King Sarvada, who lost his kingdom to a usurper and then surrendered himself to a poor brahman so he could collect a reward from the new king; and Prince Candraprabha, who gave his blood and marrow to cure a leper.[41] The stories of these heroes are presented in a matter of fact manner as paradigms of true generosity. Medieval Chinese readers surely ought not to be blamed for the fact that the stories were originally composed in a literary environment that was clearly very different from that of their own classical heritage.

That difference is all too apparent to the twenty-first-century scholar, who can survey a vast range of textual material, but must have been almost impossible to perceive at the time. The fact that Chinese Buddhists received the teachings of the Mahāyāna not as a single corpus of texts with a curriculum and reading guide attached, but piecemeal over many centuries probably only contributed to the problems of interpretation that came along with their sincere desire to make sense of material that was widely divergent and often flatly contradictory. Medieval Chinese Buddhists could not recognize Indian rhetoric when they saw it because they were not aware of the larger literary culture of India of which the Mahāyāna texts were but a part. They were, however, acutely aware that these precious teachings had emerged from the golden mouth of the Buddha himself. They could point to many places in the *sūtra*s where the Buddha had more or less explicitly instructed them to do what they or their compatriots did with such enthusiasm.

An important theme that runs through this study is the way in which the miraculous world described in Buddhist *sūtra*s and represented in Buddhist artworks took root in Chinese soil. This may be seen, for example, in the development from early accounts of monks emulating *jātaka* stories and the *Lotus Sūtra* to later direct and unmediated encounters with the Bodhisattva Mañjuśrī in China and the increasing prevalence of the spontaneous combustion of eminent monks. We may also trace this process by paying attention to the mention of relics in the biographies. Broadly speaking, in early accounts relics hardly ever appear; later the relics of the Buddha start to play significant roles, but by the tenth century self-immolators themselves were commonly depicted as being able to produce relics in vast quantities, sometimes spontaneously while still alive. I would see the changing nature of relics as part of an ongoing process in which Chinese monks grew more confident of their abilities to create bodhisattvas in China. The rise of Chan Buddhism is just the best-known example of this process, but the present study may suggest other ways in which this could happen.

Contents and Scope of the Volume

The limited scope of this book means, unfortunately, that many interesting cases have been excluded. I do not discuss in any detail, for example, the case of the holy figure of Liu Benzun柳本尊, active in Western Sichuan around the late ninth and early tenth century. Beautifully executed three-dimensional reliefs of his "ten austerities" (the burning and cutting of various parts of his body) are still to be found in Dazu 大足 and Anyue 安岳 county.[42] I touch on the mass auto-cremations of the followers of Mahāsattva Fu (Fu Xi 傅歙, 497–569) only in passing.[43] I do not have room to discuss the case of the eminent Song-dynasty Tiantai 天台 master Siming Zhili 四明知禮 (960–1028), who in 1017 vowed to burn himself along with ten of his companions and, despite a lengthy correspondence on the matter with the literatus Yang Yi 楊億 (974–1020), ultimately did not go through with his plan.[44] There are also references to self-immolation and auto-cremation in dynastic histories I have not pursued because they are not directly related to the cases I have chosen to study.[45]

There are a couple of examples of faked auto-cremation known to me. An unnamed Tang 唐 (618–907) monk is said to have conspired with the famous general Li Baozhen 李抱真 (733–794) to fleece pious donors by staging a fake auto-cremation. The plan was that the general would collect donations from the onlookers and set the pyre ablaze while the monk made his escape from a tunnel hidden beneath. However, the general had the tunnel sealed up, thus ensuring the death of the monk and not having to share the spoils with an accomplice.[46] The following story is found in the *Shasekishū* 沙石集 (Collection of Sand and Pebbles, 1279–1283), a Japanese work of edifying tales. An old lay priest from Hitachi province knew a "beggar monk" who made a tidy living out of performing the "Body Lamp Ritual." A fake dead body was covered in firewood while the hoaxer escaped through a tunnel and slipped into the crowd. The monk took the money and rice that were given as donations. Once the monk only barely escaped alive. Later he met a devout layman who had seen him apparently burn to death; the monk tricked him a second time by fooling him into believing that the layman had actually died himself and that they were meeting in the intermediate existence between re-births. Convincing the man that he could return him to the land of the living, the beggar monk relieved him of his clothes.[47]

But these episodes aside, there remains a great deal of material for us to explore. Because this book is intended to be a history of self-immolation, its six chapters run in more or less chronological order. The first offers a de-tailed examination of the earliest accounts of self-immolation as presented in the biographies of eminent monks and nuns from the fifth century. Chapter 2 examines the importance of the *Lotus Sūtra* (and related Mahāyāna litera-ture) as a source of inspiration for auto-cremation in medieval China and investigates records of self-immolation as they appear in biographical collec-tions of *Lotus* devotees.

By the sixth century Chinese Buddhists had both a large corpus of trans-lated texts and a growing repertoire of well-established practices like self-immolation on which to draw. Some were also becoming conscious that the teaching of the Buddha, which the *saṃgha* had worked so hard to plant and nurture in Chinese soil, was not only under threat from secular forces, but also losing efficacy because of the ever-increasing temporal distance between themselves and the Buddha. In Chapter 3 I explore how the political realities of a newly reunited empire, combined with fears of the decline of the *dharma*, affected the practices of self-immolation.

Although most of the book concentrates on bodily practice as recorded in biographical materials, the doctrinal and ethical dimensions of self-immolation as interpreted by Chinese monks also deserve consideration. A particularly interesting justification of self-immolation by the tenth-century monk Yongming Yanshou 永明延壽 (904–975) is the focus of Chapter 4. Although Daoshi had offered a spirited defense of the practice in the mid-seventh century, Yanshou's work provides the most extended discussion of the doctrinal meaning of self-immolation that we now possess, and as such it deserves an extended examination.

By the eighth century self-immolation was a well-established practice in China, but the increasingly unstable and fragmented state of the empire in the late Tang and Five Dynasties meant that it was often deployed for imme-diately local ends or to shore up a collapsing imperium. Chapter 5 exam-ines cases of self-immolation during this often tumultuous period.

In Chapter 6 I survey the later history of self-immolation from the Song dynasty until the early Republic—that is to say, from the tenth century to the early twentieth. The variety of cases that have been preserved for this long pe-riod of history shows that self-immolation continued to be a well-attested form of Buddhist practice that was still open to reinterpretation. In particular I note the types of self-immolation that were performed at major critical and traumatic points in Chinese history, such as the loss of North China to the Jurchen Jin in 1126, the fall of the Ming dynasty in 1644, and the end of Imperial China in 1911. In the Conclusion I offer some final reflections on the importance of self-immolation in the history of Chinese Buddhism and suggest ways in which to rethink our perspective on religious practice in China and East Asia as a whole.

There are two appendices. The first provides synopses of all the biographies I have studied in the order in which they originally appeared in biographical collections. To give some idea of how biographies of self-immolators were disseminated beyond the monastic community, I have included in the appendix details of the biographies that were reproduced in such popular Buddhist collections as the *Shishi liutie* 釋氏六帖 (The Buddhists' Six Documents) and the *Liuxue seng zhuan* 六學僧傳 (Biographies of Monks by the Six Categories of Specialization). I also present the biographies contained in the *Hongzan fahua zhuan* 弘贊法華傳 (Biographies Which Broadly Extol the *Lotus*), an important Tang collection of pious practices centered on the *Lotus Sūtra*.

The second appendix contains complete, annotated translations of the critical evaluations by the compilers of the first three *Gaoseng zhuan* collections. I have supplied translations because the allusive language and subtle arguments presented in these documents defy easy summary. I think it is important for us to know exactly what these men said about the acts documented in their collections.

CHAPTER 1

"Mounting the Smoke with Glittering Colors"

Self-Immolation in Early Medieval China

The biographies of religious practitioners in medieval Chinese are not just sources of valuable data for historians; they also gave shape to the contours of Buddhist practice and doctrine. In China, unlike India or Tibet, the biographies of monks formed a distinct genre that became an important part of Buddhist literature.[1] As collections of biographies entered the canon and were widely read, accounts of the conduct of monks and nuns recorded Buddhist practice and shaped it as well. From the sixth century onwards monastics could find exemplary models of conduct in the history of their own community in China as well as in scriptures translated from Indian languages. For self-immolators of later periods in Chinese history and the thinkers who defended them in their writings, the fact that eminent monks of the past had made offerings of their bodies conferred legitimacy on the practice. Thus a close look at the earliest sources we have for self-immolation will not only reveal much about its early history, but also show how these accounts provided inspiration and authority to monks and nuns of later generations who were aware of their illustrious predecessors.

There were three significant early collections of biographies. Two are devoted to the lives of monks: the *Mingseng zhuan* 名僧傳 (Biographies of Famous Monks), compiled by Baochang 寶唱 (463–after 514) and the *Gaoseng zhuan* 高僧傳 (Biographies of Eminent Monks) by Huijiao 慧皎 (497–554).[2] Baochang also compiled nuns' biographies to form the collection *Biqiuni zhuan* 比丘尼傳 (Biographies of Bhikṣuṇīs).[3] The individual accounts collected in these early sources are really quite diverse because they come from different locations and times and were written by people of varied backgrounds (often laymen, in fact) who were ruled by an assortment of regimes in the North and South during the first few hundred years of the Buddhist presence in China. The biographies were not written from a single point of view, and when read en masse they offer us multiple perspectives on the Buddhist order in China. Sometimes these perspectives converge to bring aspects of Chinese Buddhism into clearer view, but at other times they diverge sharply, leaving us no more than fragmentary impressions.

How, then, are we to comprehend self-immolation as represented in the biographies of medieval Chinese monks and nuns? We should not assume that because these sources now appear in three "books" they form no more than a collection of hagiographical clichés, legends, or literary tropes—although individual biographies may contain one or more of these elements. Equally, we cannot assume that they are historically verifiable in every detail. We must give some weight to the fact that they record something and that most people who read these accounts in traditional China, whether they were sympathetic to the acts described therein or not, responded as if they recorded what had truly occurred.

When we examine the biographies of men and women who performed extreme acts of devotion with their bodies, it is important to remember that we are not faced with accounts that are particularly anomalous or obscure. On the contrary, the circumstances of these events are as well supported by textual and epigraphical evidence as any other aspect of medieval Chinese life in which modern scholarship has shown an interest. If contemporary scholarship has tended to relegate self-immolation to the margins, then that tendency reveals more about nineteenth- and twentieth-century constructions of Buddhism as a rational middle way than it does about how Chinese Buddhists viewed (and continue to view) aspects of their own practice.

Many of the works studied in this and subsequent chapters are collections that concern "eminent monks" (*gaoseng* 高僧), and we should always bear in mind how very eminent these monks were, not only within the monastic community, but above all in their relations with secular authority. They were not unlettered peasants, but the confidants and advisers to rulers and generals. Local governors and aristocrats composed their memorial inscriptions and praised them in verse. Their deaths were witnessed by great crowds of all classes, including emperors and princes, empresses and concubines, as well as their fellow monks, nuns, and peasants. In the case of the *Gaoseng zhuan* in particular, the prominence of the social elite was no doubt connected to Huijiao's own experience in his native area, Kuaiji 會稽—a place of "material prosperity and cultural brilliance" where Buddhism was patronized by both the Liang court and the aristocracy.[4] But we should further note that in medieval China, as in medieval Europe, the religious practices and beliefs of the elite and the common people had more in common than not.[5]

Although the collections of biographies represent our major source of information concerning self-immolation by Chinese Buddhists between the fourth and tenth centuries, it would be naive to assume that they contain either a complete or unbiased record of these practices. After all, the individual biographies were not composed to be exhaustive and accurate, but rather to extol the conduct of the deceased and thus edify the living. The compilations are then not innocent and inert repositories of data; they were designed by their compilers to fulfill certain agendas and are highly selective and carefully arranged. For all the hundreds of thousands of monks and nuns who lived in China between the third century and the tenth—even if we include epigraphic and other sources beyond the *Gaoseng zhuan* collections—we only have biographical information for about ½₀ of 1 percent of them.[6] Thus we must always bear in mind that the monks who appear in these sources were not just common or garden-variety monks: They were famous, admirable, exemplary, and elite monks.

Biographies of Famous Monks

Although the *Mingseng zhuan* has long been eclipsed by the Liang-dynasty *Gaoseng zhuan,* this early collection of monastic biographies established many of the conventions of Buddhist hagiography in China. In particular, Baochang's classification of biographies of monks by type of religious speciality is a feature that was adopted by later collections and gave them their distinctive shape. The *Mingseng zhuan* includes biographies of self-immolators under the heading "Abandoning the body—steadfast practice in the face of hardship" (*yishen kujie* 遺身苦節).[7] Baochang evidently saw self-immolation as a practice that was as readily identifiable and appropriate for Chinese Buddhists as was the translation of *sūtra*s or the erection of *stūpa*s, to mention but two of the other categories in his collection.

Baochang, one of the most important figures in early Chinese Buddhist historiography, began compiling the *Mingseng zhuan* in 510.[8] By the time he completed it, he had a large collection of 425 biographies in 30 fascicles. His work seems to have been the most extensive of the collections of monastic biographies that were in circulation before the *Gaoseng zhuan* was completed in 531.[9] The *Mingseng zhuan* no longer survives in its complete form, but the table of contents (*mulu* 目錄; Jpn. *mokuroku*) and some excerpts from the biographies were copied out by a thirteenth-century Japanese monk by the name of Shūshō 宗性 (1202–1292). These few precious fragments survive as *Meisōdenshō* 名僧傳抄 (Manuscript Copy of the *Mingseng zhuan*).[10] Why the *Mingseng zhuan* was not transmitted is unclear, but it seems to have fallen out of favor after Huijiao's more selective collection was completed.[11] A comparison of the preserved excerpts with biographies in the *Gaoseng zhuan* reveals that Huijiao incorporated a great deal of Baochang's work into his own.[12] The table of contents, which appears to be complete, indicates that the *Mingseng zhuan* contained the biographies of nineteen self-immolators under the category *yishen kujie.* The term *kujie* is attached to six other category headings in Baochang's collection, such as *zao tasi kujie* 造塔寺苦節 ("Building *stūpa*s and monasteries—maintaining steadfast practice in the face of hardship").[13] In Baochang's system of typologies, abandoning the body is classed as the third of seven types of "steadfast practice." As far as we can determine then, the rubric of "self-immolation" as a category of worthy behavior by monks began with Baochang's collection, was adopted by Huijiao, and continued to be applied in every collection of biographies thereafter—with the exception of *Biographies of Eminent Monks Compiled under the Great Ming,* which we mentioned in the Introduction.[14] Given its significance, it is somewhat unfortunate that so little of the *Mingseng zhuan* survives.

Compilers of biographies did not just collect and organize; they evaluated and commented on their material. As we shall see, we can gather many clues about medieval hagiography from critical evaluations (*lun* 論) that the compliers wrote and appended to relevant sections of their work. Because we have no critical evaluation from Baochang for the section on self-immolation, his rationale for the creation of this category must perforce remain obscure. We may say with certainty that Baochang did include self-immolators at the heart of Buddhist practice in his scheme of monks' vocations.

Baochang not only created the category of self-immolation, but also collected much of the important early data. The biographies of many of the self-immolators collected by Baochang also appear in the *Gaoseng zhuan,* although not necessarily in the self-immolation section of that work. The full list of nineteen biographies in Baochang's collection may be found in Appendix 1.

Biographies of *Bhikṣuṇī*s

Those rare records of female Buddhist practice in fifth-century China that Baochang also preserved for us prove that it was not just famous or eminent monks who made offerings of their bodies—nuns did so, too. Baochang's *Biqiuni zhuan* is the only biographical collection exclusively devoted to Buddhist women of medieval China.[15] It is arranged chronologically, so there is no separate category for self-immolators. Of a total of sixty-five biographies, no fewer than six concern female auto-cremators, although three of these cases are intimately connected. In the absence of other collections devoted to nuns, it is frustratingly difficult to discuss female self-immolation systematically after the Liang dynasty, but we shall see more biographies of nuns who gave away their bodies in other collections discussed below. I believe that a search of biographies contained in local gazetteers would turn up many more examples of self-immolation by nuns in later periods.

Biographies of Eminent Monks

When Huijiao compiled the *Gaoseng zhuan* he discarded many of Baochang's twenty rubrics for the divisions of monastic specialization, but he did preserve a separate "self-immolation section" as one of the ten sections of his work.[16] Thus the origins of this particular rubric would seem to lie at least as far back as Baochang's conception of renowned monastic behavior, although the precise parameters of his vision remain obscure to us in the absence of a complete version of the *Mingseng zhuan*. We can at least say that because so many of the self-immolators in Baochang's collection also had biographies in Huijiao's, the latter must have considered them eminent as well as famous. The category of self-immolation was then not just an idiosyncratic invention on the part of one monastic historian; it was a mode of religious practice that evidently had some meaning for other members of the Buddhist community.

Huijiao seems to have completed his own collection around 531, about a dozen years after the *Mingseng zhuan*.[17] He took considerable pains, in his preface at least, to distinguish his work from the earlier *Mingseng zhuan* on the grounds that his compilation dealt with monks who were truly "eminent" (*gao* 高) and not merely "famous" (*ming* 名).[18] His success in promoting his own vision of the monastic ideal may be measured in part by the fact that the *Mingseng zhuan* essentially ceased to be transmitted and was superseded by his own work.[19] Nevertheless, Huijiao does seem to have owed a great deal to his predecessor, and in addition to the material that he took from funerary inscriptions and eyewitness accounts, whole biographies were lifted verbatim from the earlier work. Only the loss of Baochang's complete collection prevents us from knowing exactly how much information Huijiao borrowed from him.

The geographical bias of the *Gaoseng zhuan* in favor of monks who were based in the area corresponding to modern-day Jiangxi, Jiangsu, and Zhejiang was already noted by Daoxuan in his preface to his own collection of monastic biographies and has been confirmed by modern scholarship.[20] Because of the division of early medieval China into the alien regimes of the North and the more cultured states of the refugee Chinese aristocrats in the South, and because of his own personal inclinations, Huijiao was more interested in and better informed about monks from the South. However, his collection of self-immolators does include a fair number of biographies of monks who were active in North China. The somewhat unusual prominence of northern monks in the self-immolation part of the collection (five biographies) may mirror the broad distinction between the austere, practice-oriented Buddhism of the North and the more genteel and intellectual "gentry Buddhism" of the South. It also reflects somewhat different forms of patronage of the religion by the non-Chinese rulers of the North, who tended to favor more devotional styles of Buddhism than did the more literary and philosophical southern regimes.

We can get some idea of how Huijiao saw self-immolators as a class from his preface, in which he describes the qualities of the monks in the first eight categories of the collection. (He considered the remaining two, hymnodists [*jingshi* 經師] and proselytizers [*changdao* 唱導], to be much less important.) Huijiao extols the translators of Buddhist texts at some length and explains that he has placed them first in his collection because "the enlightenment of China was wholly dependent on them." He goes on to praise the exegetes, the thaumaturges, the meditators, the Vinaya masters, the self-immolators, the chanters, and the promoters of merit:

> When the wise explanations [of the exegetes] revealed holy [truth], then the way [of Buddhism] encompassed millions [of world systems]. When the penetrating responses [of the thaumaturges] produced appropriate transformations, thereby violent and fierce people were pacified. When [the meditators] constrained their thoughts and entered into meditation, then merit flourished. When [the Vinaya masters] propagated the Vinaya, conduct in accord with the prohibitions was of limpid purity. When [the self-immolators] were oblivious to their physical forms and abandoned their bodies, then prideful and avaricious people experienced a change of heart. When [the cantors] intoned the words of the dharma, the invisible and visible worlds tasted blessedness. When [the promoters of merit] planted and nurtured merit and goodness, then the symbols bequeathed by the Buddha could be passed on to posterity. [The monks in] all these eight categories, even though their legacies of good deeds were not all the same, and though their transforming influences were markedly different, yet were all endowed with virtue like that of the four classes of saints and their achievement lay in meritorious acts of body, mouth and mind. Therefore they are [the types of monks] praised by all the scriptures and extolled by all the sages.[21]

In this important passage Huijiao articulates his vision of the multifaceted nature of the monastic mission in China. Different types of monks performed different roles in the ideal Buddhist order. Huijiao considered self-immolation to be part of the propagation of Buddhism, as significant and as effective in its own way as exegesis of the scriptures, the working of miracles, or the maintaining of monastic discipline. For him, and in accordance with the logic of sympathetic resonance, the deeds of the monks he selected for his section on self-immolation were selfless acts that had the potential to rectify society as a whole by changing the attitudes of the selfish. Far from being nihilistic or antinomian, self-immolators were in fact not all that different from Vinaya masters. Self-immolators countered the faults of pride and avarice, while Vinaya masters worked to ensure purity and correctness of conduct in the monastery.

In his collection under the heading of "self-immolation" Huijiao placed eleven main biographies (*zhengzhuan* 正傳) and two supplementary biographies (*fujian* 附見). Of these thirteen, eight of the monks are auto-cremators, four offered their bodies in other ways, and one monk is mentioned only through association with a self-immolator. Although at first glance it may seem that Huijiao drastically reduced the overall number of self-immolators from that recorded in his predecessor's work (nineteen), in fact only four were dropped from the compilation altogether and four other biographies of *Mingseng zhuan* self-immolators were assigned to other categories. In other words, all of the self-immolators in Huijiao's collection have biographies in Baochang's, but Huijiao does not acknowledge this fact. Because Baochang's collection includes 425 main biographies and Huijiao's only 257, the exclusion of four biographies cannot really be taken as a significant reduction in the coverage of self-immolation as a vocation for monks.

To grasp what kinds of practice were considered "abandoning the body" in the early fifth century, it is worth paying some attention to these early biographies. A thematic discussion follows; details of the biographies in the order in which they appear in the *Gaoseng zhuan* may be found in Appendix 1.

The Hungry Tigress

One of the most common methods of (attempted) self-immolation after auto-cremation involved casting the body in front of a hungry tiger or tigress. The prime exemplar of this act was the Buddha himself, as seen for example in a *jātaka* contained in the *Jinguangming jing* 金光明經 (*Suvarṇaprabhāsa sūtra*, Sūtra of Golden Light).[22] This particular tale was also widely known from other Chinese translations of *jātaka*s.[23] Evidence of the popularity of this theme may be seen in the many contemporary artistic representations of the scene of the bodhisattva hurling his body before the emaciated tigress.[24]

The story of the hungry tigress in the *Sūtra of Golden Light* runs as follows. There was a king called Mahāratha (Moheluotuo 摩訶羅陀) who had three sons: Mahāpraṇada (Moheponaluo 摩訶波那羅), Mahādeva (Mohetipo 摩訶提婆), and Mahāsattva (Mohesatuo 摩訶薩埵). One day, the three princes were in a bamboo grove in the park when they saw a tigress that had given birth to seven cubs seven days before. Her body was emaciated and weak, and she was suffering from hunger and thirst. The third son, Prince Mahāsattva, was inspired by the compassionate acts of the bodhisattvas and resolved to donate his body, discarding his useless and impermanent form in exchange for a changeless one, replete with wisdom and virtue. Sending his older brothers away, he went back to where the tigress lay and stripping off his clothes made a vow: "I do this now for the benefit of all beings, to attain the supreme unsurpassable awakening, and to save all beings in the three realms." He threw himself in front of the hungry tigress, but she was too weak to move. Realizing this, the prince rose and looked for a knife but could not find one. Taking a sliver of bamboo, he slit his throat so that the blood gushed out. In response to his act, the earth shook in six ways and the sun stopped shining. There was a rain of flowers and marvelous fragrances. Then gods appeared, amazed at this unprecedented act, and they praised the prince: "Excellent, O Mahāsattva (dashi 大士), because of your true great compassion for beings, you are able to discard that which is hard to discard. You will quickly attain pure nirvāṇa." The tigress saw the blood flowing from the prince's body, licked it up, and devoured his flesh, leaving only bones.

The two older brothers, having witnessed the earthquakes, darkness, and magic rain, realized what had happened and rushed back to the place where they had last seen Mahāsattva. The scene that awaited them is described in vivid detail: They found his discarded clothes hanging from a bamboo; his bones, hair, and skin scattered all over the ground; and a big pool of blood. In shock, the two princes passed out on top of their brother's bones. On regaining consciousness, they lamented their loss. The story goes on to describe the shock and distress of the prince's parents. The king, accompanied by a large crowd, paid homage to Prince Mahāsattva's relics (śarīra) and erected a seven-jewelled stūpa. Before throwing himself before the tigress, the prince had made a vow that his relics should cause beings of future generations for many kalpas to take up Buddhism.

This particular jātaka had a deep influence on the religious imagination of medieval China. It contains at least six elements that were significant for the construction of a logic of self-immolation in China:

1. Prince Mahāsattva's donation of his body did not occur to him spontaneously; it was inspired by the actions of bodhisattvas before him. By imitating him, in their turn Chinese Buddhists became part of an infinite lineage of beings who had become buddhas through actions such as this.
2. The jātaka emphasizes that Mahāsattva did not simply discard his body—rather he exchanged an impermanent form for a permanent

one. This motif of exchange or transformation is one that we shall see repeated in many of our Chinese materials.

3. Before he offered his body to the tigress, Mahāsattva made a vow in which he stressed that his offering was not just for the animal but for all beings. Chinese self-immolators frequently made similar public vows that emphasized their belief in the salvific power of their actions.

4. The Bodhisattva's death was not an easy one: He had to slit his own throat to allow the tigress to feed on him. The *jātaka* makes clear in the most graphic and horrific way the heroic determination that was necessary to make an offering of the body.

5. In the *jātaka* the universe responded to Mahāsattva's death with earthquakes and eclipses. Biographies of Chinese self-immolators also emphasized the reactions of the cosmos and the displays of auspicious signs attendant on the moment of death.

6. The king buried Mahāsattva's relics (which had the power to convert beings in future generations) beneath a *stūpa*. Similarly, kings and officials interred the relics of Chinese self-immolators and entertained similar expectations about the power of those sacred remains.

But to understand fully the associations of the hungry tigress as a trope in Chinese accounts of self-immolation, we ought to look beyond the Indian antecedents and consider also the image of the tiger in Chinese culture. As Charles Hammond remarks in his study of the lore surrounding this animal, "One might say that in traditional China the tiger was the most savage beast one could expect to meet."[25] Because of the dread that it inspired, the tiger was also seen as a symbol of greed or tyranny, as in the famous remark attributed to Confucius: "An oppressive government is worse than a tiger."[26] In time, this saying came to be understood as implying that good government removed the threat of man-eating tigers, and in the biographies contained in the early dynastic histories one finds examples of the arrival of benevolent local officials accompanied by the rapid departure of the unwanted felines.[27] From this point of view, we might see the acts of monks who tamed man-killers with their own bodies as part of a broader history of competition for the hearts and minds of the people between religious specialists and representatives of the secular order (who of course often included religious techniques in their repertoire).[28]

An archetypal account of a monk and a tiger comes from the early fifth century. Around the year 420 the area below Jia shan 駕山 in Pengcheng 彭城 was plagued by a man-eater.[29] Every day one or two villagers were killed, so to halt these attacks a monk called Tancheng 曇稱 (d. after 420) proposed to

offer his body. The villagers tried to persuade him not to do it, but he ignored their pleas. That very night, he sat alone in the bush and called out this
vow to the tiger: "With this body of mine I will fill you with food and drink,
causing you to abandon your hateful and harmful intentions from now on. I
shall obtain [for you] the food of the unsurpassable *dharma* in the future."[30]
As presented in the biography, Tancheng's vow illustrates the premeditated
nature of his action and his conscious imitation of scriptural models. What
he offered the tiger in his vow was not just a solution to its immediate problem of hunger, but also an assurance of its future liberation from *saṃsāra*. He
made explicit the connections between his own body as food for now and the
teachings of the Buddha as the more sustaining nourishment for the future,
thus setting the tiger as well as himself firmly on the path to buddhahood.
Realizing how determined the monk was, the weeping villagers returned
home. In the middle of the night they heard the tiger take Tancheng. Rushing back to the place where they had left him, they found his body had been
completely devoured; only the head remained. The villagers interred the
head beneath a pagoda, and the tiger never attacked humans again.

There is, of course, at least one significant difference between the Bodhisattva saving the life of a starving tigress and her cubs and Tancheng, who
saved the lives of villagers threatened by a man-eating tiger. The act of self-
sacrifice, in Tancheng's case, was directed first towards human beings rather
than animals, although Tancheng did promise the tiger the food of the unsurpassable *dharma* in the shape of his own body. But details such as the erection of a *stūpa* for Tancheng's head, which mirrors the account in the *Sūtra of
the Causes and Conditions of the Erection of the Stūpa for the Bodhisattva Who Gave
Away His Body to the Hungry Tigress,* suggest that the hungry tigress theme was
a key source of paradigms for medieval Chinese forms of piety.[31] This
influence remained strong in later centuries, as we shall see in accounts that
tell of monks who attempted to get tigers to eat them without too much concern for whether the animals were starving, threatening the lives of villagers,
or just quietly going about their own business.

The Body as Food and Medicine

Indian Buddhist sources contain many stories of heroes who offered their
bodies as food or medicine to those in extremis.[32] Just as with the *jātaka* of the
hungry tigress, these accounts provided models for pious imitation in China.
Two biographies in the *Gaoseng zhuan* show how these heroic offerings were
enacted: Daojin 道進 (d. 444) offered his own flesh to feed the hungry, while
Sengfu 僧富 (d. after 385) saved the life of a child by substituting his own

body. Both monks were disciples of the leading Buddhist masters of the late fourth and early fifth centuries.

The biography of Daojin, a disciple of the great translator Dharmakṣema (Tanwuchan 曇無讖, 385–433), appears in the *Gaoseng zhuan* under the name Fajin 法進.[33] Daojin was held in high esteem by Juqu Mengxun 沮渠蒙遜 (r. 401–433), the non-Chinese ruler of the dynasty of Northern Liang 北涼 (397–440).[34] After Mengxun died, his son, referred to in the biography as Jinghuan 璟環, continued to consult Daojin on matters of state:[35] "He asked Daojin, 'Now I wish to turn and seize Gaochang 高昌, will I succeed or not?'[36] Daojin said, 'You will certainly triumph, but my only concern is that there will be disaster and famine.'"[37] Despite Daojin's warning, Jinghuan marched on Gaochang and captured it. It seems that Daojin was not just Dharmakṣema's disciple in religion, but also played a similar role to his master's as adviser to the crown.[38] If that is so, we should be alert to the possibility that his radical final gesture may have had a political as well as religious dimension.

In 444 Anzhou 安周 (?–460) succeeded to the throne, and there was a famine just as Daojin had predicted.[39] Daojin repeatedly asked for food from Anzhou to feed the hungry, but as the national granaries gradually became exhausted, he stopped asking for help. One day after bathing he took a knife and some salt and went to a remote cave where the starving people had gathered. He bestowed on them the triple refuge (*san gui* 三歸), thus formally converting them to Buddhism, then hung his robe and bowl on a tree and flung himself before them saying, "I give myself as food for all of you."[40] The people were famished but had some difficulty in accepting this unprecedented offer, so Daojin began to slice and salt his own flesh. When the flesh on both his thighs was gone, he no longer had the strength to continue. He told the starving people, "Take this flesh of mine. There is still enough for several days. If officials of the king come here they will take [my body] away, so just take [the flesh] and store it." But no one could bear to take it. A short while later, Daojin's disciples arrived, followed by officers of the king who took him back to the palace. Obviously affected by his selfless act, the ruler decreed that the granaries be reopened. In this account we see the logic of sympathetic resonance operating at the worldly level: The sincerity of Daojin's actions on behalf of the common people stirred the ruler into action.

By the next morning Daojin was dead. He was cremated (*shewei* 闍維) north of the city walls.[41] Smoke and flames shot into the sky for seven days before the fire burned out. Although his corpse and skeleton were completely consumed, his tongue remained unburned. We shall have occasion to discuss the significance of the unburned tongue in more detail later, as the trope appears again in later accounts. Suffice it to say here that the miraculous indestructible tongue was an important mark of sanctity in Chinese religious biography, and here it must be understood as a marker of the righteousness of Daojin's self-sacrifice.

Given what we know about Daojin, it is likely that his decision to offer his body was inspired by the *Sūtra of Golden Light*, a text translated by his master, Dharmakṣema, which contains the story of Prince Mahāsattva's sacrifice of his own body to the hungry tigress.[42] Another text translated by Dharmakṣema, *Karuṇāpuṇḍarīka* (White Lotus of Compassion), also contains extremely graphic scenes of flesh-giving in its accounts of the previous lives of the Buddha.[43] In Daojin's case he fed hungry human beings rather than animals, but like the prince he carved up his own body to encourage others to feed on his flesh.

Attitudes toward cannibalism in medieval China were complex and defy easy summary, so it is difficult to know where the case of Daojin belongs in the larger narrative.[44] However, we can say that in light of research by Michihata Ryōshū and Hubert Durt it seems likely that the introduction of Buddhism to China brought with it new ideas concerning the consumption of human flesh.[45] Note, for example, that Daojin sliced the flesh from his thigh, a practice that is now mostly associated with the feeding of parents by filial sons and daughters in the Confucian tradition (although in fact this particular part of the body was a favorite offering of the heroes of *jātaka* literature).[46] Certainly, Daojin's act was cast as a form of self-sacrifice in response to the real suffering of people—for which there was also ample scriptural support—rather than as an act of *pūjā* (homage) to a holy being or sacred text of the kind we shall see more of below.

The biography of Sengfu provides another example of the heroic offering of the body to save the life of another being. Sengfu was a disciple of Daoan 道安 (312–385), the most knowledgeable and charismatic Buddhist teacher of his day.[47] After Daoan died, Sengfu returned to Tingwei monastery 廷尉寺 in Wei 魏 commandery, where he became a recluse.[48] In the local village some bandits kidnapped a young child, intending to use his heart and liver as a sacrifice to some bloodthirsty god.[49] Sengfu was wandering by when he happened to see the bandits and realized what they planned to do. He asked whether the five viscera of an adult would serve their purposes just as well as those of a child.[50] The bandits still did not take his offer seriously, so Sengfu grabbed a knife and cut open his torso down to the navel. The bandits all blamed each other for this shocking outcome and ran away. Sengfu managed to send the child back home.

A person who was walking by at the time saw Sengfu and asked what had happened. Although the monk was on the point of death, he was still able to give a full account of the preceding events. The passerby went home and fetched a needle with which he sutured the skin of Sengfu's abdomen and smeared it with some ointment.[51] Sengfu was taken back to the monastery, where he is said to have recovered somewhat, although the circumstances of his death are not known.

Jātaka tales offered repertoires of bodily gifts that could be as bloody as they were bizarre. Sengfu's story has some of this almost grotesque flavor while still retaining its Chinese setting. The lack of definite information on Sengfu's death suggests that the biography was taken from a miracle tale rather than a funerary inscription, and this may give us a clue as to how to read it. Although there is no clear conversion narrative (the body snatchers simply run away), the story hints at the competition between Buddhism and bloody indigenous cults that required sacrifices.

The Transcendent and the Duck

Although it is possible to see the influence of the *jātaka*s on Chinese Buddhist practice in the biographies we have discussed so far, there are some cases that seem to owe a debt to more indigenous traditions. Huijiao's collection of self-immolators opens not with auto-cremation or a monk being eaten by a tiger, but with a biography that is rather less spectacular in scope. Sengqun 僧群 (fl. ca. 404) built a thatched hut for himself on a mountain called Huo shan 霍山 (in Luojiang subprefecture 羅江縣 on the coast of present-day Fujian), where he observed the precepts, ate vegetarian food, and chanted the *sūtra*s.[52] Huo shan's solitary peak was surrounded by the sea, and on its summit was a large stone pond. According to legend, when "Sengqun the transcendent" (*xian* 仙) drank from it he did not experience hunger, and so he was able to "abstain from grain" (*jueli* 絕粒). Reports about Sengqun's abilities came to the attention of the governor of Jin'an 晉安, Tao Kui 陶夔 (fl. ca. 404), who tried to get hold of some of this magic water for himself.[53] Sengqun sent him some, but it began to stink as soon as it left the mountain. Tao Kui tried to visit the mountain in person, but his boat was turned back by storms, which caused him to lament on being cut off from such a sage.

Sengqun's hut was separated from the pond by a small mountain stream, which he crossed by means of a narrow bridge when he went to draw water. One day a duck with a broken wing landed on the bridge, and whenever Sengqun approached, it would stretch out its wings and peck at him. Sengqun considered using his monk's staff to push the duck aside, but he was concerned that he might injure it, and for this reason he turned around and went back. Cut off from his supply of magic water, he died after

only a few days; the biography claims that he was 140 years old. As he lay dying, Sengqun explained that when he was young he had broken the wing of
a duck and that the present situation was a repayment of that karmic debt.

This biography is unusual among those of self-immolators in that it explains Sengqun's self-sacrifice in terms of *karma*.[54] As we have already noted,
self-immolation was usually understood less as a repayment of past *karma*
than as a practice productive of merit for the present and future, especially
when performed as an act of homage (*pūjā;* Chn. *gongyang* 供養).[55] The biography also contains elements that are not entirely Buddhist. Most obvious
among them is the fact that Sengqun is referred to by locals as a "transcendent," a term with a long history in China but more usually associated with
Taoism by the fifth century.

Sengqun was able to attain remarkable longevity not through the purity
of his Buddhist practice, but by drinking an elixir-like water that enabled him
to "abstain from grain." As far as I am aware, the practice of abstention from
grain has no doctrinal basis in Indian Buddhist texts but was an indigenous
Chinese idea.[56] It is recommended in a number of texts associated with longevity, such as Ge Hong's 葛洪 (283–343) *Baopuzi* 抱朴子 (The Master Who
Embraces Simplicity), for example. Another early fourth-century Taoist text,
Taishang lingbao wufuxu 太上靈寶五符序 (Explanation of the Five Talismans
of the Most High Numinous Treasure, *DZ* 388) provides a fairly typical recommendation of the practice:

> You attain the Tao by avoiding all grains. You will never again have to fol-
> low the rhythm of the moon and plant and harvest. Now, the people of mys-
> terious antiquity, they reached old age because they remained in leisure
> and never ate any grains. As the *Dayou zhang* 大有章 (Verse of Great Exist-
> ence) says, "The five grains are chisels cutting life away, making the five or-
> gans stink and shorten our spans."[57]

As we shall see in some of the biographies below, abstention from grain
could also be used as a preparatory practice for self-immolation.[58]

We might see Sengqun as representative of a type of early medieval holy
man who was not clearly perceived as either Buddhist or Taoist but as a hybrid
of the two. The fact that the account was drawn from a miracle tale collection
rather than a funerary inscription may account for this ambiguity.[59] It would be
tempting to suggest that the apparent terminological confusion involved in calling a Buddhist monk a "transcendent" represents an early stage in the history of
Chinese Buddhism were it not for the fact that even as late as the nineteenth
century other Buddhist self-immolators were still referred to by this term.[60]

Sengqun's self-immolation, like those of Sengfu, Tancheng, and Daojin, was more or less spontaneous and aimed at rescuing a fellow being from immediate danger. We have not yet seen a premeditated act of self-immolation complete with elaborate physical and ritual preparations.

Auto-Cremation

Seven biographies in Huijiao's self-immolation section are cases of auto-cremation: those of Fayu 法羽 (ca. 352–396), Huishao 慧紹 (424–451), Sengyu 僧瑜 (412–455), Huiyi 慧益 (d. 463), Sengqing 僧慶 (437–459), Faguang 法光 (447–487), and Tanhong 曇弘 (ca. 400–455). In some ways they are quite different from the biographies we have discussed so far and not just because they involved death by fire. The grouping together of these biographies may well have been a deliberate strategy on Huijiao's part because they do not seem to follow a strictly chronological order.

Fayu, who died in 396, is the earliest known auto-cremator.[61] His premeditated and publicly staged performance seems quite distinct from the more spontaneous acts we have mentioned so far. Possibly his ritualization of bodily practice was indebted to the kinds of devotion he had worked on in his earlier career. Fayu's master, Huishi 慧始 (d.u.), was particularly diligent in the practice of austerities and cultivation of *dhūta* (*toutuo* 頭陀) in which he seems to have also trained his disciple. The term *dhūta* (also written *dhuta*), which means literally "to cast off," denotes ascetic practices such as eating only once a day, sleeping in the open, and not lying down to sleep—all of which were designed to free one from attachment to the body.[62] In the early biographies, self-immolators are often described as having been trained in *toutuo,* which suggests an association between these particular modes of physical practice.[63] But *toutuo* in our medieval sources probably does not refer strictly to the twelve or thirteen ascetic practices *(dhutaguṇas)* known from the canonical sources; it is often used in the larger and vaguer sense of "austerities" in general. The term seems to be encountered most often in biographies of monks from the north of China, where Buddhists (and Taoists for that matter) had a reputation for tough physical cultivation. Perhaps practitioners from the North regarded auto-cremation as one aspect of a larger ascetic ideal.

Although the *Lotus Sūtra* is not mentioned by name in Fayu's biography, we are told that his constant aspiration was "to follow the traces of the Medicine King and to burn his body in homage to the Buddha."[64] The Medicine King, hero of the eponymous chapter in the *Lotus Sūtra,* was a major inspiration for Chinese auto-cremators as we already noted in the Introduction and as we shall discuss at greater length in the next chapter.

Fayu began by informing the illegitimate "prince of Jin 晉" Yao Xu 姚緒 (fl. late fourth century), that he intended to burn himself alive.[65] Yao Xu tried to dissuade him, but the monk was not to be put off. He swallowed chips of incense and wrapped his body in cloth, then recited "The Chapter on Abandoning the Body" (sheshen pin 捨身品).[66] At the conclusion of his recitation Fayu set fire to himself. The religious and laity who witnessed his act are described as being "full of grief and admiration."

Although Fayu's biography seems to be the earliest account of auto-cremation that we now possess, it is hard to know whether such a matter-of-fact report could represent the origin of the practice. The usual style of medieval Chinese biographies, both secular and religious, tends to be laconic, and this text in particular gives no clue as to whether Fayu came up with the idea himself or was inspired by an earlier auto-cremator for whom documentary evidence has not survived. Fayu's aspiration to emulate the Medicine King is not explained in any way, nor is the necessity of his asking for permission from the local ruler spelled out—although this precaution would have been self-evident in medieval China, where it was dangerous to do much without permission from the authorities. All of the elements that were to characterize auto-cremation in the fifth and sixth centuries—the involvement of secular powers, preparation of the body with incense or oil, the chanting of the text, and the public nature of the final act—are already present in this biography from 396. But we should note that there is no mention of any relics or miracles. Both of these elements are marked features of later accounts.

Fayu staged his performance in North China, then under the firm control of non-Han rulers, and it may be that the religious atmosphere and types of devotional practice that were in vogue in the North were particularly conducive to auto-cremation. It is also significant that auto-cremation seems to have begun around the year 400, when Buddhism was really making its mark in court circles and Buddhists were becoming more deeply involved in politics. This was around the time when translation activities first came under the patronage of the state, for example.[67] In both the North and South, rulers cultivated the power of monks in a more systematic way than had been the case in earlier centuries. This new atmosphere had well-recognized and far-reaching effects on translation and the formation of the Chinese Buddhist canon; could it not also have affected and shaped physical practices such as self-immolation?

Fifty-five years after Fayu's auto-cremation, in 451, a twenty-eight-year-old monk called Huishao hired some people to cut firewood, which he then stacked up in a grotto in the Dong shan 東山 mountains near Yangzhou in Jiangnan 江南.[68] In the middle of this pyre the monk opened a niche (kan 龕)

just large enough for his own body.[69] Later he returned to his home monastery to say farewell to his master, Sengyao 僧要 (d.u.). Sengyao played the same role as the prince of Jin in Fayu's biography and the opponents of gifts of the body in the *jātaka* tales: He begged his disciple not to go through with his plan. Huishao, like Fayu, ignored his entreaties. On the day of the auto-cremation itself, Huishao held a large-scale ceremony on Dong shan during which he administered the eight precepts (*baguan* 八關) to the laity.[70] His intended auto-cremation was well advertised, drawing huge crowds and large amounts of donations.

Why would laypeople want to witness an auto-cremation or give alms on that occasion? Clearly self-immolation was thought of as an act that was capable of generating large amounts of religious merit. The laity gave material goods in the expectation of seeing spiritual rewards at a later date. They wanted to be present at the offering itself so they could form good karmic connections with the auto-cremator. This logic was one that was constantly reinforced in the *jātaka* literature. Just as those who witnessed the Bodhisattva's offerings in his previous lives came to be intimately connected with the Buddha after his awakening, so laypeople in medieval China might have hoped to have similarly glorious careers in their future lives when their own local hero became an advanced bodhisattva and in time even a buddha. The karmic message was simple: A simple donation made now could accrue enormous interest over lifetimes and finally pay out handsomely in the future.

Huishao obviously wanted to make the most of his performance. He planned it for the hours of darkness, when the flames would be most spectacular. During the first part of the night religious ceremonies were performed, and Huishao himself took part in the ritual "procession of incense" (*xiangxing* 香行). Then he took a torch and set fire to the pyre. He got inside the niche, sat down, and began to recite the chapter on "The Original Acts of the Medicine King" (*Yaowang benshi pin* 藥王本事品).[71] Although the firewood was completely aflame, the crowd could still hear Huishao reciting. When the fire reached his forehead, they heard him chant "one mind" (*yixin* 一心), and with those words his recitation ended.[72] The pyre must have been fairly substantial; it took another three days to burn out completely.

Biographies of medieval Chinese monks do not often offer us much insight into the psychology of individuals. Motives for auto-cremation are often provided only in the briefest fashion and most conventionally pious language, if at all. But the biography of Sengyu provides perhaps a glimmer of insight into the mind of an auto-cremator.[73] In 438, together with some of his companions, Sengyu constructed a hermitage on the southern range of Lu shan 廬山.[74] He thought that being bound to the three "evil destinies"

(rebirth as a hell dweller, hungry ghost, or animal) was due to having emotions and a physical body. This somewhat pessimistic perspective, combined
with his admiration for the example of the Medicine King, led him on several
occasions to announce his vow to burn his body. Seventeen years later he
finally carried out his heartfelt wish. The biography skips over the interven-
ing years between vow and act, leaving us no idea what else he might have
done in the interval. The biography describes Sengyu's final hours thus:

> On Xiaojian 孝建 2.6.3 of the Song (July 3, 455), he stacked up firewood,
> leaving just a niche, and invited the *saṃgha* to hold a vegetarian banquet, at
> which he said farewell to the community.[75] That day clouds obscured the
> sun, and a heavy rain fell ceaselessly. Sengyu pronounced the following
> vow: "If what I intend is to be fulfilled, the sky should clear up. If it will not
> be efficacious then let the rain pour down. Thus all classes of people will
> know that the divine responses are unambiguous." As he finished speaking,
> the clouds parted to reveal a clear bright sky.
>
> In the first watch of the night he went into the niche in the pyre. He
> put his palms together and sat down calmly. He recited the chapter on the
> Medicine King. The flames continued to rise but he kept his palms to-
> gether. People who knew of this, both religious and lay, swarmed over the
> whole mountain. They all made prostrations, touching their heads to the
> ground, as they wished to make karmic connections with him. They all saw
> a purple vapor that rose into the sky and lingered for a long time.[76] At that
> time he was forty-four.[77]

The logic of sympathetic resonance is, I believe, stated quite explicitly in
this passage. Sengyu did not proceed with his auto-cremation until the
clouds had cleared, thus showing that the cosmos was in harmony with his
plan. After his death the witnesses saw the auspicious sign of purple vapor,
which not only marked Sengyu's ascent from the mundane world, but also
was another sign of the response of the cosmos to the stimulus of his burning.
Although it may be tempting to read his avowed dislike of *saṃsāra* as "nega-
tive" or pessimistic, this characterization does not seem to be borne out by
the text, which makes much of the ecstatic crowds and auspicious signs that
attended the event.

As we have seen, preparations for auto-cremation could be quite elaborate and time-consuming. They could even occupy several years. Following a
pattern that is by now becoming familiar to us, Huiyi, a resident of Zhulin si
竹林寺 in the Song capital, Jiankang 建康, practiced austerities and vowed to
burn his body.[78] Some of his fellow monks castigated him for this while

others praised him. In Daming 大明 4 (460) he began by "abstaining from ce-reals" (*queli* 卻粒) and eating only sesame and wheat.[79] Two years later he stopped eating wheat and consumed only oil of thyme.[80] On occasion, he dis-pensed with the oil and ate only pills made of incense. The biography stresses that although this diet made him physically feeble, Huiyi was still able to ex-ercise sound judgment.

No less a person than the Song emperor Xiaowu 孝武 (r. 454–464) at-tempted to dissuade Huiyi from carrying out his plans, dispatching his chief minister, Liu Yigong 劉義恭, prince of Jiangxia 江夏 (413–465), to the monas-tery to reason with him.[81] Huiyi, of course, would not go back on his vow. He planned to burn himself on the eighth day of the fourth month of Daming 7 (May 11, 463)—that day being the anniversary of the birth of the Buddha and thus frequently chosen for auspicious events including auto-cremations.

Huiyi's method provides a unique example of an explicit re-creation of the Buddha's cremation rather than the auto-cremation of the Medicine King. Nevertheless, the Medicine King was not entirely absent from this epi-sode. Huiyi began by having a cauldron full of oil set up on the southern slope of Zhong shan 鐘山. He got into the cauldron, lay down on a little couch within it, and wrapped himself in cloth. On his head he added a long cap, which he saturated with oil so that it would act as a wick. When he was about to apply the flame to it, the emperor ordered his chief minister to approach the cauldron and try to dissuade him. But Huiyi's resolve was unshakeable and he showed no remorse. The biography describes the auto-cremation thus:

> Huiyi took up the torch in his own hand and ignited the cap. With the cap ablaze, he cast away the torch, put his hands together, and chanted the chapter on the Medicine King. As the flames reached his eyebrows the sound of his recitation could still be clearly discerned. Reaching his eyes it became indistinct. The cries of pity from the rich and poor echoed in the dark valley.[82] They all clicked their fingers [in approval]; they intoned the name of the Buddha and cried, full of sorrow.[83]

The imitation of the Buddha's *parinirvāṇa* and subsequent cremation is suggested in many accounts of auto-cremation in China. In Huiyi's biogra-phy it is made quite apparent. Although Huiyi may have declared his inten-tion to imitate the Medicine King, his method of auto-cremation is indebted not so much to the *Lotus Sūtra* as to the *Mahāparinirvāṇa-sūtra,* a scripture that contains a detailed account of the Buddha's cremation.[84] According to this text, the funeral of a Buddha was based on that of a *cakravartin* (universal monarch), which required that the body be wrapped in cotton (no less than

five hundred pairs of shrouds in most versions of the *sūtra*) and placed in an
iron container filled with oil.[85] Looking at this prescription from a practical
point of view, we may infer that wrapping oil-soaked cloth around the body
may have been intended to produce a "wick effect," thus making it burn
more rapidly and completely.[86] The biographies record that many Chinese
auto-cremators wrapped their bodies in oil-soaked cloth in imitation of the
Medicine King rather than the Buddha.[87] Whether intentional or not, this
method does seem to have been an effective way of fully reducing the body to
ashes rather than producing a charred corpse, which would be the case if an
unprepared body was burned on an open fire.

The oil-filled iron vessel described in the *Mahāparinirvāṇa-sūtra* has been
the subject of some controversy and speculation by scholars of Buddhism; if
understood literally, a cremation performed in such a manner would result
in a deep-fried Buddha or perhaps yield no more than a pot containing a
mixture of oil, rendered fat, skin, and bones.[88] To make sense of the cremation process, scholars have suggested a number of alternative explanations
for the iron coffin.[89] Perhaps the auto-cremation of Huiyi, in which the
flames apparently burned within the iron container rather than the cauldron placed on top of the pyre, may offer us a glimpse into how medieval
Chinese Buddhists drew on and adapted scripture as a template for their own
practices.

Huiyi may have burned like a Buddha as he lay on a couch imitating the
posture of the Buddha passing into *parinirvāṇa,* but his bodily preparations
for the pyre have a distinctly Chinese flavor to them. Prior to his auto-
cremation, Huiyi abstained from grain and ate sesame. As we shall see below,
abstention from grain was commonly paired with the ingestion of oil and
incense, thus preparing the body as a suitably fragrant offering to the Buddha. But the consumption of hemp and sesame also echoes the ingestion of
elixirs by the transcendents described in texts such as the *Shenxian zhuan* 神
仙傳 (Biographies of Divine Transcendents) by Ge Hong.[90] This preparatory process cannot have been casual or performed at the spur of the moment: Huiyi apparently followed his special dietary regime for years. If this
diet was merely a matter of making the body more flammable or if it was
only a preparatory fast, one would not expect it to be quite so drawn out.
The procedure has much in common with the dietary practices adopted by
Huiyi's Taoist contemporaries. Especially noteworthy is the presence of "incense pills" in Buddhist materials; Taoist texts called for the making of pills
and pellets out of mineral and vegetable drugs.[91]

Buddhist auto-cremators in China clearly adopted and adapted indigenous techniques associated with transcendence. But the ingestion of oil and

incense also consciously mimics the Bodhisattva Medicine King's preparations for auto-cremation in the *Lotus Sūtra,* where he is said to have consumed the essential oils of flowers for twelve thousand years.[92] As we have
already noted, the *Lotus* was clearly the primary textual model for Chinese
Buddhist auto-cremation, especially in the fifth century. The *Lotus Sūtra* describes the Medicine King's preparations thus:

> Straightway then he applied [to his body] various scents, *candana, kunduruka,*
> *turuṣka* [two kinds of frankincense], *pṛkkā* [trigonella], the scent that sinks in
> water, and the scent of pine-tar; and he also drank the fragrant oils of
> *campaka*-flowers. When a thousand two hundred years had been fulfilled, he
> painted his body with fragrant oil and, in the presence of the Buddha Pure
> and Bright Excellence of Sun and Moon, wrapped his body in a garment
> adorned with divine jewels, anointed himself with fragrant oils, with the force
> of supernatural penetration took a vow and then burnt his own body.[93]

Note the emphasis in the *Lotus* on applying fragrant materials to the
body: "painting" and "anointing" it with oil. There is much less about actually drinking oil, and no mention of swallowing incense or incense pills or
fasting. In the *Lotus Sūtra* the body is in a sense a passive object, perhaps
even already dead. Actions are performed on the body—it is decorated and
perfumed—whereas in Chinese enactments of this drama indigenous ideas
about transforming the constituents of the body by diet took center stage.
For Chinese auto-cremators, the body itself became the site of transformation (or actively participated in the transformation) rather than a passive
substance transformed by fire. Clearly, by the fifth century, ideas about abstention from cereals and the ingestion of such things as herbs, sesame, and
honey were not items of arcane knowledge, but simply part of the cultural
background of the Six Dynasties. If one were to drink oil, as suggested in
the *Lotus,* then it also made sense to eat the other items referred to and
swallow pills made of incense. In this way the body was made into a fragrant
human candle, but the process of physical transformation had already begun even before the refining or smelting action of the flames.

In fact, the inspiration for the preparations described in the *Lotus* probably
comes from Indian cremation practices, in which the body was prepared for
the pyre by soaking it in oil—as mentioned earlier with reference to the cremation of the Buddha. In China, there really was no strong tradition of cremation prior to the ninth or tenth century, so it is not surprising that the
Medicine King's preparations were understood in a different way and that we
find a greater emphasis on internal cultivation. Although Indian scriptures

posited the body as primarily an offering to be given to the Buddhas, early medieval Chinese religious ideas interpreted it foremost as a site of transformation—as an active means of deliverance.

The biography of a monk from Shu 蜀 (present-day Sichuan) who burned to death in 459 shows that Huiyi's dietary preparations for self-immolation were not unique. Sengqing was probably not raised as a Buddhist; according to his biography his family had been members of the Taoist "Way of the Five Pecks of Grain" (*Wudoumi dao*五斗米道) for generations.[94] He began his devotions by burning off three of his fingers (the first mention in these biographies of this popular practice) and finally vowed to burn his body. Sengqing gradually ceased eating grains (*jue liangli* 絕糧粒) and consumed only fragrant oil.

> On Daming 3.2.8 (March 27, 459), west of Wudan si 武擔寺, at the walls of Shu, facing an image of Vimalakīrti (Jingming淨名) that he had made himself, he burned his body in homage.[95] The prefect (*cishi*刺史), Zhang Yue張悅 (fl. mid-fifth century), personally came and witnessed it.[96] [No matter whether] religious or laity, travellers or residents, everyone left the city empty [and went to attend the auto-cremation]. Passing clouds gathered and a heavy rain was falling gloomily when suddenly the sky cleared and fine bright weather returned. [The witnesses] saw something like a dragon come out of the pyre and leap into the sky. At the time he was twenty-three. The governor (*taishou*太守) of Tianshui天水, Pei Fangming 裴方明 (fl. mid-fifth century), had his ashes gathered and erected a *stūpa* for them.[97]

As we have seen, although public auto-cremation certainly drew crowds, there could be considerable diversity in the practices on display. The date of this offering, the eighth day of the second month, was one on which the Buddha's *parinirvāṇa* was sometimes celebrated. Sengqing burned himself before an image of Vimalakīrti, the lay bodhisattva who was very popular in early medieval China, but we find no mention in his biography of the *Lotus Sūtra* or the Medicine King.[98] It seems that from the first auto-cremation could range from self-conscious attempts to imitate the *Lotus* to more individually constructed expressions of piety. But even if Sengqing's devotion was offered not to the relics of the Buddha but to an image of a lay bodhisattva, the sympathetic resonance model was once again to the fore: The overcast sky cleared in anticipation of his auto-cremation and his ascension was marked by a flying dragon.

The concise account of the auto-cremation of Faguang contains some of the classic elements of fifth-century auto-cremation: avoidance of grain, a change in diet, the making of a vow, and recitation of a text.[99] Other elements, however, are conspicuously absent; the biography makes no mention of miraculous signs or the involvement of local authorities.

> [Faguang] diligently practiced *dhūta* (*kuxing toutuo* 苦行頭陀) and did not wear silk.[100] He refrained from the five grains (*jue wugu* 絕五穀) and ate only pine needles. Later he vowed to burn his body, and from then on he ate pine resin and drank oil for half a year. On Yongming 永明 5.10.20 of the Qi 齊 (November 21, 487), within Jicheng si 記城寺 in Longxi 隴西 [present-day Shaanxi], he piled up firewood to burn his body in fulfilment of his former vow. As the flames reached his eyes the sound of his recitation could still be heard. When they reached his nose it became indistinct. He passed away peacefully. He was forty-one.[101]

Faguang's biography only makes complete sense in the context in which it now appears—as part of a compilation of other cases with fuller descriptions of the processes of auto-cremation. Appended to his biography is an even briefer account of another auto-cremator, which shows once more the involvement of local authorities in venerating those who chose this path:

> At the same time, around the end of the Yongming reign period (483–493) in Shifeng 始豐 county, there was a monk called Facun 法存 who also burned his body in homage.[102] The prefect of the commandery (*junshou* 郡守), Xiao Mian 蕭緬 (456–491), sent the *śramaṇa* Huishen 慧深 (d.u.) to erect a *stūpa* for his ashes.[103]

Most cases of auto-cremation were public events—some very lavish and well attended as we have seen—but there could also be a furtive side to auto-cremation: There were monks who burned themselves in secret. Tanhong lived at Xianshan si 仙山寺 in Jiaozhi 交趾, which is now in North Vietnam.[104] There he recited two texts that particularly extol the virtues of rebirth in the Pure Land of the Buddha Amitābha—the *Wuliangshou jing* 無量壽經 (Sūtra of Immeasurable Life, T 12.360) and the *Guan wuliangshou jing* 觀無量壽經 (Book on the Contemplation of the Buddha of Immeasurable Life, T 12.365)—and he vowed to be reborn in the Pure Land (*anyang* 安養).[105] One day in 455 he gathered up firewood on the mountain, secretly entered the pyre, and set fire to himself. He was rescued by his disciples, although half of his body had already been consumed by fire. He survived and after a month showed some signs of improvement. But one day, when a nearby village held a religious assembly (*hui* 會) and invited all the occupants of the monastery,

Tanhong was left alone and again attempted to burn himself. By the time the villagers reached him he was already dead, so they added firewood to build up the fire, which did not burn out until the next day. Although the circumstances of a failed auto-cremation followed by a second attempt seem inauspicious and show that offering the body could be a potentially messy business, Tanhong's death (as we shall see below) was accompanied by miracles that suggest that his determination was nothing but praiseworthy.

Auto-Cremation by Nuns

The six cases of auto-cremation by women are harder for us to interpret because the biographies are relatively brief and short of detail when compared with those of their male counterparts. This is not to say that female auto-cremation was less significant, less powerful, or less productive of miracles. In fact, nuns seem to have been at the forefront of the practice in the fifth century.

The nun Shanmiao 善妙 (fl. fifth century) of Shu lived with her younger sister, a widow, and her sister's young child.[106] Her sister often heard Shanmiao lament that she had not been born at the time of the Buddha. After they had lived together for four or five years, Shanmiao wove a length of cloth and began to purchase large quantities of oil, telling her sister that it was "for a work of religious merit." Shanmiao set fire to herself at midnight on the eighth day of the fourth month, a favorite day for acts of auto-cremation. As she burned she ordered her sister to summon the other nuns. Still alive when they arrived, she had time to deliver a final speech to them, urging them to work hard to escape *saṃsāra*. Finally, she revealed that she had abandoned her body as an offering to the buddhas in twenty-seven previous lives but that only now would she attain the first fruit (*chuguo* 初果)—that is to say, she would be a "stream enterer" and no longer be reborn in the unfavorable destinies.

Shanmiao wove her own cloth whereas monks normally purchased it or received it as a donation. This relatively minor domestic detail is one of the few things that clearly distinguishes the nun's auto-cremation from that of her male contemporaries. Doctrinally speaking, Shanmiao took rather a long view of the path to enlightenment, seeing herself only at the lowest level of attainment despite having made numerous offerings of her body in previous lifetimes. Nevertheless she evidently did not doubt that this somatic path out of the horrors of *saṃsāra* was open to her as a woman. Perhaps Shanmiao considered her rebirth in a female body as a sign that her progress was not likely to be swift.

Shanmiao may have had few opportunities to enjoy a distinguished monastic career, living as she did with her sister and her sister's child, and auto-cremation may have seemed like a particularly productive alternative. Dao-zong 道綜 (d. 463) of Sanceng si 三層寺 in Jiangling 江陵 also seems to have had rather an unmemorable monastic career. A reference to her "muddled outward behavior that disguised her inner depths" may indicate that she was considered a little eccentric by her contemporaries.[107] She burned herself on the night of Daming 7.3.15 (April 18, 463), just a few weeks before the monk Huiyi did the same. The middle of the lunar month was another favorite night for auto-cremation: The light of the full moon would certainly have added to the drama. Daozong chanted steadily while she burned in front of an awestruck crowd. The scholar Liu Qiu 劉虯 (438–495) is said to have composed her eulogy in the form of a *gāthā*.[108]

Rather than being marginalized by the Buddhist establishment in the fifth century, it seems that female auto-cremators were quite the equals of their male counterparts. They chose the time, place, and means of their offerings and were celebrated in the same ways: by large numbers of witnesses and by the eulogies of literati. Just as male auto-cremators sometimes encountered and overcame opposition to their acts, so too did nuns.

The account of the auto-cremation of Huiyao 慧耀 (d. 477) of Yongkang si 永康寺 in Shu shows that people could sometimes be suspicious about the true motives of those who intended to burn themselves.[109] Huiyao is also notable for the fact that she left behind what are explicitly referred to as *śarīra*, which as we have seen were rare enough for monks in the fifth century. Huiyao became a nun in childhood and constantly vowed to burn her body as an act of devotion to the Three Jewels (*sanbao* 三寶). At the end of the Taishi 泰始 reign period (465–471) she announced her intention to the governor, Liu Liang 劉亮 (d. 472), who initially gave his permission.[110] She wished to perform the act on top of a tile pagoda belonging to a Madam Wang 王, who agreed to her plan. At midnight on the fifteenth day of the first month (the day of the lantern festival, which marked the end of the new year celebrations), Huiyao and her disciples arrived, bringing oil and cloth with them.

Before Huiyao could burn herself a letter arrived from Liu, saying that if she went ahead her convent would be committing a major offense. Madam Wang immediately suspected some collusion between the governor and the nun—perhaps a ruse designed to bring glory to Huiyao without her actually having to burn. But the nun dismissed Wang's accusations and returned to her convent. There she abstained from cereals and drank oil until 477, when she finally burned herself, reciting scriptures until the flames reached her face. Before she died Huiyao told the nuns that she would leave two *sheng* 升 of bones. They gathered exactly that amount.

The biography goes on to explain that just over a month before Huiyao burned herself, a foreign monk appeared with long black hair sprouting from his shoulder—because, he explained, he never covered that part of his body with his robe. The monk said he was from Vārāṇasī and brought a silver vase that was later used to hold the *śarīra* from Huiyao's bones.[111] Huiyao's account is as replete with signs and miracles as any of her male contemporaries. The presence of an Indian monk is especially significant as it conferred a miraculous legitimacy on the act by having it foretold and approved of by a strict practitioner from the very home of Buddhism.

One unique feature of female auto-cremation is the joint offering of bodies by two or more women. In 493 two nuns, Tanjian 曇簡 (d. 493) and Jinggui 淨珪 (d. 493), burned themselves at the same time and place.[112] Seven years later Tanyong 曇勇 (d. 501), who was Tanjian's sister by birth as well as by vocation, did the same. (In a later chapter we shall examine an account of two sisters who burned together.) Why should women in particular be linked in this way? One is tempted to imagine some deep emotional bond between Tanjian, Jinggui, and Tanyong, but the biographies do not actually mention this possibility, and as is often the case we are left only with a tantalizing glimpse into the religious lives of women of the medieval period.

Unlike Shanmiao and Huiyao, Tanjian came from a distinguished clan (the Qinghe Zhang 清河張) and was an accomplished meditator. She had her own convent, Fayin si 法音寺, which she donated to a monk called Huiming 慧明 (d.u.). She built a thatched hermitage on Bai shan 白山, went out begging, and was sustained by alms.[113]

> She often gathered firewood, saying that she was going to carry out a meritorious act, and on the night of Jianwu 建武 1.2.8 (March 11, 493), she mounted this pile of firewood and kindled a fire, thereby abandoning her *saṃsāra* body as an offering to the Three Jewels.[114] When people in the neighboring village saw the fire they raced to rescue her, but when they arrived Tanjian had already died. Religious and laity alike lamented, their cries reverberating through the mountains and valleys. Then they built a tomb for her remains that they had gathered.[115]

Jinggui had a long association with Tanjian: As a child, her parents allowed her to take up residence in Tanjian's convent. She studied both scriptures and Vinaya and like Tanjian was a skilled meditator. The biography notes that she tended to neglect her body and often looked emaciated. Although this laconic remark may suggest parallels with the role of food in the lives of medieval European women studied by Caroline Bynum, we do not yet have enough contextual evidence to come to any firm conclusions about the attitude of medieval Chinese nuns towards their own bodies.[116] When Tanjian left for Bai shan, Jinggui went with her; when Tanjian burned her body, Jinggui did the same. Jinggui's relics—again the text explicitly calls them *śarīra*—were gathered up and entombed.

Tanyong, Tanjian's elder sister, moved to Bai shan with the other two nuns. She was a meditator and a strict observer of the Vinaya. She is said to have "deeply comprehended impermanence, and highly venerated the joy of cessation."[117] On the night of Yongyuan 永元 3.2.15 (March 19, 501), she piled up firewood and burned herself in front of witnesses. Her remains—not referred to as *śarīra* but as "leftover ashes" (*yijin* 遺燼)—were entombed.

Women burned themselves in public, had their acts recorded by literati, and left relics, just as their male counterparts did. Can we really imagine that such practices did not continue after the sixth century just because the biographies ceased to be collected after Baochang? This seems hard to credit especially because we can still find scattered references to female self-immolation in other sources.

As we have seen, the biographies of self-immolators record what occurred on a particular day and sometimes events leading up to the final act, but they also give clues to the subsequent commemoration of self-immolation. The actions of the men and women they celebrate produced miracles; they changed the landscape and the monks and nuns lived on as heroes in the memories of those left behind. Let us now give some thought to how and why these performances affected those who witnessed them as we examine some miracles associated with self-immolation in the early period.

Miracles

The witnesses to Huishao's auto-cremation saw a star descend straight into the smoke of his pyre and suddenly rise into the sky. They identified it as an emissary of the Celestial Palace 天宮—meaning perhaps the Pure Land of Amitābha or Tuṣita Heaven, the home of the future Buddha Maitreya—come to fetch Huishao. This sign lends itself to a number of possible interpretations. First, it could imply simple ascent into any unspecified heaven in the way that transcendents were also said to ascend. Second, it could mean specifically that Huishao had attained rebirth in a Pure Land, a stage of non-retrogression whence he would continue the bodhisattva path without being reborn in the lower destinies. Third, Huishao may have been understood to have joined the retinue of Maitreya, ready to descend with him in glory when the time was ripe for the appearance of the next Buddha. Whatever interpretation we favor, the sign shows that some external force recognized and validated Huishao's offering of his body and again we can detect the presence of the underlying logic of sympathetic resonance.

The descending star was not the only miracle associated with Huishao's act. Just before the time of his death, he told his fellow disciples: "A firmiana tree (*wutong* 梧桐) will grow in the spot where I burn my body.[118] Don't let anyone cut it down."[119] Three days later one did indeed spring up there. The *wutong* is an important tree in Chinese mythology: According to the *Zhuangzi* 莊子, for example, it is the only tree on which the phoenix will land.[120] The miraculous growth or regrowth of a sacred tree might stand metaphorically for the miraculous production of a new kind of body by the auto-cremator or just as an appropriately rare auspicious sign indicating the response of the cosmos, but sometimes the biographies insist on providing the tree with a specifically Buddhist gloss.

The firmiana tree appears again at the end of the biography of Sengyu. Here, the tree is a sign that the biography explores and explicates in detail. In this case the reader is left in no doubt about the level of the monk's attainment. The biography tells us that fourteen days after Sengyu's auto-cremation:

> A double firmiana tree sprang up in his cell; it flourished root and branch and the proportions [of both halves] were exactly symmetrical. [The two trunks of the tree] went straight down into the ground and straight up into the air, and then became intertwined [thus forming an auspicious natural arch]. The knowledgeable claimed that they were the precious [twin] *śāla* trees that had been present at [the Buddha's] *parinirvāṇa* and because Sengyu had attained *nirvāṇa*, this proof had appeared. So people referred to him as "the double firmiana *śramaṇa*."[121]

Sengyu's firmiana tree with its twin trunks is multiply auspicious. It retains the numinous power of the perch of the phoenix and forms an auspicious arch, and it is also explicitly interpreted as the twin *śāla* trees beneath which the Buddha entered *parinirvāṇa*. Alan Cole has suggested that the appearance of the firmiana trees should be read as a symbol of agrarian fertility.[122] Although that symbol may be present at some level, it seems to me that in Sengyu's biography a greater claim is being made, one that draws on both Chinese omen lore and powerful Buddhist cosmological myths. Specifically, the double firmiana echoes the auspicious "intertwining trees" (*mulianli* 木連理), a traditional sign of the ruler's virtue and the harmony of all under heaven: "When a ruler's virtue and kindness are pure and harmonious, and when [the peoples at] the borders of the empire are united as a single family, intertwining trees grow."[123] The stress on such traditional auspicious signs in the early biographies shows how important it must have been to overwrite the polluting implications of an unlucky site of death with positive messages of hope and good fortune. The connection between self-immolation and a harmonious empire may not appear obvious to us now, but it was one that was often suggested in the biographies and was grounded in the mechanisms of sympathetic resonance.

From the Buddhist perspective, Sengyu's auto-cremation was presented as functionally equivalent to the Buddha's final exit from the world. Because the tree appeared, ergo he had entered *nirvāṇa*, just like the Indian sages of the past. This was something of a bold claim, but as we shall see, it was taken up and expanded upon in later biographies in which relics of auto-cremators increasingly came to replace stars, trees, and purple vapor as the indisputable marks of sanctity. In terms of the postmortem status of auto-cremators, in Sengyu's biography we have already progressed considerably beyond the earlier accounts where there was no hint of the possibility of entering *nirvāṇa* as a consequence of sacrificing the body. Perhaps as the practice became more widespread it had to be supported by claims to the attainment of the very highest goal in Buddhism.

In Sengqing's biography the dragon in the sky seen by witnesses gives us the clue that his auto-cremation ought to be read as a transformation of the body rather than an act of self-destruction. This kind of evidential sign of the efficacy of auto-cremation is a fairly common feature of fifth- and sixth-century biographies, but it tends not to appear in later cases, perhaps because it was so reminiscent of the transformations of non-Buddhist sages. Although the local governor had Sengqing's ashes placed in a *stūpa*, in this biography the auto-cremator's remains are not referred to explicitly as *śarīra*. They were, however, preserved for the local community and a new sacred site was created. They may even have been the focus of a cult, which was the case with the *śarīra* of some later auto-cremators.

Although Tanhong's auto-cremation was a private, secretive affair—perhaps even inauspicious because his first attempt had failed—the local community was not denied their miracle:

> That day, the villagers saw Tanhong, his body golden in color, heading west, riding a golden deer. He was in such a hurry that the villagers had no chance to exchange greetings with him. Not until then did the religious and laity realize [the meaning of] this miraculous and anomalous event (*shenyi* 神異). Together they gathered the ashes and bones and erected a *stūpa* for them.[124]

The glittering form of Tanhong serves as a sign that his body had truly transformed from that of an ordinary being to that of a bodhisattva.

Although the golden deer does not appear to be associated with any particular sage, Tanhong's departure for the west, the direction of Amitābha's Pure Land, carries with it echoes of the departure of Laozi in the same direction on the back of a water buffalo.[125] Like the firmiana trees that were equated with the *śāla* trees standing witness to the Buddha's *nirvāṇa*, Tanhong's final revelation as a "golden man" hints at a Buddhist view of transformation. Once the bodhisattva has abandoned the body made of flesh, he gains a *dharmakāya*, a body composed of pure *dharma*s. Tanhong's body of gold, with its associations of purity and incorruptibility, is surely a gesture in this direction.

State and Literati Involvement

It was not only monks and nuns who participated in and witnessed acts of self-immolation. As we have seen, literati, officials, and even royalty were all active participants. At the very least, local officials arranged the interment of remains and the composition of epitaphs for self-immolators. According to Sengyu's biography, Zhang Bian 張辯 (fl. mid-fifth century) of Wu 吳 commandery was the governor of Pingnan 平南 at the time of the monk's death.[126] He witnessed the events and composed both a biography and a verse eulogy (*zan* 贊), which is reproduced at the end of the *Gaoseng zhuan* entry.[127] In Zhang Bian we have an eyewitness, a real historical figure who, we are told, composed the biography of the auto-cremator. This kind of independent corroboration does not prove that events unfolded exactly as described in the biography, but the presence of figures whom we know from other sources does at least add to the appearance of veracity. Sengqing's biography says that his auto-cremation was witnessed by the local prefect, Zhang Yue. So we can place on the spot at the time of Sengqing's death both Zhang and Pei Fangming, the governor of Tianshui, who gathered the monk's ashes and had them interred beneath a *stūpa*.

We are not told what kind of relationship Zhang Bian and Sengyu enjoyed, but the biography of Huiyi shows him to have been very close to the emperor Xiaowu.[128] When he set out for the site of his auto-cremation in a cart, being presumably too weak to walk, it occurred to Huiyi that he ought first to say farewell to the emperor in his role as patron of the Three Jewels. He wanted to enter the palace under his own strength, but when he reached the Yunlong gate 雲龍門, he could no longer proceed on foot. Common people were never permitted to enter the imperial palace in carts or on horseback, so he could only send a message, in which he presented his farewells and entreated the emperor to safeguard the *dharma*. When the emperor heard this he was upset and immediately came out to meet him at the gate. Huiyi again entrusted the *dharma* to his care and then left, followed by the emperor and a retinue of princes, concubines, religious, laity, and officials who flooded into the valley, all of them offering donations.

Xiaowu tried to dissuade Huiyi from going through with his planned self-immolation, but the monk asked only that the emperor should permit the ordination of twenty monks. The emperor immediately issued an edict authorizing these ordinations. We have some independent confirmation that the emperor kept his promise: The biography of a monk called Fajing 法鏡 (437–500) records that he was among the twenty monks who had been ordained as a consequence of Huiyi's auto-cremation.[129] The relationship between emperor and monk is dramatically rendered in the biography. We read that after Huiyi's body had been burned:

> The fire did not die down until the next morning. At that moment the emperor heard the sound of pipes in the air and smelled a strange perfume that was remarkably fragrant. He did not return to the palace until the end of that day. At night he dreamed that he saw Huiyi, who came striking a bell. Again he entrusted to him the *Buddhadharma*. The next day the emperor held an ordination ceremony. He ordered the master of ceremonies to give a eulogy for the funeral service. At the place of the auto-cremation was built Yaowang si 藥王寺, which alludes to [Huiyi's recitation of] "The Original Acts."[130]

The lengthy descriptions of Huiyi's contacts with the court and the presence of the emperor himself at the cremation site make evident the close relationship between *saṃgha* and state in medieval China. The repeated admonitions of Huiyi that the emperor should safeguard the *dharma* and his request for the ordination of more monks show clearly what was at stake here for Huiyi: the continued survival of the *saṃgha* in China. The ability of the self-immolator to protect the whole community is a theme that we shall see taken up in many later accounts.

Huijiao's Critical Evaluation

Having examined these early biographies in some detail, we will now consider what Huijiao, the compiler of the *Gaoseng zhuan,* made of the materials he selected for inclusion in his collection.[131] How did these accounts of bodily devotion, extreme generosity, and miraculous transformation by fire fit into his vision of Buddhist practice in China? We have some clues as to how Huijiao intended his readers to make sense of these biographies. He summarized and evaluated the biographies in each section of his collection under the heading "critical evaluation" (*lun* 論), a form of appraisal he borrowed from secular historiography but which also had an immediate antecedent in the *Mingseng zhuan*.[132]

Huijiao's critical evaluation, as we would expect from this type of formal medieval prose, begins with a general statement of the subject containing learned allusions to the *Analects* and to Mencius. Next, he compares the selfishness of ordinary people to the selflessness of self-immolators: This was to become a favorite theme of later writers who expanded upon it in their own evaluations. Huijiao then summarizes the biographies and compares them to examples found in the scriptures. Finally, he offers an appraisal of the ethics of self-immolation.

Life and the physical form are precious to most people, says Huijiao. That is why many are driven to spoil themselves with the material comforts of rich food and fine clothes. Some try to hang on to life as long as they can by practicing various techniques associated with longevity: taking herbal and mineral drugs and cultivating meditational and gymnastic techniques.[133] These selfish people, who would not do the least thing to help others, are contrasted with self-immolators, who are completely selfless and extremely generous. Their charity arises from the fact that they have realized that the body is merely illusory, a temporary stopping place in *saṃsāra*. This realization of the ultimate emptiness of the self, of material possessions, and indeed of one's own family, allows them to give away everything. For Huijiao, the self-immolators in his collection are just such men.

Huijiao then summarizes the acts of Sengqun, Sengfu, Daojin, and Tancheng, with a pithy phrase for each. Their acts are explicitly compared with those of Prince Mahāsattva and King Śibi—the two great archetypes of selfless giving in the Mahāyāna literature.[134] The rest of the self-immolators, from Fayu to Tanhong, are auto-cremators. Huijiao hints that they were motivated as much by the determination to be reborn in a Pure Land as by the perfection of charity (*dānapāramitā*). He further notes that such acts were accompanied by auspicious signs such as the sudden appearance of the firmiana tree. According to Huijiao, the portents indicate that these acts were successful and thus beyond the constraints of normal morality.

The remainder of Huijiao's discussion is taken up with the ethics of self-immolation. The obvious tension between interpretations of the act of self-immolation in the *sūtras* and Vinaya was a topic that the learned Buddhist doctors of China returned to again and again as we shall see in succeeding chapters. First, says Huijiao, if there is no auspicious sign that indicates the legitimacy of the act and no benefits for other beings, then the monk's primary duty is to obey the Vinaya, which prohibits killing. The body of a monk is not

just his own but an important field of merit for the laity and thus not something to be lightly destroyed. The benefit of self-immolation is that it involves
being oblivious to the self, which is a fundamental precondition of enlightenment. The cost is that one breaks the precepts. Having set out this fundamental dichotomy between precept and practice, which was always the core of the
ethical problem, Huijiao moves on to a more detailed exposition.

Although advanced bodhisattvas may be able to make the supreme
sacrifice—as is attested in so many stories about the previous lives of the
Buddha—according to Huijiao, a bodhisattva who is just starting the path is
not able to attain such heights. Any attempt to do so leads to an unbalanced
practice. For example, Prince Mahāsattva's generosity saved the tigress but
caused his parents great distress and so was unfilial. The next objection to the
practice is one we have already met: It may cause harm to the parasites that
live in or on the human body. The Buddha had said that the body of the arhat
had to be inspected carefully for such creatures before being cremated, but
obviously burning oneself alive was sure to kill them. Huijiao presents two
possible counters to this rule. First, if an arhat, like Ānanda for example, can
burst into flames, why not an ordinary person?[135] Second, advanced practitioners can will their lives to be over before they actually enter the flames, thus
sparing the lives of their eighty thousand parasitic companions. I am not sure
if there is any scriptural support for this last idea or if it is casuistry on
Huijiao's part. Huijiao also muses on the fact that, in the early stages of the bodhisattva path, bodhisattvas are still subject to rebirth, but this does not stop
them from jumping into fires or slicing themselves up.

In the final analysis, for Huijiao there is a clear distinction between bodhisattvas who appear on earth in human form and ordinary humans. As
auto-cremation by the former cannot be censured—and as we shall see in
later chapters, some auto-cremators in China were quite clearly understood
to be bodhisattvas in human form—ordinary humans, who undertake it for
fame or notoriety, reveal their inadequacy because fear overcomes them at
the last moment. It seems, from his description, that Huijiao was familiar
with such cases, but he has certainly excluded them from his compilation.

Huijiao's verse at the end of his critical evaluation leans heavily towards
indigenous, specifically Taoist, imagery and offers us an important clue to
how self-immolators were understood in medieval society:

> If a person can stiffen his will (zhi 志), then metal and stone cannot be
>   considered hard.[136]
> Melting away what others consider important, they sacrificed it for that
>   precious city,

With its luxuriant vegetation and aromatic firmiana trees, and its fine
   floating purple buildings.
Mounting the smoke with glittering colors, spitting out tallies, and bearing
   auspicious omens.
They remain noble for a thousand years, their reputation is transmitted for
   ten thousand generations.[137]

In these lines Huijiao shows himself most impressed by auto-cremators,
who "melt away" their bodies and rise into the heavens with the smoke. He
attributes their actions not primarily to generosity but to determination—an
interpretation that squares with that found in the *Lotus Sūtra* as we shall see.
Rather than discarding their bodies, auto-cremators use them as a means of
transport to the heavens ("that precious city") or perhaps *nirvāṇa*. As if to
stress the mechanism of sympathetic resonance, Huijiao indicates the presence of the same firmiana trees that sprang up on earth to indicate a successful act of self-immolation.

Conclusion

In this chapter we have seen the significance of self-immolation as a monastic
practice for compilers of biographies in the sixth century. For Huijiao and
Baochang, self-immolation was not a deviant or marginal tendency, but a tradition that could serve the *saṃgha* just as effectively as translation, exegesis, or
miracle-working. In the actual biographies themselves, self-immolation appears to have been endorsed by the monastic establishment and by the secular powers, albeit with the occasional show of reluctance.

As for the origins of auto-cremation in China, they have proved impossible to determine. The biographies of the earliest auto-cremators show no
interest in establishing where and when their subjects learned of the possibility of re-enacting the Medicine King's offering. But as far as we can establish from the sources, auto-cremation was not the preserve of a single area
or cult activity. We have also learned that women were performing acts of
auto-cremation as early as men.

There are a number of significant themes that we shall see develop or
change over the history of self-immolation. We have noted the importance of
scriptural models to those who performed and recorded acts of self-immolation—particularly the *Lotus Sūtra* and the *jātakas*. It seems that not just individual details but also the narrative form and doctrinal logic of *jātaka* tales
were incorporated into the practices of Chinese monks and nuns. The *Lotus
Sūtra* provided not only a template for auto-cremation, but also the liturgy:

Monks chanted the Medicine King chapter as they enacted it, thus turning the scripture into a kind of performative speech. In this way Chinese monks and nuns incorporated themselves into one of the most important and beloved scriptures of the Mahāyāna. At the same time, the biographies make explicit some aspects of self-immolation that are only suggested by the scriptures, such as the power of self-immolation to convert people to Buddhism and to save beings.

We have seen in this chapter many references to and descriptions of miracles attendant on self-immolation. Descending and ascending stars, divine monks, unburned tongues, and intertwined trees were important markers of the response of the cosmos to human actions. The miracles and signs associated with our Chinese auto-cremators were open to multiple interpretations both traditional/classical and Buddhist. Intertwined trees and dragons, for example, carry more Chinese associations and show how self-immolation did not depend on a Buddhist symbolic framework but could be read and understood in terms of more indigenous schemes. The fact that relics were mostly associated with female auto-cremators, who interestingly seem to have produced few miracles, may suggest that relics were a type of miracle that could be read most satisfactorily as Buddhist. In other words, there may have been some resistance on the part of male biographers to attributing auspicious signs such as intertwined trees and dragons to the acts of females.

If there were indigenous aspects to the miracles, there were also elements in the preparation of the body, such as abstention from grain and consumption of incense pills, that suggest that self-immolators were drawing on a large and varied repertoire of techniques. Certainly by the time of Huijiao and Baochang, auto-cremation was a distinctive element of Chinese Buddhism that made a certain amount of sense to the *saṃgha* and to the secular world in part because of the practitioners' successful use of frames of reference from both Buddhist and indigenous traditions. As we shall see, as self-immolation developed in the succeeding centuries there were fewer overt references to such omens as Buddhist authors became more conscious of the boundaries of orthodoxy and orthopraxy. Likewise, references to relics increased as Chinese Buddhists became more confident in their ability to produce such marvels in their own territory.

CHAPTER 2

The *Lotus Sūtra*, Auto-Cremation, and the Indestructible Tongue

A s is immediately apparent from the many references to the scripture (both explicit and oblique) in biographies of auto-cremators, the *Lotus Sūtra* was a text that offered both rationale and model for burning the body. To understand the way in which Chinese Buddhists shaped their auto-cremation practices we will need to examine the nature of this text as a whole in addition to looking closely at the legend of the Bodhisattva Medicine King. How did a piece of literature composed in quite a different religious and cultural milieu come to affect Chinese beliefs and practices so deeply and enduringly? Why and how was the *Lotus* in particular so influential on body practices?

Auto-cremation is not unique to the *Lotus:* It appears in a variety of other Buddhist texts. Scriptures such as the *Samādhirāja sūtra* contain accounts of auto-cremation that may have been influential even if they were not attributed with inspiring the kind of devotion that the *Lotus* did. We shall examine here some of these other texts to appreciate the range of literary presentations of burning the body and how these different tableaux were understood by Chinese monastics.

Forms of bodily devotion associated with the *Lotus* can be found throughout the *Gaoseng zhuan* literature, but if we look beyond these sources we will find collections of biographies of *Lotus Sūtra* devotees that seem to have been even more popular and enthusiastically pious. These collections include accounts of lay auto-cremators as well as monks. How did the practice of auto-cremation and its textual representation change outside the monastic context?

The *Lotus Sūtra* and Its Interpretation in China

By any standards the *Lotus Sūtra* is a very odd literary work. Actual preaching never begins because it is endlessly deferred by stories, testimonials, and miracles that attest to and extol the miraculous powers of the *sūtra*.[1] The reader of the scripture is thus caught up willy-nilly in a dizzying series of recursive loops that refer back to themselves so as to produce a kind of closed system— an entirely self-contained *Lotus Sūtra* universe. The reader must perforce surrender both reason and disbelief if he is to enter that universe, which is advertised in the most enticing and hyperbolic manner. The language of the scripture seems designed not so much to convince by pure reason as to overwhelm the senses, drawing the reader (or listener) into a very different world in which the normal constraints of time and space do not apply. Textually speaking, the work is not a coherent whole, as parts of the *sūtra* were written at different times, but that fact was not immediately apparent to medieval Chinese Buddhists. They found within the *Lotus* universe dramatic stories and beautiful *gāthā*s rather than systematic presentations of profound philosophy. The words came from the "golden mouth" of the Buddha himself, so they were true, however fantastic they may have seemed. The challenge that faced Chinese monks and nuns was to incorporate the *Lotus* world into their own paths of practice.

The *Lotus Sūtra*'s stories of enthusiastic and heroic bodhisattvas and their aspirations and devotions employed a kind of rhetoric and hyperbole understood by those familiar with the Indian literary tradition, but one that many medieval Chinese—who had rather a different attitude to the writings of sages—could be forgiven for taking quite literally. The modelling of moral behavior, government, and ritual after ancient and respected norms found in the classics was, after all, the ideal in medieval China. We may remember, for example, the disastrously bookish suggestion of Fang Guan 房琯 (697–763) that the Tang army should follow the way of the ancient sages and ride into battle on ox-drawn carts rather than horses. Fang's tactic rather predictably ended in a rout at the hands of more conventionally mounted cavalry forces and forty thousand casualties.[2] This example is perhaps rather an extreme case, but it does illustrate that sometimes in medieval China the precedent of a text was elevated over experience or common sense and that such behavior was not confined to the realm of religion.

The *Lotus* defies understanding—or so the text itself claims. It is full of drama and magic. Scenes are played out against a vast cosmic backdrop, and the buddhas and bodhisattvas express themselves in emotive and highly charged language very different in tone from the cooler and more measured prose of the *Prajñāpāramitā sūtra*s. Although the individual chapters of the *Lotus* are self-contained (and parts of the *sūtra* circulated independently in China), if we look at it as a whole we may discern the following three ideas that inspired modes of Buddhist practice in China: (1) the elevation of the Buddha and his powers far beyond other beings and their abilities, (2) the ineffability of the *dharma*, and (3) the primacy of worship *(pūjā)* over other types of practice.[3] In the second chapter, "Expedient Devices," (*Fangbian pin* 方便品; Skt. *Upāyakauśalya*), the *Lotus* reveals that the omniscience of the Buddha is hard to attain and beyond the capacity of ordinary people.[4] In Chapter 5, "Medicinal Herbs" (*Yaocaoyu pin* 藥草喻品; Skt. *Oṣadhī*), the true *dharma* itself is also said to be beyond understanding.[5] The Buddha says that he alone possesses the power to save and enlighten others:

> Those not yet in *nirvāṇa* I enable to attain *nirvāṇa*. For this age and for later ages, I know things as they are. I am the one who knows all, the one who sees all, the one who knows the Path, the one who opens up the Path, the one who preaches the Path.[6]

Because the Buddha himself, as he appears in the *Lotus,* is the access to deliverance, we see other practices not focused on the Buddha, such as meditation or observance of the Vinaya, recede in importance. The worship of the Buddha and/or his relics becomes the way to attain supreme enlightenment, which the *Lotus* explains is nothing less than the attainment of buddhahood itself.

In the *Lotus,* bodhisattvas well known from other *sūtras*, such as Mañjuśrī and Samantabhadra, play somewhat subsidiary roles, although there is much celebration of newly qualified bodhisattvas who advance rapidly through their enthusiastic acts of devotion. All these characteristics of the scripture can only have encouraged the practice of worship and devotion in China and inspired ordinary men and women to join the ranks of these magnificent creatures.[7] In fact, in our Chinese sources we find that some self-immolators were presented as newly minted bodhisattvas. The fervor of their devotion and the emotional language used to eulogize them seem to be drawn from the operatic world of the *Lotus*'s bodhisattvas. If we seek evidence of the influence of the *Lotus Sūtra* on Chinese Buddhist practice and the language used to describe it, then records of self-immolation surely offer us a broad range of material.

The impact of the *Lotus* on Chinese material and artistic culture provides an instructive parallel to its influence on practice. From a purely materialist perspective, the *Lotus Sūtra* is, as Liu Xinru has so memorably described it, "virtually a workshop manual rather than a text of Buddhist philosophy."[8] In the scripture, the precious objects suitable for worshipping the Buddha (through the decoration of *stūpas*, images of buddhas and bodhisattvas, or copies of the *Lotus Sūtra* itself) are repeatedly listed in great detail: flowers, incense, garlands, ointments, clothing, necklaces, gems, jewels, canopies, parasols, flags, and banners.[9] These objects are not just decorative; according to the *Lotus* the donation of such luxuries will in itself bring certain buddhahood.[10] In a famous episode from the *sūtra,* the daughter of the *nāga* king changes sex and attains enlightenment because she presents the Buddha with a priceless gem.[11]

The obsession with material wealth and frequent mentions of moneylending throughout the *sūtra* have been noted in the scholarship and attributed to the fact that the *Lotus* was composed against the background of the rise of a monetary economy in northwest India in the early centuries of the common era.[12] The donation of the Medicine King's body, understood as his "internal wealth," thus parallels the orgiastic donation of "outer wealth" so lovingly described elsewhere in the *sūtra.* The donations of precious objects given by nobility and commoners to auto-cremators show that Chinese believers entertained similar expectations about the power of charity and the transformation of wealth into merit. Reinforcing the logic of the concept of donating material goods in return for spiritual rewards was the *Lotus Sūtra*'s insistence that a bodhisattva could share his merit with others. In the biographies of Chinese auto-cremators, the merits of abandoning the body are understood to extend far beyond the practitioners themselves, and the biographies often emphasize the benefits that accrue to other beings. Thus many of the underlying attitudes towards self-immolation in China, and not just the practice of auto-cremation itself, can be traced back to ideas found in the *Lotus Sūtra.*

But, as Eugene Wang's work on the artistic representations of the *Lotus Sūtra* universe in China has shown, medieval Buddhists were not content merely to imitate or represent the cosmos presented to them in the text.[13] The murals and inscriptions made by medieval Chinese that ostensibly depict the *Lotus Sūtra* defy any attempt by the modern viewer to anchor them firmly to the text; they rather, as Wang argues, attest to "an imaginary world that draws on not only the Lotus Sutra but a host of other domains of experience."[14] We have already seen similar evidence in the biographies: Even those who explicitly identified the *Lotus* as their inspiration, who chanted the text as they burned, manifested patterns of behavior and ways of thinking that quite clearly come from somewhere other than the *Lotus* (for example, abstention from grain and the ingestion of incense pills were combined with wrapping the body in oil-soaked cloth and chanting the scripture). The *Lotus Sūtra* did, nevertheless, supply some of the most important elements in the repertoire of the imagination upon which self-immolators and their biographers drew.

As we have seen from the frequent invocation of the Bodhisattva Medicine King in the biographies, auto-cremation was in part predicated on a literal understanding and literal (or perhaps we may say ritual) re-enactment of one episode from the *Lotus Sūtra*. However, because the term *shaoshen* (burning the body) is also used in scriptural accounts to refer to the Buddha's cremation, the act of auto-cremation always carried echoes of the most important body in Buddhism—that of the Buddha himself. We see in this imitation of the ideal the introduction of a double. At the moment of burning, the practitioner's body is that of a buddha or a bodhisattva, yet at that same moment the double is also denied: It is oneself who is burned, not the substitute. The doubling is suggested by the biographical accounts as when the auto-cremator returns in dreams or visions after his death or when he is revealed to have been a bodhisattva in disguise. This effect may also help us to understand the absence of pain: The sensations of the body are denied at the very moment when the body becomes the focus of religious practice. As auto-cremators took on the role of the Medicine King, they also took on his body with all its miraculous powers. We should therefore take a close look at the scriptural model that was part of the repertoire familiar to self-immolators.

The Original Acts of the Medicine King

To understand what some auto-cremators used as the literary blueprint for their acts, let us consider the contents of the chapter "The Original Acts of the Medicine King" (*Yaowang pusa benshi pin* 藥王菩薩本事品; Skt. *Bhaiṣajya-rājapūrvayoga*).[15] The narrative frame of this chapter is introduced by the Bodhisattva Beflowered by the King of Constellations (Xiuwanghua 宿王華; Skt. Nakṣatrarājasaṃkusumitābhijña), who asks the Buddha to explain the "difficult deeds and austerities" (*nanxing kuxing* 難行苦行) of the Bodhisattva Medicine King. The Buddha relates that in the past, innumerable *kalpa*s ago, there was a Buddha called Pure and Bright Excellence of Sun and Moon (Riyuejingmingde 日月淨明德; Skt. Candrasūryavimalaprabhāsaśrī). (The very name of this buddha seems to presage the radiance of the bodhisattva's burning body.) This buddha had eighty million *bodhisattva-mahāsattva*s, and they all had a lifespan of forty-two thousand *kalpa*s. His realm was perfectly flat and adorned with jewelled trees, banners, and terraces; women, hell dwellers, hungry ghosts, and *asura*s were absent. It was, in other words, a Pure Land. At that time in the far distant past, in a Buddha realm very different from our own, the Buddha Pure and Bright Excellence of Sun and Moon taught the *Lotus Sūtra* to the Bodhisattva Seen with Joy by All Living Beings (Yiqie zhongsheng xijian 一切眾生喜見; Skt. Sarvasattvapriyadarśana). This bodhisattva wished to cultivate austerities within the time of the *dharma* of the Buddha Pure and Bright Excellence of Sun and Moon to attain buddhahood himself, and so he practiced diligently for twelve thousand years. Through his practice he attained the "*samādhi* that displays all manner of physical bodies" (*yiqie seshen sanmei* 一切色身三昧). He was delighted with this result, which he attributed not to his own practice alone, but to his having heard the *Lotus Sūtra*.

Seen with Joy by All Living Beings resolved to make offerings (*pūjā, gongyang* 供養) to the Buddha Pure and Bright Excellence of Sun and Moon and to the *Lotus Sūtra*. First he went into *samādhi* and produced a rain of flowers and incense. Later he decided this was not as good as making an offering of his own body. The *Lotus Sūtra* describes his preparations in a way that will echo through later accounts of auto-cremation in China.

The Bodhisattva doused himself in fragrance and oil, drank scented oil, and wrapped his body in an oil-soaked cloth. He made a vow and then burned himself. (We have already seen these stages described in the Chinese sources that speak of the Bodhisattva's later imitators.) The light of his burning body illuminated world systems to the number of eight hundred million times the number of grains of sand in the Ganges. The Buddhas of all the world systems were favorably impressed and praised his action:

> Good man, this is true perseverance in vigor! This is called a true Dharma-offering to the Thus Come One. If with floral scent, necklaces, burnt incense, powdered scent, paint-scent, divine cloth, banners, parasols, the scent of the candana of the near seashore, and a variety of such things one were to make offerings, still they could not exceed this former [act of yours]. Even if one were to give realms and walled cities, wives and children, they would still be no match for it. Good man, this is called the prime gift. Among the various gifts, it is the most honorable, the supreme. For it constitutes an offering of Dharma to the thus come ones.[16]

Note here how the offering of inner wealth is described as far surpassing even the most extravagant gifts of external wealth and even the offering of one's own wife and children (well known in China and elsewhere in the Buddhist world from the story of Prince Viśvantara).[17]

The Bodhisattva's body burned for twelve hundred years before it was consumed. Because he had made such a great offering he was immediately reborn again in the realm of the Buddha Pure and Bright Excellence of Sun and Moon. He was born not in the usual manner but by transformation, and he materialized sitting cross-legged in the household of King Pure Virtue (Jingde wang 淨德王; Skt. Vimaladatta). There he introduced himself in verse:

O Great King! Now be it known that I, going about in that place,
Straightway attained the All-Body-Displaying Samādhi,
Whereby, striving and greatly persevering in vigor,
I cast off the body to which I had been so attached.
Making this offering to the world-honored one,
I seek the unexcelled wisdom.[18]

This *gāthā* tells us three important things about the Bodhisattva's self-immolation. First, it was a consequence of attaining the *samādhi*. Second, it was a practice of the perfection of vigor *(vīryapāramitā)* and not the perfection of charity *(dānapāramitā)* as we might have expected. Third, it was an offering to the Buddha. It is interesting to note that in the cases of auto-cremation described in our Chinese materials, these three aspects are not necessarily to be found—a fact that suggests that auto-cremators were in fact picking and choosing from a repertoire of the imagination rather than slavishly reproducing textual models. For example, I have not found any mention of the "*samādhi* that displays all manner of physical bodies" in the biographies. Commentators on self-immolation often chose to present it as a practice of the perfection of charity rather than vigor as in the *Lotus*. Finally, the offering of the body to the Buddha, although it may often be implicit, is not always explicitly presented as being articulated in vows or enacted before buddha images or relics in the biographies.

After explaining himself in verse, the Bodhisattva announced to his new father that he would again make offerings to the Buddha Pure and Bright Excellence of Sun and Moon. He went to the Buddha, made obeisance, and spoke a *gāthā*. The Buddha told him that he was about to enter *parinirvāṇa* that very night and immediately entrusted the Bodhisattva with the *dharma,* his bodhisattvas, the world systems of his realm, and finally his precious *śarīra*. In the last watch of the night he entered *nirvāṇa*.

The Bodhisattva cremated the deceased Buddha and collected the *śarīra,* which he placed in eighty-four thousand reliquaries inside eighty-four thousand *stūpa*s. He draped them with banners, covered them with parasols, and adorned them with jewelled bells, but again it occurred to him that he should make a further offering. He announced to the assembled bodhisattvas, their disciples, gods, *nāga*s, and *yakṣa*s, "You are all to attend single-mindedly. For I will now make an offering to the *śarīra* of the Buddha Pure and Bright Excellence of Sun and Moon."[19] He then burned his forearms for seventy-two thousand years, causing many beings to open their minds to *anuttarasamyaksaṃbodhi* (complete and perfect enlightenment) and enabling them to dwell in the "*samādhi* that displays all manner of physical bodies."

But the assembled witnesses were somewhat upset that the Bodhisattva had no arms. He then vowed, "I have thrown away both arms. May I now without fail gain the Buddha's golden-colored body! If this oath is reality and not vanity, then may both arms be restored as before."[20] His arms were of course immediately restored, the great world system shook in six ways, and all men and gods "saw something they had never seen before."

The reference to the Buddha's golden body in the Bodhisattva's vow is alluded to in some of the biographies we shall discuss below. The golden body and other physical attributes of attainment, such as the unburned tongue or the production of relics, seem to have been particularly important to self-immolators and their biographers. Without them, auto-cremation might be nothing more than a bizarre form of suicide.

With the dramatic return of the Bodhisattva's arms (echoing as it does the magical restorations of body parts that occur in the *jātukas*), the story of the former acts of the Medicine King concludes and we return to the narrative frame of the chapter.[21] The Buddha now reveals to the Bodhisattva Beflowered by the King of Constellations that the Bodhisattva Seen with Joy by All Living Beings is none other than the present-day Bodhisattva Medicine King. The Buddha describes the Medicine King's practices and then makes a recommendation to ordinary practitioners:

> Gifts of his own body, such as this one, number in the incalculable hundreds of thousands of myriads of millions of *nayutas*. O Beflowered by the King of Constellations! If there is one who, opening up his thought, wishes to attain *anuttarasamyaksaṃbodhi*, if he can burn a finger or even a toe as an offering to a *Buddhastūpa*, he shall exceed one who uses realm or walled city, wife or children, or even all the lands, mountains, forests, rivers, ponds, and sundry precious objects in the whole thousand-millionfold world as offerings.[22]

In this speech Śākyamuni explicitly states that burning the body is not restricted to advanced bodhisattvas alone but may be practiced by anyone who wishes to attain buddhahood. However, in the typical fashion of the *Lotus Sūtra*, this claim for the powers of auto-cremation is immediately undercut by a further claim that the merit accrued by one who memorizes even a single *gāthā* of the *Lotus* exceeds that gained by one who gives away a trichiliocosm full of the seven jewels. No matter what praise it heaps on other practices, the *Lotus Sūtra* always reserves a special place in its heart for itself. The chapter on the original acts of the Medicine King concludes with the usual praise for the miraculous powers of the *Lotus Sūtra,* and the Buddha entrusts this chapter to the Bodhisattva Beflowered by the King of Constellations.

By burning their bodies as prescribed by this chapter of the *Lotus,* Chinese monks and nuns literally became bodhisattvas by enacting the role of its hero. Some were careful to mimic the Bodhisattva's consumption of incense and oil and the wrapping of the body in oil-impregnated cloth that preceded his auto-cremation. Evidence of their success in emulating his example was manifested if not by the "world system shaking in six ways" then at least by lights and signs in the sky, by miraculous trees growing in their cells, or at the site of the act, by dreams and portents—and, perhaps most importantly of all, by their relics. Some self-immolators even returned and revealed their newfound (or long-established) status to their followers. All of these factors indicate that something much more significant than simple suicide was understood to have occurred. Auto-cremation was not presented as mere termination but as transformation, just as the *Lotus* had promised.

Chinese Translations and Commentaries

The *Lotus Sūtra* was so extraordinarily popular and widely circulated that it would be hard to overstate its ubiquitous influence on medieval Chinese religious life. The most important early translation was known as the *Zheng fahua jing* 正法華經 (Sūtra of the Flower of True Dharma) made in 286 by Zhu Fahu 竺法護 (Dharmarakṣa, ca. 230–308).[23] It is now known from the revised version of 290. As Tsukamoto Zenryū has pointed out, although the text was translated in North China, its influence was by no means restricted to that area. It circulated in the Central Plain, and even south of the Yangzi from quite an early date.[24] But the *sūtra* really became popular only after 406, when Kumārajīva (Jiumoluoshi 鳩摩羅什, 344–413 or 350–409) translated it afresh as the *Miaofa lianhua jing* 妙法蓮華經 (Sūtra of the Lotus Blossom of the Wondrous Dharma). Kumārajīva's beautiful and accessible prose, which incorporated many semivernacular elements, made the *Lotus* an instant and enduring success throughout China.

The popularity of the *Lotus* may be gauged from the number of artistic representations it inspired, the compilation of numerous biographies of *Lotus* devotees, and its frequent mention in other sources, but it may also be seen in the number of copies made of it. The Russian expert on Dunhuang manuscripts L. N. Menshikov made the following calculations concerning the most popular *sūtra*s in medieval China based on surviving copies:

1. The *Diamond Sūtra (Vajracchedikā)* is represented in collections of Dunhuang manuscripts in London, Paris, and St. Petersburg in 1,470 copies.
2. The *Lotus Sūtra (Saddharmapuṇḍarīka)* exists in 3,140 fragments, or 450

copies. In London and Paris collections alone we find 2,181 items, or around 310 copies. There are 100 individual copies of the twenty-fifth chapter concerning Avalokiteśvara in various locations.

3. The *Sūtra of the Golden Light (Suvarnaprabhāsa[uttama]-sūtra),* which we discussed in the last chapter, has survived in 1,200 fragments (and approximately 120 copies of the full text).

4. The *Sūtra on the Essence of the Great Wisdom (Prajñāpāramitāhṛdaya-sūtra)* exists in 150 copies.[25]

Although it is true that there are many more full copies of the *Diamond Sūtra* than the *Lotus,* the *Diamond* is a much shorter text—only a few sheets of paper are required to make a copy of it. The material evidence proves that Chinese Buddhists did exactly as the *Lotus Sūtra* itself recommended: They copied it again and again for the great merit that such an action was said to bring. The *Lotus* spread across the landscape of medieval China not only as written text but as recitation, performance, and image. We know that recitation of the *Lotus* was not restricted to religious professionals in medieval China; it was recited by laypeople, especially in ceremonies sponsored by lay societies (known variously as *yiyi* 邑義, *yiyi* 義邑, and *fashe* 法社) often led by monks.[26] Steles with images of the preaching of the *Lotus* were erected by such societies. Recitation of the text brought with it great rewards that were frequently attested in the biographies of both monks and laity.[27]

Bhaiṣajyagururāja's offering of his body by fire evidently captured the Chinese imagination, and as a tale in its own right it gained some autonomy outside its place in the *Lotus Sūtra.* We may note, for example, the independent circulation of a text about burning the body called *Shao shen-bi-zhi yuanji* 燒身臂指緣記 (Account of the Circumstances of Burning the Body, the Arm, and the Finger), which is no longer extant but was noted in Lu Cheng's 陸澄 (423–494) *Fayuan zayuan yuanshi ji mulu* 法苑雜緣原始集目錄 (Catalogue of the Original Collections of Miscellaneous Accounts from the Dharma Garden).[28] According to the catalogue, this text was excerpted from the *Lotus Sūtra.* We may say with some confidence then that whether as part of the *Lotus* or as an independent account the legend of the Medicine King was very widely known and admired throughout China, possibly even before the first known case of auto-cremation in 396.

The commentarial literature on the *Lotus* is vast but not always relevant for understanding self-immolation.[29] This is because Chinese Buddhist commentary on *sūtra*s does not work in quite the same way as, say, commentaries on the classics. Chinese commentaries often do not explain *sūtra*s word-by-word or chapter-by-chapter. Neither do they usually summarize the teachings or narrative of *sūtras* nor provide an interpretation of *sūtras* from a doctrinal point of view. Instead, commentaries tend to overlay a blueprint of the structure of the *sūtra* upon the text so that they often assume the shape of an extended list or outline. When translated into English, they resemble the table of contents of a particularly imposing piece of legislation with many sections, subsections, paragraphs, and subparagraphs. It is when they are rendered diagrammatically that they fully reveal their architectonic form with many branches nested one inside the other. In other words, commentators were more interested in the deep structure of the *sūtra* taken as a whole, than they were with individual episodes within it.

This is not to suggest that the auto-cremation of the Medicine King goes entirely unremarked by the commentators. Commentaries on texts and miracles in China that attested to the powers of those texts were not mutually incompatible. For example, Jizang 吉藏 (549–623) and Guanding 灌頂 (561–632) refer to Guanyin 觀音 miracle tales in their writings.[30] The *Fahua wenju* 法華文句 (Textual Commentary on the *Lotus Sūtra*)—attributed to Tiantai Zhiyi 天臺智顗 (538–597) but actually written by Guanding from notes taken of Zhiyi's talks and much borrowing from the works of Jizang—mentions the auto-cremation in Changsha 長沙 of a Liang-dynasty *dharma* master Man 滿 who had lectured on the *Lotus* one hundred times.[31] This brief mention was later picked up and included in a Song-dynasty collection of biographies of *Lotus* devotees, the *Fahua jing xianying lu* 法華經顯應錄 (Record of Manifest Responses to the *Lotus Sūtra*), compiled by Zongxiao 宗曉 (1151–1214).[32] But the story of the Medicine King was not just edifying; his auto-cremation was also illuminating. Zhiyi himself was said to have become enlightened on reading the Medicine King chapter of the *Lotus.*[33]

On the doctrinal aspect of auto-cremation, there is the following passage found in the earliest extant Chinese commentary on the *Lotus,* that of Daosheng 道生 (360–434). Daosheng had studied under Kumārajīva himself and had a sophisticated understanding of doctrine and the *sūtra.* Here he comments on the auto-cremation of the Medicine King:

> What does burning one's body signify? When it comes to what a man treasures and values, nothing exceeds bodily life, and when one burns it oneself, it is because there is something as treasured as much as the body. If one is capable of grasping such meaning, even though one exists with the physical form, one is burning, as it were, all the time. [If] *li* 理 (principle) is perverted in the attempt to understand it, even though one burns oneself all day long, [in reality] one is never burning. [The Buddha] hopes that they attain [*li*] free of its traces and so will not be stagnated in worldly facts (*shi* 事).[34]

It seems that Daosheng's comments were not purely theoretical and could be applied to people actually burning themselves in China. He also stressed repeatedly that all humans were bound to become buddhas in time, and this idea may have encouraged people to act like the bodhisattvas they read about.[35] A later commentary on the *Lotus* by Jizang also takes the auto-cremation of the Bodhisattva to be a real event rather than a parable of some kind. He says that the bodhisattva does not break the precepts against burning the body or the arm because he is a lay bodhisattva and not a monk.[36] Certainly this would indicate that he gave the practical and ethical ramifications of the matter some thought.

Auto-Cremation in Other Buddhist *Sūtras*

Lest anyone imagine that the description of a bodhisattva burning his body is in any way unique to the *Lotus Sūtra*—or even that it is particularly anomalous within the broader span of Buddhist teachings—let us now examine other scriptural cases, some of which were known in China and others apparently only known elsewhere in the Buddhist world. In 1963, the scholar of Indian Buddhism Jean Filliozat wrote an article in response to Jacques Gernet's piece on auto-cremation in China, which had appeared in 1960.[37] Filliozat took Gernet to task somewhat for not knowing more about the Indian textual antecedents to the Chinese cases, although in fact Gernet had given a very full account of the Chinese material and early medieval Chinese knowledge of self-immolation in the translated texts. In particular, Filliozat expressed some surprise that there was no mention of the auto-cremation described in the *Samādhirāja sūtra*, a text that was quite well known in China. It is true that this *sūtra* is scarcely referred to in Chinese accounts of self-immolation, and I can only assume that the Medicine King's offering of his own body in the *Lotus* took such a powerful hold on the Chinese imagination that it could not be usurped by other texts.

The auto-cremation found in the *Samādhirāja sūtra* is at least as dramatic as the one recounted in the *Lotus Sūtra*, and the episode centers in a similar fashion on a junior bodhisattva who offers his own body to relics. Chapter 33 of the *Samādhirāja sūtra*, which is entitled *Kṣemadattaparivarta*, appears in the Chinese translation by Narendrayaśas of 557 (*Yuedeng sanmei jing* 月燈三昧經; Skt. *Candrapradīpasamādhi sūtra*, Moonlight Samādhi Sūtra, T 15.639), although there were earlier translations of the *sūtra* by An Shigao 安世高 (d. late second or early third century) and others. Given the popularity of Prince Moonlight (Yueguang wang 月光王) as a messianic figure in medieval China, it is hard to believe that this *sūtra* did not have some background influence on auto-cremation, even if it was not mentioned as a specific source of devotion.[38]

The story goes as follows, according to the Narendrayaśas translation:[39] During the period after the passing away of a Buddha called Ghoṣadatta (Shengde 聲德), King Śrīghoṣa (Deyin wang 德音王) had erected eighty-four thousand tens of millions of *stūpa*s containing relics, which were worshipped with innumerable lamps, music, flowers, incense, and so on. A *bodhisattva* called Kṣemadatta (Anyinde 安隱德) was a young *bhikṣu* at that time. Observing all the millions of lamps that blazed in front of the *stūpa*s and the vast assembly of gods, courtiers, and commoners assembled in devotion, he vowed to make an act of homage before the relic *stūpa*s. This act, he said, should cause all gods, humans, and *asura*s to marvel and be joyous. He wanted his offering to surpass that of King Śrīghoṣa and thus cause the king and his courtiers to marvel at his act and be joyous.

That night, when Kṣemadatta saw the great assembly in front of the *stūpa*s listening to the *dharma*, he wrapped his right arm in cloth and soaked it with oil before burning it as an offering to the buddha. At that moment he aspired to perfect and total enlightenment, and thinking of nothing else, he did not move. There was a great earthquake, and the radiance from his arm spread in all directions. Kṣemadatta attained the *samādhi* in which the fundamental identity of all *dharma*s is made manifest, and with beautiful and melodious speech he preached to the assembly. Gods and *apsara*s offered him homage and sang his praises. King Śrīghoṣa, who was then observing the scene from the top of a pavilion along with his harem, saw Kṣemadatta's act and realized that he must have attained great spiritual powers. He was so delighted that, accompanied by his entire harem, he flung himself off the pavilion at Kṣemadatta's feet. Even though it was thousands of feet high, the gods, *nāga*s, and *yakṣa*s all protected him and did not allow anyone to hit the ground. Seeing the pitiful state of the bodhisattva's arm, the king and the rest of the crowd cried out and wept. When Kṣemadatta asked the reason for their tears, the king sang his praises in *gāthā*s. Meanwhile, Kṣemadatta raised his arm, and it was restored to its former state.

It is interesting that Kṣemadatta, a *bodhisattva-mahāsattva*, is explicitly and repeatedly described in the *sūtra* as a *bhikṣu* and not a layman. Given the disputes over the issue of whether or not monks could burn themselves, it does strike me as somewhat odd that no one seems to have brought up this example—which actually refutes the claims made by Yijing 義淨 (635–713) in the early eighth century that only lay bodhisattvas burn themselves in the *sūtra*s.[40] The text also repeats that Kṣemadatta felt no pain, only joy and euphoria, the same emotions experienced by the participants. We should also note the importance placed on the presence of the king and his courtiers— just as in the Chinese biographies discussed in Chapter 1. Although the text may not have been a direct influence on self-immolation in medieval China, it may well have supplied some of the logic of the practice.

There are other important Mahāyāna texts that endorse the idea of donation of the body. *Karuṇāpuṇḍarīka* (White Lotus of Compassion), despite its rather innocuous title, contains numerous tales of the extreme violence the Buddha inflicted on his body in previous lives, most of them related with meticulous attention to the goriest detail. The text seems to have been quite popular in China, and episodes from it are frequently alluded to in the biographies of self-immolators. In this scripture, for example, as part of a cycle of stories about King Pradīpapradyota, one of Śākyamuni's former lives, the Bodhisattva wraps his arm in oiled cloth and sets fire to it to light the way for five hundred merchants lost at sea. His arm burns for seven days.[41]

A story from the popular collection *Zhongjing zhuanza shiyu* 眾經撰雜譬喻 (Various Avadānas Selected from the Sūtras) tells of a disciple of a brahmin who soaks his turban in oil and sets fire to it to act as a lamp for the Buddha.[42] As a result of this he becomes the Buddha Dīpaṃkara ("he who acts as a lamp"). While the lamp is burning, the young man shows no sign of pain and continues to read the holy texts. Finally, the story of the Medicine King is told with approval as an example of the immense benefits of worshipping the Buddha *(Buddhapūjā)* in the *Da zhidu lun* 大智度論, the great compilation of Buddhist lore that was so frequently consulted and taken as an authority by the learned doctors of medieval China.[43]

Further stories of auto-cremation are preserved in other languages and seem to have no analog in Chinese. They show the popularity and persistence of the trope of self-immolation throughout the Buddhist world. The *Lokapaññatti,* a text compiled in Burma in the eleventh or twelfth century, relates the following story about King Aśoka:

> Then, King Aśoka, wishing to pay [even] great[er] pūjā to the Mahāstūpa, had his own body wrapped in cotton up to his neck and his limbs up to his wrists, and he had himself soaked with five hundred pots of scented oil. Then, standing facing the Great Stūpa, with folded hands, his head anointed with oil, and mindful of the Buddha, he had his body set on fire; and the flames rose up in the air to a height of seven persons.
>
> The king kept repeating a stanza in praise of the Buddha: "Hail to the Blessed One, the arhat, he who is altogether enlightened [namo Bhagavato arahato samasambuddhassa].... For the benefit of many he taught the Dharma.... His is the community of disciples which conducts itself uprightly, properly, and correctly."
>
> In this way, he recollected the Triple Gem, and, while he was so meditat-

ing, the flames did not burn his body in the slightest, and he remained cool as if he had been smeared with sandalwood paste. And so it was on the second, third, and up to the seventh day; the king paid pūjā to the Great Stūpa with his entire body ablaze. Then he bathed, and, adorned with all his ornaments and surrounded by his ministers, he worshipped the stūpa, circumambulating it three times. Then he listened to the preaching of the Dharma for seven days and nights, offered food to the community of monks, worshipped it and went off together with his entourage.[44]

Evidently, auto-cremation in front of relics as recounted in the *Lotus Sūtra* and *Samādhirāja* was such a powerful trope that it could be applied even to historical figures such as Aśoka and not just to bodhisattvas in other world systems.

The late Pāli text called *Dasabodhisattuppattikathā* (Birth Stories of the Ten Bodhisattvas), obviously a work of Mahāyāna inspiration, contains many stories that feature the classic themes of the offering of children, the head, the eyes, and so on. The following story is told of the Buddha Rāmarāja:

During the Dispensation of Kassapa the Perfect Buddha, this Rāmarāja was the youth Nārada, full of confidence and gladdened by the Triple Gem. Then, Sāriputta, the youth Nārada seeing the Perfect Buddha Kassapa surrounded by the assembly of gods, Brahmas and men, embellished with the thirty-two marks and eighty minor marks of a Great Being, illuminated by a halo extending a fathom, thought thus: "A Perfect Buddha is very rare; what is the use to me of this disgusting life; it is worthwhile sacrificing one's life for the Buddha." Having pondered thus, taking two pieces of cloth, he soaked them in scented oil and wrapped himself with them from head to foot and then set fire to them with a torch as an offering to the Buddha. Having sacrificed his life thus, he made the aspiration "May this light-offering help to obtain the All-knowing Knowledge."

Then, Sāriputta, the Perfect Buddha Kassapa prophesied, seated in the assembly: "Nārada, this Auspicious Aeon will end in fire; then there will be an incalculable period without Buddhas called an empty aeon. At the end of this empty aeon there will be a Maṇḍa Aeon with two Buddhas; then you will be the Perfect Buddha named Rāma." So he did prophesy. Then the youthful Bodhisatta Nārada burnt himself throughout one whole night without any agitation, maintaining a pure heart, and having expired he was born in Tusita city. On the oblation ground a lotus bud blossomed. The people seeing the lotus bud applauded, saying; "This youth Nārada is certainly an extraordinary person and will be a Buddha in the future," and they paid great homage.

Thus, Sāriputta, by reason of the offering of life and limbs, in the future he will be the Perfect Buddha named Rāma. By the merit of offering the body he will be eighty cubits in height; on account of sacrificing his life, his span of life will be ninety thousand years; from the merit accruing by burning the body as an offering throughout one night Buddha-rays will radiate continuously night and day all over the world overpowering the light of the moon and sun.[45]

The ubiquity of the theme of self-immolation in Buddhist literature shows how violence in Buddhism was often directed inwards and accepted with joy by the bodhisattva. Surrounded, as early medieval Chinese Buddhists were, by almost constant affirmation of the act in *sūtras*, *jātakas*, *avadānas*, and learned treatises, we can hardly be too surprised if people on occasion acted on these instructions to do likewise.

Lotus Miracles in China: Manifestations of Guanyin

To understand the miraculous aspects of self-immolation connected with the *Lotus,* it may be helpful to look to another well-attested set of miracles that were known in China. There exists a large body of literature that describes how the Bodhisattva Guanyin 觀音 (var. Guanshiyin 觀世音, Guangshiyin 光世音, Guanzizai 觀自在, Guanshizizai 觀世自在; Skt. Avalokiteśvara) appeared and intervened in people's lives in China in a very direct way.[46] If Guanyin could appear in the here and now, why should the acts of the Medicine King not be present in China also? The belief in Guanyin's "real presence" in medieval China took the form of "embodied devotion," as Robert Campany has shown at some length.[47] Auto-cremation—taking on the role of the Medicine King—may be conceived of as just another form of that kind of devotion. In the manifestations of Guanyin and the embodied devotion of auto-cremators, we find that the sages of the *Lotus Sūtra* were really present in China in a way that even the heroes of classical antiquity could not match. The power of the *Lotus* came not from its presence elsewhere—beyond any particular place and time—but from its reification in the present, in China, for real living human beings. As in the cult of the saints in the Mediterranean world so eloquently described by Peter Brown, we see in medieval China an ardent desire to make spiritual beings present.[48] This desire applies equally to the Buddha and the cult of his relics; to Guanyin, who frees the wrongly imprisoned; and to the Medicine King, whose self-immolation was reinterpreted and reenacted by auto-cremators in a variety of times and places. Accounts of auto-cremators were, like the miraculous accounts of Guanyin, a "cult in narrative

rather than spatial or ritual form."[49] Of course, one cannot say that the desire
for the real presence is unique to Buddhism in China; it also occurs in Taoism, and direct encounters with spiritual beings predate both religions in
China. But the immediate apotheosis of auto-cremators—and the fact that
their publicly performed transformations as well as their remains were surrounded by cultic activities—may indeed indicate a way of making saints that
first appeared only in the Buddhism of the early medieval period.

What the Buddha had declared in the *Lotus* regarding the spiritual
efficacy of that scripture was put to the test and proved to be true in China.
For example, all of the many and various stories about Guanyin releasing
people from prison that were so popular in China rested ultimately on a
single promise made by the Buddha: "Even if there is a man, whether guilty
or guiltless, whose body is fettered with stocks, pillory, or chains, if he calls
upon the name of the Bodhisattva He Who Observes the Sounds of the
World, they shall all be severed and broken, and he shall straightway gain deliverance."[50] Sure enough—as recorded in the miracle tales—when believers
held in Chinese jails called on Guanyin, their chains and fetters dissolved,
and they were released from imprisonment. Similarly, when people burned
themselves, they expected to attain buddhahood just as the Bodhisattva Medicine King had done.

The Unburned Tongue

The unburned tongue offers a peculiar and memorable example of the "real
presence" of the *Lotus* in China that deserves some explanation. In his study
of biographies from the *Xu gaoseng zhuan* and of stories of *Lotus* devotees contained in the *Hongzan fahua zhuan* 弘贊法華傳 (Biographies which Broadly
Extol the *Lotus*) and the *Fahua jing chuanji* 法華經傳記 (Accounts of the
Transmission of the *Lotus Sūtra*), Suwa Gijun has found twenty cases (including those of auto-cremation) in which the tongue either does not rot or remains intact, pink and moist, after the cremation of the body.[51] Suwa's cases
are all associated with people who recited the *Lotus Sūtra,* although as we
have seen, this miracle was also attributed to monks such as Dharma-kṣema's
disciple Daojin.[52] The tongues were treated as relics, enshrined in reliquaries, and placed in *stūpas.* They may remind us in some ways of the miraculously preserved tongue of St. Anthony of Padua (ca. 1193–1231), still
venerated to this day by pilgrims to his shrine.[53] Although St. Anthony's
tongue appears to have been an unusual relic in medieval Europe, there
must have been quite a few indestructible tongues in medieval China.

What could account for the miracle of the incorruptible tongue? If we consult the *Lotus* itself, in "The Chapter on the Merits of the Preacher of the Dharma" (*Fashi gongde pin* 法師功德品) we discover that reading, reciting, interpreting, and copying the *sūtra* all bring physical rewards to the body and sense organs of the practitioner. In particular, the Buddha, in addressing the Bodhisattva Satatasamitābhiyukta (Changjingjin 常精進, Ever Persevering), promises that the tongue will have twelve hundred virtues:

> Further, O Ever Persevering, if a good man or good woman accepts and keeps this scripture, whether reading it, reciting it, interpreting it, or copying it, he shall attain a thousand two hundred virtues of the tongue. All things whether good or ugly, whether delicious or foul-tasting, or even bitter and astringent, shall all change for his lingual faculty into things of superior flavor, like the sweet dew of the gods, none failing to be delicious. If in the midst of a great multitude he has anything to expound, then, producing a profound and subtle sound, with his lingual faculty he shall be able to penetrate their hearts, causing them all to rejoice and be cheerful.[54]

The text goes on to list all the deities, *nāga*s, *yakṣa*s, *garuḍa*s, monks, nuns, kings, and others who will come to listen to the preacher. It is true that preservation of the tongue after death is not mentioned explicitly, but the scripture does promise definite changes in the power of that particular organ. This passage, together with others from the same chapter of the *Lotus,* evidently supplied the imaginary world of medieval Buddhists with the idea that the six sense organs could be made literally incorruptible by chanting the *sūtra.* There are several examples of this concept in the biographies of pious devotees of the *Lotus.*[55] The basis of this belief in the passage quoted above is actually made explicit in a story originally contained in the *Jingyi ji* 旌異記 (Citations of Marvels) by Hou Bai 侯白 (fl. ca. 600) and later collected in the *Xu gaoseng zhuan.*[56] Conversely, Buddhist histories ascribed to those who spread heterodox teachings or slandered the *sūtra*s tongues that rotted away prematurely.[57]

The *Da zhidu lun* contains the following story that indicates that the miracle of unburned tongue may not only have appeared in China:

> Once, in a certain country, there was a *bhikṣu* who used to recite the *Amituo fo jing* 阿彌陀佛經 (*Amitābhabuddhasūtra*) and the *Mohebore boluomi* 摩訶般若波羅蜜 (*Mahāprajñāpāramitā* [*sūtra*]). When he was at the point of death, he said to his disciples, "Here is the Buddha Amitābha, who is coming with his great *saṃgha.*" His body shook, and he took refuge and died soon afterwards. After his death his disciples stacked up firewood and burned him.

The next day, among the ashes, they found the *bhikṣu*'s tongue, which had not been burned. Because he had recited the *sūtra* of Amitābha, this Buddha personally came for him. Because he had recited the *Prajñāpāramitā*, his tongue could not be burned.[58]

The *Da zhidu lun* was a compendium for much Buddhist knowledge in medieval China and a source of legitimation for practices that was at least as important as the *sūtra*s themselves. We may see the influence of the text in the fact that Kumārajīva, the translator of the *Da zhidu lun,* was also said to have left behind an unburned tongue after his own cremation.[59] Suwa credits Kumārajīva with importing the belief in the indestructible tongue to China, but perhaps the cremation of Daojin, who died thirty years or so later, also played a role. It is likely that later citations of the *Da zhidu lun* in the context of discussions of such miracles must have helped spread the belief.[60]

Not only sages but also quite ordinary men and women were able to produce the miraculous relic of the indestructible tongue, and this prodigy must be taken as a sign that virtually anyone could be a "preacher of the *dharma*" if they were devout enough. The power of the *sūtra* itself was what lay behind the determination of some people to go even further than just preaching and to enact the role of the bodhisattva by burning themselves.

Lotus Miracle Tales

Let us return now to the Chinese biographical material, this time to a specific genre: collections of miracle tales that attest to the power of the *Lotus* in China. They contain biographies of self-immolators who were inspired by the *Lotus Sūtra* and were often based on materials compiled in the *Gaoseng zhuan* collections but also include some biographies that no longer exist elsewhere.[61] We will examine here a few of these collections to see what kinds of miracles were associated with auto-cremation.

In Huixiang's *Hongzan fahua zhuan,* the biographies of self-immolators are grouped together under the familiar rubric *yishen*.[62] They appear in the middle of the collection, the fifth section in the fifth fascicle, immediately before the category *songchi* 誦持 (chanters and upholders). Clearly then, self-immolation was an important and meaningful category in the context of pious devotion to the *Lotus*.

The biography of Sengming 僧明 (fl. ca. 502–519) shows how baroque the miracles associated with auto-cremation could become. On the peak of Shimen shan 石門山 in Zhaoyi xian 招義縣, Hao zhou 濠州, Sengming built a "Heavenly Palace of Maitreya" (Mile *tiangong* 彌勒天宮) out of bricks and made an image of the future buddha.[63] There he constantly recited the *Lotus Sūtra,* and as he did so he always heard the sound of fingers snapping in approval and the sound of someone saying "Excellent" (*shanzai* 善哉)! Some time during the Tianjian 天監 period (502–519), he memorialized the emperor Liang Wudi several times, asking his permission to burn his body. Wudi finally approved his request and Sengming burned himself on a rock in front of the Maitreya palace.[64]

Sengming's cremation was followed by a remarkable series of miracles, including healing, spontaneously blooming flowers, and a moving statue:

> His body was completely reduced to ashes; all that remained was one fingernail (*jia* 甲). When the burning was over, the ground surrounding the rock to a radius of four or five feet (*chi* 尺) sank, thus forming a pond. Two or three days later, flowers bloomed there; bright and luxuriant, they were unmatched in beauty. All those who drank from this pond were cured of their illnesses. Later, people gathered up the ashes and made an image of him with them. They also made a small wooden image. They burned the nail again, took the ashes, and made a paste. When people smeared it on the image, it moved away. In all the places where it went, flowers bloomed. They were as big as pear and jujube trees, and there were more than a hundred thousand. Now there is a *stūpa* that marks this, [its inscription] completely describes the story in detail.[65]

Although Sengming's biography is included in the collection as that of a *Lotus* devotee, clearly the miracles associated with his auto-cremation do not map precisely onto any episodes recounted in that text. Rather, they emerged out of that world of the imagination in which the *Lotus* was but one of many elements with antecedents both Buddhist and indigenous. Nor were Sengming's practices "orthodox" in terms of what the scripture prescribed: He combined chanting the *Lotus* with a personal cult to Maitreya, before whom he burned his body. One might imagine that he had vowed to be reborn in Tuṣita Heaven, where Maitreya dwelt in his Heavenly Palace, but this is not explicitly stated. Also the details of the many miracles following Sengming's auto-cremation would argue against this interpretation because he seems to have been very present at a specific site on earth after his death.

These few lines of biography contain an extraordinary number of miracles, some of them quite unique. For example, Sengming left but a single relic, a fingernail. The fingernail relic is fairly unusual, although the *Mūlasarvāstivāda Vinaya,* for example, contains a reference to the Buddha giving away his hair, nails, and teeth while alive, and these would presumably have been treated as relics.[66] The site of his auto-cremation sank into the earth, forming a miraculous pond. The connection between Buddhist thaumaturges and the discovery of springs is well attested in the sources and has been studied by Michel Soymié, but the connection between auto-cremation and water is certainly less common.[67] Beautiful flowers miraculously bloomed at the site only a few days later. This trope recalls the sudden appearance of miraculous trees that we noted in Chapter 1. But in addition the water of this pond was magical and had the ability to cure people—perhaps like the water drunk by Sengqun the transcendent. Thus the merit of Sengming's self-immolation was shared rather tangibly with others and in a way that hints at his identification with the Medicine King.

When the ashes of the nail relic were smeared onto a wooden image of Sengming, the statue came to life. The animation of icons by placing relics inside them is well known in East Asian Buddhism and continues to this day; the powers of this "relic paste" must be a related case.[68] Not only was an image of Maitreya the site of Sengming's auto-cremation, but the power of his act introduced another, even more potent, image onto the local religious scene. That image went on to produce further miracles itself as flowers as big as trees sprang up wherever it walked. These miracles were not slavishly reproduced from the scriptures but rather attest to the virtuoso nature of the religious imagination in the medieval Chinese world, where miraculous acts, texts, relics, and images came together to produce a remarkable and unprecedented variety of effects.

Appended to Sengming's biography is another odd account of an image produced by auto-cremation. A layman from Pinglu 平陸 district in Jiaozhou 交州 chanted the *Lotus* and aspired to follow in the footsteps of the Medicine King.[69] After he burned himself, the earth swelled up in the shape of a human body. His father dug up the mound and within it found a golden statue as big as a man. After he had excavated the image, he wanted to raise it so that it would stand upright, but suddenly it disappeared.

The meaning of this brief account appears obscure at first, but I suspect that the biography combines the idea of the bodhisattva revealing his true form in the shape of a golden image and the idea of bodhisattvas "welling up out of the earth" as described in the eponymous chapter of the *Lotus Sūtra*.[70] These bodhisattvas, described as golden in color, dwell beneath our world sphere and appear out of cracks in the earth as the Buddha is preaching. The discovery of the image also echoes the exhumation of dynastic treasures, Aśokan *stūpa*s, prophetic steles, and images so frequently encountered in medieval Chinese sources. The sudden disappearance of the image only adds to its numinous power, pointing to its nonworldly origins.

Yet another story connecting auto-cremation with images is that of Tanyou 曇猷 (d. 666), who became a monk after he conceived a profound "disgust for the world."[71] He was a devout reciter of the *Lotus Sūtra* and would only begin to chant it after setting up a purified altar and decorating it with banners. He later learned to recite the *Huayan jing* while being guided through its verses by a figure who appeared in his dreams. Later he heard that in Changsha si 長沙寺 there was a miraculous Buddha image that had been made by Aśoka himself and had flown to China.[72] He decided to burn his body in homage to the image just like the Medicine King.

In Qianfeng 乾封 1 (666), Tanyou visited the image and made his vow in front of it. He heard the sound of fingers snapping in approval. At first it looked as if wet weather would prevent him from carrying out his vow, but he saw this as no impediment. Sure enough on the night of the fifteenth of the second month (March 26, 666), the clouds cleared, revealing the light of the full moon. Tanyou wrapped himself in waxed cloth and set fire to his hands and the crown of his head. He wanted the flames to last a long time so that he would not die too quickly. As he burned, his expression did not alter and he kept preaching the *dharma.* He kept his eyes on the image and vowed to see the Buddha Pure and Bright Excellence of Sun and Moon, the one to whom the Medicine King had offered himself in the *Lotus.* When people asked him how he felt, Tanyou replied that his mind was like a diamond and that he felt no pain. As the flames finally flared up and consumed him, he could still be heard preaching.

The monks in attendance were worried that he would leave no relics and earnestly requested him to leave a single sign. In the ashes they found his skull. The local officials from the provincial seat arrived at dawn, performed prostrations, and circumambulated this miraculous object. But when they left, the skull suddenly exploded. The dozen or so remaining witnesses prayed fervently for relics. Eight grains of *śarīra* appeared, rising and sinking in the air. The biography concludes by stating that "the relics are now inhumed in the monastery, and the response of snapping fingers is still heard." This biography spells out quite unambiguously the connections between miraculous images, the *Lotus Sūtra,* and relics. It points to the deeply felt need not only to have all those holy objects in China, but also to make them alive— to make the cult an active one rather than a passive remembrance of things past. Tanyou's desire to see the same Buddha that the Medicine King worshipped makes explicit his assumption of the role of that great Bodhisattva.

It is rare that our sources preserve information about individuals from the lower orders of medieval society, but we do have one account of a man of very modest rank who burned himself. In the household of the prince of

Jiang (Li Yun 李惲, d. 675), there was a personal retainer (*buqu* 部曲), a man whose status was barely above that of a slave.[73] He had been devoted to the *Lotus* from the age of eight or nine and recited it from memory day and night, forgetting to eat or sleep. When the prince was serving as the regional inspector of Ji zhou 箕州, his retainer vowed to burn his body. As it happened, his daughter was a favorite concubine of the prince. When she told the prince of her father's wish, he gave his permission. Then her father went into the mountains, bathed and purified himself, and also purified an altar. There he burned his body, apparently alone. A month later, the daughter ordered some men to gather up her father's ashes. His body and bones were completely consumed, and all that was found among the ashes was a tongue, still fresh and moist. The prince's son-in-law Wei Zheng 韋徵 (d. after 674) saw the miraculous object, and deeply moved, he reported it to the prince. The prince saw the tongue himself, and he too was impressed. Even several years later it remained intact. Thus the incorruptible tongue was not reserved for monastics and high-status laypeople but could be manifested even by quite lowly individuals. It would be interesting to know how the class dynamics of this biography were understood by contemporary audiences, but certainly it seemed to promise that the power of the *Lotus* could be bestowed on even those who had no other avenue for gaining status and autonomy.

Conclusion

The popularity of the *Lotus Sūtra* in China is beyond question. It was widely known through being copied and through collective recitation and visual representation. The *Lotus* made very powerful claims for its unique status and efficacy that evidently stimulated fervent devotion to it. The *sūtra* seems to have taken hold of the religious imagination like no other scripture, and the miraculous appearances of Guanyin in China may be seen as analogous to the equally miraculous re-enactments of the Medicine King's fiery transformation. The *Lotus* may have been a unique scripture, but its story of the auto-cremation of the Medicine King is actually not all that rare. The many analogous cases in the Mahāyāna literature must have convinced Chinese Buddhists that the Medicine King's was a perfectly orthodox form of offering and, furthermore, that auto-cremation was an option open to the ordinary practitioner. The works of the commentators do not offer a significantly different reading of the Medicine King's offering.

The *Lotus Sūtra* provided much material for the repertoire of images, concepts, and ideals upon which auto-cremators, their audiences, and biographers drew. Auto-cremators declared their devotion to the text even as they acted out key elements from it. The biographers' descriptions of enthusiastic donations of lavish material goods (jewels, clothing, banners, flags) echoed the *sūtra*'s own fascination with money and commerce. The logic behind these donations—that they actually facilitated the rapid journey to buddhahood—was one that was also drawn from the scripture. Although the *Lotus* was but a part of the literature of self-immolation, it was an essential element that provided both legitimation and script for medieval auto-cremators.

The *Lotus* biographies show how the miraculous took on an extraordinary life of its own in China. They reveal a great deal of religious creativity, and we find in them accounts of miracles sometimes even more complex and difficult to interpret than those found in the *Gaoseng zhuan* collections. The stories themselves must surely have impressed people with the efficacy of auto-cremation and encouraged others to try it for themselves. Seen through the lens of these biographies it appears that *Lotus* devotionalism was an important mode of belief and behavior within Chinese Buddhism that spanned apparent divisions between monastic and lay practice. Details in the biographies, such as the revelation of a golden body or the miraculously unburned tongue, did not have to be explicitly traced back to the text; it was enough to allude to the parallels between our world and the miraculous universe of the *Lotus Sūtra.*

CHAPTER 3

Saṃgha and the State

The Power(s) of Self-Immolation

For mid-seventh-century metropolitan monks the world and the *saṃgha*'s place within it looked very different from what Baochang and Huijiao had known. China had been unified since 581, first under the pro-Buddhist Sui 隋 (581–617) and then under the Tang 唐 (618–907), a dynastic house that dared not challenge the strength of the Buddhist institution despite its ideological commitment to Taoism. As a consequence of these developments, self-immolation looked different, too. By the seventh century it was a well-established practice, but in contrast to earlier periods—when rulers apparently colluded in the acts of self-immolators—it now sometimes took on a more overtly confrontational aspect. Also Buddhists of the sixth and seventh centuries were on occasion made acutely aware that the teaching of the Buddha was not only under threat from secular forces, but also losing efficacy because of the ever-increasing temporal distance between themselves and their great teacher. Fears of the decline of the *dharma* or the impending end of the eon *(kalpa)* affected the practices and interpretation of self-immolation. For some Buddhists self-immolation offered nothing less than a renewal of the waning power of the *dharma*.

Daoxuan, compiler of the *Xu gaoseng zhuan* 續高僧傳 (Continued Biographies of Eminent Monks, T 50.2060), employed the self-immolation section of his collection to laud the sacrifices made by the heroes of recent anti-Buddhist persecutions and to remind the Tang rulers (albeit obliquely) of the necessity of their continued patronage of the *saṃgha*. He wrote from a perspective that recognized that Buddhism in China appeared to be stronger than ever, but at the same time acknowledged the fact that he and his contemporaries were far from the Buddha in time and space and at the mercy of fickle political forces that they might hope to influence but not control.

Continued Biographies of Eminent Monks

Daoxuan was much closer in time to the majority of his subjects than any other compiler of monastic biographies before or since.[1] His work thus reflects many of his particular concerns as an elite monk of the capital who was witness to the interplay of religion and politics under the Sui and Tang dynasties. As both a Vinaya master and one of the most prolific Buddhist writers of the seventh century, he composed works that provide a unique view of Buddhism at a particularly crucial time in Chinese history. No longer was the *saṃgha* patronized only by local aristocrats and rulers of smaller states; it now had an empirewide mission and a complex and often uneasy relationship with the imperium.

The preface to his collection of biographies is dated 645, although Daoxuan continued to add material up to his death in 667, and some additional biographies were interpolated centuries later.[2] Compared to the first *Gaoseng zhuan* and the later *Song Gaoseng zhuan* 宋高僧傳 (Song Biographies of Eminent Monks), Daoxuan's work is easily superior in terms of literary style, historical accuracy, and organization. Even by contemporary standards, Daoxuan deserves to be credited as a diligent and very well-informed historian.[3]

Daoxuan was much better informed about the religious situation in other parts of China than was Huijiao or Zanning 贊寧 (919?–1001?), compiler of the *Song Gaoseng zhuan*. Nevertheless, in the case of his section on self-immolators there remains a definite geographical bias. Much of his information was drawn from stele inscriptions and eyewitness accounts of monks who lived on Zhongnan shan 終南山, a mountain range not far from the Tang capital.[4] Daoxuan even investigated some acts of self-immolation in person on his visits to the area.

The self-immolators in Huijiao's collection were not the compiler's contemporaries: They were already somewhat remote historical figures. In contrast, Daoxuan's collection includes biographies of men and women who were very much part of the world around him. The biography of Xuanlan 玄覽 (613?–644) of Hongfu si 弘福寺 in the capital provides a particularly vivid example of how close compiler and subject could be.[5] Given that Xuanlan drowned himself in 644 (just before the first draft of the *Xu gaoseng zhuan* was completed) and that he was attached to a major imperially sponsored monastery in Chang'an, his biography preserves a sense of immediacy that we do not find in earlier sources.

The Self-Immolators of Mount Zhongnan

In contrast to the section on self-immolators in the earlier *Gaoseng zhuan*, which includes biographies of monks from all over China, the *Xu gaoseng zhuan* contains a disproportionate number of biographies of monks whose religious activities centered on the same place: Mount Zhongnan. This was an area with which Daoxuan was very familiar; he resided there on several

occasions and finally retired there towards the end of his life.[6] Around 630
Daoxuan withdrew into the Zhongnan mountains in response to the anti-
Buddhist policies adopted by the new Tang emperor Taizong 太宗 (r. 626–
649).[7] That period in his life, as well as a continued sense of disquiet at the
emperor's policies towards Buddhism, may have been on his mind while he
was compiling the biographies ten years or so later. Out of a total of ten main
biographies in the section on self-immolators in the original text of the *Xu
Gaoseng zhuan*, no fewer than five of them lived and died on Zhongnan shan.

Daoxuan seems to have been particularly concerned to make clear the
links between self-immolation and the persecution of Buddhism by Zhou
Wudi 周武帝 (r. 560–578), which began in 574.[8] By bringing together a number of biographies of self-immolators who were active on Mount Zhongnan
during the persecution, he shows how self-immolation could be deployed on
occasion as a Buddhist response to government constraints on the practice
of the religion. The biographies of three of these monks—Puyuan 普圓 (fl.
ca. 560) and two of his disciples, Puji 普濟 (d. 581) and Puan 普安 (530–
609)—also suggest that self-immolation was a practice that could be passed
down through a lineage.[9]

Puyuan's self-immolation echoed a mode of body offering found in the
*jātaka*s but attested only rarely in the Chinese biographies. Active around
central Shaanxi at the beginning of the reign of Zhou Wudi, Puyuan had particular skill in reciting the *Huayan jing* 華嚴經 (*Avataṃsaka-sūtra*) and in meditation.[10] One day, an "evil person" begged Puyuan for his head. The monk
was about to chop it off and hand it over, but the other did not dare take it
and begged for his eyes instead. Puyuan was willing to gouge them out and
give them away. The person wanted Puyuan's hand, so the monk lashed his
wrist to a tree with a rope, cut off his arm at the elbow, and gave it away. He
died by the Fan vale 樊川, south of Chang'an, where the local villagers could
not agree who should get his remains. In the end they divided Puyan's body
into several pieces and built a pagoda for each of them.[11] The division of the
relics recalls what occurred after the Buddha's cremation, but this must have
been a more bloody process as Puyuan's body had not been reduced to ashes
and bones. It has many parallels with the amateur dissections of the bodies of
saints in medieval Europe described so well by Piero Camporesi.[12] The competition to secure fragments of the holy body shows how important relics
were to the medieval Chinese, and how taboos on the handling of the corpse
could be transcended in the case of these "very special dead."

Puyuan's disciple Puji made a vow that reveals how self-immolation
could be understood as a potential mechanism for political change. After the
"destruction of the *dharma*" (that is, Zhou Wudi's persecution of Buddhism),

Puji went to live among the peaks of Mount Zhongnan. There he made the following detailed declaration of intent:

> He vowed that if the images and teachings [Buddhism] should flourish, he would relinquish his body in homage *(pūjā)*. He cultivated the practices of Puxian 普賢 ("Universal Goodness," the Bodhisattva Samantabhadra) so as to be reborn in a most worthy state *(xianshou guo* 賢首國*)*.[13] At the beginning of the Kaihuang 開皇 reign period [of Sui Wendi 隋文帝, 581–600], the *dharma* gate was greatly propagated [that is, Buddhism was restored], and he considered that his vow had been fulfilled. Then he arranged his own offering. He led a crowd to assemble on the western cliffs of the Tan 炭 valley of Taibai shan 太白山 (Zhongnan shan). Loudly pronouncing his great vow he threw himself off and died. People from afar flocked there, filling the cliffs and valleys. They built a white pagoda for him on a high peak.[14]

Puji's vow and subsequent leap provide us with a vivid example of how medieval Chinese Buddhists thought of their place in society and the occasionally hostile reactions that they provoked from the authorities. His actions suggest that by the late sixth century Buddhists were becoming confident of their ability to influence history in quite profound ways by bargaining with their bodies. In particular, the phrase *xianshou guo* in Puji's vow carries the sense not only of a Pure Land, but also quite literally "a most worthy state," one that propagated Buddhism. Certainly the Sui, at least under Wendi, could be characterized as just such a state.[15] I have found no explicit antecedent in the *jātaka* or *avadāna* literature for a bodhisattva giving up his life in exchange for the restoration of the *dharma*, and we may see Puji's self-immolation rather as a particularly Chinese response to persecution in which a new dynasty was invoked as the guardian of the *dharma*.

The long and detailed biography of another of Puyuan's disciples, Puan, was probably included in the self-immolation section because of his lineage rather than any spectacular act of self-immolation.[16] Like Puji, he went into hiding to escape the persecution of Zhou Wudi; he sheltered *dharma* master Jingyuan 靜淵 (544–611) and some thirty other renegade monks with him in the Zhongnan mountains.[17] The biography describes his attempts to give away his body:

> Also he cultivated ascetic practices, abandoning his body for the sake of beings. Sometimes he exposed his body in the grass, donating it to mosquitoes and gadflies. Flowing blood covered his body, but he had no fear at all. Sometimes he would lie among the discarded corpses, hoping to give himself to

wild dogs (*chai* 豺) and tigers. In the hope of giving himself away while still alive, this is what he prayed for as his fundamental intention. Although tigers and wildcats (*bao* 豹) came, they just sniffed at him and would not eat him. He always regretted that his heartfelt vow had not been fulfilled. Alone he followed the tracks of wild animals, hoping to find one that would eat him.[18]

Puan's donation of his body to insects, which might appear to be a bizarre and ad hoc invention, was probably inspired by stories of King Śibi and others and became a common feature in the biographies of later self-immolators.[19] Being eaten by tigers was apparently much harder than it looked in the *jātakas*, although the implication is that by not being eaten Puan was being saved for an even greater task.

Failure to be eaten by wild animals proved to be the least of his worries, as Puan found himself responsible for the material needs of the monks he was hiding in the forest. Because there was a bounty for the capture of monks at that time, he was taking a considerable risk in showing himself to beg for food and clothing on their behalf. He had a couple of narrow escapes and on one occasion was released from custody by Zhou Wudi himself.[20] Puan attributed his miraculous good fortune to the power of the *Huayan jing*.[21] When Buddhism prospered again under the Sui, Puan was free to resume his former solitary and austere way of life. I suspect that Daoxuan deliberately chose to feature the monks of Puyuan's lineage as self-immolators over such figures as Jing'ai, who disembowelled himself on Mount Zhongnan in despair over Wudi's persecution signaling the end of the *dharma* and whose biography Daoxuan placed instead with "defenders of the *dharma*." Puji and Puan showed a much more optimistic spirit in comparison to Jing'ai's somewhat defeatist attitude.

The last in a series of tales concerning Puan brings us back to the theme of the bodily offering. Troubled by the number of blood sacrifices made at local altars, Puan was in the habit of buying back sacrificial animals to save them from slaughter. On one occasion, Puan attempted to pay the ransom for three pigs in a local village. But the members of the altar society who were planning to sacrifice them wanted the outrageous price of 10,000 cash for them. Puan could only offer 3,000 and this caused an argument among the crowd. Suddenly a young child, clad in a sheepskin, miraculously appeared and helped Puan buy back the pigs. He distracted the crowd by getting drunk and dancing around. Puan took quick advantage of their confused state:

Then Puan pulled out a knife. He sliced the flesh of his thigh and said, "Mine and theirs [the pigs'] are both flesh. Pigs eat shit and filth yet you still eat them. Furthermore, if people ate grain [instead of meat], then human flesh would be more valuable." The people of the altar, having seen and heard this, simultaneously released [the pigs]. The pigs, having attained their escape, circumambulated Puan three times. They snuffled at him with their snouts as if out of love and respect. The result was that within fifty *li* 里 southwest of the suburbs pigs and chickens had their lineages discontinued [that is, they were no longer raised domestically].[22]

In this account, self-immolation goes hand in hand with a kind of militant vegetarianism and the ongoing Buddhist campaign against the bloody cults of local religion. It reminds us of Sengfu, who substituted his own body for that of a child, and of Daojin, who sliced off his own flesh. By offering his own "meat" to the villagers, Puan used his body to stage a dramatic performance of the teaching of the fundamental identity shared by all beings, whether human or animal. The pigs as well as the humans apparently recognized this fact: They circumambulated the monk, foretelling his future Buddhahood in the same way as the animals saved by the actions of the Bodhisattva in the *jātaka* literature.

There were self-immolators on Zhongnan shan in Tang times as well, but their acts do not appear to carry the same kind of political message as those examined above. Fakuang 法曠 (?–633) of Hongshan si 弘善寺 in the capital was a truly serious ascetic like Puan, but he also had a considerable reputation for scholarship and memorization.[23] His self-immolation was a private affair and was grounded in his personal view of the endless cycles of birth and death:

He always said, "I think that attachment to birth and death constitutes *saṃsāra* without beginning. Those who detest life are rare, but those who detest death are even fewer." He always felt that he had had enough, and he wanted to attempt to discard [his life]. On Zhenguan 貞觀 7.2.21 (April 5, 633), he entered Zhongnan shan. More than forty *li* within the Tan valley, he took off his robes, hung them on a tree, and cut his throat with a knife.[24] Because he died all alone, no one knew where he was until the middle of the eighth month, when, after an extended search, his friends found his "Eulogy on Abandoning the Body" (Yishen song 遺身頌).[25]

This relatively rare case of private self-immolation, which was attributed to a weariness with *saṃsāra*, throws into relief the public and political cases that characterize Daoxuan's selection as a whole. Fakuang was a man deeply immersed in scriptural knowledge. Two texts that he studied in particular—the *Da zhidu lun,* with its many accounts of the heroic renunciation of the body by bodhisattvas, and the *Sūtra of Infinite Life,* with its message of hope of deliv-

erance from *saṃsāra* and rebirth in the Pure Land—may have shown him a
path that offered an alternative to the endless rebirth he found so wearisome.

Self-immolation on Zhongnan shan was still occurring even as the *Xu
gaoseng zhuan* was being compiled. Huitong 會通 (d. 649) has a short biography that was added after the date of the preface (645). He led a secluded and
ascetic lifestyle in the Baolin 豹林 valley on the mountain.[26] When he read the
Lotus Sūtra he was inspired by the example of the Medicine King, whose self-
immolation he vowed to enact for himself. His biography recalls those of the
fifth century that we examined in Chapter 1, but by the middle of the seventh
century the hagiographical tropes of auto-cremation were well established.
Huitong's auto-cremation took place at night; he sat and chanted the *Lotus
Sūtra* in a niche within the pyre and a celestial light entered the flames. This
miracle will remind us in particular of the star seen in the biography of
Huishao. Again, the presence of this sign shows that Huitong's death was no
act of suicide, but one of miraculous transformation in a cosmos that responded through the mechanism of *ganying*:

> In the last year of the Zhenguan reign period (649), in the still of the night
> he stacked up firewood in the middle of the forest and made a cavity within.
> He chanted as far as the Medicine King [chapter] then ordered that the fire
> be started. The wind made the blaze flare up suddenly, and the smoke and
> flames raged all over. With outstanding dignity, he sat in the lotus position
> chanting as before. An instant later there was a large white light in the south-
> west, which flowed into the mass of flames. His body fell onto its back. By
> dawn both body and fire were burnt out. People gathered his remaining
> bones and raised a white *stūpa* for them. The inscription is still there.[27]

Huitong's auto-cremation is presented as an act of devotion to the *Lotus Sūtra* without any overt political message. Yet, when read in combination
with the other biographies of self-immolators on Zhongnan shan, it serves
as a reminder that auto-cremation was very much a living tradition for monastics who lived close to the capital. If we consider geography an important element in the history of self-immolation, we can see that a certain area
could shape and determine not only local practice but also the empire-wide
relationship between state and *saṃgha*.

Self-Immolation in Defense of the *Saṃgha*

Even after the Sui restoration of Buddhism there was a sense of insecurity
about the safety of the *saṃgha*, and individual Buddhists continued to

present a variety of responses to threats both real and imagined. The idea that monks would lay down their lives to protect the monastic community as a whole against the depredations of the state is nowhere better exemplified than in the biography of Dazhi 大志 (567–609) of Lu shan.[28] Dazhi was a monk of a truly famous lineage, being one of the disciples of the most revered monk of the sixth century, Tiantai Zhiyi.[29] It was Zhiyi himself who gave him the *dharma* name Dazhi (Great Determination). After his initial training on Tiantai shan, Dazhi travelled in 590 to Mount Lu, where he resided at Fengding si 峰頂寺.[30] There he lived the life of a solitary ascetic, concentrating on recitation of the *Lotus Sūtra*. Like other aspiring self-immolators, he tried to offer his body to tigers, but they would have none of it. In 609, Sui Yangdi 隋煬帝 (r. 604–617) decreed the imposition of some limits on the number of monks, nuns, and monasteries after nearly thirty years of unrestricted growth—first under his father, Wendi, and then in the earlier years of his own reign.[31] Dazhi reacted with extraordinary passion:

He lamented that the deterioration of the *dharma* should have reached a point such as this. Then he changed his clothes and inflicted injuries on his body. He wore a mourning cap (*xiaofu* 孝服) on his head and a robe of coarse cloth. In the middle of the Buddha hall he began to wail mournfully in a loud voice. He continued for three days and three nights without ceasing. When the monks of the monastery came to console him, Dazhi said, "I am lamenting that bad *karma* should have reached such a state as this! I should exhaust this body of mine to glorify the true teaching!"

Accordingly he went to the Eastern Capital (Luoyang 洛陽) and submitted a memorial that read, "My wish is that your majesty might cause the Three Jewels to flourish. In which case I shall burn one arm on Mount Song 嵩岳 to repay the compassion of the state."[32] The emperor assented to this, and he ordered a great *zhai* 齋 to be held at which the seven assemblies all gathered.[33] Dazhi did not eat for three days. He climbed on top of a large canopied platform (*peng* 棚). He heated a piece of iron until it was red hot and used it to burn his arm, charring it completely black. He used a knife to cut off the flesh, peeling it off so that the bones were made visible. Then he burned the bones, charring them black as well. He wrapped them in cloth, which was saturated in wax, and set fire to them. The light sparkled off the peaks and summits. At that time, a large crowd was watching this performance of austerities. They were all distressed, pierced to the marrow, and felt unsteady on their feet. Yet, although he continued to do more burning and branding, neither Dazhi's speech nor expression changed—he talked and smiled as before. From time to time he recited

verses of the *dharma,* and sometimes he praised the virtues of the Buddha.
He preached the *dharma* for the benefit of the crowd and his speech never
faltered. When his arm was completely incinerated, he climbed down from
the platform as before. After remaining in *dhyāna* for seven days he died in
the lotus position. At that time he was forty-three *sui.*[34]

Although Dazhi's fears about the state of the *dharma* may look like an
emotional overreaction to Yangdi's attempt to rein in the *saṃgha* a little, they
were clearly in keeping with the kind of anxiety experienced by other monks
of the sixth and early seventh centuries. From the rather fragmentary evidence available to us about this episode, it is hard to understand quite what
Yangdi hoped to achieve by allowing Dazhi to burn off his arm in front of a
large public audience given that he apparently did not change his policy as a
consequence. It is likely of course that the biography was rewritten in such a
way as to recast Yangdi as a tyrant and Dazhi as a heroic martyr for the *saṃgha.*
Rather than an act of protest Dazhi's sacrifice of his arm was perhaps a form of
atonement for some perceived misdeeds on the part of his fellow monastics.

At the end of this extremely detailed, and slightly gruesome, account of
Dazhi's offering, Daoxuan appended his own opinions on Dazhi's talent and
physical beauty.[35] These personal and eulogistic comments strongly suggest
that Daoxuan did intend Dazhi to be seen as some kind of martyr for the Chinese *saṃgha.* Finally, we learn that in Daoxuan's own day Dazhi was still being
commemorated at Lu shan, nearly forty years after his death:

> He compiled the text of his vow, which was more than seventy pages in
> length. His purpose was that through this text all sentient beings might be
> his good friends (*shanzhishi* 善知識; Skt. *kalyāṇamitra*). Even those monks
> who were tough and stubborn and found it hard to uphold [Buddhist prac-
> tices] with faith, none of them could help shedding tears on reading this
> votive text. Now, on the peak of Lu shan, at the end of every year, the
> monks and nuns who are present in all the monasteries gather together for
> one night.[36] They read the vow that he left behind, using it to teach both re-
> ligious and laity. All of them sob with grief.[37]

Like the monks of Lu shan, Daoxuan wanted to suggest that Dazhi's act
still carried an important message in his own day. In Dazhi's biography we see
a monk using his body in the most spectacular and public fashion to ensure
the continuation of the *dharma.* Dazhi's personality, his vow, and his dramatic
gift of his body were still being publicly remembered in the Tang, when the
protection of the *saṃgha* was by no means assured. By commemorating

Dazhi's death the monks of Lu shan not only remembered his personal act, but also the bargain that had been struck with Sui Yangdi—a bargain that presumably the monks of Lu shan and Daoxuan himself wished the Tang rulers would respect. Daoxuan's presentation of the biographies of Puji and Dazhi may not have been entirely ingenuous. The texts might in fact represent a kind of moral blackmail—a way of saying to the Tang rulers (probably to Taizong in particular), "You see what happens when you do not support the *saṃgha:* Eminent monks jump off cliffs or they publicly burn off their arms and die."

The possibility that Daoxuan had a hidden agenda in his compilation of the self-immolation section of his collection may help explain his inclusion of a biography that does not appear to belong among those of eminent monks. Zhiming 智命 (?–619) was a monk only on the very last day of his life, and he seems to have had no formal master.[38] He spent most of his career as a bureaucrat, but he was doubly unfortunate in that he happened to live during the political turmoil that occurred between the end of the Sui and the founding of the Tang and that, in hindsight, he backed the wrong man. His secular name was Zheng Ting 鄭頲, and the biography refers to him by this name throughout.[39] Although he had long had an interest in Buddhism, after the fall of the Sui Zheng found himself serving as censor-in-chief (*yushi dafu* 御史大夫) to the general Wang Shichong 王世充 (d. 621), who declared himself emperor of the Zheng 鄭 dynasty (618–621), based in Luoyang.[40] Wang Shichong was the last of the military claimants to the empire to be defeated by the forces of the nascent Tang dynasty under Li Yuan 李淵 (Gaozu 高祖, r. 618–626) and his son Li Shimin 李世民 (Taizong 太宗, r. 626–649), with help from the monks of Shaolin si 少林寺.[41] Not unnaturally then, Wang is portrayed as a cruel and capricious tyrant in Tang sources.[42]

Zheng eventually realized his mistake and attempted to leave his position and renounce the householder's life. Wang Shichong was not impressed with this act of treason and ordered his execution:

> Zheng Ting was worn out by this disorder and he earnestly wished to leave home. He repeatedly requested of the Zheng ruler that he might cultivate the Way for the benefit of the state. But when he could not accomplish this intention, he thought only of taking the tonsure and did not worry about the punishment. Therefore, at night he secretly read *vaipulya* (*fangdeng* 方等) *sūtra*s.[43] During the day he continued to discharge his public duties. He did not change his mind even for a moment, so he spent forty days in a complete recitation of the *Lotus Sūtra.* This soothed his heart and made him determined to leave secular life. He also encouraged his wife to take refuge in

Buddhism. His words were to the point so she followed him and they gave each other the tonsure. Zheng Ting said to his wife, "My wish has been fulfilled! I will not die and be reborn. I must inform the Zheng ruler. It is not fitting for me to be this way [that is, a monk in government office]." He put on his *dharma* robes and picked up his *khakkara*.[44] He went to the palace gates and he said, "I, Zheng Ting, have just left home! So I have come to pay my respects." Wang Shichong could not overcome his anger, and he ordered him to be executed. When Zheng Ting heard this he was delighted and said, "Again, my wish has been fulfilled." He smiled imperturbably and joyfully. He walked to the banks of the Luo river. At that time, it was still only daybreak and not yet time for the execution. Zheng Ting said, "If you are my good friend, please deliver me to the other shore as soon as possible. If not, I will soon be released, and thus I will not be able to fulfil my fundamental aspiration." At that time religious and laity were circumambulating him, and they exhorted him to wait until sunset. But Zheng Ting, with a stern expression and a loud voice, would not agree. So then he was executed. Soon after, there was an imperial order for his release. [The officials of] the whole court felt regret that this did not save him. This all took place in the early years of the Kaiming 開明 reign period of the pseudo-Zheng.[45]

The case of Zheng Ting provides us with a rare opportunity to see how the same event was reported in Buddhist and secular sources. Although the two official Tang histories do mention Wang Shichong's execution of Zheng Ting and his subsequent regret, they do not recount the circumstances and certainly make no mention of any Buddhist inclinations on Zheng's part.[46] Was Wang Shichong's act particularly anti-Buddhist then? There are some indications that he may have severely curtailed Buddhist activities under his regime, but given the biased nature of the sources concerning the founding of the Tang it is difficult to know how much credence to give this picture.[47] If we examine the account given in the *Zizhi tongjian* 資治通鑑 (Comprehensive Mirror for the Aid of Government), we find substantial confirmation for the *Xu gaoseng zhuan* account at the end of the narrative of Li Shimin's campaign against Wang Shichong.[48] But this version of events is slightly less laudatory towards Zheng Ting; his flattery of Wang Shichong seems a little excessive, even if he was using it as a means to escape an intolerable situation. But overall, even the historian Sima Guang 司馬光 (1019–1086) saw Zheng's faith in Buddhism as sincere, and his death as heroic and widely admired:

Earlier Zheng Ting, the censor-in-chief, had grown unhappy with serving Wang Shichong. He often refused to attend state affairs on the pretext of illness. Then he told Wang Shichong, "I, your servant, hear that the Buddha has an indestructible adamantine body. Your majesty is truly like this. I must have many blessings indeed to be reborn during the time of a Buddha, and so I wish to resign from office, take the tonsure, and become a *śramaṇa* and so strive diligently to aid your majesty's divine martial ability (*shenwu* 神武)." Shichong said, "Great minister of state, your reputation has long been respected. When you desire to enter the Way, this will come as a great surprise to public opinion. Wait until the battles have ceased, then you may follow your wish." Zheng Ting made determined requests, but [Wang] would not agree. He went back and told his wife, "I have served in office since I became a man, and in my mind I have aspired to fame and integrity. Due to ill fortune, I have encountered these turbulent times, I have become a refugee here, and I have to stay in this land of danger and death. My intelligence and strength are too weak to protect us. People are born, and then they die, what difference is there whether it is sooner or later? If I could follow what I liked, I would have no regrets if I died."

Then he shaved off his hair and put on monk's robes. When Wang Shichong heard of this, he was furious and said, "Is this because you think I am certain to be defeated, and you wish to escape by improper means? If I do not execute you, then how can I control the masses?" Accordingly he had Zheng Ting executed in the marketplace. [Before this] Zheng Ting laughed and talked unaffectedly, and the onlookers admired his courage.[49]

Unlike the rather bleak picture presented in this source, the *Xu gaoseng zhuan* biography claims that Zheng Ting had long nurtured the idea of escaping the horrors of *saṃsāra,* and it reproduces a long speech to this effect. The speech is given in response to a monk who had made a prediction based on Zheng's physiognomy at a lecture given by Jizang.[50] In the *Xu gaoseng zhuan* biography Zheng speaks of seeing many dead people; because he lived through some remarkably bloody and unsettling times, one can only sympathize with his unenviable predicament. Daoxuan's biography, however, does seem determined to read his execution as an act of self-immolation rather than merely the result of being in the wrong place at the wrong time. The latter part of the account also contains what is, I believe, one of the earliest death verses recorded in the context of self-immolation.[51] In time, the verse composed just before death was to become a significant trope in the biographies of self-immolators. Zheng's verse provides a nice example of the deeper doctrinal underpinnings of self-immolation. Ultimately, he says, there is no self to immolate:

Thus when Zheng Ting was on the point of execution he made obeisance
to the ten directions and chanted the *Bore* 般若 [*jing* 經].[52] He took up his
brush and composed this poem:

> Illusory arising returns to illusory destruction.
> But this great illusion does not last beyond the body.
> There is a place where the mind can be pacified,
> One may seek for a "person," but there is no such "person."[53]

After bidding farewell to his friends and acquaintances, he closed his eyes
and in a short while he said, "You may let the blade fall." When they heard
his words they executed him. His expression was mild and pleasant, even
more so than usual. His wife became a *bhikṣuṇī* and now resides at Luozhou
si 洛州寺.[54]

As with most of the biographies selected by Daoxuan for the self-immolation section, it is almost impossible to avoid the political implications of this
piece. One scarcely has to read between the lines to get the message that
only the cruelest of tyrants would refuse to allow a decent man to join the
saṃgha. Because Tang Taizong (Li Shimin) had defeated just such a cruel
tyrant, he was in a sense morally obligated to uphold and patronize his Buddhist allies. Daoxuan was only too willing to remind Taizong of his obliga-
tions, although for obvious reasons he chose an oblique approach rather
than direct confrontation.

Millenarian Fears

As we have seen, a number of sixth-century self-immolators seem to have
been inspired in their actions by what they perceived to be the newly urgent
and perilous situation faced by their religion. These fears and the consciousness that in such parlous times new forms of Buddhist teaching were demanded drove Sengyai 僧崖 (488?–559?), a monk from a non-Chinese tribe
in Sichuan, to burn himself publicly on the fifteenth day of the seventh
month of Wucheng 武成 1 of the Zhou 周 (September 2, 599).[55] The choice of
date was probably not accidental; it was the day of *yulanpen* 盂蘭盆, the so-
called "ghost festival" that has been so well studied by Stephen Teiser.[56] Because large crowds traditionally assembled at monasteries to make offerings
on that day, Sengyai would have found a ready-made audience for his act.
The choice of the ghost festival may also be related to Sengyai's expressed intention "to enter hell to suffer vicariously for all sentient beings." But if we examine Sengyai's farewell speech, a rather more specific and eschatological
vision is unveiled:

"At the end of the *kalpa* people are lightweight and sluggish, and their minds become attenuated and weak. When they see images [of the Buddha] they are just blocks of wood and when they hear *sūtra*s it is like the wind blowing through a horse's ear. Now, in order to inscribe (*xie* 寫) the teachings of the Mahāyāna *sūtra*s, I burn my hands and will destroy my body because I wish them to respect the *Buddhadharma* with faith."[57]

Sengyai seems to be suggesting here the need for strong action in a time when people's capacity to understand the *dharma* through the normal means of images and texts was severely restricted. We may be able to point to a specific moment in history that made evident the urgency of this need: the fall of the pro-Buddhist Liang dynasty in the late 550s. Similar beliefs articulated in a similar way at around the same time may be detected in the career of the man known as Mahāsattva Fu. Because he was drawn, somewhat anachronistically, into the history of early Chan, he is remembered now as rather an unthreatening and benign figure, but the reality is probably somewhat different.[58] In 548, during the disorder of Hou Jing's 侯景 (?–552) rebellion, Fu, who was regarded by many of his contemporaries as an incarnation of the Buddha Maitreya, vowed to burn himself as a living candle.[59] Rather than allow him to do so, large numbers of his disciples burned themselves alive; others burned off fingers, cut off their ears, and fasted.[60] They were convinced that the period of *xiangfa* 像法 (counterfeit *dharma*) had come to an end, and they wanted their leader to remain in the world to save sentient beings. In 555 the situation had not improved and the people of the Liang were faced with constant warfare, banditry, disease, and starvation. Fu appealed to his followers to offer their bodies "to atone for the sins of sentient beings and pray for the coming of the saviour."[61] Three more of his disciples burned themselves to death, becoming flaming lamps by hanging themselves from metal lantern frames. In 557, when the Liang was on its very last legs, Fu asked his disciples to burn off their fingers "to invoke the Buddhas to save this world."[62] In 587, long after Fu's death in 569, one of his sons burned himself to death. We can see then that the fall of the Liang resulted in a veritable orgy of blood and fire, not just in Sichuan but also in Dongyang 東陽 (Zhejiang) and its environs, where Fu and his devotees were based.

But the political disorder of the 550s and consequent religious panic that swept through South China may just have been a fairly local manifestation of a catastrophe that seems to have affected other parts of the world.[63] David Keys, for example, has suggested that a massive volcanic eruption in what is now Indonesia may have resulted in sudden and disastrous climatic change—the effects of which would have been hard to ignore in South China—and may well have been attended by crop failure, famine, and disease.[64] Whatever the causes for the deep sense of impending doom felt by Fu and his devotees, the situation for most people around the 550s and 560s must have appeared extremely bleak, especially if they remembered the much more prosperous, more civilized, and safer days of Liang Wudi's reign.

Sengyai's auto-cremation, on the other hand, was not presented as an act of despair but rather as the herald of a radical new direction in Chinese Buddhist practice that seemed to offer a total renewal of the *dharma*. Witness the following remarkable statement attributed to him, which is reminiscent of similar exhortations made at a slightly later period by members of the Sanjie jiao 三階教 (Teaching of the Three Stages):[65]

> Then he said to his attendant, Zhiyan 智炎 (d.u.), "After my extinction, it would be good to do homage *(pūjā)* to sick people. It is hard to fathom all their roots because many of them are buddhas and sages who have temporarily transformed themselves in response [to circumstances]. If one does not have great equanimity of mind, how can one honor and respect them? This is true practice."[66]

Sengyai promised that his auto-cremation would usher in a new age in which the bodhisattvas known through scripture would manifest among those who had previously been separated from them by time and space. As a lowly, illiterate barbarian who became known as "Bodhisattva Sengyai," this monk offered a potent example of this new dispensation. He seems to have had an attentive and appreciative audience to judge from the length of his biography, the number of miracle stories it contains, and other texts composed about him.[67]

Scriptural Models

In Puyuan's biography we saw the appearance of an "evil person" who begged for parts of the monk's body. This extreme form of giving, to anyone who asks no matter how evil their intention, was a common theme of the *jātaka* literature popular in North China in the fifth and sixth centuries. The donation of the head or the eyes is often encountered in these stories, and the theme has been explored most productively by Reiko Ohnuma.[68] Puyuan's tale seems to be most indebted to stories told of a prince called Candraprabha and to some accounts of King Śibi. Candraprabha was a wise and enlightened ruler who was very generous. An evil ascetic decided to test

Saṃgha and the State 93

his charity and demanded his head. The prince then tied his hair to a tree, and the ascetic charged at him with his sword.[69] Puyuan, we will recall, tied his wrist to a tree and chopped off his arm when an "evil person" requested it. Puyuan's death also recalls the story told by Xuanzang 玄奘 (600–664) about the death of the philosopher Nāgārjuna, who cut off his head to offer it to a prince who had requested it.[70]

King Śibi's gift of his body is one of the best-known *jātaka* stories in the Buddhist world and like the story of the hungry tigress was a popular subject for pictorial representation in India, Central Asia, and China.[71] We should not discount the power of these representations in an age when, because of its relative scarcity, the image had much more power than it does today. As is often the case with the exemplary heroes of the Buddhist tradition, many different stories are told of the same figure. Generally speaking, in the Pāli sources King Sivi [*sic*], a past birth of Śākyamuni, is remembered for giving away his eyes; in the Northern tradition, he is celebrated for giving away all of his flesh. If we examine the story as it appears in a Chinese translation of the *Mahāyānasūtrā-laṃkāra* of Aśvaghoṣa (*Dasheng zhuangyan lun jing* 大乘莊嚴論經 T 4.201), we read of a virtuous king known for his generosity.[72] Two gods, Śakra and Viśvakarman, decide to put his charity to the test. Viśvakarman takes the form of a pigeon, and Śakra becomes a falcon. The pigeon flies away from its pursuer and hides under Śibi's arm. Śibi promises to protect the bird, but the falcon complains that Śibi has stolen his food. Śibi offers the falcon a portion of his own flesh equivalent to the weight of the pigeon. The falcon agrees to the deal. Śibi places the pigeon on the scale and starts cutting off his flesh (beginning with his thigh) and adding it to the other balance. But no matter how much flesh he gives, he cannot match the weight of the pigeon. Śibi ends up giving his entire body. The gods reveal their true identity and encourage King Śibi to declare the sincerity of his gift. As a result of this "act of truth," Śibi's body is magically restored. There are similar magical restorations of body parts in the biographies that suggest the enduring influence of the *jātakas*' logic and narrative structure. Sengyai, for example, burned his fingers off; the bones regrew and when he was asked for relics, he bit them off and spat them out.[73]

The biography of Puyuan represents a re-enactment on Chinese soil of stories told about the heroes of Indian Buddhist literature. As such, it displays a literal quality that is actually rather unusual in the Chinese sources. Other biographies present forms of self-sacrifice that are not so much copies of Indian stories but more nuanced reinterpretations of those themes. For example, the evil person or god who demands the head of a bodhisattva is a common character in the *jātaka*s but appears very rarely in these biographies.

The biography of Xuanlan shows how self-immolators sometimes explicitly cited scriptural models. In 632 Xuanlan came to receive ordination in Chang'an, where he often spoke to his fellow monks of his intention to abandon his body. In the fourth month of Zhenguan 18 (May–June 644), he began by taking off his clothes and making them into a bundle, which he gave to the monks of his home monastery. After approaching the Wei 渭 river with recitations, prostrations, and prayers, he threw himself in, but a crowd of people pulled him out.[74] Xuanlan explained to them,

> "I have vowed to discard my body and life for a long time.[75] My intention is that I wish to revere and learn from the *mahāsattva*s (*dashi* 大士). The ability to discard that which is hard to discard is [extolled as] correct practice in the *sūtra*s. I hope you will not prevent me, as it would impede both your *karma* and mine."[76]

The crowd apparently accepted this explanation and allowed him to throw himself in again. Three days later, his corpse came to the surface. Some villagers pulled it out and erected a pagoda for him. Meanwhile, back at his home monastery, his fellow monks were puzzled when he did not return. When they were still unable to find him they opened the bundle of clothes and saw the text he had left behind:

> It said, "Homage to the buddhas of the ten directions and the three time periods. It has been twelve years since I, the disciple Xuanlan, left home. Although I have added to the number of the *saṃgha,* my great purpose has not yet been completed. Now I wish to cultivate *dānapāramitā* (perfection of charity) like the Bodhisattva who formerly cast away his body as King Śibi, like the Fish King, or the story of the mountain of flesh. These are all recorded in the scriptures. I ask that I might follow the former sages so that their teachings might be passed on to later times. As for my clothes and other possessions please dispose of them in accordance with the Buddha's instructions. As I am going to die, [please forgive me for] leaving so many things uncompleted."
>
> His fellow disciples, when they saw the text he had left behind, went to [the place of his death] to investigate what had happened.[77]

Xuanlan provided clear textual authorities for his aspiration, thus revealing how some self-immolators related their own actions to those performed by the sacred models of scripture. We have already mentioned King Śibi's gift of the body, but the other two examples given by Xuanlan—the fish king and the mountain of flesh—are perhaps a little more obscure.

For the story of the fish king, we turn to the *Liudu ji jing* 六度集經 (Sūtra of the Collection of Six Perfections, T 3.152.33c15–25).[78] Once, in a past life, the Buddha was a fish king. He had two ministers who were very noble (in fact, they were none other than the Buddha's major disciples Śāriputra and Mahāmaudgalyāyana in a previous life). The two fish ministers observed the teachings of the Buddha, kept a vegetarian diet, and tried to protect and proselytize to all the king's subjects. One day, a fisherman caught them all in his net. All the fish were seized with fear, but the fish king saved them by sticking his head in the mud and lifting up the edge of the net with his tail.

In the *Karuṇāpuṇḍarīka* (White Lotus of Compassion), the following story is told of two of the previous lives of Śākyamuni.[79] As King Durdhana he lived during the time of the Semblance Dharma (*xiangfa* 像法) of the Buddha Gandapadma. He split his country between six of his sons, but because they had not listened to him preach the *dharma*, they quarrelled and the state was overrun with wars, disasters, disease, and famine. Durdhana vowed to save beings by sacrificing himself. He climbed to the top of Mount Dagapāla and jumped off, vowing to transform himself into a mountain of meat for beings to eat. He became such a mountain with thousands of heads. He was constantly eaten by humans and animals but still the meat mountain grew larger. His self-sacrifice lasted for ten thousand years. He was able to do so, the text explains, as a consequence of an earlier vow that he had taken as King Ambara, who ruled in a continent called Rūḍhavaḍa.

There is no doubt then that the heroic acts recounted with such relish and exuberance in *jātaka* and *avadāna* tales directly inspired Xuanlan and Puji. But rather than react to the suffering of others as the heroes of the *jātaka*s did, these monks deliberately sought out death. Thus their acts take on a rather fanatical cast, which is not so evident in the Indian materials. How Xuanlan's act could have saved anyone, or anything, remains somewhat obscure—even the fish in the river did not seem to have been interested in eating him. But we can be sure that the villagers who erected a pagoda for his remains and the monks who wept while reading his last testament were quite certain of the heroism of his death.

Two Sisters

As we noted in Chapter 1, female self-immolation seems to have been very poorly documented. However, the *Xu gaoseng zhuan* does contain one account of two sisters who burned themselves in public. We meet again here the motif of the unburned tongue, which by Tang times was becoming particularly associated with recitation of the *Lotus Sūtra*. Like Fakuang, the two

sisters registered some disgust at having to live in *saṃsāra,* perhaps because
of their female bodies:

> At the beginning of the Zhenguan reign period (627–649), in Jingzhou 荆州,
> there were two sisters who were *bhikṣuṇī*s.[80] Together they recited the *Lotus*
> and they had a deep loathing for their physical form. Both wished to aban-
> don their bodies. They restricted their food and clothing and admired the
> practice of austerities. They consumed incense and oil and gradually cut
> out grain from their diet. Later they completely abstained from grain and
> ate only incense and honey. They were filled with strength of essence, their
> spiritual determination was bright and vigorous.
>
> They widely advertised, to both religious and laity, that on the ap-
> pointed day they would burn their bodies. On Zhenguan 3.2.8 (March 8,
> 629), they set up two high seats on the main road of Jingzhou. Then they
> wrapped their bodies in waxed cloth right up to the crown of the head;
> only their faces and eyes were visible. The crowds massed like mountains,
> their songs and eulogies like gathering clouds.
>
> They recited [the *Lotus*] up until the point where [the Medicine King]
> burns. The older sister first applied a flaming wick to her younger sister's
> head, then she asked the younger sister to apply a burning wick to her
> head. In the peace of the night the two torches blazed away together simul-
> taneously. The fire burned down to their eyes, but the sound of their recita-
> tion became louder. [The flames] gradually reached their noses and
> mouths and then [the recitation] came to an end. This was just at daybreak,
> and they were still sitting together and intact. Then, simultaneously the
> fires flared up, and their bones were smashed and broken, but the two
> tongues remained intact. The assembled crowd sighed admiringly and raised
> a high pagoda for them.[81]

Aside from the mention of their deep loathing for their own bodies,
there is little in this account that appears to mark out any gendered vision
of auto-cremation. It does not seem to have been a problem that the sisters
imitated the Medicine King, who was a male hero of the *Lotus Sūtra.* But this
scripture also contains the famous story of the *nāga* king's daughter who
changes her body from female to male and becomes a buddha. This message about the ultimately empty nature of gender may have encouraged
women to take up such "advanced" practices as self-immolation. The sisters
burned themselves in public, just as monks did, and they left the same kinds
of miraculous signs. Their auto-cremation was celebrated with a pagoda,
just as monks' remains were commemorated. We still have a very indistinct

picture of the religious lives of women in medieval China, but this kind of evidence suggests that they were not always excluded from the highest ranks of the heroes.

Self-Mummification

One biography from Daoxuan's collection introduces us to a new means of self-immolation: self-mummification, truly the gift of one's body to the community as Jacques Gernet noted so perceptively.[82] Like the majority of self-immolators in this collection, Daoxiu 道休 (d. 629) lived not too far from Chang'an, at Fuyuan si 福緣寺 in Xinfeng 新豐, Yongzhou 雍州.[83] He was a true ascetic and a heroic meditator. His regular practice was to sit for seven days before emerging from *samādhi* and then, holding his bowl and carrying his staff, come off the mountain to beg for food, preach, and bestow the precepts. He kept this up for forty years. But one day in the summer of 629, he did not appear at the expected time. The villagers went to look for him at his meditation hut, which he had built in a secluded valley on Li shan 驪山. Daoxiu had died, sitting erect with his hands folded, but the villagers imagined that he was still in *samādhi*. They kept guard overnight by his side and continued to do so for a further two nights. It was only when they eventually examined him close up that they realized he really was dead. His body remained upright in the lotus position and did not rot. The villagers left him there and closed up his hut, placing thorny brambles outside the doors to discourage animals from damaging his body. The next year, he had an honored guest:

> At the beginning of winter in the fourth year (of Zhenguan, 630), I (Daoxuan) went to have a look at him.[84] The people north of the mountain had taken him back to their village, where they had raised a hut for his mausoleum and installed his body. Although his skin had turned leathery and his bones had fused together, his facial expression had not changed, and he sat cross-legged as before. They had added lacquer-soaked cloth to the surface of his body.[85]

Daoxuan continues the biography with special attention to Daoxiu's clothing. He used only the three robes, as approved for practitioners of *dhūta,* and sometimes dispensed with them, sitting naked in the depths of winter. He also earns Daoxuan's respect for his avoidance of silk and is compared favorably with the monks from "Western regions," whom Daoxuan had known in his days at the translation bureau. We can see here the special affection that villagers had for advanced meditators and ascetics.

Shandao and Self-Immolation

The *Xu gaoseng zhuan* contains what appears at first glance to be a contemporary account of the teaching of Shandao 善導 (613–681), the well-known Pure Land preacher.[86] It does not seem to be all that flattering and was probably not part of Daoxuan's compilation but added at a fairly late date:[87]

> Recently there has been a mountain monk by the name of Shandao who has wandered all over the world in search of a taste of the Way. This led him to Xihe 西河, where he encountered the group around Daochuo 道綽 (562–645).[88] They practiced solely the pure practice of reciting the name of the Buddha Amitābha. When he entered Chang'an, he broadly promoted his teaching. He copied out several tens of thousands of scrolls of the *Mituo jing* 彌陀經 (*Amituo jing* 阿彌陀經, *Sukhāvatī*[*amṛta*] *vyūha*, T 366). Countless people, both men and women, had faith in him. Once, when he was preaching the *dharma* at Guangming si 光明寺, someone said to him, "Now, if I recite the name of the Buddha, will I definitely be reborn in the Pure Land or not?"[89] Shandao said, "If you recite the name of the Buddha, you will definitely be reborn there." After making his obeisances this person began to chant "Namu Amituofo" incessantly, and he went out of the gates of Guangming si. Then he climbed to the top of a willow tree. With his palms together and facing west, he threw himself off. He died when he hit the ground. The matter was reported to the Department of State Affairs (*taisheng* 臺省).[90]

From this brief anecdote of dubious authenticity came a tradition that linked Shandao, the Pure Land, and self-immolation in legend. A Song source completed in 1084, the *Xinxiu jingtu wangsheng zhuan* 新修淨土往生傳 (Newly Compiled Biographies of Those Who Attained Deliverance in the Pure Land) by Wang Gu 王古 (d.u.), expanded on the account by claiming that in response to Shandao's teachings monks, nuns, and laypeople hurled themselves off mountains, drowned in wells, or burned themselves on pyres.[91] There does not appear to be any contemporary evidence for such an outbreak of mass self-immolation, but it is interesting that the legend seems to echo the accounts of Mahāsattva Fu and his followers. The later story that Shandao himself committed suicide is apocryphal and based on a misreading of the above biography.[92] Certainly this biographical aside does not seem very complimentary to Shandao and *nianfo* practice in general and is rather at odds with the biographies that were in the original *Xu gaoseng zhuan*.

Daoxuan's *Critical Evaluation*

Let us turn from the biographies to Daoxuan's own views of what self-immolation meant.[93] Daoxuan's prose is notoriously difficult to translate, especially the high-flown style of his critical evaluations in the *Xu gaoseng zhuan*. His composition is elliptical and densely allusive, very much in the manner that was admired in the early Tang. His lengthy remarks therefore require considerable unpacking but repay serious consideration—not least for his digression from self-immolation into the topic of funerals. This source may be particularly important for the history of Chinese funerals and cremation.[94]

Daoxuan begins by broaching the subject of self-immolation in the same general way as Huijiao does, with two parallel sentences comparing the difficulty of dying well with the ease of running away. Then he explains that the biographies given above, like those in the dynastic histories or the sayings found in the classics, serve a dual purpose: as warnings to the beginner and as models to the spiritually advanced. For Daoxuan, as for Huijiao, successful self-immolators were beyond ordinary morality because they had directly awakened to the fact that life is temporary and, ultimately, empty. The summary of cases that follows, accompanied by allusions to the *jātaka*s and *sūtra*s, implies that there were many more examples of self-immolation than are actually included in the collection.

Although Daoxuan points out that, according to the scriptures, self-immolation means exchanging the temporary and impure human body for an indestructible *dharma* body of a Buddha, he is quick to restate the fundamental dichotomy between advanced bodhisattvas like the Medicine King, who made a powerful vow and had cultivated the *pāramitā*s over many lifetimes, and the ordinary people who imitate him but are unable to maintain the same level of determination. For Daoxuan, it seems, determination or will was an important factor in judging the correctness of practice. He states that Sengyai, Dazhi, Xuanlan, and Puan did not waver in carrying out their intentions; because of this they clearly distinguished themselves from ordinary beings. Arhats and bodhisattvas were able to burn themselves, but their acts were also beyond criticism and productive of merit for others. Puyuan, Fakuang, and Puji recognized the empty and provisional nature of their own bodies and selves and were thus able to perform the same acts as those "former sages."

Next Daoxuan deals with the objection that self-immolation merely attacks the fruit, or effect, of suffering (that is, the human body) instead of attacking the seed, or cause, of that suffering (craving). He concedes that this is a good point, but because the present self and the body are a result of past *karma,* they must be dealt with in the present. Self-immolation, like medicine, can correct problems with the body. In fact, he claims, it may be just as good as meditation for correcting one's unenlightened mind. But if one is ignorant of the actions one undertakes then the result is just more delusion. In that case it is better to do as the *Lotus Sūtra* suggests and memorize a single stanza of the scripture. However, Daoxuan then identifies a further class of people who are unable to practice what is preached. For them, he suggests, it might be a good idea to sever a finger to break their attachment to the human body. In the final analysis, it is a matter of knowing one's limits and one's spiritual capacity. If one does not have the spiritual power, one simply cannot emulate the self-immolation of bodhisattvas.

As Daoxuan admits, there were certainly cases of people whose self-immolation was unsuccessful because they had insufficient power or determination. Their failure was betrayed by a groan of pain at the point of death. There were even monks who castrated themselves to limit their sexual desire. But they attacked the problem in the wrong way and should have regulated their minds instead. We may recall that self-castration is attested in the Vinaya, most famously in the case of the monk who pounded his unwanted erection with a rock in the *Mūlasarvāstivāda Vinaya.*[95] The Buddha rather wittily pointed out to the *saṃgha* on that memorable occasion that this foolish monk had "cut off the wrong thing": He should have cut off desire instead of his penis. Daoxuan most likely has this case in mind here when he declares that castration should definitely be considered an offence that brings expulsion from the order because it is certainly not productive of merit.[96]

A large part of Daoxuan's evaluation is taken up with a discussion of funerals and methods of disposing of the corpse. First, he mentions six methods for dealing with the corpse that were common in medieval Chinese Buddhism: exposure in forests; water burial, which provided food for fish and birds; burial in tombs and mounds or marked by tall stelae; cremation; and pulverizing the bones to make images. He contrasts these exemplary forms of "abandoning the body" with boring holes in the skin and cutting off noses and feet, perhaps alluding to types of practice current in his own day. In particular, Daoxuan notes approvingly the practice of exposure. The sight of bodies wasting away in the wilderness and being devoured by animals, birds, and maggots, he says, "inspires feelings of compassion and pity." We know that exposure of the corpse was a fairly well-attested practice in the Sui and early Tang, and Daoxuan must have seen many such remains on Zhongnan shan.

Four types of funerals were known to the Chinese from the "Western Regions" (Central Asia and India): cremation, water burial, earth burial, and exposure in forests. Daoxuan says that because kings of the *dharma* and *cakravartin* monarchs were cremated, this form of funeral was especially highly regarded, often at the expense of other forms of disposal. In China, on the other hand, cremation and water burial were unheard of in ancient times: Only earth burial and exposure of the corpse were known. During the reign of the legendary emperor Shun 舜, earthenware coffins first appeared, and the practice of forest exposure was forgotten. Although the history of funerals in China is somewhat obscure, as Daoxuan admits, burial in the earth, especially in a tumulus, became the dominant method for disposing of the dead. In particular, Daoxuan praises the practice of erecting engraved stelae so that accounts of the deceased's conduct might inspire the living. In addition, burial near *stūpa*s and making images or miniature *stūpa*s out of pulverized bone —practices that originated outside China— had been adopted by Daoxuan's time and are deemed particularly praiseworthy by him. In Daoxuan's day there were, he says, people who wanted to imitate the practices of forest exposure but did so insincerely, acting only out of a desire for personal fame and recognition. They made a great show of announcing their intention to die in the forest but never actually carried it out, content to reap the admiration of their peers for their ostentatious asceticism.

This excursion into funerary customs leads Daoxuan back to the question of the validity of self-immolation. Death by jumping from a cliff is, he claims, *pārājika*. But like those who practice forest burial, one has to examine the intention of the self-immolator. Those who are still affected by impure desires, and who secretly do not wish to die, are wrong, and so Daoxuan has not included their biographies. As he stresses again and again, one's intention must be good for the act to be considered permissible and exemplary.

Some people choose death; others try desperately to stay alive by practicing techniques of longevity and transcendence. They abstain from grain and practice alchemy, breathing techniques, and gymnastics. They seek magic fungi, herbs, and minerals in the mountains. Whether they wish to see Maitreya or just increase their knowledge of magic, these people's efforts are in vain. In a clear reference to Taoism, with which such techniques were clearly identified in his mind, Daoxuan says they have been clearly rejected in Buddhism (although they were, of course, practiced by Tang Buddhists). Because *saṃsāra* is so long, all efforts to live forever are ultimately doomed to failure. Much better, says Daoxuan, to practice cemetery contemplations to awaken to impermanence. But, as in all cases, there are good practitioners and bad ones, such as those who appear to be pure but reveal their attachment by staging extravagant funerals.

Conclusion

Examining our seventh-century biographies we can see how the imitation of scriptural models from the *Lotus* and the *jātaka*s mingled with pragmatic and sometimes desperate attempts to defend the *dharma* against the depredations of the state. In both his carefully crafted selection of biographies and his critical evaluation, Daoxuan hints strongly that the moral power and charisma of self-immolators allowed them to act as guardians of the community. As a monk who spent much of his career close to the center of political power, he was particularly interested in self-immolators who demonstrated these attributes within sight of the court—hence his marked attention to the self-immolators of Mount Zhongnan.

The shape of the self-immolation section of the *Xu gaoseng zhuan* as we have it in the received text has somewhat obscured the implicit message of Daoxuan's original composition which, I believe, had a certain polemical intent. His aim was to remind his readers of those who had fought to maintain the integrity, indeed the very survival, of the *saṃgha* under previous regimes. More specifically, he may very well have wanted Taizong to take notice of the fact that Buddhist monks had the means to oppose tyrants and usher in just rule by their physical acts. Thus the political dimensions of self-immolation, which we already noted in Chapter 1, took on a significantly new cast. The powers of self-immolation could now be harnessed to protect the *saṃgha* as well as generate merit.

The power of self-immolators in the sixth and seventh centuries found expression not only in relics and miracles but in the writings they left behind. From Dazhi's seventy-page vow to Zheng Ting's death poem and Xuanlan's hidden farewell message, self-immolators increasingly left written justifications and commemorations of their actions. We know from the case of Dazhi that such a text could be as much an object of emotional devotion as a body relic. Self-immolation in China was beginning to acquire a certain aesthetic.

Despite the literary aspects of self-immolation—explicit references to obscure *jātaka*s, written vows-cum-manifestoes, death verses—there was another strain of medieval self-immolation that stressed the power of the physical act. The charismatic and illiterate "barbarian" Sengyai and those in the Mahāsattva Fu cult seem to have been convinced that their style of "action Buddhism"—often manifested in the form of burning fingers and bodies—had the power to extend or renew the vitality not only of the Buddha's teaching but the very world itself.

Self-immolation was a well-entrenched aspect of Buddhist practice by the mid-seventh century, but it did not remain static. Monks and nuns brought to it a deeper appreciation and knowledge of the scriptural antecedents as well as a confidence that it was a practice that could meet their personal requirements and was desperately needed by a monastic community whose continued existence depended on the sometimes precarious patronage of rulers and a cosmos that was moving entropically from order to chaos. Self-immolation was not just the transformation of a single monk; it could be a ritual force for social and cosmic renewal.

CHAPTER 4

Is Self-Immolation a "Good Practice"?

Yongming Yanshou on Relinquishing the Body

So far we have viewed self-immolation largely through the lens of biographies—that is to say, through literary descriptions of monks' actions. But if self-immolation did in fact offer a somatic path to liberation, as I believe it did, then what did Chinese Buddhist authors who worked with doctrine make of the practice? How did they fit self-immolation into the larger framework of valid and orthodox praxis? In this chapter we shall examine two such attempts to do so. The first is the enthusiastic defense of self-immolation offered by Daoxuan's contemporary Daoshi in his "encyclopedia" *Fayuan zhulin*. The second is the more sophisticated and extended discussion offered by Yongming Yanshou in the *Wanshan Tonggui ji* 萬善同歸集 (The Common End of the Myriad Good Practices, T 48.2017, hereafter *Tonggui ji*).

Yanshou's approach to self-immolation will occupy most of our attention in this chapter. By the time he was writing, he could look back on nearly six hundred years of self-immolation in China. But while the practice was well attested, the question of its orthodoxy continued to vex the Buddhist community. In addition to occasional criticisms from without levelled at self-immolators by rulers and officials, the Buddhist translator, pilgrim, and Vinaya master Yijing had composed a sharp critique of the practice based in part on his experiences in India. Yanshou brought his extensive knowledge of scripture and the history of the Chinese *saṃgha* to bear on the potentially divisive issue of whether monks could or should burn their bodies.

Before we come to grips with Yanshou, let us first consider a mid-seventh-century perspective on self-immolation composed by a monk who, like Daoxuan, viewed such matters from a metropolitan monastery close to the center of political power. Daoshi's writing combines scriptural sources, scholarly opinion, and biography to offer a comprehensive vision of self-immolation.

A Grove of Pearls in a Dharma Garden

The *Fayuan zhulin* is the largest, most exhaustive Buddhist compendium that survives in the Chinese canon and is a fascinating source for the study of Tang

Buddhism and Tang social history. Daoshi was a close associate of Daoxuan and was familiar not only with Buddhist literature that had been translated into Chinese, but also with Chinese works, both religious and secular.[1] The *Fayuan zhulin* was an ambitious attempt to integrate Buddhist theory and practice with Chinese culture and values.

Chapter 96 of Daoshi's work covers self-immolation in a self-consciously encyclopedic and didactic manner. The chapter on self-immolation (*sheshen pian* 捨身篇) follows the *Fayuan zhulin*'s standard format: It opens with an "overview" (*shuyi bu* 述意部); continues with "evidence," or the citation of scripture (*yincheng bu* 引證部); and concludes with "stories of stimulus and response," or biographies (*ganying bu* 感應部).[2] Although Daoshi showed that he was aware of objections to self-immolation, he was unequivocally in favor of the merits of the practice. His overview makes no attempt to define self-immolation, nor discuss the practice, but proceeds along the following lines, now familiar to us from the critical evaluations of Huijiao and Daoxuan: The universe itself is impermanent and so is the body. Any notion of a "self" is fundamentally illusory. However, unlike the bodhisattva who works tirelessly for others, lifetime after lifetime, ordinary people are fundamentally greedy and try desperately to amass possessions, which like themselves are inherently devoid of any real existence. The bodhisattva, on the other hand, is always aware that the body is but a phantom or a dream.[3] Daoshi ends this short argument by comparing secular and Buddhist ideas about the value of life:

An outer text [*Zhuangzi* 莊子] says, "When alive I take the body as a lodging, when dead I take heaven and earth as a coffin."[4] We Buddhists say, "When the prince discarded his body the merit [allowed him to] pass over nine *kalpas,* when he sliced his thigh and exchanged [the flesh] for a pigeon, the shock reverberated through the trichiliocosm."[5] When we take cases from the present and compare them with these from the past, [we find that self-immolators] all had the same intention. They wanted to enable the white ox[cart] to have the capacity for the long journey, and the precious raft to have the ability to reach the other shore.[6]

In this passage Daoshi forcefully advances the idea that Chinese self-immolators are just as good as the bodhisattvas described in translated scriptures. Their acts are part of the greater propagation of Buddhism. Their intention is no less than to drive the great vehicle ever forward.

In the following section, Daoshi quotes from the scriptures that support the practice of self-immolation. Not surprisingly he adduces the Medicine King chapter of the *Lotus Sūtra* here, but he begins in fact with another *sūtra,*

which we have already mentioned more than once.[7] He takes as his fundamental text the story of the hungry tigress in the *Sūtra of Golden Light*. This
sūtra was notably employed for state protection in East Asia, although it also
offers a wide variety of instruction on Buddhist practices such as expression
of faith and repentance. There are five Chinese translations; most important
are those by Dharmakṣema, Baogui 寶貴 (d. after 597), and Yijing.[8] The frequency of its translation attests to the deep interest in this *sūtra* by Chinese
monks and laypeople. Because it was used for state-sponsored rituals, we may
suppose that even those with little knowledge of Buddhism would have had
some familiarity with its contents.

The popular story of the hungry tigress from this much-translated text
shows just what kind of claims were being made for self-immolation in
Daoshi's day. The act of offering the body—for the benefit of a tigress, for
other beings, or in homage to buddhas—was guaranteed to result in enlightenment, often expressed in the form of a new permanent body replete
with wisdom and virtue, and the ability to save other beings. In the legend,
Prince Mahāsattva himself is conscious of imitating the bodhisattvas just as
Chinese self-immolators later imitated him, King Śibi, and the Medicine
King. The universe responds to his sacrifice just as the acts of Chinese
monks were accompanied by magic rain, the blossoming of trees and flowers, light shows, earthquakes, thunder, and so on.

Daoshi's quotations from the two major Mahāyāna *sūtras*, the *Lotus* and
the *Sūtra of Golden Light*, are followed by a passage that attempts to resolve
the key problem for Chinese monastics. Is self-immolation allowed by the
Vinaya, the code that regulates the behavior of monks and nuns? Daoshi's
argument and choice of scriptural authority are perhaps less than convincing, and other authors brought heavier guns to bear on the question, as we
shall see:

> QUESTION: When a bodhisattva gives up his body, does he commit the
> wrongdoing of suicide or not?
>
> ANSWER: According to the Vinaya, if one makes use of some expedient
> before giving up one's life then it is a lesser offence of *sthūlātyaya* (*toulanzhe*
> 偷蘭遮). But if one has already given up one's life, then there is no offence
> involved. Therefore, one does not commit the major offence of killing a
> person. If one bases oneself on the [acts of the] bodhisattvas of the
> Mahāyāna then one leaves *saṃsāra* in disgust to worship the buddhas, and
> one also gives rise to a mind of great compassion towards all beings. One
> has no intention of harming others, but on the contrary will invite merit.
> So how could one commit any offence?

So, as the *Mañjuśrīparipṛcchā* (*Wenshushili wen jing* 文殊師利問經, Questions of Mañjuśrī) says, "The Buddha said, 'If one kills oneself there is no retribution. Why? It is just like a bodhisattva killing himself; he only obtains merit as his body comes from himself. As one [who hurts his body] receives retribution, then the acts of cutting one's fingernails or hurting one's fingers would receive punishment. Why? Because one injures one's own body. The bodhisattva's giving away his body is not a neutral act. Rather, it only results in merit, since it extirpates *kleśa* (defilement) and extinguishes the body, and one obtains a pure body. It is just like when you wash stained clothes with ashes and water: The stain is eradicated, but the clothes remain.'"[9]

For Daoshi the power of the precedents from the Mahāyāna literature simply outweighs the Vinaya and trumps its proscription of suicide. The bodhisattva cannot receive karmic retribution for something he does to his own body. Lest we imagine that this is a particularly heterodox position or one written from a position of ignorance, we should remember that Daoshi (like Daoxuan and Zanning) was well versed in the Vinaya and wrote extensively on correct monastic behavior. Certainly as Daoshi presents his argument here, it seems to be a fairly straightforward matter: The bodhisattva acts selflessly so he does not experience retribution for his actions. When the bodhisattva gives away his body, he does away with a defiled body—one that is born of *karma*—and exchanges it for a pure *dharmakāya*. The act does not bring karmic retribution but rather generates merit. This passage is followed by a note in smaller characters that indicates some other scriptural sources that Daoshi does not discuss in the self-immolation section:

Other scriptures that recount [tales of] bodhisattvas abandoning their bodies are far from few. There is Prince Moonlight (Yueguang wang 月光王, Candraprabha), who gave away his head, and Śibi, who cut his thigh. Also there is the elephant king Saḍḍanta (Shizi xiangwang 師子象王), who gave away his tusks and skin to benefit others. Also there is the deer king Qin 禽, who ferried a woodcutter in peril over a river. Also there is the case of [the bodhisattva who became] a great turtle who saved people from danger at sea. Also there are [the stories of] the great fish who drove out disease, and the mountain of meat who donated himself to feed people. These examples have not been laid out together but have been scattered and distributed in other chapters [of the *Fayuan zhulin*]. I fear that it would complicate the text and so it has not been possible to recount them again here.[10]

Daoshi's laconic references to the *jātakas* require a little patient unpacking. We have already encountered the story of Śibi, the flesh-donating
king, but we should become familiar with the other stories, too.[11] The cycle
of legends about Candraprabha is extremely complex, as many different
tales concerning offerings of the flesh are associated with this figure.[12] We
discussed the story of Candraprabha donating his head in connection with
Puyuan's self-immolation.

The story of the six-tusked elephant Saḍḍanta emphasizes not only
charity but also patience and respect for the robe of a *śramaṇa*. A wise and
benevolent six-tusked elephant king had two principal wives.[13] Because he
presented one with a lotus, the other grew jealous and vowed to kill him in a
later life. Dying in a fit of rage she was reborn as the daughter of a good
family and the favorite wife of a human king. One day she told the king that
she had dreamed of a six-tusked elephant and that she wanted the ivory
from its tusks. He had all the hunters gathered together and found one who
knew of this elephant. The queen told him to shave his head and beard and
wear the robe of a *śramaṇa*. Thus the hunter was able to approach
Saḍḍanta, kill him, and saw off his tusks. When the queen saw the tusks,
there was a mighty clap of thunder, and spitting blood she dropped down
dead to be reborn in hell.

The story of the deer king who saves a man from drowning also appears
to extol the perfection of vigor rather than charity.[14] The story of a giant tortoise who saves five hundred merchants on his back and is then killed and
eaten by their leader is told in *Za baozang jing* 雜寶藏經 (Sūtra of the Storehouse of Sundry Treasures).[15] The story of the Rohita fish is somewhat similar to that of the meat mountain we discussed earlier.[16] According to the
Zhuanji baiyuan jing 撰集百緣經 (*Avadānaśataka*, One Hundred Selected
Avadānas, T 4.200.217a), a virtuous and charitable king called Padmaka
(Lianhua 蓮華) rules in Vārāṇasī.[17] An epidemic breaks out, and the doctors
tell the king that the only cure is the flesh and blood of the Rohita fish. The
king sends people to search for such a fish, but it cannot be found. He throws
himself off the roof of the palace, vowing to be reborn as the fish. He is reborn and the people feed off his flesh for twelve years until the famine ends.

These then were among the accounts of the gift of the body that were
most widely known in China. They showed the ability not only of humans,
but also of animals (albeit animal princes and kings, of course) to save others
by their own heroic self-sacrifice. In light of the range of such accounts,
widely attested in a variety of sources, self-sacrifice might quite reasonably be
understood as a necessary stage on the path to Buddhahood—not merely an
optional part of the bodhisattva's career. Chinese Buddhists sincerely

wanted to study and cultivate that path. If they learned that self-immolation was so important to their heroes, one can hardly be shocked that some of them put it into effect.

Although Daoshi was able to bring together the key exemplars of self-immolation in the scriptures, a host of *jātaka* tales, and some eminent Chinese self-immolators of the past (beginning with a non-Buddhist transcendent) and to sketch out the beginnings of a kind of Mahāyāna ethics for the practice, his defense of self-immolation was by no means grounded in the fundamentals of doctrine. To compete with Yijing's diatribe against the practice, something much more developed was required.

The Common End of the Myriad Good Practices

Yanshou's *Tonggui ji* has to date been approached by scholars mainly as a work that has a specific syncretic agenda. Modern Japanese scholarship in particular, influenced in part by the image of Yanshou presented in sectarian hagiographies, has promoted him primarily as a harmonizer of Chan and Pure Land practice. For this reason, the contents of the first fascicle of the three-fascicle recension of the text, which does indeed contain discussion of Chan and *nianfo* 念佛 practice, have been privileged over the contents of the other two fascicles, which have been more or less ignored.[18]

The *Tonggui ji* consists of 114 sections in question-and-answer format (not numbered in the original text) and covers such diverse practices as worshipping the Buddha, preaching the *dharma,* chanting *sūtra*s, worshipping *stūpa*s, repentance, Chan meditation, *nianfo,* building temples, building roads and bridges, and performing general acts of altruism. The first seven or so sections of the second fascicle, in particular sections 34, 39, and 41, address the issue of self-immolation as a "good practice."[19]

Earlier authors such as Huijiao and Daoxuan tended to shy away from a systematic doctrinal approach to the problems and paradoxes of self-immolation. In his Buddhist encyclopedia, Daoshi drew together scriptural accounts and biographies to show that it was indeed a valid practice, but he did not attempt to draw out the doctrinal and ethical ramifications. Yanshou's writing on the topic therefore provides a rare opportunity to explore how an elite monk who was well versed in Buddhist doctrine could make sense of the practice within the framework of the mature Chinese tradition. Below we shall focus on sections 34–41 of the *Tonggui ji* because this sequence of questions and answers is particularly revealing of Yanshou's thoughts on the matter. We shall also examine his justification for self-immolation from several perspectives.

First, how does Yanshou justify self-immolation? What scriptures does he cite in support of the practice, and how does he put them together? Specifically, how does he defend the practice against the charge that it contravenes the Vinaya? This issue seems to have been a perennial cause for concern in China, although the objection rarely was made in discussions recorded in the actual biographies themselves. Second, how does Yanshou's argument relate to the overall taxonomy of the *Tonggui ji*? Is the inclusion of a discussion of self-immolation merely an aberration, or does Yanshou truly see the issue as one that was deeply embedded in Buddhist practice? Third, how does his endorsement of self-immolation compare with other statements concerning the practice found in other Chinese Buddhist texts? Specifically, how does his opinion differ from statements made by the compilers of the *Biographies of Eminent Monks* and the *Fayuan zhulin*? Is Yanshou's attitude towards the practice actually unique? Finally, can one find historical reasons for his endorsement of this practice? Did he know any self-immolators, or was his argument purely theoretical?

Yanshou's Justification of Self-Immolation

Before we can analyze the way in which Yanshou makes sense of self-immolation, we must establish the nature of the text with which we are dealing. The image of Yanshou as a synthesizer of Chan and Pure Land practices is one that first began to take shape during the late Song, was crystallized in Tokugawa-period (1603–1867) Japan, and remained unchallenged by Buddhist scholars until very recently. Yanshou was an extremely prolific writer and compiler, and the *Tonggui ji* in particular has long been recognized as one of his two major works along with the *Zongjing lu* 宗鏡錄 (Record of the Principle that Mirrors [the Ten Thousand Dharmas], T 48.2016), the widely read compendium of Chan lore and scripture, which was completed in 961.[20] The *Tonggui ji* has, however, largely been read from the point of view of the later tradition, in effect reducing it to a treatise on two "good practices" (Chan and *nianfo*) rather than the ten thousand originally envisaged. This reductionist view of Yanshou has unfortunately obscured the breadth of his knowledge and the originality of his thought.

Biographies of Yanshou can be found in some thirty Buddhist compilations, but many of these were composed centuries after his death and are clearly sectarian in motivation.[21] However, two early biographies were composed by men who quite possibly knew Yanshou personally: those by Zanning, compiler of the *Song gaoseng zhuan,* and Daoyuan 道原 (fl. ca. 1004), compiler of the *Jingde chuandeng lu* 景德傳燈錄 (Jingde-era Record of the

Transmission of the Lamp).[22] Zanning quite clearly regarded Yanshou not as a Chan master, but primarily as a promoter of Buddhism in general and placed him in the *xingfu* 興福 (promoters of merit) section of his compilation; of the many works attributed to Yanshou he accorded pride of place to the *Tonggui ji*.[23] In contrast, the purpose of the *Jingde chuandeng lu* biography was primarily to promote the Fayan 法眼 lineage of Chan (Daoyuan was a third-generation successor to Fayan Wenyi 文益 [885–958]) and more particularly to establish Yanshou's position as the third patriarch of that lineage. The *Tonggui ji* is not mentioned at all in this biography, although the *Zongjing lu* is cited. Nevertheless, the *Jingde chuandeng lu* (composed after the *Song Gaoseng zhuan*) presents Yanshou as a Chan master who did not simply indulge in rhetorical sparring matches with other Chan monks, but rather bestowed bodhisattva precepts on the laity, fed hungry ghosts, set free birds and fish, and recited the *Lotus Sūtra* thirteen thousand times.[24] The picture that emerges from these two early biographies is of a Buddhist monk who practiced what he preached, with the possible exception of self-immolation; according to his biographies he died of natural causes, and if Yanshou burned off any limbs that fact is not mentioned.

Throughout the *Tonggui ji* Yanshou aimed to resolve doubts concerning Buddhist teachings by responding to questions with quotations from the scriptures interspersed with his own comments and judgments. We may note that Yanshou uses a good deal more technical language and Buddhist-style argument and examples than do Huijiao, Daoxuan, or Daoshi, who tended to favor secular language and allusions to Chinese literature. We may surmise then that Yanshou was writing for a different audience—one composed of monks—but also that he was grounding his defense of Buddhist self-immolation solidly in his understanding of Buddhism rather than Chinese cultural norms. His argument is certainly forceful, but at the same time it is nuanced and sophisticated.

In his study of the *Tonggui ji,* Albert Welter tabulates the occurrences of the scriptural quotations, and the overwhelming importance of those works considered central to the Huayan and Tiantai schools is evident at a glance.[25] It cannot be argued, therefore, that the interpretation of self-immolation is actually offered from either a Chan or Pure Land perspective. Rather, self-immolation is presented as one of the myriad "good practices" (*wanshan* 萬善) that leads to the common end (*tonggui* 同歸) of enlightenment. The title of Yanshou's work in fact derives from the phrase Zhiyi used to describe the teaching of the *Lotus Sūtra,* and we have already noted the importance of that text in Yanshou's practice.[26] But Yanshou takes Zhiyi's formulation a stage further by equating *wanshan* with the concept of *shi* 事 (phenomena) and *tonggui* with *li* 理 (principle). This phenomena/principle dialectic was a favorite device of Huayan thinkers. Once we grasp the fact that this blend of Huayan and Tiantai concepts is Yanshou's primary means of justifying a broad range of Buddhist practices, the framework of the *Tonggui ji* as a whole becomes much more important to our discussion of a single topic within it. However, because this lengthy and complex text has still not received the scholarly attention that has been directed towards the works of other major synthesists of East Asian Buddhism, we must remain somewhat cautious about making statements concerning the larger taxonomy of the *Tonggui ji*.

Nevertheless, one might well ask whether this Huayan/Tiantai epistemology offers the basis for Yanshou's vindication of self-immolation. Albert Welter argues, with some justification, that for Yanshou self-immolation was primarily a manifestation of *dāna* (charity), and that as the ultimate expression of this *pāramitā* (perfection) the gift of one's body is an act of *li* as opposed to *shi*, which is to say that it takes place at the level of ultimate truth rather than the level of conventional phenomena.[27] This argument is true, as far as it goes, but it is neither a unique formulation nor the main thrust of Yanshou's primary argument as expressed in Section 34 of the *Tonggui ji*.[28] One might go so far as to say that the definition of self-immolation as *dāna* of the ultimate level looks almost like a secondary argument added in an attempt to make the discussion fit into the overall taxonomy of the text. It is true that Zanning, Yanshou's close contemporary, also seems to have understood self-immolation as an act of *dāna* in his *Song Gaoseng zhuan,* but as we shall see that was not his only interpretation of the act.[29] In fact, Yanshou begins with neither principle nor *dāna;* rather his primary argument is expressed in terms of the precepts, specifically the superiority of the Bodhisattva precepts of the apocryphal *Fanwang jing* 梵網經 (Book of Brahmā's Net) over the "*śrāvaka* precepts" of the *Sifen lü* 四分律 *(Dharmaguptaka Vinaya)*. In this section of the *Tonggui ji,* Yanshou is not offering a phenomenological approach to a Buddhist practice; he appears to be arguing that because the practice is vindicated by the bodhisattva precepts, it is ipso facto a "good practice."

Self-Immolation and the Precepts

In Section 34 of the *Tonggui ji* the "question" (*wen* 問) concerning self-immolation is expressed in terms of the precepts, and it is answered (*da* 答) in terms of the precepts.[30] Yanshou begins by citing the sixteenth of the forty-eight lesser precepts of the *Fanwang jing,* which was given the rubric *wei li daoshuo jie* 為利倒說戒 (the precept on making inverted statements for [one's own] gain) apparently by Zhiyi himself.[31] The text of this precept is admittedly a little difficult to construe and seems to have been open to different interpretations, but in Yanshou's reading the following part is fairly unambiguous: When bodhisattvas who are new to the practice come in search of teaching one who has taken the bodhisattva precepts, then:

> In accordance with the *dharma* he should explain to them all the ascetic practices, such as setting fire to the body, setting fire to the arm, or setting fire to the finger. If one does not set fire to the body, the arm, or the finger as an offering to the buddhas, one is not a renunciant bodhisattva.[32]

But at least according to the received text of the *Fanwang jing,* the meaning of this precept is that if one does not explain the true *dharma,* point by point, then one is guilty of a lesser transgression. The ascetic practices that are detailed in the precept are merely an example of the true teaching; they are not what the precept requires one to do oneself. Here Yanshou omits twenty-five characters towards the end of the precept and replaces them with *ruo bu ru shi* 若不如是 ("if one does not do so"). Thus the reader is left with the impression that by not burning the body one is breaking a bodhisattva precept. This is surely not the thrust of the original precept, which is actually concerned with the necessity of transmitting the teachings correctly and not "inverting" them. One needs only turn to a commentary on the *Fanwang jing,* such as that of Fazang 法藏 (643–712) for example, to confirm that the conventional reading of the text was that the precept concerned the correct teaching of the *dharma* to students of the Bodhisattva path.[33]

On this question of precepts, we should also consider the close parallels between the statements Yanshou makes concerning the Vinaya's proscription of suicide and those made slightly later by Zanning. Yanshou says of self-immolation: "Forsaking the body, or ending one's life, to repay the compassion of the *dharma* profoundly accords with the Mahāyāna and deeply resonates with the true teaching." Later he adds, "So the Hīnayāna clings to appearances, it restricts but it does not allow. But the Great Teaching is perfect and comprehensive, fundamentally it has no fixed *dharma.*" As we shall see, Zanning took a similar line in the self-immolators section of the *Song Gaoseng zhuan:*

> The teachings of the lesser vehicle hold that suicide contravenes the major precepts and is an offence that takes precedence over all expedient means. Therefore, no one dares take up a torch to burn himself. However, there are two types of suicide. The first is that one kills oneself out of fear of punishment. This entails *sthūlātyaya* (an indeterminate offence) or *duṣkṛta* (a feeling

of remorse).[34] The second is that one vows to be reborn in the Pure Land
with a powerful and bold mind. When life ends, the body is reborn, so how
could *sthūlātyaya* or *duṣkṛta* act as obstacles to that? Furthermore, when one
unifies and arouses the great mind, this single lamp can dispel even the darkness of a hundred years. What offence is present in that? For this reason,
practitioners should not impede the great roots by taking the lesser way![35]

In this interesting passage, Zanning recognizes that suicide is technically
an offense, but says that this really only applies to those who commit suicide
with the wrong intention of escaping *saṃsāra*. For those in the Mahāyāna, the
vow to be reborn in the Pure Land is so powerful that it transcends all petty
restrictions. There can be no counter to this; when one's earthly life ends,
one is instantly reborn in the Pure Land. Minor transgressions of the precepts cannot prevent this from happening. The fact that these remarks were
appended to the biography of a monk from Tiantai shan who was a contemporary of both Zanning and Yanshou and was himself one of Tiantai
Deshao's 天臺德韶 (891–972) students makes one wonder if the matter of
self-immolation was a frequent topic of discussion on Tiantai shan in the late
tenth century. Zanning's comment, however, does not necessarily imply that
the precepts of the *Fanwang jing* supersede those of the *Sifen lü*. In fact it is
much more analogous to the statement made by the Tiantai exegete Zhanran
湛然 (711–782) that the attitude of the practitioner, not the type of precept,
was the basis for judging whether a practice was Hīnayāna or Mahāyāna.[36]
But in any case, there are intriguing similarities between the positions of
Yanshou and Zanning regarding the relevance of the precepts to self-
immolation.

Leaving aside this particular case of precepts and self-immolation, an argument could be made to the effect that the *Tonggui ji* and the *Song Gaoseng
zhuan,* produced as they were by two contemporaries from the kingdom of
Wu-Yue 吳越, were both written to present Buddhism as a very broad church
made up of different practitioners and diverse practices. The practices of
self-immolators may seem anomalous, but Yanshou was able to argue fairly
convincingly that their activities were perfectly in accord with the teachings
of the Buddha. Something analogous seems to be at work in Zanning's attitudes towards monks who break the precepts (or perhaps who appear to
break them). As John Kieschnick notes, for Zanning, "there was no such
thing as a bad monk; there were only misunderstood monks."[37] As we shall
see, the *Song Gaoseng zhuan* was directed towards the Song court and was intended to present Buddhism in the most sympathetic light possible, but we
simply do not know the audience for which *Tonggui ji* was written.[38]

Aside from the fact that the *Tonggui ji,* like the *Song Gaoseng zhuan,* was intended to legitimate a broad range of practices by defining them as properly Buddhist, there is another possibility that would explain why Yanshou was so interested in defending self-immolation. He could have been responding to a specific charge that self-immolation was not appropriate for monks because it contravened the Vinaya. Just such a charge had been made in the Tang by Yijing, but there is no surviving evidence of any such attack on self-immolation originating within the Buddhist community in Yanshou's time, more than two hundred and fifty years later. We should therefore turn to Yijing's attack. As it is somewhat lengthy, it may suffice here just to quote the opening lines:[39]

> Burning the body is not fitting. Among renunciates there is a group of practitioners who, on commencing their studies, want to be brave and keen. They are not familiar with the sacred books but put their trust in people who have gone before them. They consider burning the fingers as the practice of vigor (*jingqin* 精勤; Skt. *vīrya*) and the burning of the flesh as the production of great merit. They follow their own feelings, go by what is in their own minds. Although they are extolled in the *sūtra*s, such actions are for the laity who may offer their own bodies, not to mention any external possessions that they have. This is why in the *sūtra*s it simply says, "If someone gives rise to such a thought . . ." Thus it does not apply to renunciates. The meaning is that renunciates should abide by the Vinaya. If they do not transgress the precepts then they are in accordance with the *sūtra*s. If they do transgress then I see no reason to justify [their acts]. Even if the whole *gandhakuṭī* is covered in grass, they should not destroy even one blade.[40] Even if they are starving alone in the wilderness they should not steal even half a grain of rice. But for Sarvasattvapriyadarśana [the Medicine King], who is classed as a layperson, to burn his arms is considered perfectly permissible. Bodhisattvas may give up their sons and daughters, but *bhikṣu*s need not seek for sons and daughters to surrender. The *mahāsattva* donates his eyes and body, but [does it follow that] the person who begs for the *mahāsattva*'s eyes and body should use them to donate [to a third person]?[41]

Having set out his case by drawing a clear line between the *bodhisattva-mahāsattva*s of scripture, who were free to do as they chose with their bodies, and ordinary Chinese monks, who were not, Yijing attacked self-immolation for the following reasons. Human rebirth is hard to attain, and one should not give up the body before one has really begun to study.[42] Suicide is not permitted in the Vinaya.[43] The Buddha did not even permit castration but encouraged the "releasing of living beings" (for example, releasing fish into ponds).[44] Self-immolation means going against the teachings of the Buddha, although this does not apply to those who follow the bodhisattva path without being ordained to the Vinaya.[45] Those who burn their bodies are guilty of a *sthūlātyaya* (indeterminate) offense, but those who then imitate them are guilty of *pārājika* (defeat) because their intention is worse.[46] There were suicides in India at the time of the Buddha, and he declared them "heretics" (*waidao* 外道).[47] The rest of Yijing's argument, which unfolds across some seven frames of *Taishō* text, can be summed up as follows: "My teachers were all wise and virtuous men, they never burned their bodies, and they told me it was wrong to do so."[48]

Yijing's attitude towards self-immolation was not merely theoretical; he berated at least one self-immolator whom he knew personally. A story preserved in the *Jin'gang bore jing jiyan ji* 金剛般若經集驗記 (Collected Evidential Accounts of the *Diamond Sūtra*) by Meng Xianzhong 孟獻忠 (?–718+) records that in 707 Yijing recommended to the emperor Zhongzong 中宗 (r. 705–710) a monk called Qingxu 清虛 (d.u.) who conducted rituals to bring a fall of snow.[49] When Qingxu's early attempts produced only disappointing results, he resorted to burning off two fingers. Although the two fingers were miraculously restored in a manner that is now familiar to us, and both snow and rain did fall, Yijing bitterly condemned his actions.

Certainly Yijing's polemic against self-immolation begged a similarly comprehensive response, and it is telling that he began his thesis, as did Yanshou, with the question of the precepts. But if we look beyond the Buddhist world in search of a text to which Yanshou might be responding, there is another candidate in the form of the edict promulgated in 955 by Emperor Shizong 世宗 (r. 954–959) of the Later Zhou, one of the "Five Dynasties" that ruled North China in the period between the final collapse of the Tang in 907 and the restoration of a unified empire by the Song in 960. Although admittedly we cannot date the *Tonggui ji* with any degree of certainty, the consensus of scholarly supposition is that it was written during the second half of Yanshou's monastic career, when he was at Yongming monastery in the capital of Wu-Yue, from 961–975.[50] Shizong's edict was responsible for setting in motion what is regarded as the last of the four major suppressions of Buddhism in Chinese history (the others being those that occurred in 446, 574, and 845); according to the official histories, 33,336 monastic institutions are said to have been destroyed.[51] Exaggerated though these figures may be, Yanshou could hardly have been unaware of the problems his fellow believers were experiencing in North China. In the eighth clause of Shizong's edict we read:

Previously, *saṃgha* and laity have been practicing self-immolation, burning their arms and igniting their fingers or cutting off their hands and feet and then carrying them on pikes like flaming torches . . . all this must now cease. These are very serious offences as defined in the Vinaya.[52]

Because the edict cites the Vinaya as the authority on correct practice, it is entirely possible that Yanshou's defense of self-immolation, which endeavors to prove that the practice accords with the so-called "Mahāyāna Vinaya" was conceived of as a direct response to the wording of this particular section of Shizong's edict. Yanshou need not have actually seen the text itself to have been aware of its contents. Indeed, might not the whole of the *Tonggui ji* have been conceived as an apologetic for Buddhism at a time when, protected and privileged as it was under stewardship of the kings of Wu-Yue in the South, the religion was under severe attack in the North? Without even a definite date for the composition of the *Tonggui ji* this remains, of course, pure conjecture.

Leaving aside the possibility that endorsement of self-immolation by citing the *Fanwang jing* was intended as a response to a particular text or edict, what other evidence is there that Yanshou advocated the superiority of the bodhisattva precepts over those contained in the *Sifen lü*? His penchant for the bodhisattva precepts would seem to be fairly well attested. In the preface to the *Zongjing lu,* Yanshou is described as being an advocate of the precepts, and the fact that he frequently held bodhisattva precept ordination ceremonies is mentioned in his *Jingde chuandeng lu* biography.[53] In 974 he is said to have administered the precepts to ten thousand people on Mount Tiantai, and throughout his life he regularly administered the precepts to religious and laity alike. Three works on the bodhisattva precepts are attributed to him and one of them, the *Shou pusa jie fa* 受菩薩戒法 (Protocol for Transmitting the Bodhisattva Precepts), is still extant.[54] In the preface to this text he declares that "the bodhisattva precepts establish the land of a thousand sages, form the basis for the myriad good deeds, open the gate of sweet dew, and allow one to enter the path to *bodhi.*"[55] There is, of course, nothing particularly startling about a statement such as this, but it does at least demonstrate some internal consistency regarding the precepts in Yanshou's writings. Moreover, Yanshou's works sometimes reveal quite a critical attitude towards the "Hīnayāna" *Sifen lü.* In addition to the statements in Section 34 of the *Tonggui ji* that compare this Vinaya unfavorably with the "Mahāyāna Vinaya," we also find a ten-point critique of Vinaya masters in his *Zongjing lu.*[56] This evidence raises the outside possibility that Yanshou considered that monks should conform primarily to the precepts of the *Fanwang jing* and should not be bound by the *Sifen lü* at all, which if it could be proved would indeed challenge our notions of Chinese Buddhist attitudes towards the bodhisattva precepts. More research needs to be done, although a start has been made on this question by Jan Yün-hua.[57]

Moving on from Yanshou's use of the "Mahāyāna Vinaya" to justify self-immolation, let us examine the rest of his argument, which takes us away from the precepts and into the loftier and more abstruse reaches of Chinese Buddhist doctrine.

Self-Immolation and Its Paradoxes

The question addressed in Section 35 begins by comparing self-immolation to the practices of non-Buddhist (*waidao* 外道) ascetics in India, such as "those who roast themselves with five sources of heat" (*wure zhishen* 五熱炙身).[58] These, says the interlocutor, are heterodox practices, censured by the buddhas, so why should they be adopted when Buddhists have correct modes of practice on which to rely? Yanshou begins his answer with the contrast between the "path of complete emptiness" (*bijing kong dao* 畢竟空道) and the "path that discriminates between good and bad" (*fenbie haoe dao* 分別好惡道) as outlined in the *Da zhidu lun,* one of his favorite sources for questions concerning cultivation of the Buddhist path.[59] Discrimination of any kind—choosing between right or wrong, orthodox or heterodox—is counterproductive and prevents one from reaching the full attainment of wisdom. Moreover, the "special application" *siddhāntha* (*duizhixitan* 對治悉檀), which is a mode of teaching *(siddhāntha)* aimed at destroying the deep defilements or bad *karma* of certain beings, dispenses with logic altogether. Thus, says Yanshou, we are led to this apparent paradox:

> If you say [auto-cremation] is completely right, then Nigrantha [Niganzi 尼乾子, the Jain founder] perfected the orthodox true path, and all the buddhas are wrong to criticize him. If you say it is completely wrong, then the Medicine King falls into the error of inversion, and all the buddhas are wrong to praise him.[60]

This line of argument—that auto-cremation, if performed while on the path of complete emptiness, is essentially beyond such worldly and provisional categories as right and wrong—is one to which Yanshou returns again and again in his discussion. But despite having established this point, Yanshou does go on to distinguish between the meanings of self-immolation as performed by Buddhists and non-Buddhists. For each type of practitioner, he says, the act has two meanings. For Buddhists, it first illustrates that the nature of both self and others is empty, and it negates the idea that either the self or *dharma*s have any inherent existence. Second, Buddhist self-immolators only offer themselves to the Three Jewels and repay the four kinds of kindness (*si en* 四恩): kindness of parents, kindness of beings, kindness of rulers, and kindness of the Three Jewels. These offerings actually help them to attain unsurpassed *bodhi*. Self-immolators do not seek to be reborn among *deva*s or humans because they have a higher goal. On the other hand, non-Buddhists still retain the view of a self that has inherent existence, and thus their act remains essentially a selfish one. Also, Yanshou claims, they are motivated by the idea of fame in their present rebirth and a beneficial future rebirth; in particular, he says, some of them vow to become rulers of the *kṣatriya* caste or to be reborn in the Heaven of Extensive Rewards (*Guangguo tian* 廣果天).[61]

Yanshou next cites Zhanran's subcommentary on the *Lotus Sūtra*, the *Fahua wenju ji* 法華文句記, to support his contention that if self-immolation is performed in a way that is empty and untainted by duality, the act is essentially correct.[62] It is the intention behind the act that determines whether it is orthodox or heterodox. Finally, he paraphrases the *Questions of Mañjuśrī*—the same proof text that Daoshi had cited—to the effect that the actions of bodhisattvas who discard the body are not karmically "indeterminate" (*wuji* 無記).[63] Bodhisattvas just obtain good fortune and virtue, and by the extinction of the afflicted (*kleśa*) body they attain a pure body in exchange.

Self-Immolation as Phenomena and Principle

Section 36 moves us further into the more abstract doctrinal issues of self-immolation.[64] The question advances the view that self-immolation is a phenomenal *(shi)* act that does not take into account the perspective of the ultimate principle *(li)*. From the point of view of principle, the good fortune and virtue gained by the self-immolator are themselves ultimately empty. Yanshou responds that to advance a single practice or doctrine at the expense of others is dangerous, citing in support a line from the *Huayan jing:* "Accepting a single thing and rejecting the remainder, this is what demons uphold."[65] Rather than do that, he says, the bodhisattva takes a broad view of an extensive range of practices because (paradoxically) rejecting the peripheral and taking only the middle way leads to heterodox ideas. Yanshou stresses that principle and phenomena have to be cultivated equally, just as teaching and morality or compassion and wisdom go hand in hand. A single doctrinal stance is to be avoided because one may thus lose everything and fall into the error of holding a personal view. He goes on to cite texts that speak of two practices or paths: a path of wisdom, which means direct entry into enlightenment by means of emptiness, and a path of practice, which involves cultivation at the phenomenal level. Likewise, he says, there are two suchnesses, two minds, two marks, and (in Tiantai philosophy) two goods: the good of cessation, which is the ability to penetrate emptiness, and the good of practice, which means the cultivation of expedients. Clearly he understands self-immolation, from the perspective of principle, to be a case of "the good of cessation."

Thus we appear to have a strong case from within the mature tradition for self-immolation as a somatic path to liberation. Not only is the practice definitely not marginal or heterodox, it is not even an expedient practice. Yanshou is claiming that self-immolation offers a direct access to emptiness and thus awakening.

Self-Immolation and the Single Vehicle

The question that begins the next section presents the counterargument to the position laid out by Yanshou in the preceding passage—namely that the buddhas and patriarchs have but a single vehicle, that the buddhas gain access to wisdom, and that beings leave *saṃsāra* by only a single path.[66] The very concept of there being two accesses to the *dharma* surely just obscures the true teaching and encourages heterodox views. Yanshou responds that these two accesses are apparent only from the perspective of function (*yong* 用). The two accesses complement each other like root and branches. From the point of view of essence (*ti* 體) there is no dividing line between unity and duality, and all beings enter buddhahood by the access of non-duality. Emptiness and existence are not in contradiction, and with the first step on the path of practice one has already reached the final destination of emptiness. This view of the path as a closed system that is complete at the instant it is begun clearly owes a debt to the ideas articulated in Tang-dynasty Huayan thought.

Self-Immolation and the Perfection of Charity

Sections 36 and 37 in a sense lay the doctrinal groundwork for Yanshou's position in Section 38, in which he steers the argument from the fundamental issues of principle and phenomena back to the specific case of self-immolation.[67] The question that commences this section is, however, still rather theoretical. The questioner maintains that while different phenomena are distinct from one another, principle has only a single taste and is "deep and still." Therefore, the inherent nature (*xing* 性) and "marks," or external appearance (*xiang* 相), are not identical with each other. How then can there be no distinction between phenomena and principle or between the inherent nature and external appearances? Yanshou begins with the basics: He points out that phenomena are dependent on principle for their formation, and conversely principle is made manifest by "going along with" phenomena. Similarly essence and function mutually contain each other. At this point his argument switches tack and he begins to speak of *dāna*, which he extols as chief of the ten *pāramitā*s and first of the ten thousand practices, the primary cause for entering the path, and the essential principle for protecting beings. He continues with a lengthy quotation from the *Da zhidu lun* that enumerates some of the qualities of *dāna:*

> *Dāna* is a precious treasure that always follows its author. *Dāna* destroys suffering and increases happiness for humans. *Dāna* is the good ruler who shows the heavenly way. *Dāna* is the good governor who encompasses all good people. *Dāna* is security; when approaching the end of one's life the mind [of the giver] is free of fear. *Dāna* is a mark of compassion, capable of saving all beings. *Dāna* is an accumulation of happiness, capable of destroying suffering. *Dāna* is a great general capable of destroying avarice. [One attribute is missing here, that of "fruit."] *Dāna* is a pure path traversed by noble Āryans. *Dāna* is an accumulation of good acts, the access to merits and virtues. [Some attributes are missing here.] *Dāna* protects the fruit of merit. *Dāna* is the first condition of *nirvāṇa*. It is the method for entering the assembly of good people. It is a storehouse of praises and elegies. It is the virtue that permits entry to the assemblies without pain. It is the root of good *dharma*s and the practice of the Way. It is the jungle of multiple goodnesses. It is the field of merit that assures one of richness, nobility, and security. It is the point of obtaining the Way and *nirvāṇa*.[68]

Having thus stated the position for *dāna* as the root virtue in Buddhist practice, Yanshou adds that correct donation relies on correct intention. Here he quotes from a text identified as the *Liuxing ji* 六行集 (Collection of the Six Practices), which I have been unable to trace:

> When ordinary people make a donation, if they give rise to a conceited mind, they complete a bad action. If they give rise to a reverent mind, they complete a meritorious action. When [followers of] the two vehicles make a donation, they only see dusty *saṃsāra*. When a lesser bodhisattva makes a donation, he considers that the substance of the form is empty. But when a great bodhisattva makes a donation he knows that [any view of] "mind" is itself a false view. If a buddha [makes a donation] he will say that all awakening

is achieved through the mind; constant purity is achieved through abstaining from concepts.[69]

Having distinguished between the donations made by different levels of practitioner, Yanshou continues: *Dāna* has many types. There is inner *dāna* and outer *dāna,* the *dāna* of principle and the *dāna* of phenomena, and so on. But by relying on either principle or phenomena alone, one is lost. It is only when principle and phenomena interpenetrate that one can avoid error. According to the teaching of the buddhas, the *dāna* of principle is primary and the inner *dāna* is most important. Yanshou explains that this is why the *Lotus* says, "If there is one who, opening up his thought, wishes to attain *anuttarasamyaksambodhi,* if he can burn a finger or even a toe as an offering to a Buddhastūpa, he shall exceed one who uses realm or walled city, wife or children, or even all the lands, mountains, forests, rivers, ponds, and sundry precious objects in the whole thousand-millionfold world as offerings."[70] Yanshou thus understands self-immolation or the gift of the body as an example of inner *dāna.* But, according to the *Lotus,* self-immolation is practiced correctly only if the person aims at attaining complete and perfect enlightenment.

Yanshou goes on to discuss this kind of inner *dāna* in more depth. Compared to fine words, which are "mere speech and easy to say," the body is hard to give up because one has a strong emotional attachment to it. So ending one's samsaric existence is only possible as a consequence of understanding the "comprehensive teaching." If one discards the body while still being attached to it, this cannot be an act of "pure donation." Moreover, he says, this particular kind of donation embraces the whole *dharma* realm, not just the self-immolator. He insists that the true practice of self-immolation involves both principle and phenomena and thus leads to complete awakening. He points out that the *Lotus* refers to "bodhisattvas by whom heads and eyes, torso and limbs, are joyously presented in quest of the Buddha's wisdom."[71] If self-immolation were heterodox, then how could these beings attain the wisdom of the Buddha? Yanshou further points out that self-immolation is attested in the former lives of Śākyamuni and performed by bodhisattvas, therefore it must be completely selfless and have no inherent nature of its own. In short then, for Yanshou, self-immolation is a perfectly valid practice if performed in an empty manner.

Self-Immolation of Bodhisattvas and Eminent Monks

In this section the questioner points out that the praise of the Medicine King's act in the *Lotus Sūtra* is immediately followed by a statement that seems to qualify, or undermine, it entirely: "Giving away bodies to the number of grains of sand in the river Ganges is not as good as receiving and upholding one four-line *gāthā*."[72] So surely then *dāna* is inferior to *prajñā* (wisdom)? Why should practitioners expend effort on the practice of self-immolation, which is ultimately futile? Again Yanshou counters that one cannot reject any one of the ten thousand practices because this involves discriminating between them. He reiterates that this particular practice has a precedent in the lives of all the buddhas and especially in the former lives of Śākyamuni. The karmic fruit of all these actions in his former lives is nothing less than the attainment of the triple body of a buddha.

Next Yanshou cites some cases of self-immolation in China which, he says, all accorded with Śākyamuni's example and imitated the Medicine King's style. It is interesting to note here that Yanshou was clearly familiar with more cases than are contained in the sections on self-immolation in the *Gaoseng zhuan* and the *Xu gaoseng zhuan*. He begins with the case of Jing'ai, who eviscerated himself on Zhongnan shan, and he quotes at length from Jing'ai's death verse, which he wrote in his own blood.[73] As we have noted before, this biography was contained not in the self-immolators section of Daoxuan's work but under the rubric of "defenders of the *dharma*." The next case he cites is that of Sengyai. He quotes here part of a debate between Sengyai and Baohai 寶海 (474–after 559) on vicarious suffering and Sengyai's instructions to his attendant on doing homage to sick people.[74]

The next three examples are not found in the self-immolation sections of the *Gaoseng zhuan* and the *Xu gaoseng zhuan*, and their presence here shows that Yanshou was familiar with a wide range of Chinese self-immolators:

> *Dhyāna* master Man 滿 of the Tiantai school spent his whole life lecturing on and chanting the *Lotus Sūtra*. In response a divine person appeared, who fixed [the meaning of] the *sūtra*'s *dhāranī* and words. Later he burned his body in homage to the *Lotus*. Also there was Zhiyi's disciple, the *dhyāna* master Jingbian 淨辯. He burned his body in front of the repentance hall in homage to the Bodhisattva Samantabhadra. Fu *dashi* of the twin trees 雙林 傅大士 wished to burn his body to save beings from suffering. Forty-eight persons, both his disciples and others, successively burnt their bodies in place of their master. They begged their master to remain in the world and teach beings.[75]

Yanshou adds that there are "too many examples to cite in full." For him, these are not the acts of deluded people; if buddhas and bodhisattvas merely appeared to abandon their bodies, then they would be guilty of tricking people. The sages, he says, are truly compassionate and do not deceive people. Thus the later imitations of earlier acts are quite orthodox. He concedes that the self-immolator must know whether he has the power to accomplish the act, but for some Buddhists (Yijing?) to criticize the religious practices of others or judge them in any way is certainly quite wrong. He points out that people who burn their arms or their bodies would not be able to obtain a response if they had not yet perfected the quality of forbearance, even if they knew how to use the fire of wisdom to burn defilements, had completely comprehended the emptiness of self and *dharmas*, and held no view of the self.

Yanshou insists throughout these sections that self-immolation is just as valid and efficacious as *dhyāna* or any other Buddhist practice. He stresses that principle and phenomena must operate in conjunction—like the mixture of pills and powders to cure an illness or the combination of cloud and sun, which causes things to grow. As long as one is not attached to any particular form of practice, he holds that people can attain complete awakening by means of the single practice of self-immolation. He quotes from the *Da zhidu lun* to support this idea:

> Beings find salvation by all kinds of different means. Some are saved by *samādhi,* some by upholding the precepts, some by preaching the *dharma,* some are saved by being touched by rays of light [from the Buddha]. Like a city with many gates, the entries are different but the point of arrival is the same.[76]

As for the specific claim made in the question, that wisdom (*prajñā*) is more important than charity (*dāna),* Yanshou admits that wisdom is certainly powerful and chief among the teachings. But although wisdom can appear at the head of the ten thousand practices, it cannot function without those practices. In Yanshou's eyes there is always danger in exclusive reliance on a single *pāramitā,* unsupported by other practices. He quotes his favorite source, the *Da zhidu lun,* on this point:

> Śakra gave rise to this thought: "If *prajñā* is the ultimate *dharma,* the practitioner just practices *prajñā.* What is the point of any other *dharmas*?" The Buddha answered, "In the six *pāramitās* of the bodhisattva, one takes *prajñāpāramitā* along with the other non-discriminating *dharmas.* This is just this *prajñāpāramitā.* If you just practice *prajñā* and do not practice other *dharmas,* then the merit is insufficient; it is neither wholesome nor miraculous. This is like a stupid person who does not know all the varieties of food.

He hears that soy sauce is the master of all flavors. So he only drinks soy sauce, loses his sense of taste, and becomes ill. This kind of practitioner is just the same. If you wish to get rid of the attached mind and just practice *prajñā,* you fall into heterodox views and cannot accumulate good *dharma*s. If you jointly promote it with the other five *pāramitā*s, then the merit is complete and the flavors of the ideas are in harmony."[77]

Yanshou concludes with a passage from the *Dasheng jiaye shanding jing* 大乘伽耶山頂經 (Mahāyāna Summit of Mount Gaja Sūtra) that distinguishes between the two swift bodhisattva paths:[78]

The first is the path of expedients and the second is the path of *prajñā:* If one has *prajñā* but no expedients, one drowns in the pit of the unconditioned; if one has expedients but no *prajñā,* one falls into the net of phantom transformations.[79]

Thus the practice of *prajñā* alone is not only insufficient but also dangerous. Yanshou reiterates that the perfection of wisdom must be combined with the other *pāramitā*s, and it must be put into action at the phenomenal level.

Self-Immolation, the Body, and the Self

The interlocutor suggests that relinquishing the body perpetuates the false idea of a self, thus contradicting one of the fundamental teachings of Buddhism—that there is no self. Yanshou's answer begins by indicating that ultimately there is no existence, but on the phenomenal level, there is the illusion of birth that arises from various causes and conditions.[80] He says that although ultimately there is no actor and good and evil have no inherent nature, *karma* operates just as if these things existed. From the beginningless past, beings in *saṃsāra* have in fact lost countless bodies, but they just continue to be reborn and their deaths do not create any merit. Also he suggests that the body people lose when they die is one that they have inherited from their mother and father, so this is not really their own body anyway. But if a person has even a single intention of cultivating morality, meditation, and wisdom (the three trainings of Buddhism), then this body does become their own. The body that the self-immolator discards is formed by conditions and exists within the phenomenal world, but when the self-immolator dies he produces merit.

Yanshou says that if one is only attached to the idea of there being no self, while still subject to defilement, then this is a pointless stance, and one has not penetrated the true *dharma*. Yet again he stresses that the practitioner has to put the *dharma* into action before he can speak of it. To practice in response to the *dharmas* of the phenomenal world, without conforming to the function of true suchness, merely creates a self-centered mind, and one falls into error. This is why texts such as the *Sūtra of Benevolent Kings* (*Renwang jing* 仁王經) and Zhiyi's *Mohe zhiguan* 摩訶止觀 (Mahāyāna Calming and Contemplation) lay out stages of practice. Because of the importance of practice and accumulating good roots, the *sūtras* can speak of burning a finger joint or a stick of incense on the body to wipe out accumulated *kalpas* of error or of someone who offers a single flower in praise of a buddha and eventually attains full awakening.

Yanshou moves on to discuss the activities of bodhisattvas in *saṃsāra*, who, according to *Śūraṃgama sūtra*, are able to operate unimpeded even if they are thieves, butchers, prostitutes, or widows.[81] A passage from the *Wusheng yi* 無生義 (Meaning of the Unborn[?]) confirms that bodhisattvas can manifest form bodies and can appear to be noble or base, ordinary or sagely.[82] All *dharmas* are available to the bodhisattva for teaching purposes; he does not reject any of them. Also all the sages who discarded their bodies were subject to censure for their actions, although they were not affected by such slanders.[83] The bodhisattva's relinquishing the body is like exchanging poisonous herbs for pure ghee or swapping an earthenware vessel for jewels because he acquires a new, pure *dharma* body. However, without a correct view of the self, self-immolation cannot be practiced properly.

Yanshou thus argues that self-immolation is a bodhisattva practice par excellence. Having set out on the path to liberation, the practitioner has some claim on his or her body and is thus able to use it to generate merit. The bodhisattva rises above the criticisms of the practice from others and moves inexorably towards buddhahood by discarding the defiled body and acquiring the permanent and pure body of awakening. Here Yanshou puts into doctrinal terms what self-immolators had been doing in China for centuries: building bodhisattva bodies by acts of extreme and selfless generosity.

Self-Immolation and Regret

The final section we shall consider here starts from the premise that although the body is (ultimately) void and provisional, it is afflicted by suffering, and because of that suffering beings want to, and are able to, attain awakening.[84] As one *sūtra* says, "If one does not enter the great sea of passions (*kleśa*), one cannot obtain the priceless precious pearl."[85] The interlocutor asks, "If one discards this body, will one not regret it later?"

Yanshou answers that what arises will inevitably decay, and all the marks of existence are inherently empty. If the self-immolator gives rise to a single thought of giving away his body with determination and sincerity towards the Three Jewels, then he exits *saṃsāra* and exchanges his weak impermanent body for a solid adamantine one. He concludes one should use wisdom to determine whether to discard the body or retain it.

Ultimately, self-immolation is not an obligation but an option. As one of the ten thousand *dharmas* that leads to the good end of liberation or as a distinct somatic path, it can be selected only by a practitioner who understands exactly what he or she is doing.

Historical Considerations

So far we have discussed Yanshou's endorsement of self-immolation mostly in terms of how it functions doctrinally, how it relates to the question of bodhisattva precepts versus the Vinaya, and how it might form part of a greater apologetic for Buddhist practice in response to the persecution of Buddhism in North China by Shizong. There is a further consideration to be made, which revolves around a single event, or in fact non-event, that occurred in Yanshou's home state of Wu-Yue in 961. We have noted throughout this study that it was often considered necessary to ask permission from the emperor before carrying out the act. This tradition is significant in light of the events related below.

In 961 a monk by the name of Shaoyan 紹巖 (d. 971)—who had studied under Fayan Wenyi together with Deshao, the preeminent Chan master in Wu-Yue—made a vow to emulate the Bodhisattva Medicine King. But King Zhongyi 忠懿 (r. 948–978) of Wu-Yue, despite his well-known patronage of Buddhism, declined to give his permission.[86] Shaoyan then threw himself in a river but was hauled out by fishermen. After these two unsuccessful attempts he seems to have given up on the idea of self-immolation. Given that Yanshou had studied under Deshao it is entirely possible that he knew Shaoyan personally, and even if he did not, he could hardly have been unaware that the king had turned down the monk's request. Assuming, as seems likely, that the *Tonggui ji* was composed after 961, this raises the intriguing possibility that Yanshou's endorsement of self-immolation was directed at the ruler himself as he had so obviously failed to grasp that what Shaoyan proposed was a "good practice." In the absence of any other evidence, a historical explanation for Yanshou's composition of this part of the *Tonggui ji* seems quite likely. It could have been written either in response to the persecution of Buddhism in the North by Shizong or in response to the king of

Wu-Yue's refusal to allow Shaoyan to burn himself alive. Possibly, it was in fact the combination of the two events that inspired Yanshou to defend the *dharma* and endorse the practice so forcefully.

Conclusion

Self-immolation is a topic that has been little explored by scholars of Buddhism and to find the practice so unequivocally endorsed in a text by such a major Buddhist figure as Yanshou may appear somewhat counterintuitive. But I would argue that, aside from the fact that self-immolation was quite literally a matter of life and death to a significant number of Buddhists in East Asia, if it was important to Yanshou we cannot afford simply to dismiss it as an aberrant, unimportant, or grotesque aspect of Chinese Buddhism. Nor can we relegate it to the category "little tradition" because it is given such serious consideration in the major works of key representatives of the "great tradition."

Yanshou was not the first Chinese monk to endorse self-immolation, but he was the first to attempt to seek out the doctrinal foundations for the practice and think through some of the ethical ramifications. Whereas the compilers of biographies had given a cautious endorsement by assembling materials, writing critical evaluations, and citing scripture, Yanshou actually attempted to grapple seriously with the issues and paradoxes that self-immolation seems to present. For him, self-immolation was not an abstract issue confined to the scriptures and records of the past. Rather, he was able to look at a living tradition and boldly to secure its legitimacy not as a subsidiary practice, minor curiosity, or subset of asceticism, but as nothing less than a path to liberation on an equal footing with meditation, recitation, and ritual.

We have noted that Yanshou began his exploration of self-immolation with the question of the precepts, reflecting a common concern shared by Chinese Buddhist authors that suicide was *pārājika*, or in some way proscribed by the Vinaya. Yanshou's solution was a bold one, but one that made perfect sense in the context of the Chinese tradition: He turned to another (Mahāyāna) set of precepts and found a rule that not only permitted body-burning practices but seemed to require them.

Aside from claiming that the precepts taken by an aspiring bodhisattva simply outweighed or invalidated the precepts of the lesser vehicle, Yanshou's argument for self-immolation depends on the premise that if self-immolation is performed in a completely empty manner then the practitioner is essentially beyond such worldly categories as right and wrong. Yanshou's daring position provides further evidence for the idea that by burning their bodies as prescribed in scripture, Chinese self-immolators could indeed take on the role, and mental attitude, of advanced bodhisattvas. Because their aspirations were to become buddhas by offering themselves to the Three Jewels of Buddha, Dharma, and Saṃgha, they would in time attain awakening in a pure body and not suffer any adverse karmic consequences for killing themselves.

Yanshou takes the argument back to the fundamental nature of the practice of giving *(dāna)*. He claims that when the giving of the body is rooted in the true "inner *dāna*," which embraces all the Buddhist teachings, then self-immolation affects not just the practitioner but the whole universe and brings buddhahood. Thus, for him, self-immolation was a valid path to awakening that is confirmed not just by the precedent of the Buddha's many body offerings, but also by the logic of the perfection of charity; in other words, it is performed in an empty manner by advanced bodhisattvas. What greater evidence of emptiness is there than the ability to give up that which is hardest to surrender?

Yanshou shows no hesitation in linking the actions of famous (and obscure) Chinese self-immolators with the heroes of the *jātaka*s and the *Lotus Sūtra*. For him these men and women were not deluded, foolish, or extremist ascetics; they were the inheritors of a noble and spiritually productive tradition. In short, self-immolation was as valid a practice as any other of the time and should not be criticized by those who might prefer other types of practice themselves.

I have suggested two events to which Yanshou might have been reacting in his strong defense of self-immolation: namely the persecution of Buddhism in 955 and King Zhongyi's refusal to allow a monk to burn himself alive in 961. I would suggest that the history of Buddhism in Wu-Yue needs further research to better answer the question of the circumstances in which the text was written. As for Yanshou, his attitude towards the bodhisattva precepts needs to be more clearly evaluated if one is to fully understand his thought. Nevertheless, it is clear that Yanshou was able to marshal a rational and well-supported argument in favor of self-immolation as a good practice.

Translation from the *Wanshan tonggui ji* (Treatise on the Common End of the Myriad Good Practices), SECTION 34, T 48.2017.969b26–c19

QUESTION: The body is the basis of the path, and bondage is the cause of release. So how can one cultivate the path while turning one's back on the path by burning the fingers or setting fire to the body? In the *Biographies*

of Eminent Monks and in the Vinaya of the Hīnayāna this is explicitly condemned. So what is the sacred scriptural basis [for these practices]?

ANSWER: Forsaking the body, or ending one's life, to repay the compassion of the *dharma* profoundly accords with the Mahāyāna and deeply resonates with the true teaching. The Mahāyāna *Fanwang jing* (T 24.1484.1006a)
says:

> If a son of the Buddha is to practice with a good mind, he should start by
> studying the proper decorum, the scriptures and the regulations of the
> Mahāyāna so that he thoroughly understands their meaning and sense.
> Later he will meet Bodhisattvas who are new to this study and who have
> come a hundred or a thousand *li* in search of the scriptures and regulations
> of the Mahāyāna. In accordance with the *dharma* he should explain to them
> all the ascetic practices, such as setting fire to the body, setting fire to the
> arm, or setting fire to the finger. If one does not set fire to the body, the
> arm, or the finger as an offering to the buddhas, one is not a renunciant
> Bodhisattva. Moreover, one should sacrifice the feet, hands, and flesh of
> the body as offerings to hungry tigers, wolves, and lions and to all hungry
> ghosts.
>
> Afterwards to each of them in turn one should preach the true *dharma*,
> so that one causes the thought of liberation to appear in their minds. If one
> does not behave in this way, then this is a lesser wrongdoing.[87]

The Mahāyāna *Śuraṃgama sūtra* (T 19.945.132b) says:

> The Buddha said to Ānanda,"After my death, if there is a monk who gives
> rise to a mental state wherein he is determined to cultivate *samādhi,* and he
> is able to burn his body as a torch or to set fire to a finger joint before an
> image of the Tathāgata, or even to burn a stick of incense on his body, then
> in a single instant he will have repaid the debts of his previous existences
> since the beginningless past. He will always avoid [being reborn] in the
> world and he will be eternally free of all outflow (*lou* 漏; Skt. *āsrava*). Even if
> he has not yet understood the supreme path of awakening, such a person
> has already focused his mind on the *dharma.* But if he does not have the
> subtle underlying cause for sacrificing the body, then even if he attains the
> unconditioned he must be reborn again as a human to repay the debts
> from his previous lives. Just as when we [had to] eat horse fodder."[88]

So the Hīnayāna clings to appearances; it restricts but it does not allow. But
the Great Teaching is perfect and comprehensive, fundamentally it has no

fixed *dharma.* According to the *Pusa shanjie jing* 菩薩善戒經 (T 30.1582. 961c25–26):

> The precepts of the *śrāvaka*s are stringent, whereas the precepts of the bodhisattvas are tolerant. The precepts of the *śrāvaka*s are restrictive, whereas the precepts of the bodhisattvas are expansive.

And [another] sūtra says, "To adhere to the precepts of the *śrāvaka*s means breaking the bodhisattva precepts." This is the meaning of the above passage.

If one follows the scriptures that reveal the whole meaning (*liaoyi* 了義), then all the Buddhas joyously approve. But if one clings to the provisional teachings (*yishuo* 宜說), then all the sages are disappointed and do not approve. What is appropriate is that one praises the great [vehicle] and honors the perfect [teaching], thus benefiting oneself and others. What is inappropriate is that one should cling to the provisional and remain stuck in the lesser [vehicle], being deluded about both the fundamental and its traces.

CHAPTER 5

Local Heroes in a Fragmenting Empire

Self-Immolation in the Late Tang and Five Dynasties

Many of the biographies in the self-immolation section of Zanning's *Song gaoseng zhuan* relate the tales of local heroes in a world that was often unstable, frightening, and hostile towards Buddhists. We can find in the many accounts of self-immolation from the eighth to tenth centuries no overarching narrative of religious persecution and dynastic legitimation such as we perceived in Daoxuan's collection. Probably the most significant theme that recurs throughout the section, and one that Zanning develops with enthusiasm in the critical evaluation, is the miraculous power of the relics of the Buddha, in which the compiler had a great personal interest. In tandem with the importance of the Buddha's remains, we can detect in our sources a growing interest in the relics of self-immolators themselves.[1] In the biographies we find relics created in ever-increasing numbers and in ever more miraculous ways. Self-immolators were able to produce *śarīra* not only through cremation, but now also by spontaneously exuding them from their skin while still alive. Along with this very marked "relic inflation," miracles were recorded in abundance and in great detail. As the Buddha receded farther and farther in time and space so conversely did Buddhist miracles on Chinese soil become ever more important.

Zanning and the *Song gaoseng zhuan*

Zanning was the most important monk official in the coastal kingdom of Wu-Yue during the period of disunion after the fall of the Tang dynasty. This small state was a haven of safety during the violence and disorder of the period, and Buddhism flourished there under state protection and patronage.[2] But when the Song emperor Taizong 宋太宗 (r. 976–997) ascended the throne of a dynasty that controlled most of China, King Zhongyi (Qian Chu 錢俶, 929–988) realized that he had little choice but to bring his state under the direct control of the Song empire. The submission of Wu-Yue to Song hegemony was accompanied by a significant gift to the new emperor of the relics of Śākyamuni, formerly in the possession of Wu-Yue and handed over by

Zanning himself, as he relates in his critical evaluation to the self-immolation section.

A collection of biographies of eminent monks was commissioned by Zanning's new master, Taizong, in 982 and was completed in 988.[3] It was the first such collection to be written under imperial orders. Because of his standing at court, and particularly because of his involvement in the diplomatic negotiations between Wu-Yue and the Song empire, Zanning was able to step fairly easily into an equally influential position in the new order. Taizong, much impressed by the breadth of his knowledge, appointed him to the Hanlin 翰林 academy. But Zanning, while undoubtedly a clever individual who was well versed in both secular and religious literature, was simply not as talented a historian as Daoxuan, although the inadequacies of his work may in part be attributed to the problems in compiling a vast collection very rapidly at the end of a period of division.[4] Zanning compiled the *Song gaoseng zhuan* not in the Song capital but in his native Qiantang 錢塘 and clearly did not have access to as many documents, or as many eyewitnesses, as Daoxuan. He was not able to cross-check his sources with the diligence shown by his predecessor, and so we find many contradictions between the biographies.[5] The collection was written for the emperor to assure his support for the Buddhist establishment and for that reason it is apologetic in nature. On the other hand, Zanning did go out of his way to explain and interpret in a way that perhaps Huijiao and Daoxuan, writing for a more Buddhist audience, may not always have thought necessary.

The section on self-immolators is entitled *yishen*. There are twenty-two main biographies and two supplementary: These include five acts of autocremation and seventeen by other means. As we might expect from the circumstances under which the collection was compiled, there is a certain geographical bias in favor of the South, and many of the later biographies concern monks from Wu-Yue in particular. We may also note the presence of a number of quite well-known Chan masters in this section, which will confirm that there was more to Chan in the Five Dynasties than the clever word games found in the records of the transmission of the lamp (*chuandeng lu* 傳燈錄) and recorded sayings (*yulu* 語錄). The presence of such men in this collection further shows that no one was immune to the lure of self-immolation.

Sacred Sites: Pagoda and Mountain

The biographies display a variety of themes and tropes that in their complexity and interrelatedness offer some rare glimpses of a diverse and often

rapidly mutating religious world. What they have in common is a shared
sense that China was at the center of the Buddhist world. Two examples in
particular allow us to appreciate the role of sacred space in self-immolation.
In the first case, a pagoda became a site of transformation, and in the second a Chinese mountain gave access to an alternative reality.

Zhengshou 正壽 (d. ca. 710) was a disciple of a certain Chan master Zao
愷 of Nanta si 南塔寺 .[6] Later he became a recluse at a mountain monastery in
Suibu 隨部, where the local people did not know him.[7] Li Chongfu 李重福,
prince of Qiao 譙王 (680–710), the second son of Emperor Zhongzong 中宗
(r. 705–710), was then serving as the prefect of Junzhou 均州, where Zao
lived.[8] Li, who later died in an attempted coup, became a patron of master
Zao, for whom he constructed the *shengzang* 生藏 pagoda.[9] This pagoda, with
its suggestive name ("living repository"), seems to have been an impressive
edifice at some seventy feet in height. By the time it was complete Zao was already dying, and Li Chongfu asked whom he intended to make his successor.
Zao named Zhengshou, whom of course Li did not know since he was in reclusion. Informed of his whereabouts, the prince sent a messenger, ordering
him to come. But first Zhengshou consulted his master:

> "I am glad that the prince is our benefactor (*tanyue* 檀越; Skt. *dānapati*). His
> pagoda is already complete, and I wish to test it first. Is this appropriate or
> not?" Zao said, "Please test it for me carefully." At that time Zhengshou ad-
> justed his robes, put his palms together, and entered the pagoda, his ex-
> pression impassive, his eyes closed. With his legs crossed, thus he attained
> *nirvāṇa*. His body was intact and did not decay. At that time he was called
> "the Upādhyāya who tested the pagoda." When the prince of Qiao heard of
> this, he sighed with grief all day long and said, "Even one of his disciples
> was already [as advanced as] this." He changed his mind and altered the
> plan and constructed [another pagoda] for *dhyāna* master Zao.[10]

Rather than being inauspicious as one might think—having his disciple
attain *nirvāṇa* in his own pagoda—the event seems to have reflected well on
Master Zao and enhanced his status in the mind of his royal patron. Zanning's
appended comment (*xi* 系) to this biography lauds Zhengshou's achievement:

> If one precedes someone else, he might be suspected of intending to take
> advantage of the other person. Here Master Shou preceded his [master,]
> Zao. [Let us see if he should be blamed for this:] Now, one who leaves
> [*saṃsāra*] directly must be able to arrive straightaway [at *nirvāṇa*]. Accumu-
> lated *karma* did not detain him, nor did traps ensnare him.[11] He escaped

from detention, opened up the snares, and was free from *saṃsāra*. Thus he was liberated and has already ascended to the final stage [of the bodhi-sattva path]. From the secular perspective, Master Shou was "the blue that comes from the indigo plant," and so he was able to ride the mind along the direct path and come out ahead of his teacher.[12] This is what one calls "a thousand *li* in a single day!"[13]

Such stories of the direct, willed attainment of *nirvāṇa* were told of Bud-dhist saints in India, but up until the Tang they seem to have been relatively rare in China.[14] The biography of Zhengshou may represent a newly develop-ing conception of how advanced practitioners were understood to die. As we have already noted, much of the biographical material of the Tang and Song is very much concerned with the death that was exemplary, miraculous, and controlled, and this seems to have affected the concept of "abandoning the body" in the Song and later dynasties. The death verse in particular came to exemplify mastery over the grave. In the case of Zhengshou, we know noth-ing else of his spiritual achievements other than the manner in which he died. His whole religious career and charisma are encapsulated in this single moment.

The *stūpa*, or pagoda, intended to house the remains of the special Bud-dhist dead, had become a place for staging the special Buddhist death. In a similar fashion, Indian literary models were recast with Chinese actors, and Chinese mountains were made into important centers in a larger Buddhist sacred geography. The Tang monk Wuran 無染 (d. ca. 836–840) was fasci-nated by manifestations of the Bodhisattva Mañjuśrī on Mount Wutai 五台山.[15] In particular he wanted to follow in the footsteps of the Kashmiri monk Budh-hapālita (Fotuopoli 佛陀波利, d. after 677), who had allegedly gone to Wutai in search of Mañjuśrī in 676.[16] Wuran arrived on the mountain in 791 and de-cided to stay there. Over more than twenty years he made more than seventy-two complete circuits of the sacred places on the mountain, during which he heard bells and chimes and saw many amazing sights. One day to the east of the central terrace he suddenly saw the apparition of a monastery that bore the name Fusheng 福生 (Produced by Virtue).[17] Within were tens of thou-sands of Indian monks and the Bodhisattva Mañjuśrī himself, who also ap-peared as a monk. Mañjuśrī told Wuran that he had karmic connections with the place, and that he needed to support the Buddhist community on the mountain and not abandon his body in vain, which would achieve nothing. After he finished speaking, the monastery and the monks disappeared. Stim-ulated by this spiritual encounter, Wuran determined to organize donations for vegetarian feasts. When he succeeded in organizing banquets for one million monks, he burned one finger to record the event. Eventually he provided ten million meals and burned off all ten fingers.

Some time during the Kaicheng 開成 period (836–840), Wuran said farewell to the other monks in a long speech. He looked back on his religious career, taking satisfaction in the fact that he had not left the mountain throughout. Now, he said, at the age of seventy-four and after fifty-five years as a monk, he was growing old and weak. He announced his intention of saying farewell to the *tathāgatas* of the ten directions and the ten thousand bodhisattvas by "burning one stick of incense on the summit of the central terrace." He ended by telling the monks that they were all disciples of bodhisattvas and close attendants of *nāga* kings, that they had planted good karmic seeds in their former lives and so had attained the reward of living on Wutai shan. He urged them to strive day and night to control their production of *karma* and await the coming of Maitreya. He put his palms together, wished them well, and left. His fellows did not catch his rather broad hint about burning incense on the mountain and told him to return early.

Taking with him just his bowl, his staff, and some incense, Wuran ordered a layman called Zhao Hua 趙華 (d.u.) to carry waxed cloth, coarse hemp, and fragrant oil to the summit of the central terrace. All day long he made prostrations and burned incense, chanting the name of the Buddha and not stopping to rest, eat, or drink. By the middle of the night, Zhao had grown puzzled by what his master was about. Climbing up the rocky peak, he saw that Wuran had not shifted from his former spot but was increasing his devotional efforts. Then Wuran revealed his plan and urged Zhao to make a beneficial karmic connection with him. He told Zhao to wrap his body in oil-soaked cloth and promised that if he attained awakening, he would deliver Zhao to liberation in return. Zhao begged him not to go through with it, but he could not stop him. As Wuran began to burn from the crown of his head down, he instructed Zhao to scatter his ashes and bones and not have them displayed as miraculous relics. Only when Wuran's body had burned down to his feet did it fall over—just like the stick of incense that he had declared himself to be. Notwithstanding Wuran's explicit instructions about his remains, his disciples gathered the "true bones" (*zhengu*真骨, that is, relics) and placed them in a *stūpa* that they raised on the south side of Fanxian shan 梵仙山. The pagoda was still extant in Zanning's day.

In the long and detailed biography, Wuran is presented as a monk who had fully entered an alternative reality in which the confines of his immediate space and time were completely dissolved. He was able to commune directly with Mañjuśrī and his retinue, who are explicitly described as Indian monks (*fanseng* 梵僧). His practice of burning off his fingers shaped his body into a living memorial of his religious service to the Wutai Buddhist community. By the time he offered his whole body in homage, he was almost entirely part of that other world in which the true *dharma* of the Buddha and the ideal (Indian) monastic community existed on a Chinese mountain, unimpeded by the apparent barriers of historical time and conventional geography. In this context he really was a bodhisattva like the Medicine King except that, tellingly, he did not offer himself to the relics of a Buddha but to the numinous mountain of Wutai shan and its inhabitants, both Indian and Chinese. In this biography we see how the drama of the Mahāyāna literature was adapted and played out on a Chinese stage with actors from throughout the Buddhist universe: Chinese and Indian monks (both human and divine), *bodhisattva-mahāsattva*s, and even a layman.

Scriptural Models

We noted briefly in an earlier chapter how Chinese Buddhists had adopted the practice of feeding insects with their bodies from *jātaka* accounts of King Śibi. This mode of giving is increasingly visible in Zanning's collection. Sengzang 僧藏 (d.u.), for example, was a very humble monk; if monks or laypeople bowed to him, he would bow and run away, as if he dared not stand in the way of his superiors.[18] His physical practices consisted of stripping off his robes in the heat of summer and offering his body to be bitten by a variety of insects: "The blood flowed and he bore it patiently although sweating profusely, all the while he constantly recited the name of Amitābha. Even the most skilled mathematician could not reckon the number [of recitations]."[19] The biography presents Sengzang as one convinced of his own salvation in the Pure Land: On his deathbed he spoke of seeing the heavenly emissaries who had come to escort him there. Thus self-immolation in a minor key was combined with a devotional practice of extreme humility that recalls the actions of the Bodhisattva Never-Disparaging in the *Lotus Sūtra* and the more conventional recitation of Amitābha's name.[20]

The biography of Dinglan 定蘭 (d. 852) brings together some interesting themes and episodes: mortification of the flesh for the purposes of filial piety, a rather startling miracle, and recognition by a Tang emperor.[21] Dinglan was a native of Chengdu 成都 and a butcher by trade. But having repented of the transgressions in his former lives that had led to this unhappy rebirth (butchers were particularly reviled in Buddhist sources), he vowed to conduct himself well and to proselytize the people of Sichuan.

Dinglan's mother and father had died young and he had no money with which to perform the necessary ancestral rites for them. Whenever the anniversary of their death came round, he would silently weep with grief. Then one year he stripped himself naked and entered Mount Qingcheng 青城山.[22] There he allowed mosquitoes, gnats, gadflies, and flies to bite at his bare body, saying, "I am giving away my inner wealth. I am using it to repay the travails (*qulao* 劬勞) [of my parents]."[23] The references to "inner wealth" (*neicai* 內財) in this and later biographies, as well as in Zanning's comments, no doubt reflect the rise of the monetary economy in the late medieval period and a greater awareness of the possibilities of "outer wealth" (*waicai* 外財). The self-immolator could draw on his inner resources and direct them to ends that were otherwise only really obtainable through external resources —that is, money.

Dinglan's name is nearly homophonous with Ding Lan 丁蘭, a paragon of filial piety who famously carved an image of his dead mother that came to life.[24] Although it appears that this Buddhist biography borrows from the native tradition in order to co-opt the virtue of filiality, in fact this process often occurred the other way around. Buddhist stories, especially *jātaka*s, were the source for some of the behavior of filial children that appears most famously in the later *Ershisi xiao* 二十四孝 (Twenty-four Exemplars of Filial Piety) by Guo Jujing 郭居敬 of the Yuan 元 dynasty (1260–1368). One of the twenty-four, Wu Meng 吳猛, a filial eight-year-old boy of the Jin 晉 dynasty (265–420), offered his own body to mosquitoes because his parents could not afford mosquito nets.[25] Although filial piety is often claimed as the Confucian virtue par excellence, in fact many of the heroic deeds such as donating the body to insects and feeding flesh from the thigh to one's parents turn out to be of Buddhist origin.

Feeding the body to insects and the cultivation of humility (both drawing on a repertoire that partook of the *Lotus* and the *jātaka*s) were sometimes combined with a range of other bodily practices. Toyuk 道育 (Chn. Daoyu, 858?–938) was an eccentric monk from the Korean kingdom of Silla who, in 892, travelled to Mount Tiantai, where he stayed for the rest of his life.[26] He prepared baths for the other monks, brewed tea, and saved the lives of insects he found wriggling in the woodpile. He always wore a thick, coarse robe, but at the beginning of every summer and the end of every autumn, he would expose his chest, back, and legs in the afternoon, saying, "I am giving mosquitoes, gnats, gadflies, and leeches something to nibble." There were so many insect bites that Toyuk's blood would flow to the ground. He continued this practice for more than forty years. In 935 Zanning met this monk for himself, and his account confirms Toyuk's habit of saying only "Yiyi," along with other bizarre behavior.[27] Also he reports that a group of tigers came to sniff at Toyuk but did not eat him.

In addition to feeding himself to mosquitoes, Dinglan also copied *sūtra*s in his own blood, burned off his arm, tore off his ears, and finally gouged out his eyes and fed them to birds of prey and wild animals.[28] This last donation had rather unfortunate consequences because he tended to bump into things and fall over unless he had someone to lead him. But later a strange man appeared holding in his hands some pearl-like objects, which he placed in the monk's empty eye sockets. Dinglan was then able to see again. The gift was accompanied by the mysterious announcement "The King of the Southern Heavens has returned the master's eyeballs."[29]

As we have seen, King Śibi, who gave away all his flesh, was a much-imitated role model for Chinese self immolators. Another story told of this king relates that after giving away material wealth, he wished to give away parts of his body. The god Śakra, hearing of this, disguised himself as a blind brahmin and begged for one of Śibi's eyes. Ignoring the entreaties of his ministers, Śibi gave away both eyes. Later Śakra returned and magically restored the king's eyeballs.[30] The god's return of the eyeballs, combined with the fact that Dinglan fed insects with his body surely shows that, consciously or not, the monk's offerings were directly equated with those of the famous king.[31] The miraculous return of his eyes affirms that the power of selfless charity in China was depicted as no less than it had been in mythical India. The biographies thus echo the claims that were made more explicitly by Yanshou and others.

The biography of the forest dweller (*lanruo* 蘭若; Skt. *āranyaka*) Xingming行明 (fl. ca. 900) of Nanyue南嶽 illustrates that self-immolators not only measured themselves against the exemplary acts of the *sūtra*s and *jātaka*s, but also against those found in the biographies of earlier self-immolators.[32] During the declining years of the Tang, there was much bitter fighting, and Xingming ended up at Qibaotai si 七寶台寺 (Monastery of the Terrace of the Seven Precious Materials) on the Zhurong 祝融 peak of Nanyue, the Southern Marchmount, where he intended to spend the rest of his life. There he became friends with the distinguished Buddhist author Xuantai 玄泰 (d. after 901):[33]

> Once, he said to his companion in the Way [Xuantai], "I do not wish to follow the example of Sengyai, who burned himself on a wooden tower. I do not wish to do as Qu Yuan 屈原 (d. ca. 315 BCE) did and be entombed in the bellies of fish.[34] Ultimately, I vow to discard my body in emulation of the Prince Mahāsattva (*saduo taizi* 薩埵太子), who attained the stage of the sage, [quickly] passing over many *kalpa*s.[35] Should I not make an effort to accomplish this?" He said this again and again, but [his fellow monks] did

not believe it. Suddenly, in the forest, he abandoned his body before a group of roaring tigers. They vied to eat him, and in an instant the flesh was gone.

At that time, Master Tai gathered up his remaining bones, burned them, and collected the *śarīra*. Then he picked flowers, poured out water, and composed a text to pay homage to him. In this text he extolled his bravery; his ability to donate his inner wealth; his way of destroying meanness; his sudden and empty perfection of *dānapāramitā* in its three aspects of giver, recipient, and gift; and his attainment of the great result, which he accomplished as easily as if he were bending down to pick up a mustard seed.

Zanning writes in his appended comment:

> The Buddha commanded that if *bhikṣus* gave [themselves as] food to beings, in the next life there would be successive benefits, and the rewards produced thereby would be great. In just this way, Master Ming perfected the great *dānapāramitā* and avoided meanness. He perfected great bravery and attained fearlessness. He perfected the emptiness of the three aspects [of *dāna*], thereby attaining the merits and virtues (*gongde*功德) of non-action (*wuwei* 無為). He perfected the mind of [giving away] that which is hard to abandon, thereby purifying the Buddha land. His instant casting away of his body has brought abundant merit. "Those who are good at rewarding people spend little yet encourage many."[36] Is this not a perfect example of this saying?[37]

In the eulogy and the comment both Xuantai and Zanning vie to heap praises on Xingming for his accomplishment of the selfless perfection of charity. Xingming's donation of his body to tigers was not an easy task, as we know from other monks who tried to do likewise and failed. How his act benefited others is not immediately apparent until we remember that, by feeding himself to the tiger, Xingming became functionally equivalent to Prince Mahāsattva and was assured of Buddhahood in the future, when the benefit to other beings would presumably be made manifest.

Shouxian 守賢 (ca. 890–ca. 968) was a tenth-century Chan master who gave away his body in a similarly scriptural manner.[38] The monk was ascetically inclined and did not wear silk; he wore trousers made of coarse cloth, which he never changed whatever the season. He never lay down to sleep but sat on his rope bed with his eyes closed all night. At the age of seventy-four he announced to his fellow monks: "I have an outstanding vow that has not yet been fulfilled, and my mind cannot rest until it is." The next day he threw himself to a hungry tiger. When his disciples went out to look for him, they found that all that remained were his two legs encased in his trousers. They gathered them up and cremated them, obtaining countless *śarīra*. Zanning reports that in his day Shouxian's remains were still enshrined in a small *stūpa*.[39] We will recall that in some traditions, it was Prince Mahāsattva's head that remained uneaten and was enshrined as a relic. Is it going too far to see in Shouxian's leg relics a kind of Chan reversal or visual pun on the scriptural account?

It is interesting that it was not until the late Tang and early Song that monks actually had much consistent success in enacting *jātaka* stories. Like King Śibi they fed themselves to insects and plucked out their eyes, but successfully imitating Prince Mahāsattva's feeding of the hungry tigress was still fairly difficult. Shouxian's biography shows a greater sense of confidence about performing these old legends in China. By actually managing to be eaten by a tiger, this Chan master took on the role of the Bodhisattva in the same way that in other contexts Chan masters ritually assumed the part of the Buddha himself.

State Recognition

Whereas many self-immolators of the late Tang appear to have been local heroes with posthumous cults, some also attained nationwide prominence. For example, the emperor Xuanzong 宣宗 (r. 846–859) invited Dinglan to court in 849 and received him with a great deal of courtesy because of the miraculous return of his eyeballs. Dinglan's disciple Youyuan 有緣 (835–907) went with him, and their visit to court is confirmed in his own biography.[40] In 852 Dinglan vowed to burn his shoulder—his arm of course had been removed earlier. The emperor repeatedly exhorted him not to do so, but Dinglan did not obey his edict; he burned his shoulder and subsequently died. Youyuan requested that the emperor bestow a posthumous name on his late master and have a pagoda built for him. Xuanzong obliged and Dinglan's posthumous title was decreed to be Juexing 覺性 (Enlightened Nature) and his pagoda was named Wuzhen 悟真 (Awakened to the Truth). At the end of the biography we hear that "in Shu it is simply called 'Dinglan's pagoda,' and the offering of donations [literally, 'incense and fires' (*xianghuo* 香火)] there has not ceased up until today."[41] By honoring Dinglan, Xuanzong may have been recognizing the strength of sentiment towards the self-immolator in his native land as shown by the posthumous cult at his pagoda. But bestowing on Dinglan an imperial title would also have provided a form of legitimation for Xuanzong, who had worked hard to reverse the effects of the Huichang 會昌 persecution of Buddhism in China.[42]

Dinglan practiced a number of types of self-immolation simultaneously by imitating both King Śibi and the Medicine King and following the practice called "unsurpassed giving" (*wushang shi* 無上施) in the *Shanjie jing* 善戒經.[43] His initial motive of filiality appears to have given way to a more generalized charity and ever more dramatic and extravagant offerings. His story shows how self-immolation offered a way for a man of obviously humble and obscure background to become an eminent monk who was honored by the emperor and remembered by posterity.

Self-Immolation for the Empire

In the late ninth century the Tang empire was plagued by internal rebellion. Some monks who died resisting the rebels are remembered in Zanning's collection specifically as self-immolators. We should consider that accounts of monks who remained loyal to the Tang must have been as significant to Buddhist historiography as the biographies of loyal officials were for official histories. During the Guangming 廣明 reign period (880–881), when Huang Chao 黃巢 (d. 884) and his rebels overran Huangbo shan 黃蘗山 in Min 閩 (Fujian 福建), Hongxiu 鴻休 (?–880/881) came out of his monastery to meet them.[44] While proclaiming "I vow not to stain this place of purity," he calmly stretched out his neck and awaited the blow of a sword. When no blood fell from the blade, the rebels fell back in amazement, and prostrating themselves they confessed their transgressions.

One has to suspect at least some political propaganda in this account, although unlike other monks who resisted rebels, Hongxiu does not seem to have received a posthumous title from the emperor. Howard Levy, in his introduction to the translation of Huang Chao's biography, notes the staunch resistance on the part of some local officials who preferred death rather than collaboration with the rebels.[45] Hongxiu's biography may represent the religious equivalent of that loyalty. Certainly it was difficult to have a quiet life in the late ninth century, either as a monk or an official, and this text should remind us that in imperial China violence was often endemic outside the monastery.

Quanhuo 全豁 (828–887), like Hongxiu, died at the hands of bandits during the turbulent and violent years of the late Tang.[46] But unlike Hongxiu he had a posthumous name bestowed on him by the emperor. Another record of his life contained in the *Jingde chuandeng lu* presents his Chan say-

ings and provides a slightly different perspective of the man, although the account of his death is essentially the same:[47]

> From the time of the Guangqi 光啓 reign period (885–888) onwards there
> were many problems on the Central Plain, the feudal lords were in stale-
> mate, and violent rebels arrived to plunder and loot.[48] Lay[people] all fled,
> he alone remained unperturbed. Blaming him for their lack of supplies,
> the rebels had him executed in a fit of anger. He showed no sign of fear
> whatsoever. This happened on Guangqi *dingwei* 丁未 4.8 in the summer
> (May 4, 887). His disciples [subsequently] buried him temporarily. After
> burial, they gathered the remains and burned them. They obtained forty-
> nine (seven times seven) grains of *śarīra*. Xizong 僖宗 (r. 873–888) be-
> stowed on him the posthumous name Qingyan 清嚴 and his *stūpa* was named
> Chuchen 出塵. The patron (*tanyue* 檀越; Skt. *dānapati*) of the funeral was
> Brother Tian Yong 田詠, who supplied the money and organized it.[49] The
> monk Xuantai of Nanyue composed the stele inscription, which praises his
> virtues. His way of delivering sermons and lectures was lofty and stern. His
> contemporaries called him Yantou fadao 巖頭法道, and he was hard to
> understand.[50]

Although Quanhuo may have had quite a different reputation within
the later Chan tradition, this biography makes it clear that his posthumous
title, and maybe even his relics, were acquired as a consequence of his loyalty to the Tang. This is far from the iconoclastic image of the Chan master
that is so familiar to us from other sources. Zanning supplies an appended
comment that compares the biographies of Hongxiu and Quanhuo and
shows how he considered their actions in light of those of heroes of the
past:

> How were the two masters Hongxiu and Quanhuo able to approach danger
> without [wanting to] avoid it? My interpretation says, "What is difficult for
> an ordinary person is easy for a bodhisattva. The burdens accumulated
> throughout their lives were abandoned. But why should one consider them
> rare? In the past An Shigao 安世高 (d. late second or early third century) re-
> peatedly paid his debts, getting rid of them like sweeping dust, and his
> *karma* got increasingly lighter.[51] The body on which suffering is dependent
> is exhausted and one exchanges it for a solid and durable form. As for di-
> vine transcendents (*shenxian* 神仙), some of them die by means of the blade
> and this is called *jianjie* 劍解 (sword liberation).[52] How much more so does
> this apply to people who have correct cultivation and [attain] a true result?

Because they contemplate and depend on the Way and the principle, even if they do not die in a decent manner, there is no disgrace."[53]

This comment shows how conversant Zanning was with not only Buddhist history—his comparison of the two monks with the famous translator An Shigao would not have occurred to most people—but also with Taoist practice. Like Daoxuan before him, he calls on Taoist methods of liberation from earthly existence to make a point about the efficacy of Buddhist self-immolation while also drawing a distinction between the capacities of ordinary people and those of bodhisattvas. Because Hongxiu and Quanhuo were able to die without flinching, they clearly demonstrated the required determination that pushed their acts beyond the category of mere suicide.

Relics

The value of the self-immolator's relics may be seen in what occurred after Hongxiu's death. His disciple Jingxian 景先 (d.u.) cremated his corpse and collected seven grains of *śarīra,* which he put into a bag for safekeeping. But in an interesting case of *furta sacra,* some devout layperson swapped them for an equal number of beans and made off with them. Unable to pursue the miscreant, Jingxian and his fellows sought help from a fortune-teller who was able to locate the relics. When they were retrieved the relics were placed in a pagoda and each was sealed in a container made of beryl (*liuli* 琉璃), in which they glowed radiantly.[54] Thus the relics of the self-immolator were imbued with all the properties of Buddha relics, even to the extent of being objects of envy. The fact that the fortune-teller could not read from them is meant to suggest, I suspect, the unknowable nature of the master's mind.

By the tenth century relics were produced by means other than cremation. Toyuk, the eccentric monk from Silla who fed his body to insects, spontaneously exuded multicolored pearl-like *śarīra,* which people sought after avidly. He died in 938 aged over eighty, and after his cremation countless *śarīra* were found among the ashes. We see another example of relic inflation here—not only did Toyuk produce "countless" *śarīra* after death, he also sweated relics while alive, so saintly was he. Like Toyuk, Jingchao 景超 (d. ca. 936–943), who was a devoted reciter of the *Lotus Sūtra* and the *Huayan jing,* spontaneously exuded many round and shiny *śarīra.*[55] People picked them up from the mat where he sat and the places where he walked. Zhitong 志通 (d. after 939), who survived jumping from a cliff, later spontaneously produced *śarīra* from his body as he cultivated Pure Land practices.[56]

Relics of eminent monks were in turn productive of more self-immolation practices. Huaide 懷德 (d. 983) was devoted to chanting and memorizing the *Lotus*.[57] He travelled to Sizhou 泗州 to do obeisance to the image of the mummified Sogdian thaumaturge Sengqie 僧伽 (d. 710).[58] At the time of his visit the Song emperor Taizong had sent the eunuch of high rank (*gaopin* 高品) Li Shenfu 李神福 (947–1010) to present banners and flowers to the same image.[59] In response to this imperial act of homage, *śarīra* were produced, and they were buried under the foundations of a new pagoda in a deep shaft. Impressed by the numinous power of Sengqie, Huaide vowed to burn his body in homage. First he gave away his robes, his bag, and other necessaries. Then, clad in paper clothes, he covered his body in oil and wax and bowed in farewell to the assembly of monks. Holding in his hands two candles, he climbed into a stack of firewood and recited *sūtra*s as he set fire to it. As the monks heard the faint sound of Huaide reciting *sūtra*s, his body was enveloped in the roaring flames, and the onlookers wiped away their tears. Later many *śarīra* were collected from the ashes. The biography concludes, "This took place on Taiping xingguo 太平興國 8.4.8 (May 22, 983, the Buddha's birthday). When the emissary returned to court and reported to the throne, the emperor's expression changed [in other words, he was moved]."[60]

    Huaide's biography vividly demonstrates the significance and productivity of relics in late medieval China. Let us consider the cycle of production here. The numinous mummy of a Sogdian monk was honored by the court and in response produced relics. Impressed by the miraculous power of the image, another monk offered himself in homage to the whole-body relic, and his own fiery death produced yet more relics, further enhancing the status of the original cult. Sengqie was both a local and national hero, and despite Huaide's reverence for the (Indian) *Lotus Sūtra,* the biography describes an almost entirely closed system in which relics produced in China bred more relics. The role of the Buddha in this system was peripheral to say the least, although the cult of the Buddha's *śarīra* remained alive and well in the ninth and tenth centuries alongside cults centered around more locally produced relics.

    The relics of the Buddha were an essential part of the identity of Chinese Buddhism and were also frequently wielded as symbols of political power. During the chaos of the ninth and tenth centuries, they were often beacons of hope for a return to a more stable order, both spiritual and temporal. The acts of Yuanhui 元慧 (819–896) offer us a vivid example of the potency thought to reside in the tangible presence of the Buddha. Yuanhui practiced a method of esoteric Buddhism known as the "Three Whites" (*sanbai* 三白). In addition to reciting the mantras of the five divisions of the Diamond Realm, he burned sticks of incense on his arm.[61] In 845 the devastating Huichang persecution began, and he was forced to return to lay life until the restoration of Buddhism in 847. In 853 he again burned incense on his arm in homage to the relic of the Buddha's tooth at Bao'en shan si 報恩山寺 in Wujun 吳郡 (present-day Suzhou 蘇州, Jiangsu).[62] Then he went to Tiantai shan and crossed the famous stone bridge there—a sure sign of his sanctity.[63] A few years later:

> During the Xiantong 咸通 reign period (860–873), following the sending there of the relic of the Buddha's middle finger bone, he went to Chongzhen si 重真寺 in Fengxiang 鳳翔 and burned off his left thumb while reciting the *Lotus Sūtra.*[64] This thumb grew back just as it had been before in less than a month.[65]

In the *Lotus Sūtra,* the Medicine King's arms grow back after he burns them in homage, and in sixth-century Sichuan Sengyai's fingers were also restored after he incinerated them. The heroes of the *jātakas,* such as King Śibi, also had donated body parts magically regenerated. So the restoration of Yuanhui's thumb had precedents in scripture and Chinese Buddhist history, but we may suspect that this miracle could also have been read as a sign of the hoped for restoration of Buddhism after the Huichang persecution.

Zanning addresses both the unusual regrowth of the thumb and Yuanhui's esoteric practice in his appended comment:

> When he burned his thumb, the fire consumed it and the ashes flew away. How could the flesh and bone quickly regrow from the charcoal to be as they were before? This is the same type of occurrence as a lotus growing in the middle of a fire, although it manifested in a different form.
>
> What is meant by "Three Whites?" The answer is that there are two categories, that of worldly phenomena *(shi)* and that of principle *(li).* The first means the worldly phenomena of white rice, white water, and white salt. As for the second, the body does not have contact with external objects, the mouth recites true scripture, and in one's thoughts there are no deluded attachments. These three things [body, speech, and mind] are bright and white, and there is no black *karma,* hence the name.[66]

Zanning's caution is evident here. He does not make any explicit claim that the magical regrowth of the thumb was just the same as the Medicine King's arms growing back instantaneously in the *Lotus,* although he may be hinting at that precedent. In this case, perhaps for Zanning the miracle might be partly attributable to the physical and spiritual purification implied in the practice of the "Three Whites," which may be seen as a dietary practice more solidly grounded in Buddhist sources than the abstention from grain we noted in the *Gaoseng zhuan* biographies.

Public ritualized auto-cremation before the relics of the Buddha was also recorded in the mid-tenth century. During his earlier career Pujing 普靜 (887–955) had been to Famen si in Fengxiang to pay homage to the relics of the Buddha. In 943, he fasted and pronounced this vow:

> "I vow to sacrifice one thousand bodies that I might quickly attain true awakening." In Xiande 顯德 2 of the Zhou (955), it happened that [the relics of] the true body were invited to enter [Ciyun 慈雲] monastery. Then he reported to Lord Yang 楊, the metropolitan governor (*zhoumu* 州牧), "I vow to burn my body in homage."[67] Lord Yang consented to his plan. Then he went to Guangsheng si 廣勝寺, where he attracted the admiration of the people of that prefecture.[68] Some presented him with incense and fruit, others laid out banners and flowers, some wept as they followed behind him, others preceded him, singing. On the eighth day of the fourth month [May 2, 955, the Buddha's birthday], he loudly pronounced his great vow before the *stūpa* of the True Body: "I vowed to burn one thousand bodies, and this is one of that thousand." He entered the firewood hut slowly and deliberately and set fire to it himself. At that time gloomy-looking smoke rose into the air, forming fragrant mists and melancholy clouds. The assembled crowd sighed, and the multitudes wept with grief. He was sixty-nine at the time of his death. His disciples gathered his remaining ashes and paid homage to them.[69]

We have here a very full and rather moving account of auto-cremation in homage to the relics of the Buddha, incorporating many of the elements that have become familiar to us: permission from secular authorities and a vow followed by a large-scale public event attended by an emotional audience. The biography paints a vivid picture of Pujing's procession towards the place of the burnt offering, accompanied by weeping and singing crowds and gifts of banners and flowers. The heightened emotions and the drama of this account show how the monk's sacrifice replayed in ritual time the similar offerings of the body described in the *Lotus Sūtra* and other Mahāyāna scriptures.

Spontaneous Human Combustion

The *Song gaoseng zhuan* contains one biography of a monk who was supposed to have spontaneously combusted. This form of miraculous transformation was to become a marked feature of later collections of biographies of self-immolators. By effectively removing the element of human agency from auto-cremation and instead presenting the fire as a manifestation of the power of *samādhi*, such accounts may have been intended to forestall accusations of suicide, which were problematic for the *saṃgha* as a whole.

In the middle of the ninth century a mysterious monk known as Master Bundle of Grass (Shucao shi 束草師, d. before 853) arrived suddenly at Puti si 菩提寺 in the Pingkang 平康 quarter of Chang'an.[70] No one ever knew where he was from or his real name. He preferred his own company and did not mix much with others. He always carried on his back a bundle of straw and sat in the corridors of the monastery's veranda rather than in a room. Some people said that this was a form of *dhūta* practice. After several years the monastery's administrators urged him to take up proper accommodation, but he took umbrage at their suggestion:

> Some people reproached his disorderly behavior. He said to them, "Why do you dislike me? It is not worth being attached to this life, why should I prolong it?" That evening he used his bundle of straw to set fire to his body. The next morning only ashes and cinders remained. Moreover, there was no remaining skeleton, and the stench of corruption was virtually absent. Also there had been no sounds of prolonged burning or cries of fear. In view of the limited amount of straw there, it was not enough to have incinerated his entire body. Given that there was not the slightest remainder, he must have burned himself by giving rise to a *samādhi* fire.[71] The assembly all gasped in admiration, and many people came to see and to do obeisance to him. Laypeople in the capital made a paste of his ashes and formed it into the image of a monk. It was set up at the side of the Buddha hall. People of the time called [the image] Master Bundle of Grass, and he made many responses to their prayers.[72]

This biography provides further evidence that some auto-cremators had cults in which their remains were enshrined in monasteries and worshipped by laypeople in search of worldly benefits. By the mid-ninth century, such miracles as spontaneous combustion happened not just in the remote countryside or on sacred mountain sites, but even in the worldly heart of the Tang capital. Zanning's comment on Master Bundle of Grass attempts to explain the wild talent of the eccentric monk in terms of scriptural precedents:

> In the *Chutai jing* 處胎經 (Sūtra [Spoken while] in the Womb), the bodhisattva meditates and enters the *samādhi* of the fire realm.[73] Deluded beings

thought that the bodhisattva was being burned by the fire [at the end of the] *kalpa. Bhikṣus* who have not yet attained this level should not manifest such signs to puzzle common people. But an achievement like being able to use a small amount of hay to burn the whole physical frame, this is something that might convince people [of the validity of the act]. It is as the (*Shang*)*shu* 尚書 (Book of Documents) says, "[When the sages instruct them] people will no longer fall victim to confusion, and they will not create illusions through extravagant language."[74] Alas![75]

Once again Zanning was able to find a scriptural precedent for what might appear at first to be a completely anomalous event. Yet at the same time he distinguished qualitatively between the bodhisattva, burning through many *kalpa*s, and the monk, who burns only once yet provides a sign of the miracle by using only an impossibly small amount of fuel. In his view—and this opinion would seem to hold true for self-immolators in general—just as one has faith in the heroes of scripture, so even an eccentric monk can provide something for beings in a later age to rely on.

Burning Off Fingers

Zanning's collection includes biographies of monks who practiced a kind of gradual auto-cremation that involved burning off the fingers over many years. Monks offered their fingers to relics or texts, often burning one to commemorate a round of reading or recitation. We have already mentioned the case of Wuran who burned off a finger for every million vegetarian meals he supplied to monks on Mount Wutai, and so ended up with no fingers left.

Xichen 息塵 (875?–937?) once attempted to give his body to wild dogs and tigers, regularly exposed his body to the bites of gnats, and once a month allowed fish to feed on him in a river or pool.[76] In addition to these offerings he repeatedly burned off fingers. For example, after reading through the canon many times over at the cliff temple Xianyan si 仙巖寺, he held a vegetarian banquet and burned off a finger as repayment for his blessings.[77] In 931, after prostrating to every character of the *Huayan jing* and the *Da Foming jing* 大佛名經 (Great Sūtra of the Names of the Buddha, T 14.441)—a total of 120 fascicles—he then burned off another finger.[78] By this time, he had burned off five fingers altogether.[79] Because of these practices, he became a great favorite of the new emperor, Jin Gaozu 晉高祖 (r. 936–942), who bestowed on him the imperial purple robe and prestigious titles.[80]

Xichen heard that Famen si in Fengxiang prefecture held the relic of the Buddha's middle finger bone. While gazing at this amazing object he burned off yet another finger; by the end of his life only two remained.[81] After he died his disciples cremated him and obtained several hundred relics, with which they returned to Taiyuan. Jin Gaozu ordered that they be interred in the mountains west of the Jin river 晉水, where Zanning says a small *stūpa* was still preserved in his time.[82] The emphasis on burning fingers as a marker of other devotional practices is interesting and may represent a way of reshaping the body in the same way as the mind would be reshaped through recitation and prostration.

Jingchao also paid homage to the *Huayan jing*, making a full prostration to each and every character.[83] To record the completion of two rounds of this practice he burned one finger, and then he paid homage to the *Lotus Sūtra* in the same manner. In his appended comment to Jingchao's biography, Zanning takes up the question of whether this kind of gradual self-immolation, finger by finger, was a true imitation of scriptural models. His answer reveals something about Zanning's criteria for inclusion in his collection of biographies:

> [Someone might say,] "Speaking of those who abandon the body, they ought to give up the whole body, like Prince [Mahā]sattva, should they not? Now these people just use a finger as a lamp, lighting the forearm as a burning wick. How can you use these examples [in the self-immolation section]? Is this not too fortunate for them?"
>
> I answer that burning off the fingers and chopping off the forearm are subsidiary practices (*jiaxing* 加行) of abandoning the body. In the time of the semblance *dharma* and the end of the *dharma* (*xiangmo* 像末), these acts have become even more difficult [to perform]. So [they are included here] just as those who were able to maintain, even to a lesser extent, [the principles of] honesty and uprightness are entered in the biographies of the worthy officials.[84]

So for Zanning the practice of self-immolation had grown harder rather than easier as the *dharma* had declined. Thus burning the finger was a method suitable for those living in such an age, who were unable to achieve the levels that advanced practitioners had managed in earlier, more fortunate times. This view contrasts somewhat with that of sixth-century self-immolators such as Sengyai, who had tended to view self-immolation as a practice particularly appropriate to the period of the semblance *dharma* or final *dharma*. Yanshou, interestingly, did not make any mention of the decline of the *dharma* in his discussion of self-immolation. He seems to have regarded it as no impediment to the imitation of the self-immolation of bodhisattvas.

In the passage above Zanning explicitly compares the biographies in his collection to accounts of conduct of upright officials in the dynastic histories. Of course, like his predecessors, Zanning was well aware of the meaning and function of the secular antecedents to his own work, but as a Hanlin academician he may have been particularly conscious of the parallels between a career serving the emperor and a lifetime serving the Buddha. He also draws some very similar comparisons in his critical evaluation, as we shall see.

Foiled Attempts

Some attempts at self-immolation did not succeed. Monks could be thwarted by divine intervention or mundane obstacles. A particularly vivid example of the former is that of Zhitong.[85] When Zhitong was on Tiantai shan, he stayed at Zhiyi's former monastery. There he read a collection of miracle tales called the *Xifang jingtu lingrui zhuan* 西方淨土靈瑞傳 (Accounts of Numinous Signs of the Western Pure Land) and was converted to practices designed to ensure his rebirth in the Pure Land (for example, not sitting with his back to the west). On Tiantai there was a certain rock known as "the Beckoning Hand" (*zhaoshou shi* 招手石), which was associated with a legend told of the famous Tiantai master Zhiyi. Once Zhiyi had dreamed that on this rock there was a monk who looked as if he were waving towards the sea. When Zhiyi came to Tiantai he saw this very monk, whose name was Dingguang 定光 and who was evidently some kind of divine being because the tips of his ears extended higher than the crown of his head.[86] Zhiyi recalled him clearly from his dream.

Zhitong climbed up to this auspicious site and threw himself off the rock, vowing to be reborn promptly in the Pure Land. He did not die but landed in a large tree. At this point he was still uninjured, so he jumped again. This time he fell off the cliff onto some soft, thick grass and was only slightly hurt, although he was unconscious for quite a time.

The monks who were looking for him thought that he must have been eaten by wild dogs and tigers. Eventually they found him and took him back, but they only managed to locate him after consulting a local (female) spirit medium (*wu* 巫):

A god [speaking through the medium] said, "That monk is to the southwest. Now there is a god in golden armor (*jinkai shen* 金鎧神) who is aiding him with his magic powers so he does not die. I went there, but my *qi* is becoming exhausted, it is difficult for me to approach them." The facts tallied exactly with what the god had said.[87]

The idea of monks consulting a medium for knowledge about the unseen world may sound surprising, but probably this was much more common than we are used to imagining. Perhaps we may tentatively identify the armor-clad god in this biography as Weituo 韋馱, the god who protects Chinese monasteries, although Zanning does not make that connection himself. Zhitong later went to Fahua shan 法華山 in Yuezhou 越州, where he cultivated Pure Land practices more quietly and died sitting on his meditation seat.[88] When he was cremated a five-colored cloud of smoke covered the crown of his head, and everybody smelled a remarkable fragrance. Zanning compares his lucky escape with some other examples of divine providence:

> In the past there was Bakkula (Bojuluo 薄拘羅), who did not die on five occasions.[89] Now we have Master Tong, who did not die on two occasions. In the past, there was Fachong 法充 (d. 600), who hurled himself off Xianglu peak香爐峰, which is a thousand *ren* 仞 high, and yet did not die.[90] Zhitong's case is just the same. When not a single hair was harmed, did he not have the help of a heavenly dragon? Instead he was able to extend his life and did not terminate his physical mind. But how did this help him to increase his cultivation of Pure Land practices?[91]

We may infer from this comment Zanning's understanding that if some attempts at self-immolation did not succeed because the monks concerned were not ready, or were not supposed to die, then conversely successful acts must have been completed because the cultivation of those monks was complete. In his final remarks, Zanning seems to suggest that extending one's life does not help one at all in the cultivation of practices leading to rebirth in the Pure Land.

As we have noted in previous chapters, when monks petitioned for permission to burn themselves emperors usually acquiesced, albeit with a show of reluctance. Sometimes, however, they declined to do so, as in the following case. Even in his youth Hongzhen 洪真 (fl. ca. 947–950) was convinced that the world was defiled and he resolved to leave it.[92] When he had completed about ten thousand recitations of the *Lotus Sūtra,* he memorialized the Later Han (947–950) emperor, asking for permission to burn his body as an act of homage to the *stūpa* of the Buddha. The emperor declined, and there was some debate about the matter at court. When a decree was promulgated that strictly prohibited his act, Hongzhen retreated to Guang'ai si 廣愛寺 in Luojing 洛京 (Luoyang) and gave away his robe, bowl, and other belongings. He vowed to end his life that very year. It turned out that he did in fact die while sitting upright without any sign of illness, thus fulfilling his vow. Several days passed, but his expression remained as if he were still alive. When his body was cremated, only the tongue remained, as moist and red as ever. The unburned tongue stands witness to the special sanctity of Hongzhen, which had not really been recognized by the court but manifested itself all the same. Hongzhen's biography hints that no one, not even the emperor, could actually prevent the death of a self-immolator merely by withholding permission. This conviction may be discerned in some other biographies in which the secular authorities refused to cooperate.

As we noted in the previous chapter, King Zongyi's refusal to give Shaoyan permission to burn himself may well have inspired another monk from Wu-Yue, Yongming Yanshou, to compose his strident defense of the merits of self-immolation. Shaoyan's salvation from drowning echoes other accounts of miraculous rescues and indicates that the time was not right for this eminent monk to die, whatever his own heartfelt wishes. He does not seem to have been considered a failure by his contemporaries. On the contrary, he had an illustrious career, had disciples of his own, was lavishly patronized in both life and death, and left behind relics.

War and Other Natural Disasters

As we have seen, the ninth and tenth centuries were eventful times, and bloody conflict was the backdrop against which many self-immolators performed. Some of them employed their bodies to try and avert warfare, drought, and famine. Daozhou 道舟 (864–941) used his own blood to paint a standing image of Guanyin with one thousand arms and one thousand eyes.[93] When there was a drought he stopped eating and closed his eyes. Only when the rain brought widespread relief on the day he had forecast did he start taking food again. The next threat that faced Daozhou's community was that of war:

In Zhonghe 中和 2 (882), he heard that there was trouble in the pass and the capital districts (*guan fu* 關輔).[94] Then, below the *stūpa* at Nianding yuan 念定院, south of the city, he cut off his left forearm and burned it in homage to an image of Guanyin. He vowed to stop the contending spears and shields and that peace would soon be seen on the central plain and strategic points along the frontier. When he finished speaking, there was a sudden clap of thunder, a gust of wind, and a great downpour. Also he once cut off his left ear to pray for rain for the people. He repeatedly abstained from food for seven days to pray for snow. All his wishes were fulfilled. Even the Fanluo 番落 [barbarians] revered him. During the night of Tianfu 天福 6 (*xinchou* 辛丑).2.6 (March 6, 941), he gave his final instructions to his disciples and, having accomplished everything, he died seated in the lotus position.[95] He was seventy-eight years old. His remains did not decay and he looked as if he were in meditation, so [his disciples] added some lacquered cloth to his body.[96]

During the Jianlong 建隆 reign period (960–963), there was a certain Guo Zhongshu 郭忠恕 (?–977).[97] He was widely versed in all kinds of literature, and he was particularly good at the minor arts (*xiaoxue* 小學). He was skilled in seal and clerical scripts. But he often bullied people and as a consequence was exiled to the northern frontier. He enquired into Daozhou's previous feats and composed a stele inscription for him.[98]

We know from his biography and his writings that Daozhou's biographer, Guo Zhongshu, was a man of considerable education and intelligence, so we may be assured that the usual practice of having eminent men of letters compose memorial inscriptions for auto-cremators was still in effect in the late tenth century. Daozhou's acts combined homage to images with a more generalized sense of charity: He burned his arm to bring peace and rain. He burned his body and left a mummy, satisfying the religious needs of the populace twice over. We do not know if his mummy was itself able to bring rain, but this ability is known to have been attributed to other mummies, such as that of the Chan patriarch Huineng 慧能 (638–713), for example.[99]

Chan Master Self-Immolators

One of the striking features of the self-immolation section of the *Song gaoseng zhuan* is the number of biographies it contains of monks who were also celebrated as members of the classical Chan tradition. No fewer than six Chan masters have biographies in the self-immolation section: Quanhuo, Huiming, Shouxian, Shiyun 師蘊 (ca. 893–973), Shaoyan, and Wennian 文輦 (895–978). Many Chan masters are mentioned in passing: For example, Qinghuo, who composed a text extolling Hongxiu's virtue, has a biography in the early Chan collection *Jingde chuandeng lu.*[100]

Huiming was a Chan master who has some sayings preserved in the *Jingde chuandeng lu.*[101] He had studied under the well-known tenth-century Chan master Fayan Wenyi and was a tough debater with a reputation for attacking anyone who came to visit him and destroying their points of view. He was patronized and given an official title by King Zhongyi. He died sometime during the Xiande reign period (954–959).

An account of Huiming's bodily acts is not incorporated into his Chan-style biography but comes at the end, suggesting that perhaps Zanning was working with more than one source. Earlier in his career, Huiming had burned his finger like a lamp to worship Mañjuśrī on Mount Tiantai. Later he diligently continued this vocation by burning three more fingers. From such biographies we learn that among the major figures of the maturing Chan tradition in tenth-century South China, the burning of fingers and other forms of self-sacrifice were really quite unexceptional. Physical practices that dated back five hundred years or so went hand in hand with new styles of teaching.

Shiyun was a companion of the Chan master Deshao 德韶 (891–972).[102] He was in great demand among the laity for his jokes—a detail in his biography that shatters any illusion that self-immolators were always rather gloomy fellows. Because he got on best with other joke-tellers, the more serious-minded of Deshao's community looked down on him, but Deshao recognized his true qualities. However, Shiyun was not just a prankster: He chanted *sūtra*s and *dhāraṇī*s and could explain many texts.

Once Shiyun told his companions that he planned to throw himself off the stone bridge on Yanzuo peak 宴坐峰. The aim of his vow was apparently so that he could "join rapidly the class of worthies and sages"—in other words, he wanted to become a bodhisattva. Many of his comrades discouraged him from carrying out his plan, and apparently their arguments were successful:

> During the seventh month of Kaibao 開寶 6 (973), he passed away, sitting upright without any illness—just as if he were in *dhyāna*. At that time the weather was very hot, and his body was kept for fourteen days. The body did not sag, and no vile substances came out of his orifices. Then [the other monks] moved the holy seat (*shenzuo* 神座) to the eastern edge of the monastery and cremated him.[103]

In addition to the *śarīra*, which they retrieved from among the ashes, Shiyun's tongue was undamaged. When the ashes were cool they picked it up; it was like a red lotus in color. It was soft and pliable and evoked feelings of tenderness. Someone said, "This monk was not especially remarkable, this thing has just survived by chance." So they burned his tongue again and it responded by taking on the same color as the fire. They waited a long while, and once again it became like a lotus. Following this it was decided to establish a small *stūpa* within the monastery, and [the tongue] was inhumed in it. Later there was another person who did not believe what had happened; he burned [the tongue] and smelted it dozens of times over.

While Shiyun was alive he never revealed his family name or his age. People judged by his appearance that he was over eighty years old.[104]

In this biography, the unburned tongue makes its appearance once again as a mark of sanctity, and one that stood up to the usual testing applied to relics. One would like to think that it was Shiyun's jokes that made his tongue so miraculous, but probably it was his mastery of *sūtras* and *dhāraṇīs* that was responsible. Once again we see how similar these Chan monks were to monks of any other affiliation in late medieval China. They chanted, recited, and confessed; they desired to join the sages as quickly as possible; and their bodies produced relics when cremated.

Another monk in Deshao's circle was Wennian.[105] He first attained awakening under the Chan master Mingzhao 明昭 (d.u.).[106] He then went to Tiantai shan, where he followed Deshao for the next thirty years. Although Wennian was really on the cutting edge of the Chan tradition as it was developing in Zhejiang in the late tenth century, he did not eschew the traditional methods of auto-cremation:

> In Taiping xingguo 太平興國 3 (978), he grabbed his axe and said he was going to cut some sandalwood. He ingeniously joined exquisite carvings, which he put together as if making a burial chamber (*ticou* 題湊).[107] He called it a "Buddha *stūpa*" (*futu* 浮圖). In the middle he opened a door, through which he entered and sat down inside with his legs crossed. He grasped a flaming torch, and he spoke this vow: "I burn this [body of mine], which is breathing its last, in homage to the buddhas of the ten directions and all the sages and worthies." At the end of his speech, flames shot into the sky, their smoke was five-colored, and it spiralled round in thick clouds. All that could be heard was the sound of *sūtras* being recited, which lasted only for a short time. The onlookers cried and wailed. When the embers cooled, they gathered countless *śarīra*. He was eighty-four years old.
>
> Earlier Wennian had once told the monks of Shanjian si 善建寺, "When I die, I will not occupy ground that the monastery (*qielan* 伽蘭; Skt. *saṃghā-rāma*) could use for growing food—that is not as good as burning oneself in homage. It is my hope that, at that time, all of you will gather at the base of the pyre of firewood and assist my rebirth [in the Pure Land] by chanting *nianfo* [for me]. I will only trouble you with this [request]." Now within Shanjian si, they have piled up stones to serve as a small *stūpa*.[108]

Because Wennian was already eighty-four, he may not have expected to live much longer and perhaps did not wish to delay his departure. But he must have been rather a hale and hearty old man if he could carve his own fancy funeral chamber unaided. His religious life combined Chan styles of discourse with a thorough knowledge of the scriptures, and he died in the expectation not of *nirvāṇa* but of rebirth in the Pure Land. Chan in the tenth century may have been radical in rhetoric, but it was quite mainstream in terms of practice and aspirations.

The Moment of Death

A notable trope that came to dominate later biographies was the focus on the moment of death and the importance of the ideal posture as life ends: Seated upright with the palms together. Although the changing conventions of biography require further study to understand why this interest in the final moments arose, it seems that the increasing presence of this trope was part of a shift that occurred around the mid-Tang. The attributes of the moment of death, which had been noted in the biographies of earlier figures, came to be understood as almost a required part of the funerary inscription and consequently began to appear repeatedly in biographical collections. In other words, it appears that by the mid-Tang the Buddhist funerary inscription had acquired certain conventions of genre. This does not mean that the biographies themselves were stale and formulaic, but only that certain elements were almost expected from the authors of the inscriptions. The ability of the saint to die while sitting upright was singled out as a particular mark of sanctity in Daoxuan's collection and is often found in later biographies.[109] This is not merely a medieval phenomenon: Information about the death of a great monk is still important to the Buddhist community today. The two most commonly asked questions are "Did the monk leave relics?" and "Did he die sitting upright?"[110]

Descriptions of the following monks' deaths in the *Song gaoseng zhuan* stress their physical control at the point of death: Sengzang died peacefully, sitting upright with his palms together and reciting the name of Amitābha; Hongzhen died upright without any sign of illness, as did Shiyun;[111] Shaoyan also passed away peacefully seated upright, although not for want of trying other means.[112]

Zanning's *Critical Evaluation*

Daoxuan used part of his evaluation to discourse on funeral practices, and in similar fashion Zanning gives us an account of the history of the Buddha's relics in China and his personal involvement with them. Zanning's preoccupation is hardly surprising given the number of references we have seen in the biographies to the relics of the true body at Famen si and those held in Wu-Yue. The relic at Famen si had been the object of similar kinds of devotion in the seventh century, as Daoxuan and Daoshi had noted in earlier collections.[113]

Zanning attacked Confucianism and Taoism much more explicitly than did either Huijiao or Daoxuan. This strategy was no doubt determined by the fact that he was trying to offer Buddhism as an imperial ideology to the new Song regime. Overall Zanning had more space in which to explore self-immolation than his predecessors because his appended comments throughout the chapter allowed him to give more direct opinions on individual cases.

Like his Huijiao and Daoxuan, Zanning begins by broaching the topics of the body, self, and life. However, he uses much stronger language to contrast the meanness of ordinary people with the selflessness of Buddhist self-immolators. He compares people jealously guarding their own lives to a dragon guarding a pearl or a peacock its feathers. Interestingly, Zanning singles out Confucians for particular criticism, suggesting that their mourning restrictions and taboos on the body keep them isolated from their students. Self-immolators, on the other hand, are far beyond such petty and worldly restrictions. Because they obtain such great merit, whatever minor transgressions they might have committed are irrelevant.

Zanning makes reference to some famous cases of heroic suicide and selflessness from Chinese history. First, he alludes to some positive statements about altruistic suicide in the *Book of Rites* and the *Analects*. Then he mentions the case of Xu You 許由, the archetypal recluse mentioned in the *Zhuangzi*, who refused the throne when the sage-king Yao offered it to him. He was so disgusted by Yao's offer that he famously had to rinse out his ears.[114] Qu Yuan 屈原 was banished from the Chu 楚 court by Zilan 子蘭 (d.u.), the prime minister. In disgust and frustration, Qu "clasped a stone to his bosom, threw himself in the River Miluo 汨羅 and perished. . . . [F]rom this time onwards Chu declined with ever-increasing rapidity and within half a century was completely overthrown by Qin."[115] As Zanning remarks, such well-known cases from China's own past did not accord with the Confucian ideal and were in fact much closer to the Buddhist model. He next brings in the Buddha himself, whom earlier commentators had seemed to shy away from. He says that the Buddha's selfless offering of his own body for the sake of others is quite different from those who begrudge a single hair from their heads. It is the selfless action for the benefit of others that determines whether a practice is correct or not.

An interest in wealth runs like a thread through Zanning's accounts of self-immolation, probably reflecting the rise of a monetary economy since Daoxuan's day.[116] In an explicit reference to money, Zanning says that self-immolation is like banking: The more capital one lends out, the more interest one receives. It was by giving up his inheritance—carriages and fine clothes, fertile land and territory—that the Buddha was able to reap the reward of enlightenment. Those who offer their bodies to insects, gouge out their eyes, burn their fingers, slice their bodies to ribbons, or feed their flesh to tigers and fish are just the same as the Buddha. Thus self-immolation is a path to buddhahood like any other.[117]

Zanning points out that cultivation of *dāna* was the fundamental precondition for all cases of the attainment of buddhahood by the buddhas of the past, up to and including Śākyamuni. Bodhisattvas begin by giving up their external wealth but must also give up the inner wealth of their own bodies. A possessive attitude towards the material trappings of external wealth dooms one to remain an ordinary person. It is the ability to give up one's inner wealth without a second thought that makes one a bodhisattva. Zanning identifies this principle as one that had been taught by all the buddhas and exemplified by the actions of self-immolators of earlier ages, such as Sengyai and Zhiyi's disciple Dazhi. Although their actions may have troubled those who witnessed them, these self-immolators gave up their lives without any reluctance. The bodhisattva path means giving up one's life again and again. Those who practice it not only attain the indestructible body of a buddha, but also leave behind relics. Thus Zanning puts Chinese self-immolators on the same ontological level as the buddhas of the past.

Zanning then summarizes the characteristics of the various self-immolators in his collection in just the same way as Huijiao and Daoxuan had done. He goes a little further by explaining that the variety of phenomena associated with self-immolation—the unburned tongue, spontaneous human combustion, and so on—is due to the different causes and conditions that form the *karma* of the individual self-immolators. The ability to carry out the act depends on being able to see the body as empty like a bubble. Because of this ability, he says, bodhisattvas are able to give away their bodies lifetime after lifetime, unlike arhats who preserve the body for a single life until they reach extinction or Taoists who see the body as either a husk or dust and ashes. Zanning makes some interesting comparisons with the secular careers of civil and military officials—an analogy that would surely have been familiar to the audience at court. The student devotes himself to studying for the examinations, is recruited, and rewarded by the state, just like the bodhisattva attaining the reward of buddhahood.

Between Daoxuan's time and that of Zanning two very specific attacks on self-immolation had occurred—one from outside the Buddhist order and one from within. Zanning's discussion deals with the official Han Yu 韓愈 (768–824) first. In his infamous Memorial on the Buddha Relic (*Lun Fogu biao* 論佛骨表) submitted to the throne in 819, Han Yu complained to the emperor Xianzong 憲宗 (r. 805–820) that if he should honor the Buddha's relic as he proposed to do then the common people, being easily misled, would "in their tens or hundreds burn the tops of their heads and burn off their fingers in sacrifice." He goes on to add:

> Unless there is an immediate prohibition to check and control the various monasteries, there will inevitably be those who will cut off their limbs or slice up their bodies in making offerings, which will pervert our customs and destroy normal usages, making us a laughing stock to the world. This would be no small matter.[118]

It appears that Han Yu may not have simply been waxing rhetorical here. There are accounts of laypeople burning their scalps (*shao ding* 燒頂) and branding their arms (*zhuo bi* 灼臂) when the relic of the Buddha was brought to Chang'an in 819, and the biography of Li Wei 李蔚 (d. 877) speaks of common people cutting off their fingers in 873 when the relic was again brought to the capital.[119]

Zanning responds to Han Yu's attack on Buddhism by pointing out that his view of the world is one-sided. Because he is concerned with the Confucian qualities of benevolence and righteousness, naturally he does not discuss the Way and its Virtue—just as Buddhist teachings on suffering and emptiness do not make much mention of the Confucian values of loyalty and trust. Zanning rather pointedly turns Han Yu's use of the metaphor of a frog sitting at the bottom of a well and being unable to see the whole sky back on this opponent of Buddhism. In any case, he continues, Confucians do not claim to be experts on what happens after death as this is something that Confucius specifically declined to comment on. The sage Zhuangzi suspected that something went on after death—witness his famous drumming and singing after the death of his wife. The teachings of Confucius and Zhuangzi do not discuss *karma,* and it is *karma* that enables self-immolators to exchange a weaker body in one life for a stronger one in the future, growing ever more powerful and magnificent as they continue on the bodhisattva path. They gouge out human eyes but acquire the eyes of a buddha; they slice up a body of flesh and thus build a golden body. Although Zanning does not actually give any canonical references here, this kind of direct exchange or trading up from human organs to the thirty-two marks of the Buddha is actually spelled out quite explicitly in texts like the *Karuṇāpuṇḍarīka.*[120] He compares the actions of self-immolators to tiny ficus seeds, which grow into mighty trees.

The next objection to self-immolation is slightly unexpected but may serve as a salutary reminder of what a violent place tenth-century China was. The interlocutor suggests that although good people will be suitably awed and edified by the sight of a monk going up in flames, bad people, used to witnessing corporal punishment administered in public, will just laugh or see it only as a stage act. Does witnessing self-immolation actually inspire the right kind of feelings in the witnesses? Zanning replies that although the dull-witted may be so insensitive that they enjoy the sight, even the most evil people cannot bear to see that much injury to others. They may not be aware of it, but seeing something so shocking will implant a good seed and eventually bring forth a good karmic result. Zanning gives examples from the scriptures of people who attained enlightenment even after only putting on a monk's robe in jest or while drunk.

Although Han Yu attacked self-immolation from a Confucian perspective, the strongest objection to the practice came from the Buddhist monk Yijing, whose lengthy diatribe against auto-cremation in his *Nanhai jigui neifa zhuan* 南海寄歸內法傳 (An Account of the Dharma Sent Back from the Southern Seas, T 54.2125) we discussed in Chapter 4. In Zanning's critical discussion the interlocutor points out that Yijing had come out strongly against auto-cremation and that he had knowledge both of the scriptures and of Buddhist practice in India, the heartland of the religion. Zanning replies that Yijing's understanding is drawn solely from the rather basic scriptures of the *Āgama*s. In the Mahāyāna on the other hand, the attainment of the perfection of charity is dependent on giving away inner wealth. He cites the *Mahāyānasūtrālaṃkāra* in support of this and points out that exemplary individuals existed in China even long after the Buddha. The implication is that it was still possible in Zanning's day to cultivate the bodhisattva path, including self-immolation, just as the sages of the past had done.

The idea that such miracles could still occur in China, although distant from the Buddha in space and time, leads Zanning on to his final remarks, in which he recounts his own personal involvement with the imperial cult of relics. In 979 Zanning says that the state of Wu-Yue sent to the court of Song Taizong a reliquary made by King Aśoka for the relics of the Buddha. After being worshipped in the imperial palace, it was carried by the emperor himself to a wooden pagoda at Kaibao si 開寶寺, where it was interred in a deep brick-lined shaft and produced a bright light that lit up earth and sky.[121] In response to this miracle people burned their heads and fingers and burned incense on their bodies just as they had in Tang times. Zanning says that no one could have forced them to do such things, so their actions must owe everything to the bodhisattvas and heavenly kings. He takes pleasure in the fact that China now had the true relics of the Buddha and briefly recaps the history of the imperial patronage of relic cults. He ends by once again extolling the acts of the self-immolators who, he says, still live although they are dead and gone.

Conclusion

The biographies of late Tang and Five Dynasties monks provide numerous examples of self-immolators whose actions and their commemoration have a distinctly local cast to them. Rather than express hopes about renewing the cosmos or seeking a new dynastic order, these monks seem to have been concerned with particular places, such as Wutai shan, or their own monasteries. Like loyal officials, monks who chose death rather than surrender were commemorated as local representatives of a larger moral structure. Temporal as well as spatial order looked different to Buddhists of this period—the end of the *dharma*, rather than demanding renewal through self-sacrifice, was now invoked as a special situation that allowed subsidiary practices such as burning the fingers to stand in for the more advanced path of auto-cremation.

Not unrelated to the change in the power structure and in patronage networks that were partly responsible for these new attitudes to Buddhist practice was the rise of Chan. The number of Chan self-immolators in Zanning's collection reflects the dominance of this new style of Buddhism south of the Yangzi in the period from the late Tang to the early Song. Many of these monks shared lineage connections with each other and with Zanning. The distinctive style of their practice clearly did not replace other types of traditional training. The Chan monks here chant scriptures, burn off their fingers, and set fire to themselves; in these respects they are just like any other kind of monk. A consideration of Chan self-immolators offers us an interesting perspective that complements our examination of the Chan master Yanshou's opinions of the practice. Both types of evidence would seem to confirm that there was nothing particularly distinctive about "Chan" self-immolation.

The ubiquity and multiplicity of relics in the late Tang and Five Dynasties are apparent from even a cursory reading of the biographies. In these accounts self-immolators offered their bodies or body parts to not only (imported) relics of the Buddha, but also (domestically produced) relics of eminent monks. Both these relics and the relics produced by self-immolators themselves were miraculously self-multiplying. Self-immolators were now able to produce relics by spontaneously manifesting them via their already sanctified bodies as well as by burning themselves.

As well as a sense that the miraculous had escaped the bounds of the act of self-immolation and found expression in other aspects of the monk's life, we find considerable inventiveness on display in the imitation of scriptural and historical models. Self-immolators self-consciously picked and chose the type of offering from both models; they could also combine practices, offering their bodies to insects and fish while burning off fingers or plucking out eyes. By the late Tang the virtuoso self-immolator had arrived and was able to choose from a full repertoire of body practices appropriate for time, place, and personal inclination.

The many cases preserved in Zanning's text remind us what an open-ended category self-immolation was. It covered an ever-changing range of practices, aspirations, and concepts that could be applied to multiple ends. The means and the end were open to negotiation and reinterpretation by practitioners, biographers, and audiences, depending on circumstances and worldviews. As we noted in the previous chapter, by the time Zanning was writing, self-immolation in China had a long history and the arguments in its defense were getting more sophisticated and less apologetic. Despite the diversity and number of cases—and the fact that the *Gaoseng zhuan* genre was displaced by new forms of biographical collections—we should not be fooled into thinking that these biographies marked the end or even the high point of self-immolation in China.

CHAPTER 6

One Thousand Years
of Self-Immolation

We have now discussed in some detail how self-immolation was constructed and shaped by practitioners, biographers, and compilers up
to about the year 1000. We have seen that self-immolation was a fluid concept that embraced a range of practices and interpretations. Even after the
tenth century the concept of self-immolation never solidified but continued
to be reinvented and renegotiated. Although after the *Song gaoseng zhuan*
more sectarian collections, especially those of the Chan school, became the
primary repositories of biographies, monastic biographical collections did
not disappear entirely. In this chapter, we shall examine how self-immolation
was conceptualized and performed in late imperial China, from about 1000
to 1914. In particular we will note how self-immolation was represented at
times of national crisis such as the loss of North China to foreign invaders in
1126 and the Manchu takeover in 1644.

In the later sources we see both notable continuities with and radically
new conceptions of self-immolation practices. In particular, there seems to
have been a marked turn towards explaining or presenting auto-cremation
as a form of spontaneous human combustion that was initiated by mastery
of the *samādhi* of fire. We can speculate as to possible reasons for this newfound emphasis on the spontaneity of incineration, but it seems to have
mirrored a broader fascination with the moment of death and with those
who were able to will their own passing instantaneously or naturally. Also by
removing the element of human agency from the picture—auto-cremators
did not have to light the pyre themselves or have others light it for them—
self-immolation was safely distanced from the potentially problematic categories of "suicide" or "killing."

Post-Song Biographical Collections

In this chapter we shall focus mostly on material from two collections of biographies that have been little studied but have much to offer our understanding of post-Song Buddhism. The first, *Bu xu gaoseng zhuan* 補續高僧傳

(Supplement to Continued Biographies of Eminent Monks, *XZJ* 134.160b-163a), was a late-Ming attempt to continue the tradition of the first three *Gaoseng zhuan* collections that suffered from the need to cover more than six hundred years of Buddhist history. The second, *Xin xu gaoseng zhuan siji* 新續 高僧傳四集 (New Continued Biographies of Eminent Monks, Fourth Collection), which covers mostly the Qing and early Republican periods, is more of a collection of raw data than a fully conceived work but is nevertheless valuable for understanding how self-immolation continued to be reconceptualized into the twentieth century.[1]

The *Supplement to Continued Biographies of Eminent Monks* contains a great deal of fresh and interesting material, very little of it explored in the scholarship.[2] It was compiled towards the end of the Ming dynasty by Minghe 明河 (1588–1641) in response to two factors: The inadequacy of the *Da Ming gaoseng zhuan* (which is eight fascicles in length and has only three categories of religious specialization) and the dominance of biographies of members of the Chan school, which tended to overshadow the acts of other eminent monks. It took Minghe thirty years to compile and was largely based on inscriptions that he had seen in person on his travels around major Buddhist sites, but he does mention other literary sources. It is broadly inclusive and does not exclude Chan masters, although they may appear rather differently in this work than in their "Collected Sayings" or the "Records of the Transmission of the Lamp" of the time. Minghe was a diligent and intelligent compiler but unfortunately, because his work did not enter either the Jiaxing 嘉 興 canon or the Qing canon, it has been largely overlooked by scholars with the notable exception of Hasebe Yūkei.[3]

There are a number of themes in this collection that we have seen before in earlier biographies. Monks offered their bodies to save the populace from war or flood; in an echo of Dazhi's public burning of his arm before Sui Yangdi, a Ming monk offered his own life to the emperor to ensure a promised ordination of novices. In addition, monks died by auto-cremation, starvation, and drowning. There is also a significant new theme: A number of monks who died more or less spontaneously, having predicted their own deaths, subsequently remained incorruptible and were enshrined as mummies. On the whole though, Minghe's collection is much more interested in death as a mark of sanctity in itself. This probably represents part of the post-Tang Buddhist cult of death, which so far has not really been studied although Paul Demiéville sketched the outlines of the topic in his final work.[4] It also reflects the fact that many of these biographies were drawn straight from funerary inscriptions, which did tend to focus on the death of a master rather than providing an account of his career.

For biographies from the Qing and early Republican periods we are dependent on a collection that is certainly broad in scope but often falls short of the standards set by earlier collections. The *New Continued Biographies of Eminent Monks* was put together by the monk Daojie 道階 (1866–1934) and the layman Yu Qian 喻謙 (d.u.).[5] It drew on a wide variety of literary sources and especially on gazetteers.[6] It is an interesting compilation in that it assembles scattered sources, but the organization and the principles of selection fall somewhat short of Daoxuan's high standards or even those of Minghe. For instance, a number of biographies are reduplicated in different places in the collection.[7]

As with the *Bu xu gaoseng zhuan,* most of the biographies provide only the barest details of their subjects' careers, focusing instead on the moment of transformation. There are many *gāthā*s and verses preserved in this collection, and although they would probably not be ranked as the finest examples of Chinese poetry, they can be revealing of the ways in which self-immolation was understood and commemorated by other monks and by the laity. In particular the verses composed for a Ming nun are rather striking in that they do not even mention her gender. Auto-cremation is once again the predominant means of self-immolation (one monk drowned himself and another died of exposure), but there are no less than twelve cases of spontaneous combustion. This may reflect a widespread confidence during the Ming and Qing that Chinese masters were every bit as advanced as the buddhas and arhats of the past. Or, on the other hand, it may be due to a deep-seated, almost unconscious, sense of unease that such was not in fact the case. Yet another possibility is that spontaneous self-combustion was not technically suicide, and thus the act would escape the censure of any authorities (be they religious or secular) that might be opposed to such acts. It is interesting to note that at least one biography sounds a note of scepticism about whether spontaneous combustion really occurred at all or whether it was just an act of auto-cremation misperceived by witnesses.

Auto-Cremation

The *Lotus Sūtra* continued to exercise a fascination for some early modern self-immolators and was still cited occasionally as an inspiration. One biography, found not in the sources discussed above but in a collection devoted to upholders of the *Lotus,* provides a wealth of detail about not only how and why auto-cremation was enacted, but also what happened afterwards as the relics of the monk became valuable commodities and the ensuing religious fervor attracted unwelcome attention from the authorities.

People called the monk Fahe 法和 (?–1134) "Lotus" because he was always chanting the *sūtra*.[8] At the lantern festival on Shaoxing 紹興 4.1.15 (February 10, 1134), he consulted a lecturer called Keyi 可依 (d.u.) who lived in his cloister about the meaning of the Medicine King burning his body. Keyi explained that this episode was an illustration of the "true veneration of the *dharma*." Fahe walked away, pleased with this answer. A few days later, on the twenty-fourth of the month (February 19th), a great fire filled the night sky at the northeast corner of the central cloister. The monks came running to help and found "Lotus" sitting cross-legged in the middle of the fire. His mouth was moving as he continued to chant the *sūtra*:

> Before him he had set up incense and lamps as offerings to the *Lotus Sūtra*. He had also placed there a verse on leaving the world and the text of his vow. The verses said:
>> Swift-running water floats the laden boat,
>> The current ceases as it arrives at the other shore.
>> The remaining snow melts away in the red flames,
>> The feet of my purified body follow the former traces of the sages.
> The votive text reads, in outline:
>> I, Fahe, vow to burn this phantom body and to make from it the priceless incense. First, I offer it to the [buddhas of the] ten directions, the Three Jewels, and the supreme vehicle of the Marvellous Dharma. Next, I offer it to the eight classes of *deva*s and *nāga*s.[9] I wish first that the two sages should return to the capital and that the altars of grain and soil (*sheji* 社稷, that is, the state) might be restored.[10] After this I vow to be reborn in the world, always to expound the great vehicle and broadly saving all classes of beings.[11]

Fahe's vow thus explicitly expressed not only his intention to offer his body as incense to the buddhas, the *dharma,* the deities, and so on (echoing Wuran's auto-cremation on Wutai shan), but also his wish to see the Jurchen Jin invaders driven out of North China and the empire reunified under the Song emperors. The idea that an act of auto-cremation could be efficacious for the whole empire as well as the practitioner was one that had already found expression on many occasions in the preceding centuries. In 1134 South China was still reeling from the shocking loss of the North to the Jin, and we do not have far to seek for a sense of crisis that might have stimulated Fahe's action. But his impeccably patriotic ideals unfortunately did not spare his fellow monks from the wrath of the local authorities, as we shall see.

Fahe's auto-cremation precipitated a display of atmospherics and the
site was particularly productive of relics. From the flames of the pyre a five-
colored radiance flared into the sky. That night there was absolutely no
wind; suddenly people heard the sound of a terrifying ripping and drums
beating like thunder. These sights and sounds were accompanied by an unusual fragrance that wafted through the air. The next day, at dawn, pious
women went to do obeisance at the place of Fahe's transformation, where
they found the ashes shaking. After groping around and dusting off the
ashes, they found more than twenty grains of śarīra. When news of their find
spread, the relics kept increasing in number. Whoever requested them
found yet more relics. One person got a tooth and enshrined it in a casket;
a wealthy person offered thirty thousand cash for it. The head of the cloister could provide no explanation for these miraculously multiplying śarīra.
Eventually, the sheer numbers of people coming to the site in search of the
wondrous relics attracted the attention of others:

> At the time, the worshippers of the true body (zhenshen真身, that is, the Bud-
> dha relics) at Yuji peak 玉几峰 considered this a hindrance [to the cult of
> the Buddha relic] and filed a lawsuit with the authorities on the grounds
> that these people were promoting abnormal phenomena. The governor,
> Junior Guardian (shaobao 少保) Duke Guo 郭公, had the head monk ar-
> rested.[12] A few days later, when he was formally drawing up the charges, a
> fly flew into the room and landed on the tip of his brush. It sounded as if it
> were weeping. Then it left and came back again. The marshal realized that
> this was a miraculous response caused by the self-immolator, so he laid
> down his pen and released the head monk.[13]

Twelfth-century auto-cremators were obviously just as magically powerful as their earlier counterparts. Although Fahe's auto-cremation did not
bring about the restoration of Song rule, it did have potent effects on the local scene—evidently the attraction of his śarīra to the laity was seen as competition by those involved in a nearby cult dedicated to the Buddha's relics.
Zongxiao's account also reminds us that not all local officials were well disposed towards Buddhist practice, but they were not completely insensitive
when faced with evidence of the efficacy of certain acts. The pathos of the
scene with the weeping fly that moved the stone-hearted governor is particularly memorable and a tribute to the richness and sentimentality of the early
modern religious imagination.

As we have noted, biographies of female auto-cremators were not sought
out and collected after the sixth century, and we find only the occasional

mention among monks' biographies. Even nuns who were clearly quite well known remain anonymous in our sources. These brief accounts, which mention the miracles and relics so familiar to us from monks' biographies, offer only a tantalizing glimpse of what must have been a continuing practice for female religious. One such account tells of a nun who died at Guihua 歸化 in Fujian; her biography is appended to that the monk Kangzhai 康齋 (fl. ca. 1628–1644).[14]

In the last year of the Chongzhen 崇禎 reign period—which was in fact the year in which the Ming dynasty was overrun by the Manchus (1644)—this nun gathered fuel to burn herself. Although people did not believe that she would actually do it, she stacked up a tower of firewood and sat on top of it, chanting the name of the Buddha. She ordered the crowd to light it and was rapidly "transformed":

> The witnesses that day all gasped in admiration, and their praise for her spread through the alleys and lanes. Later people revered her and founded a nunnery for her. It was called Xinchuan 薪傳 (Firewood Passing On).[15] They also erected a *stūpa* to demonstrate their veneration. Famous scholars and poets heard of her ascetic act and composed many verses on the subject.[16]

The verses quoted in the biography praise this follower of Siddhārtha who was able to continue his teachings and note that the true nature of fire is empty. "Like hard ice that lasts through the winter, this bundle of bones" was able to light up the whole universe like a bright torch. "The numinous turtle lives under its shell and attains long life," while "the true person without rank (*wuwei zhenren* 無位真人) bathes in fire."[17] As the radiance of the fire spreads across the earth and expands into emptiness, like a flash of sudden lightening in a mirror, "the three thousand worlds are completely burned up, and the nine grades of lotuses open, glowing." The verses heap lavish praise on the nun and her auto-cremation, using the most refined language and most flattering allusions to both Buddhist and classical literature. It seems significant that the poet makes no specific reference to her gender but refers to her instead as "a true person without rank." This is strong evidence that female auto-cremators could be seen as acting just as heroically and powerfully as their male counterparts.

One suspects that the timing of the nun's auto-cremation on the eighth day of the fourth month of 1644 (the Buddha's birthday) cannot have been entirely unrelated to the death of the last Ming emperor in the third month of that same year. The nun's auto-cremation may have been celebrated later as much as an act of defiance (or perhaps of escape) in the face of the foreign

invader as a purely religious act. Given the cult that grew up around Ming loy-
alists it is perhaps not surprising that such a female "suicide" would attract
the notice of some later poets, although one must admit that the vocabulary
employed in the surviving poem is largely Buddhist. Whatever the case, one
cannot doubt that 1644 must have been a year of considerable uncertainty
and fear for the inhabitants of Guihua and very likely for the nun herself.
This brief account at least demonstrates that female self-immolation was not
confined to medieval China, and whatever the status of women in society as a
whole, this nun was commemorated not only in verse, but also had a nunnery
built in her honor and a *stūpa* erected for her relics. I suspect that this kind of
remembrance was actually a lot more common than the most readily available sources suggest. We cannot say that female auto-cremation never happened or that it was ignored when it did occur, but the fact that we have no
name recorded for this nun may reveal a certain determination on the part
of the monastic establishment not to accord these women the same status as
male self-immolators.

As with the fall of the Northern Song and Ming dynasties, it should not
surprise us to learn that the end of the Qing dynasty and the foundation of
the Republic in 1911 brought feelings of acute distress. One could almost expect that someone might attempt to sacrifice himself for the *dharma* at such a
time. The biography of Changhui 常慧 (1845–1914) of Tianning si 天寧寺 in
Changzhou 常州 offers a detailed account of just such an offering.[18] Changhui was a native of Huo shan 霍山 and in his youth became a novice at Jingdu
si 淨度寺 on Jiuhua shan 九華山.[19] After being ordained in 1875, in 1891
Changhui went to Tianning si, where he took up Pure Land practices, reciting the name of the Buddha and keeping to a strict practice of austerities. In
1906 he moved to Putong yuan 普同院, where there was a monk in sealed retreat.[20] Changhui kept guard outside his retreat, and together the two monks
passed many days reciting the *Lotus*. In this scripture Changhui came across
the account of the Medicine King burning his body and made a vow to give
up his body to save the world. The *Lotus* is scarcely mentioned elsewhere in
this collection, and although this is the last case of auto-cremation dealt with
in the monastic biographies, in some ways it harks back to the very earliest
cases we saw in Chapter 1.

In 1911, conscious that revolution was in the air throughout the land
and that "the Way and Virtue were declining every day":

He wished to truly carry out his intention to cause the *Buddhadharma* to
flourish, to turn people's minds around, to turn conflict into compassion
and fortune, to defeat desire and anger before they appeared, and to cause

all the tendencies for killing between heaven and earth to cease. He was resolute in this desire but for a long time could not put it into effect. At midnight on *jiayin* 甲寅 4.17 (May 11, 1914), at the eastern boundary of the cloister wall, he stacked up firewood like a small seat and sat erect and cross-legged on top. He lit the fire and transformed himself. At that time he was sixty-nine.[21]

Changhui had a disciple whom he had asked to light the fire, but on that day the man failed to arrive.

When the cremation was about half way through, his *kāṣāya* had been completely burnt to ashes, but the bronze hook [on the robe] was still hanging on right under his shoulder, bright and untainted. His enlightened mind was so strong that he was determined to show that death was like returning home. Fire shot forth from his whole body, every joint was burning but he was completely without pain, not moving an inch. If he were not completely endowed with true liberation and had attained great sovereignty, how could he remain upright and steady, not moving from his position and departing in such a manner as this?

By the side of a tree was set an incense altar; the incense in the burner had not yet been extinguished. One could imagine that Changhui had reverently paid homage to the Buddha before he transformed. At that time, the onlookers were all impressed and amazed and sighed admiringly. They all made donations and erected a pagoda at the place where he burned his body. On it Di Baoxian 狄寶賢 (d. 1941) wrote an account of this affair.[22]

It is perhaps startling to see the many points of continuity between this biography and those from hundreds of years earlier. Although Changhui was inspired by the *Lotus*, reappeared after his death, and had his biography composed by an eminent layman in the traditional manner, there is perhaps just a hint of a self-consciously "modern" attitude to the practice in the biographer's insistence that the lack of pain must be proof of his enlightened mind. As we have seen, any mention of pain in the earlier literature is quite rare. Likewise, it is tempting to see in Changhui's awareness of "the tendencies of killing" just months before the outbreak of the Great War of 1914–1918, a newly emergent global perspective on some of the particular horrors of *saṃsāra*, although in fact Changhui would not have had to look far in search of violence closer to home.

Despite the associations we find between auto-cremation and periods of empirewide upheaval such as the fall of the Northern Song and Ming dynasties, some auto-cremators were inextricably linked with much more local events—even such mundane matters as the maintenance of infrastructure. Wuming 無名 ("No Name," ca. 1590–1674) of Jingmen 荊門 in Hubei was a promoter of social projects like bridge building.[23] His most famous accomplishment was the Wanshan 萬善 (Ten Thousand Good Deeds) bridge. In October 1674 he stacked up firewood south of the Jingmen city walls and sat on top, holding the wooden fish. After he had the pyre lit he predicted that someone would have to repair the foundations of the bridge in forty years time. In 1714 (forty years later) Song Sisheng 宋思聖 (d.u.) arrived to administer the area. After noticing that the Wanshan bridge was listing slightly, Song paid for its repair from his own subsidies (*lian* 廉), thus fulfilling the prediction.[24] The biography concludes triumphantly, "What the mad monk said was true: The evidence is truly amazing!"

Although Wuming's biography shows a concern for the world beyond the cloister, even if only for the local community, other biographies show what auto-cremators could hope to achieve for their own monasteries. Zhian 止安 (d. 1740) was a serious and diligent practitioner of austerities, but he lived in a poor monastery that was falling down and always short of food.[25] No one else seemed to care about this, so he vowed to give up his own life for the *dharma*:

> He gathered firewood in a tall stack and sat upright on top. He proclaimed to the assembly, "After I, Zhian, leave, I vow that affection and response should occur between heaven and humans, causing the cloudy buildings to be lofty and bright, and the fragrant kitchen to be full." Then he took up his torch and burned himself. In clear tones he recited the name of the Buddha, and he was cheerful and unafraid. The onlookers were massed around him like a fence; they all praised him admiringly, amazed by this rare sight.[26]

The account ends at this point, so we do not know if there was any miraculous response to his call. It may be that, as with earlier cases we discussed, pious laypeople made donations during or after his auto-cremation that might have paid for the repair of the monastery. In this way self-immolation could sometimes be directed towards very parochial ends indeed, even if it appeared to invoke the cosmic principles of sympathetic resonance as Zhian's vow did. The interest in maintaining monasteries, which is not stressed in earlier collections, undoubtedly reflects real concerns about patronage within the Buddhist establishment in late imperial China.[27]

We have encountered many examples in which auto-cremation was prefaced by a vow and followed by weeks, months, or even years of preparation. But sometimes the act could occur almost randomly. Zhaizi 齋子 (d.u.) of

Zhusheng si 祝聖寺 on Nanyue led an austere life, never speaking or smiling and begging every day for a single bowl of rice.[28] One day he visited Tiefo si 鐵佛寺, where someone had left some lumber to make a fence. "Affected by this inducing cause," he set fire to the wood while sitting cross-legged within the pile, beating the wooden fish, and chanting the name of the Buddha. A couple of lines devoted to a monk called Huiming and appended to Zhaizi's biography recount a similar case of unannounced auto-cremation. The biography of Xingkong 性空 (d. 1807) is similarly brief.[29] The monk had recited the *Huayan jing* continuously for several decades, and the image of an arhat is said to have been seen among the flames of his pyre.

We have noted throughout this study that there really was no consensus of opinion on what exactly auto-cremation did for the practitioner. Did auto-cremators become buddhas or bodhisattvas? Were they bodhisattvas in disguise? Were they reborn in the Pure Land? Or were they perhaps primarily substitute sacrificial victims whose death provoked a response from a higher power? Evidently a wide variety of opinion was still being expressed in the Qing, when auto-cremation had been part of the religious scene for well over a thousand years. The story of the Spinner Monk (Luosi seng 絡絲僧, d.u.) offers a case in point.[30] This monk had been a spinner before he left home, hence his name. He lived alone in a derelict hermitage and chanted the name of the Buddha. When he found that he could not support himself, he went back to his old boss and agreed to spin in exchange for food. He did this for several years, then one day he turned up at the house of the layman Wu Xiling 吳西泠 (Wu Shuxu 吳樹虛, eighteenth century) and tried to sell him a basket full of useless scraps of paper.[31] Understandably bemused by this, the layman asked what he needed the money for. The monk replied that he needed to buy a load of firewood so that he could "return to the West." Apparently nonplussed by this response, Wu paid for the firewood. Later, when he arrived at the monk's hermitage to witness his promised "return," he found him sitting on top of a pile of blazing firewood:

> The monk was right in the middle of the fire. He raised his hand to Xiling in a gesture of farewell. Suddenly he wiped his face with his hand, immediately revealing its golden color, and he was instantly transformed. Xiling sighed and said, "Excellent! The amazing traces of the sages of the past have appeared again today." There were several hundred other onlookers who were all affected and lamented incessantly.[32]

In presenting the classic trope of the golden bodhisattva in disguise as a poor and simple monk, the biography uses the voice of the layman to underline how rare such a miracle was in late imperial times. In fact, as we have seen, there were many miraculous occurrences surrounding auto-cremation even if they did not correspond to the mode of earlier miracles.

Although one might think that the various methods of auto-cremation would have been exhausted by a certain point, we continue to find some quite bizarre twists on the means of transformation. The Qing monk Xiang-ying 香英 (d.u.) one day gathered his fellow monks and sat cross-legged, holding his bowl.[33] He used incense to light his toes, and the flames sprang up, lighting the whole room. All day long the fire burned up to his abdomen, but he continued to recite and chant. When the fire reached his chest he threw down his bowl and was transformed. That same day someone met him at Jifu si 集福寺 and asked where he was going. He replied, "To the Western lands." This person passed Xiangying's message on to one of his disciples, who found that his master's remains were about to be placed in a *stūpa*. He asked when Xiangying had died and realized that it was precisely when he had met the layman on the road. The miracle of Xiangying's bi-location here recalls the motif of the double that we mentioned above: Xiangying was si-multaneously burning and on his way to the Pure Land, which was not infre-quently named as a destination for late imperial auto-cremators. As for what inspired Xiangying to set fire to his toes, the biography offers us no clues.

The *Lotus Sūtra* clearly continued to be available as part of the repertoire of auto-cremators, but virtuosos were able to draw on an ever-expanding body of inspirations, justifications, aspirations, and methods. The discreet mention of going to the West as they prepared to depart or even as they did so was a trope that reflected a generalized aspiration for rebirth in Amitābha's Pure Land and one common to Buddhist practitioners of late imperial times.

Self-Immolation for the *Saṃgha*

We saw in our discussion of Daoxuan's collection, the *Xu gaoseng zhuan*, how the body of a single monk could be bartered with the state for the de-fense of the *saṃgha* as a whole. That this theme was not so discernable in Zanning's *Song gaoseng zhuan* is probably due to a couple of significant fac-tors: first, the lack of a strong and enduring central authority in the period from the mid-Tang to the early Song documented in that collection; and second, the fact that the Song compilation was commissioned by the em-peror. Self-immolation as a public act of atonement for the perceived mis-deeds of the *saṃgha* makes a dramatic reappearance in Minghe's collection with the biography of Yonglong 永隆 (1359–1392), which recalls specifically the example of Zhiyi's disciple Dazhi, who burned off his arm and subsequently died in an attempt to stop Sui Yangdi's proposed limit on the number of ordinands.[34]

The first Ming emperor, Taizu 太祖 (r. 1368–1398), who had himself been a monk before taking up arms against the Yuan regime, attempted to exercise tight control over the size of the *saṃgha* and in 1373 ordered that prospective monks and nuns be examined to test their knowledge of scriptures. In 1391 the Ministry of Rites was ordered to regulate Buddhism and Taoism even more thoroughly: From then on ordination was allowed only every three years, and there was a limit on the number of new monks ordained for each prefecture, department, and district. Male ordinands had to be over the age of forty, females over fifty. In 1392, as a further safeguard against people fraudulently claiming monastic status and thus exemption from taxes, a monastic register (*sengji ce* 僧籍冊) was prepared that listed the name, year of ordination, and ordination certificate number of every monk. It is against this background of legislation that the following events occurred.[35]

In 1392 there was an imperial ordination for monks, so Yonglong led his disciples to the capital, Jinling 金陵 (later called Nanjing 南京), to be examined on their scriptural knowledge and be presented with ordination certificates.[36] More than three thousand novices presented themselves for examination, but many of them had no knowledge of the scriptures and wished to obtain ordination certificates fraudulently. Taizu was irritated by this deception and dispatched the imperial bodyguard to arrest the novices and conscript them into the army.[37] Yonglong, not unnaturally distressed at this turn of events, submitted a memorial offering to burn his body to secure their release. As with Dazhi's burning of his arm, if we read between the lines we may assume that this action was designed to atone for the fraudulent actions of the few and provide an example of true monastic behavior that would shame the impostors. Of course it is hard to be certain about what happened exactly; because this record comes from a collection compiled under the Ming it is unlikely to contain anything that would reflect badly on the founder of that dynasty.

Taizu apparently assented to Yonglong's offer and ordered civil and military officials to escort him to Yuhua tai 雨華臺 .[38] There Yonglong bowed in the direction of the palace and composed the following verse:

As for this thirty-three-year-old phantom body,
The fire of the nature (*xinghuo* 性火) will clearly manifest true reality.
When the *Buddhadharma* of the great Ming prospers,
I will pray that the August Lineage (*huangtu* 皇圖) will last for a hundred
    million years.

He also took a stick of incense and wrote four characters on it: *fengtiao yushun* 風調雨順 (the wind and rain will be favorable [for crops]). This he gave to one of the officials and urged him to present it to the emperor, saying that it would be most efficacious if used to pray for rain. Then he burned himself. There was an unusual fragrance, and flocks of cranes soared over the pyre. Countless grains of *śarīra* were collected afterwards. As a consequence, the three thousand novices were pardoned and given ordination certificates. Sometime later there was a drought and Taizu ordered the officials of the Central Buddhist Registry (*senglu si* 僧錄司) to fetch the incense that Yonglong had left. The emperor led the people in praying for rain for three days and was rewarded with a heavy downfall. Taizu was delighted and told his assembled ministers, "This was truly the rain of Yonglong." He composed a poem, "Luopo seng" (落魄僧, The Monk Who Shed His Soul), to glorify his reputation.[39] Yonglong's disciples took his remains home and interred them beneath a *stūpa* on Yin shan 尹山.[40]

This is a very detailed and fascinating account, but so far I have been unable to correlate it with any event known in the official histories.[41] I suspect that something happened, but I would remain cautious about accepting Minghe's version of events without question. The story does at least show that the ideal of a monk sacrificing himself both to defend and to reform the *saṃgha* was still alive and well in the late Ming. It seems to steer a middle course between the kinds of public auto-cremation with the ruler in attendance that we saw in the fifth century and the slightly more confrontational nature of Dazhi's arm-burning. In this account, Yonglong's auto-cremation serves multiple purposes. The imprisoned are released, the emperor is mollified, the state prospers, later rainfall ensures continued fertility, and Yonglong earns a poem composed by no less a figure than the emperor himself.

Auto-Cremation and Rainmaking

Burning the body to pray for rain, alluded to in the story of Yonglong and also found in some cases discussed in earlier chapters, is an important element in the history of self-immolation.[42] The *Xin xu gaoseng zhuan* contains three interlinked accounts, which provide evidence of a powerful local tradition of rainmaking by Buddhist monks. Mingxing 明星 (ca. 1478–1568) became a novice at Bolin si 柏林寺 in Changsha (Hunan), where one day he fed a beggar.[43] The head monk did not approve of this act of charity, so he expelled him from the monastery. The beggar (who was of course no ordinary vagrant) took Mingxing into the mountains, where he taught him his occult techniques for influencing the weather.

In 1568 there was a severe drought and it did not rain for three months. The people were getting restless, and the governor was growing concerned. Mingxing vowed that if it did not rain in three days he would burn his body. The official built an altar, put firewood on top, and ordered him to climb onto it. The monk performed his rituals devoutly and sincerely but at the end of three days the sun was still blazing in the sky. The governor thought that he had been misled and angrily ordered that the fire be lit. When the fire was a few feet from the altar, suddenly a great wind sprang up and blew away the dust, and then the rains fell. The biography concludes, "Later people founded a monastery to commemorate this. Whenever there is a drought many 'carriages and canopies' (that is, high-ranking officials) come to the monastery [to pray for rain]. Even on a scorching day there will be clouds there."

Two biographies are appended to that of Mingxing. The first is of a monk known as "the Worthy of the Maṇḍala" (Mantuluo zunzhe 曼荼羅尊者), who lived sometime during the Wanli 萬歷 period (1573–1620) of the Ming.[44] His *dharma* name was Zhou Fu 周福. He was also commonly called Zhou Transcendent (Zhou xian 仙) or Master Zhou the True Man (Zhou gong zhenren 周公真人), both titles having Taoist associations. The biography describes him as an "outstanding person (*longxiang* 龍象) of the esoteric lineage (Mizong 密宗)," an unusual designation for the period long after the supposed heyday of esoteric Buddhism in China. The biography explains that Chan was the most fashionable form of practice at the time, but many people merely stole examples from *yulu* and imitated them as if that would make them enlightened. It also goes on to say that there was a certain amount of disillusionment with this kind of "wild fox" Chan. Zhou Fu particularly despised this fashion and instead applied himself to a kind of practice that had fallen out of favor: Reading Mahāyāna *vaipulya sūtras*, *dhāraṇī*, and the esoteric section of the canon. In a simple hermitage below Heimi 黑糜 peak he concentrated on his esoteric study and built an altar, which he called a *"maṇḍala."* After having cultivated such practices for several decades:

> One day he announced to his followers, "The causes that underlie my teaching in the world are about to come to an end. I must follow the Buddha's example and join the bath of fire." He sent them into the mountains to fetch firewood. He stacked it up several yards (*zhang* 丈) high, bathed and changed his clothes, and sat cross-legged on top. He ordered his disciples to light the fire, but they were all afraid and none dared approach. Fu held the wooden fish, chanting spells clearly, and the fire suddenly and spontaneously burst

into flames. Again he addressed his followers, "If there is a drought in the future, you should call my name, and rain will fall heavily." From the Wanli period of the Ming onwards, when the villagers pray for rain they just call out
"Zhou xian!" or they shout "Zhou ye" (周爺, Father Zhou)! When this happens there are many numinous responses. It is related that when the rain
comes, mixed up with the wind and rain are the sounds of the wooden fish
and chanted spells—just as at the time of his fiery transformation.[45]

Burning the body to pray for rain was a practice with roots in ancient
Chinese history. Buddhists co-opted this speciality and made it part of their
repertoire of thaumaturgy. In the case of both the esoteric practitioner and
Mingxing the places associated with their offerings became new sacred sites
imbued with the power to bring rain in response to the demands of local
people. It is interesting that Yonglong, Mingxing, and Zhou Fu were able to
cause rain to fall even after they had apparently departed the scene, suggesting that their deaths had given them something of the power of local
deities—men who had died yet were able to answer the prayers of the living.

Canling 參靈 (d. 1644) was a contemporary of Zhou Fu and also from
Changsha.[46] The biographer refers repeatedly and indignantly to the fact
that Canling's name had been miswritten in the local gazetteers as 餐苓 (eating numinous fungus), "as if he were a divine immortal—which he was not!"
Like Zhou Fu he favored the esoteric *sūtras*, and when he grew up he travelled as far as Western Shu (Eastern Tibet) to obtain transmission of the
mudrās. While there he got hold of a copy of the major Tantric text *Yujia da-
jiao wang jing* 瑜伽大教王經 *(Mahāyoga tantra),* which he studied intently.
When he returned to Changsha, he lived as a hermit on Jilong shan 集龍山 in
Hunan for more than forty years. He allowed his nails and hair to grow long
and people who encountered him took him for a transcendent.

At the beginning of the Shunzhi 順治 reign period (1644–1662) of the
Qing, Canling came off the mountain and stacked up firewood on the
banks of the Baisha 白沙 river. He bathed and lit the fire, then sat and recited the *Mahāyoga tantra* as usual. Suddenly there was a great gust of wind
and peals of thunder, and in an instant his body was transformed before the
eyes of the assembled witnesses, winning the admiration of the Buddhist
community. The fact that this happened at the beginning of the Qing
might lead one to suspect that this was an act of loyalty to the Ming, but subsequent events may argue against this interpretation. A monastery was
founded to commemorate Canling on Jilong shan and there the monks
fashioned an image of him and made offerings to it: "Whenever there was a
drought, a flood, or an epidemic, the gentry and the masses prayed for sal-

vation and always obtained a response. Right down to today, the burning of incense continues to be abundant."

In time Canling actually became a local deity. The biography relates that in 1867 the villagers and gentry of the area composed a written account of his deeds, which they submitted to the court requesting that he receive imperial recognition. Canling was accordingly granted the title "True Man All-Encompassing Protector" (Puhu zhenren 溥護真人). If he had in fact been some kind of Ming loyalist, this detail had obviously been long forgotten by this time. The biography concludes with another heartfelt protest against "successive monographs and documents" that had incorrectly placed him in the category of transcendents and those who had mistakenly classified him as a "Buddhist immortal" (fomen xianzi 佛門仙子). The case of Canling shows us that there was not only competition within Buddhism to claim certain self-immolators for Chan or Pure Land, but that other ideologies, those of Taoism and the state, also had interests in taking these figures into their own pantheons. The substitution of the *Mahāyoga tantra* for the *Lotus Sūtra* as a text to chant while burning offers an interesting twist on the power of recitation and the transformational powers of the ritual text.

Spontaneous Combustion

Cases of auto-cremation described in the later biographical collections often employed the conceit that the act was a form of *samādhi* rather than the mundane lighting of a stack of wood. We noted an earlier example of this idea in the biography of the eccentric Tang monk Master Bundle of Grass and in the scriptural precedents supplied by Zanning in his comments on that text. In the biography of Ningyi 寧義 (d. 1583) we read:

> In the *guiwei* 癸未 year of the Wanli reign period (1583), he stacked up firewood and burned himself. As soon as the torch was raised, his body started to burn "like a rotten root" and was soon completely consumed. A wise person declared, "He has entered the fiery *samādhi*."[47]

Thus was auto-cremation conflated with the *samādhi* of fire. But in other biographies this *samādhi* came to be invoked with increasing frequency as the actual means of auto-cremation. The *Bu xu gaoseng zhuan* contains two examples of this phenomenon, and the *Xin xu gaoseng zhuan* even more. The Yuan monk Delin 德林 (fl. mid-fourteenth century), a native of Dongou 東甌, resided at Zheze si 柘澤寺 in Shanghai 上海 during the Zhizheng 至正 period (1341–1367).[48] One day he suddenly asked for a coffin (*kan* 龕), saying that he would burn his body on the first day of the ninth month.[49] People did not believe him and ignored his request. On the appointed day he traded his bag and bowl for some firewood, which he placed around him. Fire rose from his body, and the shocked onlookers prostrated themselves. They were concerned that his auto-cremation would not bring good fortune to the locale, but Delin replied from amidst the flames that "there will be no problem after the rain passes." The suggestion that the rain should wash away his ashes seems to be an interesting admission that the remains of an auto-cremator could be a source of ill fortune rather than the precious relics we usually see in such biographies.

The second case, from the Ming, is somewhat more detailed and reveals more of the doctrinal implications of spontaneous auto-cremation. According to the *Bu xu gaoseng zhuan,* Shanxin 善信 (*zi* Wuyi 無疑, No Doubt, d.u.) became a monk at the age of twenty-nine and being illiterate he engaged solely in Chan meditation. He suddenly attained awakening and announced, "Since I left home I have not lain down on the mat, and today I have done all that ought to be done." (Traditionally this was what arhats said before they entered *nirvāṇa.*) Sometime later he appeared to be slightly ill and asked to be bathed and placed in a coffin. A fire sprang up instantaneously and consumed his body. The biographer comments, "This was surely a case of someone who attained awakening and who was eager to enter *nirvāṇa.*" The verse eulogy appended to the biography compares Shanxin favorably with the Medicine King, who left *saṃsāra* only to re-enter it. For Shanxin, on the other hand, "ultimately, how could there be any further coming or going?" It is somewhat surprising that the claim that a Chinese monk should have reached such a level as to enter *nirvāṇa* immediately after attaining awakening is rather rare. We saw an analogous case in the biography of the "monk who tested the pagoda" in Chapter 5.

The biography of Shanxin in the *Xin xu gaoseng zhuan* is slightly but significantly different from that in the *Bu xu gaoseng zhuan,* suggesting that competing traditions had co-opted his story for their own ends.[50] First, the *Xin xu gaoseng zhuan* makes him a practitioner of *nianfo* rather than *dhyāna* and attributes his enlightenment to reading *sūtra*s and *śāstra*s. Second, it claims that his awakening came at Fangshui an 放水庵 in Shanghai under a master called Zhide 智德 rather than on Xuanmu shan 玄墓山 under the *upādhyāya* Wanfeng 萬峰和尚. Third, it omits the verse eulogy comparing him with the Medicine King. Fourth, the *Xin xu gaoseng zhuan* maintains that a *stūpa* was erected for him and that his fellow monks had his image painted. But both biographies agree on the fact that he was bathed and placed in his coffin and that a blaze spontaneously sprang up and burned him. The existence of two biographies with quite different religious pedigrees for Shanxin shows that the sectarian interests of Chan and Pure Land biographers drove them to claim auto-cremators for their own traditions.

But are these cases of spontaneous combustion quite what they appear to be? A biography of the Ming monk Mingxiu 明秀 (d.u.) of Jingmen suggests otherwise.[51] The account begins conventionally enough: After forty years in Jingmen, one day Mingxiu bathed, did obeisance to the Buddha, and announced that he was going to the West. As he sat cross-legged on his meditation mat, fire shot out from within his body, rapidly consuming him while he chanted the name of the Buddha. The account goes on to reveal that the meditation mat was actually placed on top of a large stack of firewood and kindling that was used to supply the kitchens. Mingxiu's disciples had apparently failed to notice that he was sitting on top of a fire that was already lit, and so they suspected nothing. The biographer concludes, "Not until the flames blazed up did they feel frightened and amazed. He had accumulated devotion [to the Buddha] for so long, it was really no coincidence [that this happened]."

Perhaps all cases of spontaneous combustion can be explained in this manner, but many accounts speak of monks exhaling jets of flame from the nose or mouth and give no hint of any suspicion of trickery. Witness the case of Kangzhai 康齋, who suddenly announced one day that he had to leave and begged for a bundle of firewood from the local villagers.[52] This he stacked up in a vacant spot. Seated on top of the wood, he covered his head in an oil-soaked turban and "spat out *samādhi* fire to burn himself." But then he lifted off the turban and shouted that there was a pious woman in the audience whose "*qi* of birth within her" was conflicting with his attempt to burn himself. Sure enough, a pregnant woman was in the audience. After she was pointed out and had retreated, blushing, Kangzhai replaced the turban and was able to burn himself.

The fact that female pollution was able to prevent the successful completion of Kangzhai's act is rather revealing. Whereas there is never any hint in the Indian literature we have discussed that the miraculous powers of buddhas and bodhisattvas could be hindered by natural forces, especially by impurity, the situation on the ground in late imperial China was clearly somewhat different. It was understood, for example, that incendiary magic, such as that performed by the Boxers in the rebellion of 1898–1900, could be frustrated by impurities in the surrounding conditions.[53] Women in particular were regarded as sources of contamination. The power of naked, menstruating, or urinating women to negate or destroy ritual and magic was well known in the Ming and continues to be attested today.[54] We should perhaps look for explanations and understandings of spontaneous combustion in

China in the larger religious scene of the post-Song period and not just in the Buddhist sources.

The transformation of the Ming monk Langran 朗然 (d.u.) was doubly miraculous: He spontaneously combusted and managed to leave behind a whole-body relic.[55] The biography describes him as dull and stupid but very upright in conduct. Despite, or perhaps because of, this he was highly respected by the local populace. One day he met an old monk on Pan shan 盤山 in Hubei and received from him a certain method of chanting the name of Amitābha, which he then practiced for the next three years. In response to his chanting, "an internal fire burned him, but his body was not destroyed. [The skin] looked like old copper, and it made a sound when struck. Nowadays it is worshipped in the hermitage." The early-Qing Chan poet-monk Zhuoan Zhipu 拙庵智樸 (fl. 1671) composed a poem about him, which is preserved in the biography.[56] The poem reiterates that Langran was dull-witted but extols his constant "upholding of the six characters" (Namu Amituo fo 南無阿彌陀佛) and his wish to see Amitābha. Zhipu also praised the preservation of his body, which he saw as proof that even in the end times (moshi 末世), a person of limited capacity was able to attain awakening. Zhipu's accolades might very well be applied to all of the later examples of self-immolation. Whatever else they meant, these extraordinary acts were often taken as signs that the highest awakening could still take place on Chinese soil, even in a time and place far removed from the Buddha or the great Chinese sage-monks of the past.

Langran's biography suggests that his spontaneous combustion was a direct result of his diligent chanting of nianfo, which accords with the ubiquity of the practice in post-Tang Buddhism. This supposition also holds true for some related biographies of the seventeenth century. Hairun 海潤 (d. 1690) arrived on Huashan 華山 in Jiangning 江甯 in the third month of Kangxi 康熙 29 (April 4–May 8, 1690).[57] Asked what his practice was, he replied simply, "Nianfo." Asked why he had come to Huashan, he answered, "For a matter of life and death at noon on the first day of the fourth month." On that day people saw a fire blazing on the summit of the mountain and found Hairun sitting cross-legged on Guiren peak 貴人峰 with fire rushing out of his eyes, ears, mouth, and nose. His body remained upright and did not fall over even when the fire had burned out. This biography ambitiously connects nianfo, spontaneous combustion, the correct posture at the moment of death, and a mountain site.

There are two biographies appended to that of Hairun, and they make similar connections between nianfo and spontaneous combustion. The first is of an unnamed monk of Changjing 長涇.[58] Like Langran he is described as dull and stupid, but unlike him he was not held in high esteem by others. He practiced only *nianfo* and one day he suddenly announced that he had to leave the next day. On the morrow he kept asking his disciples whether it was midday yet. As soon as they told him that it was noon he sat cross-legged on a seat; fire shot out of his mouth and incinerated him. High noon seems to have been a preferred time of death in many late imperial biographies and may be related to earlier Taoist ideas of the transcendent who "ascends in broad daylight."[59] Presumably this monk "ascended" by fire to the Pure Land.

An unnamed monk of Luoshu 羅墅 chanted *nianfo* single-mindedly, just like Langran and Hairun.[60] When he knew that his time had come, he gave away his bowl and begged for a bundle of firewood. The faithful supplied a large amount of fuel, which "he stacked up for several days until it was like a mountain." More than a thousand people came to witness his departure. Fire shot out of his mouth and burned his body. The fact that all these miraculous transformations are attributed to the power of *nianfo* may represent an upping of the rhetorical stakes designed to promote this particular practice as efficacious even for the least able practitioners. Suddenly illiterate and dull-witted monks were able to make the highest attainments of the buddhas and arhats of the past who had spontaneously combusted at the end of their earthly lives.

Spontaneous combustion could represent a way of burning the body in situations where help in igniting it the usual way was not forthcoming. One day Liaoan 了庵 (fl. Qianlong 乾隆 period, 1736–1795) stacked up firewood in front of the monastery courtyard and sat upright on the top.[61] Repeatedly chanting the name of the Buddha, he ordered the monks to light the fire, but none of them obeyed. When the distant smell of a burning candle reached his nose, he exhaled and fire shot straight out of his nose, burning his face, robes, and body. All the while he continued to chant, and facing the west, he was quickly transformed into smoke and flames.

Xingcan 惺參 (1742–1818) became a monk at forty after the death of his parents.[62] One day, after a long and successful career, he addressed his disciples, reminding them that all the buddhas and arhats had awoken to the teaching of the *Diamond Sūtra*. He urged them to bear the *sūtra* in mind constantly and informed them that at the age of seventy-six he no longer wished to remain in the impure realm and that he was about to "depart for the West." He ordered his disciples to stack up firewood in the monastery. In the autumn, on Jiaqing 嘉慶 *wuyin* 戊寅 7.15 (August 16, 1818)—the day of the ghost festival—Xingcan climbed on top of the pyre and recited his death verse:

> Right from the beginning there is no coming,
> Now how could there be any going?

The lamp of wisdom is not extinguished,
Like a single torch on the "numinous terrace."[63]
The wind sweeps through the branches,
The moon is reflected at the bottom of the pond.
People protect the *dharma* well,
What is the difference between life and death?[64]

Xingcan's poem points to the connection between the lamp of the *dharma,* passed down from master to disciple in the Chan lineage, and the flames soon to consume his body. After he had recited the verse, flames shot out from within him and a plume of fragrant smoke rose into the sky. Among his remains, seven grains of *śarīra* were found, and they were interred in seven *stūpa*s in front of Ciyun si 慈雲寺. The elements of this biography—the emphasis on the *Diamond Sūtra,* the death verse, and the spontaneous combustion —seem calculated to present Xingcan's death as a quintessential Chan master's performance of self-immolation, and yet even he announced his intention to leave for the Pure Land to the West.

As we have seen, spontaneous combustion in late imperial China seems to have become almost an expected theme in the repertoire of the monkish imagination. Although it evoked powerful claims to the powers of an advanced practitioner, it simultaneously allowed self-immolators and/or their biographers to sidestep the question of agency. If the flames arose spontaneously, there really was no "self" in self-immolation.

Spontaneous Death and Mummification

The cases of spontaneous combustion we have seen may have been inspired by scriptural accounts of arhats and bodhisattvas who went up in flames of their own volition.[65] But they are also part of what appears to have been an increased interest in the larger theme of spontaneous death. Several such cases are included in the self-immolation sections of the later biographical collections. Self-immolation remained so flexible a category that it could incorporate modes of dying in which there seemed to be almost no conscious effort to discard the body for any particular purpose. To die effortlessly seems to have been accounted sufficient, although to leave behind a mummy was always appreciated and to use one's own death as a means of preaching the *dharma* was clearly considered ideal.

For example, a nameless Huaseng 化僧 (Transformation Monk) was well known to the people of the marketplaces in Pi 郫 and Fan 繁 in Sichuan.[66] At dawn on Chongning 崇寧 5.12.2 (December 28, 1106), he came into the city to beg for food. Having worked out that it was afternoon from the position of the sun in the sky, he suddenly put his clothes in a bag as if he were about to leave. He went to the eastern end of the market and begged for some soup. Then he straightened his clothes and sat cross-legged. Before the soup was served he was pronounced dead. The biographer records "his jadelike bones stood there like a mountain, not leaning to one side or another," thus emphasizing the importance of his upright posture in death. His body was taken back to a valley north of Pi and enshrined in a niche (*kan* 龕). Minghe notes that his mummy was still there in his day.

Appended to the biography is a written account by Yang Tianhui 楊天惠 (doctoral candidate, 1080), a native of Pi. Yang praises the unknown monk at length, and records his feelings of joy and fond remembrance on seeing the mummy's face. It is not surprising to find literati writing of such marvels, but what may surprise some are the personal sentiments expressed and the emotive language employed here. Once again we are reminded that peasants and men of letters participated in the same cults in traditional China. Yang's eulogy reads:

> Remarkable! This is something I have never seen before. This great master did not keep separate from the din and clamor of the marketplace yet manifested tranquillity. He did not despise butchers and wine sellers as defiled and deluded but manifested purity and righteousness. He did not cast aside the stains and evils of *saṃsāra* but manifested ultimate truth. He did not take pleasure in external appearances or like to display ornamentation but manifested a tough solidity. In speech his accent was harmonious and gentle, close to that of the local area, but no one knew his family or personal name. His skin was emaciated and tough, looking like a person of around seventy, but no one knew his age or the length of his ordination. His robes and boots were simple and rustic, making him look like a patch-robed practitioner in the forest, but no one knew where he lived. Oh dear! When he was alive I did not know to follow the master and associate with him; not until he is gone does it occur to me to record his traces. This is a case of the saying "Carving the boat [to find the sword]."[67] However, by virtue of what I say here, one might see the master's appearance and give rise to thoughts of joy and fond remembrance, perfecting the actions of purity and faith. Hopefully this may provide a way for people to enter [the Buddhist path].[68]

In this lengthy eulogy Yang speaks admiringly of the monk's ability to remain detached from the world and sees his mummy not as a curiosity or even a memorial, but as an opportunity to feel happy and nostalgic about the master and to turn one's mind to the teachings of Buddhism. Even for those who were not members of the *saṃgha,* self-immolation and its relics could be seen as ways of propagating the faith. What is worth noting here is the tone employed in writing of such matters: "Joy and fond remembrance" are not the emotions one might expect when gazing at a preserved corpse.

The Jin-dynasty Chan master Faqing 法慶 (1071–1143) of Dajue si 大覺寺 in Xianping fu 咸平府, whose master was Foguo Weibo 佛國惟白 (fl. 1101), taught his disciple a lesson in how to die.[69] One day the disciple was reading through the account of the "Vegetarian Feast for the Foolish" (*yuchi zhai* 愚癡齋) in the *Dongshan lu* 洞山錄 (Record of Dongshan) and commented that the Chan masters of the past were truly amazing.[70] Faqing told him that when he died his disciple was to shout and he would come back again, thus proving that spiritual power could still be generated by religious cultivation. He correctly foretold the time of his death, composed a verse, and gave away his possessions. On the appointed day, at the sound of the first bell of the night, he died sitting upright:

> His disciple shouted as promised, and the master opened his eyes and said, "What?" The disciple said, "Master, why have you stripped off and departed?" The master said, "What did I have when I came into this world?" The disciple wanted to make him wear his robes, but the master said, "Stop. Leave them for later people." The disciple said, "What is it actually like right now?" The master said, "It's just as it is." He composed another verse:
> Seventy-three years have been like a flash of lightning.
> Before leaving, let me get a thread through for you.
> [It is like] an iron ox leaping to Silla,
> Breaking the empty sky into seven or eight pieces.
> He was seventy-three. This was on Huangtong 皇統 3.5.5 (June 19, 1143).[71]

There is a self-consciously unconventional Chan flavor to this account. Faqing stripped himself naked, symbolizing his complete detachment from the world. He transcended the distinction between life and death, showing it to be ultimately empty. But he commented on his experience in verse, thus creating another literary artefact to be passed on in the Chan tradition and to provide opportunities for later students to be awakened. Thus even death could be co-opted into Chan's own story about itself.

The Ming monk Dayun 大雲 (fl. mid-sixteenth century) also used his own death as a form of teaching.[72] He began his career as a monk at Jixiang si 吉祥寺 in the northern capital (Beijing 北京, Beiping fu 北平府), where he was a junior fellow disciple of Daji 大極 (d.u.). In the Jiajing 嘉靖 reign period

(1522–1566) he lived at Guangde si 廣德寺, where he kept order over the other monks. There were two monks in particular who would not stop fighting each other. Dayun provided a feast for them to try and calm them down:

> And he told them, "On one occasion in the past in the northern capital my elder brother Daji put his hands together and chanted this: 'I wish to be re-born in the Western Pure Land, to have the nine grades of lotuses as my mother and father.' After which he passed away, sitting up. Now to solve your argument for you, I will emulate my elder [*dharma*] brother in dying of his own will." Accordingly, he sat cross-legged with his palms together and recited the two stanzas above. As he finished speaking, he passed away.[73]

Clearly the Chan tradition did not own a monopoly on dying in a way that was both controlled and "natural," simultaneously predicted and spontaneous.

The Yuan monk Jueqing 覺慶 (fl. ca. 1341–1367) followed his disciple into death and became a mummy.[74] Jueqing stressed the merits of practices such as surfacing roads, digging wells, donating hot water, running tea stalls, and providing acupuncture and medicine.[75] During the Zhizheng era, he went to Yunjian 雲間 (Songjiang 松江, Jiangsu). During a meeting of the Pu-zhao fohui 普炤佛會 (Buddha Assembly of Universal Radiance), he set his date of death as the twenty-third day of the first month (the precise year is not specified). Subsequently he wrote letters of farewell to his friends in the wine shops (*quyuan* 麴院) of Siming 四明 and Hangzhou. Two days later, Jueqing announced:

> Although I have stood under the bright moon until beyond the third watch,
> How few people come, defying this bone-chilling cold.
> Now that I have already announced that I shall return home,
> Why should I remain?

After Jueqing finished reciting these lines, he died. His followers at first wished to cremate him but found his body was still sweating. Ten days later he still looked as if he were alive and his hair and whiskers were still growing. A pious layman, Chen Yuanjian 陳源堅 (d. after 1341), donated his home as a chapel in which Jueqing's mummy was enshrined and lacquered.

Martyrs for the People and Empire

The biography of the Song monk Sijing 思淨 (before 1070–1137) recalls those of the late-Tang monks Hongxiu and Quanhuo, which we discussed in the previous chapter.[76] Like them, he lived in violent times and offered his body to save the lives of others when confronted by attackers. In 1126, ten years before his death, the Jurchen Jin suddenly occupied the whole of North China, driving the remnants of the Song forces south of the Yangzi river. Sijing—known by the sobriquet Yu Mituo 喻彌陀 because of his secular surname, Yu 喻, and his skill in painting Amitābha 阿彌陀—lived on the northern frontier.[77] He went in person to the enemy stronghold and offered his life if the enemy would spare the city (which city is not clear from the biography). According to the text, "the enemy were so astonished they reduced their attacks and many lives were saved."[78] Appended to Sijing's biography is an account of Jingzhen 淨真 (fl. 1237–1240), who "also donated his life for beings and had Master (Si)jing's style of going to the stronghold and offering his life."[79] The threat this time came not from invaders to the north but floodwaters in the south, and Jingzhen solved the problem in a remarkable manner. Arriving in Qiantang 錢塘 (in Hangzhou) he found that the river had burst its banks. Zhenjing wrote in verse to the military commissioner (*anfu* 安撫) Zhao Duanming 趙端明 (Zhao Yuhuan 趙與懽 [*jinshi* 1214]), announcing his intention to visit the palace of the *nāga* beneath the sea to petition him to stop the flood.[80] He threw himself into the sea, and right after reporting the success of his mission, he dived in again, never to re-emerge. His act of heroism was reported to the court, and the emperor bestowed on him the title "Dharma Master Protector of the State" (*huguo fashi* 護國法師) and set up a memorial to him in Huiling 會靈.[81]

The fact that these two biographies are paired in our source alerts us to the fundamental assumption that warfare and banditry were classified as natural disasters, just like floods. The stronghold of rebels and the palace of the *nāga* are explicitly compared by Minghe. Monks who protected the state against barbarians from the North or aquatic monsters from the South, against flood, famine, drought, or bandits, often received comparable rewards such as posthumous titles. Sijing and Jingzhen countered war and flood with very similar acts because those disasters were seen as expressions of the same kind of disruption of natural cycles.

Death by Water

Self-immolation by water was never as popular as auto-cremation in China, but a few examples will suffice to show that it could be just as public and emotional an event as mounting the pyre in front of a weeping crowd. The following biographies present monks who chose to stage their own deaths with a truly dramatic flair.

The Southern Song monk Miaopu妙普of Qinglong an青龍庵in Huating
華亭 was a Chan monk, and all his life he had great admiration for the Tang
Chan master known as the Boatman Ācārya (Chuanzi *heshang*船子和尚), who
had also lived in Huating.[82] He built a hermitage on the plain of Qinglong,
along the banks of the Xiu river 秀水, which runs through Zhejiang from the
Grand Canal in the north. His only possession was an iron flute, with which
he composed song lyrics. (Some examples are preserved in his biography.)
Towards the end of the Northern Song, rebel troops under Xu Ming 徐明 (d.
1128) passed through the nearby town of Wuzhen 烏鎮, pillaging and killing.[83] The population took fright, but Miaopu presented himself to the bandits, wrote his own funerary memorial, and invited them to behead him.
They let him go and the population was saved.

In the winter of 1142, he made a big basin with holes, which he plugged
up because he wished to die in the water. He then wrote to a colleague on
Mount Xuedou 雪竇.[84] This person replied with the following *gāthā*:

> Oh, come on, old Xingkong!
> You wish to feed the fish and turtles?
> Why don't you go ahead,
> Instead of just keeping on telling people about it?[85]

When Miaopu saw that his colleague understood his intention, he laughed.
He preached his final sermon in verse:

> Sitting down to attain liberation, standing up to die:[86]
> Nothing compares to water burial.
> First, one saves on wood for burning,
> Second, one avoids having to dig a pit.
> Then let me drop my responsibilities so that I may go.
> Why should I not take pleasure in it?
> Who understands my music?
> The Boatman is my true teacher![87]
> It is certainly not easy to maintain refined manners for hundreds of
>   thousands of years;
> But very few people can sing the song of the fishermen![88]

Miaopu sat cross-legged in the basin and, playing his flute, he started to
sink into the waves. His disciples urged him to turn around, but they noticed
that not a drop of water had yet entered the basin. Then, turned around by
the current, he sang his swan song:

After more than sixty years, I am returning to my hometown;
Marvellous, immeasurable is this place where my traces are sinking.
My true manner I entrust to whoever knows music:[89]
Playing my flute puts an end to this scene.[90]

The people watched him drift away until they could no longer see his
flute but could hear its notes drifting up into the sky. Then they saw him
throw the flute into the air and sink beneath the waves; they cried and wept.
Three days later they found his body on the sand, sitting upright as if still alive.
They kept him for five days and then cremated him, obtaining *śarīra* as big as
beans. Two cranes flew continually over the pyre. His remains were interred
in a *stūpa* at Qinglong an.

The verses that are preserved in this biography suggest that the ideal
model of death for a Chan master was one in which he performed literally
until the final curtain. The emphasis is on the ease and naturalness of death—
something that is probably a good deal easier to present in verse and by volun-
tary termination than in the kinds of spontaneous passing away we saw above.

Our Ming collection contains the biographies of two other drowners:
Yetai夜臺 (d. 1610) and Qiuyue秋月 (d. 1621).[91] Their narratives appear together and Minghe's appended comment explores what he sees as an interesting contrast between two types of self-immolator. Yetai had a long and
eventful career, roaming all over the empire and gaining imperial recognition, whereas Qiuyue was a complete recluse who refused to talk to anyone.
Yet they met the same ends. We have noted throughout this study how self-
immolation was a practice that cut across the whole of the *saṃgha* in China.
From Chan monks, to scholars, to Pure Land believers, all kinds of monks
and nuns found valid reasons for offering their bodies.

Yetai was a native of Western Shu and in his youth had "cultivated techniques of gymnastics and avoidance of grain." This suggests that he had Taoist training of some kind, although whether he was actually an ordained
priest or only a dilettante remains unknown. But when he met a Buddhist
master on Emei shan峨眉山, he took the tonsure. Immediately afterwards he
began his travels around the major mountain sites of Buddhism. He spent
some time on Mount Wutai, where he often fasted and consumed only water.
His habit of sitting in meditation all day and roaming the mountain by night
earned him the nickname "Yetai" (Night Terraces). His practice recalls the
repeated circuits of the mountain made by Wuran, whom we discussed in
Chapter 5, and perhaps Yetai was even aware of his predecessor's story.

Unlike Wuran, Yetai left Wutai shan and gained considerable fame at
court. After some twenty years of roaming around on his beloved mountain,

he came to the capital in 1603, where the empress dowager Cisheng 慈聖 (1546–1614) bestowed on him a bowl, a staff, and a purple *kāṣāya*.[92] Earlier he had held a thousand-bowl assembly (*qianpan hui* 千盤會) at Tayuan si 塔院 寺 and a dragon-flower assembly for the Buddha's birthday at Longquan si 龍 泉寺.[93] He had two huge bells cast for Emei and Wutai shan and requested from the court two Buddhist canons for Mount Putuo 普陀 and Mount Emei. On Jiuhua shan he established a ritual space (*daochang* 道場) for the water-land assembly (*shuilu hui* 水陸會).[94] He donated money and grain to hermitages and poor monks and won the respect of both religious and laity for never pocketing any for himself.

One day, after arriving in Guangling 廣陵, Yetai suddenly fell ill, and a certain "man of the way" (*daoren* 道人) cut off his finger to make a soup to cure him.[95] Yetai was not impressed with this vain attempt to postpone the inevitable and declared that his time was near. When he recovered from his illness, he bought a large boat and placed a "water-land" image in it.[96] In the tenth month of the *gengxu* 庚戌 year (1610), he dismissed his followers and kept by him only one old disciple. As they were climbing into the boat, two merchants arrived and asked if they could travel with them. Yetai replied that they had some karmic connection with him and allowed them to board his boat. At midday he fed his two guests and they gave him some alms in exchange.

> Then he bowed to the buddhas of the ten directions and said, "I wish to return home to the sea." The witnesses were startled and said, "We are already in the middle of the sea now, how can you return?" The master said, "I have heard that the Bodhisattva Jietuo 解脫, as he was nearing the end of his life, admonished his disciples to divide his body into three.[97] One part he donated to the birds and beasts; one he donated to the fish and turtles; one he donated to crickets and ants. I shall now do the same." The witnesses wailed and cried and pulled him back. The master produced a letter and handed it to his guests. It contained those very words of the Bodhisattva Jietuo. They would not stop wailing and pulling at him, so the master said, "Bow to the Buddha for me." They all bowed, and the master jumped into the sea in a single bound. They wanted to take in the sails and save the master. The master was sitting upright on the waves. He waved his hand and said, "If you take the sail down, you will capsize!" In the next instant a white and yellow mist closed over the master and he was gone. This was on Wanli 38 (*gengxu*) 10.25 (December 9, 1610). The old "man of the way" came back and reported it. Chen Meigong 陳眉公 of Huating 華亭 composed a written record of this occurrence.[98]

Yetai's monastic career involved ascetic practices, but he was not an obscure hermit known only to his neighbors. He was recognized by the court
and active on behalf of the *saṃgha* as a whole throughout the empire. His offering of his corpse to the fish and turtles at the end of his life is not in sharp
contrast to the dedication he showed others throughout his life. The man who
composed his biography was Chen Jiru 陳繼儒 (1558–1639), a well-known
contemporary poet, calligrapher, painter, and recluse.[99] Obviously, self-immolators continued to attract literati to compose their memorial inscriptions.

Qiuyue was an old monk who had spent his whole career on Xuanmu shan
in Suzhou. His practice focused on the precepts, prostration, and recitation,
but he also made drinking tea a Buddhist practice. If high-ranking and refined
visitors called, Qiuyue would not see them, or if he did see them he would not
drink tea with them. In 1621 he took his leave of his fellow monks for the sea. As
he was sailing along the coast, he suddenly stood up at the prow of the boat and
performed prostrations, calling the name of the Buddha in a loud voice. Then
he jumped into the waves. The crew tried in vain to pull him out. "At the time
the wind and waves were strong. The master appeared and sank between the
waves; he still had his palms together and was calling the name of the Buddha.
The sound gradually drew further away from the boat and was lost."[100]

Minghe comments on these two biographies, explicitly contrasting the
active public service of Yetai with the more passive reclusion of Qiuyue. Although this contrast is made explicit only here, it probably applies to many
earlier biographies. For Minghe, although their lives may have been very different, their final achievement was the same and they were thus equally
praiseworthy. He concludes:

> Yetai travelled around the four famous mountains, and his footsteps cov-
> ered the whole country. Qiuyue remained quietly ensconced in a single
> chamber, unaware of matters beyond his own door. Yetai broadly cultivated
> meritorious *karma*, whereas Qiuyue did not do a single thing. In their lives
> the two masters differed from each other so strikingly, but they were not
> the slightest bit different in the last act of their lives.
>
> Generally speaking, Yetai concealed quietude beneath activity, while
> Qiuyue hid action beneath tranquillity. The traces of these two masters, ac-
> tivity and tranquillity, enabled them to escape the boundaries of *saṃsāra*, to
> be without bondage or hindrance. These minds of the two masters truly
> cannot be judged as to which is superior and which inferior.[101]

Minghe's comments are instructive when considering all of the biographies we have explored: They may seem diverse, but for their compilers there

was a sense in which all of the subjects were equal in the offering of their bodies. Self-immolation as a somatic path, interestingly, never seems to have become the preserve of one tradition, lineage, or even type of monk. In late imperial times we see it adopted by Chan masters, *nianfo* reciters, eccentric hermits, and more sophisticated and worldly monks. Liberation through abandoning the body was open to all of them and could be translated into any idiom that was appropriate. Chan masters used shouts and verbal play as part of their death rituals. Esoteric adepts chanted tantric texts as they burned. Although scriptural antecedents continued to be cited (as by Yetai), the spontaneous act of Qiuyue could still be understood as self-immolation without the need to mention such justifications or models.

Conclusion

Self-immolation clearly never died out but continued to be an important practice right through the Song, Yuan, Ming, and Qing periods. Overall, we get little sense from these later biographies of Buddhism in decline. On the contrary, the many cases of spontaneous combustion would appear to indicate that individual practitioners were reaching stages of cultivation that were actually rather rare in earlier periods. The increasing importance of the death verse, and of holy death in general, adds another aesthetic dimension to the story of self-immolation. The self-immolator was so in control of his body and emotions that he could compose poetry at the very moment of departure from the world. The intersection of religion and politics, which was such a strong feature of the earlier biographies, remains as important as ever in these accounts.

Minghe's collection, which was mostly drawn from inscriptional evidence that he collected, shows that the cult of the Buddhist saints was not just a medieval phenomenon. Miracles continued to occur on Chinese soil and were marked by two signs of sanctity in particular. One was literary (the death verse), and the other was more physical (the mummy). Buddhism was not patronized by the state in quite the same way as it had been in the Sui and Tang, but we continue to see the close involvement of local elites in Buddhist cult practice and the support of the imperial family. The shape of Buddhism may have changed considerably since the medieval period, but, if anything, the significance of a holy death had only increased.

Of course it remains difficult to assess the true significance of many of these biographies simply because we know so little about the contours of Buddhist practice in the post-Song period. We have seen that there was considerable creativity in self-immolation practices, which would seem to suggest that Buddhism remained a powerful and innovative force. Certainly the self-immolators themselves were fully convinced of their own abilities to affect both those around them and the cosmos as a whole. If we consider the number of poems about self-immolators and death verses in our later sources, it could almost be said that the authors had produced nothing less than an indigenous literature of self-immolation that owed little to the *Lotus Sūtra* and the *jātaka*s. By the Song, it appears that self-immolation had acquired an aesthetic of its own that continued to develop over the centuries. But to understand and appreciate that aesthetic we would need to learn a good deal more about Buddhist literature and practice in the late imperial period.

Conclusion

Over the years that I have been studying and writing about self-immolation, the question I have most often been asked is "Why did they do that?" I hope this study has shown that there can never be a single answer to that question. Now that we have a better sense of the range of practices, variety of practitioners, and the vastly different times and places in which they acted, it will be apparent that both the "they" and "that" of the question are meaningless. We need to ask better questions of our sources.

The reader who has reached this point in the book may be forgiven for asking why I have insisted on amassing so much detail relating to the biographies of self-immolators. Apart from my own never-ending sense of wonder at the possibility of recovering even a tiny fraction of the experience of men and women who lived long ago and far away, I would point to four reasons for doing so. First, it seemed necessary to show irrefutably that self-immolation was not a marginal or deviant practice indulged in by a handful of suicidal losers. The evidence I have presented shows, I believe, that it was not only relatively common but also enduring and respected. Second, the sources presented en masse reveal that self-immolation was not a single phenomenon, but a category that allowed Chinese Buddhists to think about a diverse range of practices, ideals, and aspirations that were open to constant negotiation and interpretation. Third, I am interested in making apparent the ways in which self-immolators interacted with others and affected the world around them, especially the various institutions and worldviews of Chinese Buddhism and premodern Chinese society. Fourth, I believe it is important for us, as scholars who seek to understand religions through texts, to confront at length material that makes us most uncomfortable: Writing about what people do to and with their own bodies. Most premodern Chinese Buddhists lived in a world in which the body and its actions were intensely meaningful. If we cannot learn to appreciate how and why that was so, what can we hope to say about Chinese Buddhism as a whole?

Self-immolation was not confined to the monastery. It affected the state and had ramifications for China's intellectual and political history: Han Yu's essay about the body practices indulged in by devotees celebrating the Buddha's relic became a famous and influential text. Modes of "Confucian" filial piety, such as slicing the thigh, were indebted to Buddhist practices and ideas. Auto-cremation was sometimes co-opted by officials in late imperial China: Some local magistrates, and even a Song emperor, threatened to burn themselves to bring rain.[1]

Thus, I have avoided imposing uniformity on what was always a diverse set of practices and ideals—from burning the body to dying spontaneously in the marketplace. I have endeavored to seek the deeper meaning in the details by carefully unravelling the scriptural and historical precedents for apparently bizarre and inexplicable behavior such as feeding the body to insects or burning the fingers. By concentrating on the biographies of self-immolators, their scriptural models, and learned defenders, I have aimed to show that the category "self-immolation" is a virtual one. It was the compilers of biographies who determined what practices should constitute that model. At times, the category could include types of death that were scarcely even intentional (death in monastery fires, for example); at other times compilers such as Daoxuan could select biographies strategically to construct a larger narrative with a polemic or didactic intent.

I have also been hesitant to present self-immolation as a subset of some larger interpretive category. For example, I remain to be convinced that in China self-immolation was primarily an ascetic tradition. In the early accounts at least, the preparation of the body seems to emphasize its positive aspects: It was not something to be subdued but rather cultivated and transformed. Despite references to terms such as *dhūta* or *kuxing* (austerities) in the biographies, I have not found strong evidence of self-immolation as part of a larger and fully articulated program of asceticism.

Paying close attention to the biographical sources brings out the gulf between the ideal Indian models, which were known through scripture and artistic representation, and the realities faced by Chinese monastics. This is particularly noticeable with regard to the *jātaka* tales. The hero of these legends was most often a ruler, or at least a prince. Even if his ministers objected to his offering his head, his eyes, or his body, ultimately he had temporal power. He had the agency to do as he wished, to give away not only his body but his wife and children. In China, the monk or nun had no temporal power. He or she was necessarily beholden to the ruler, hence the need to ask permission from the emperor before burning one's body. But more than that, self-immolators had to find some way to square their actions with precepts that constrained their abilities to do as they wished with their bodies. This explains why so much discussion revolved around the precepts as Chinese monks strove to locate the correct source of authority: Was it the "Hīnayāna" Vinaya, which (apparently) told them not to harm or kill themselves, or the Mahāyāna scriptures, particularly the bodhisattva precepts, which told them they *should* burn their bodies? Interestingly, there does not seem to have been much effort to locate legitimacy in India itself or in the Indian *saṃgha*. The exception that proves the rule is the Indian monk from Vārāṇasī who appears in the biography of the nun Huiyao. Yijing's complaints about the practice of burning the body not being attested in India seem to have carried rather little weight and could seemingly be countered by reference to textual sources— even if those sources on occasion had to be fabricated.[2]

The question of authority, agency, and constraints on behavior points to another possible distinction between the Indian and Chinese situation. To speak in the very broadest terms here, in India, Buddhism's self-image was in part posited on offering a middle way between the "extreme" renunciation of other śramaṇic traditions and the priest-centered ritual path of the brahmans. Buddhists were particularly keen to distance themselves from their more ascetically inclined brethren, and this no doubt was a powerful constraint on the types of practices they considered productive and appropriate.[3] In other words, in India Buddhists could not be fanatical; they had to play the role of "moderates." In China Buddhists were not competing against other traditions characterized by ascetic practices. Thus it was possible there for some Buddhists to act as fanatics, constrained in their behavior only by their imagination—which to judge from the actions of Mahāsattva Fu's followers and others could be quite vivid. References to burning the body like a lamp or stick of incense (from the top down), clearly modelled after the offerings of light and good odors one makes to a buddha image, abound in the biographies and show the ways auto-cremators brought both enthusiasm and conceptual creativity to their practices.

The issue of the validity of self-immolation was never satisfactorily resolved. The eminent Ming cleric Zhuhong 株宏 (1535–1615) wrote an extremely critical piece on the practice of burning the body contained in his *Zheng'e ji* 正訛集 (Rectification of Errors, 1614). It is entitled "Huo fen" 活焚 (Burning Alive). The essay endeavors to move the discussion away from the question of precepts and authority towards more basic "buddhological" issues, attributing the ability to withstand the pain of auto-cremation to the archenemy of awakening, Māra. Incidentally, it seems from the content of this piece that Zhuhong may have actually witnessed auto-cremation firsthand:

> There are demonic people (*moren* 魔人) who pour on oil, stack up firewood, and burn their bodies while still alive. Those who look on are overawed and

consider it the attainment of enlightenment. This is erroneous. In the thoughts of ordinary humans there is attachment, and this is where Māra arises. If one has a single moment of thought of admiration for the wonder of this burning while alive, then before this [thought of] admiration is complete, Māra enters the mind and one is no longer self-aware.

As they sit upright in the midst of the flames, it seems as if they have no suffering. They do not realize it is Māra's power that aids them. They temporarily attain suchness, but when their life force is exhausted Māra departs. Then they are miserable and in pain that is quite indescribable. For hundreds of *kalpa*s and thousands of rebirths they are always in the midst of flames, screaming and wailing as they run. They are dead ghosts to whom one should give compassionately.

Some might say, "The *sūtra*s extol the Medicine King, who burned his body, so what of that?" Alas! How can a green insect surpass [a bird with] golden wings? When the Medicine King burned his body, the radiance was illuminating. It lasted for many *kalpa*s and extended to the ten directions. But these people who burn themselves alive, their light is negligible. When the follower of Guifeng (Zongmi 圭峰宗密, 780–841) burned his arm in praise of the *dharma,* Qingliang (Chengguan 清涼澄觀, 738–839) admonished him that it was not appropriate. So how much worse for burning the living body?[4] This is what Wenling 溫陵 calls "a cause of suffering returning as an effect of suffering."[5]

One cannot help but feel somewhat underwhelmed by Zhuhong's argument here, as it appears to revolve around two somewhat dubious propositions: (1) that self-immolators were somehow possessed by a demon, and (2) that an eminent Tang monk had once urged a little restraint in body-burning practices. I have found little evidence to suggest that his remarks had much effect. It was Yanshou who was able to articulate most clearly and fearlessly what the biographies suggest—that not only was self-immolation common, it was a valid practice. Yanshou was certainly no ill-informed propagandist for self-immolation. He had an unparalleled command of the relevant texts, history, and practice. At the time he was writing, he was not nostalgically looking back on some earlier age of "good practice," but was on the cutting edge of tenth-century Buddhism in South China.

Self-immolation in China is much better attested than we had previously imagined, and also more complex than we might have suspected. In the preceding chapters we considered a large number of biographical accounts of men and women who made offerings of their bodies from the fourth century to the early twentieth, examined the scriptural models for these offerings, and weighed up doctrinal arguments in favor of self-immolation together with polemics against the practice. It has become clear that for many monks and laypeople in Chinese history, self-immolation was a form of Buddhist practice that modelled and expressed a particular bodily or somatic path that led towards Buddhahood.

The history of these physical devotions and their formation and transmission as literary artefacts brings to light conflict between Buddhists and their opponents as well as areas of considerable tension within the religion itself. Placed in their historical context, the acts of self-immolators and those of their biographers and compilers were never separate from the larger history of imperial China—especially the history of the relationship between Buddhism and the state in the medieval and early modern period. An examination of the biographies as historical data reveals the existence of previously unknown cults and provides important new evidence for such topics as the history of relics, responses to natural disasters, drought and disease, attitudes towards the corpse and its disposal, eschatology and messianism, and the importance of local histories within the larger development of Buddhism in China.

This study has stressed the importance of understanding self-immolation as a construct that was continually being remade by historical actors who were themselves shaped by social, political, and geographical forces. As we have seen, self-immolation was invested with a variety of meanings depending on how, when, and where it occurred. The compilers of biographical collections selected biographies and used them for their own polemical purposes whether subtle or overt. This rule holds true not just for self-immolation but for other monastic specializations, although this fact has not yet been sufficiently appreciated by scholars. We still use the *Gaoseng zhuan* collections as if they were neutral databases rather than the highly structured and rhetorically charged documents that they are. Until we learn to stop looking only at individual biographies and instead attempt to understand the collective nature of the sources, much of the overall shape of Chinese Buddhism will continue to remain obscure to us.

Although some monks did offer their bodies in periods of relative prosperity and peace, we have seen a marked coincidence between acts of self-immolation and times of crisis, especially when secular powers were hostile towards Buddhism. In Daoxuan's collection this is particularly marked, and we have observed how he used the biographies of self-immolators to pay homage to the martyrs of the Northern Zhou persecution, celebrate the influence that their sacrifices had on the restoration of Buddhism under Sui Wendi, and warn the Tang rulers against taking further measures against the *saṃgha*. But the presentation of self-immolator as martyr was not just a medieval phenomenon; this is apparent from the much later case of the monk who offered his body to protect his co-religionists in the early Ming. Although self-immolation was not the only response open to the Buddhist order, and probably not even the most effective response, it is interesting to note that this form of protest did have a continuing tradition. From the perspective of the state, and those self-appointed defenders of orthodoxy such as Han Yu, the enthusiastic, almost orgiastic, offerings of the body, especially to the relics of the Buddha, were not only morally disturbing but were also seen as a threat to public order. The compilers of self-immolators' biographies were able to present these same bloody acts in the hyperbolic and aesthetic language of the Mahāyāna, rendering them part of a cosmic drama that had as its goal nothing less than the liberation of all beings.

The physical practices of the monastics we have met throughout this book can tell us a great deal about the nature and vicissitudes of Chinese Mahāyāna Buddhism. One is struck initially by the violence that some practitioners directed towards their bodies, but what lies beneath this are the graphic and gruesome depictions of self-sacrifice recounted in the Mahāyāna literature that was translated in such vast quantities and picked up with such enthusiasm in the early medieval period. The nature of the transmission of Buddhist texts from India and Central Asia was such that the Chinese were never presented with a fully resolved system of practice, monastic discipline, and religious doctrine. They had to piece this together for themselves as texts became available. By the early fifth century Chinese Buddhists had begun to embrace the idea that it was possible for them to become bodhisattvas and buddhas through religious cultivation. But when they turned to the texts to investigate the parameters of that cultivation, they found that it included not only meditation and wisdom, but also forms of worship, devotion, and extreme charity that involved giving away the body in whole or in part. The *Lotus Sūtra*, the *avadāna*s, and the *jātaka*s simultaneously proffered the highest rewards of enlightenment and provided detailed descriptions of the trials of blood and fire by which those rewards had been attained by sages of the past. Wrenched from the context of Indian devotional literature, there was no real indication that they should be taken in any way other than literally. This was not just a feature of the early medieval period, when a Chinese Mahāyāna might be said to have been in formation. We still see this consciousness in the late-tenth-century writings of Yanshou, who had a profound knowledge of a broad range of scripture and a well-articulated doctrinal position.

From the early medieval period onwards Buddhists extracted these accounts from the scriptures and implanted them in the religious landscape of

China. The heroes of Mahāyāna literature were to some extent supplanted by local heroes, and many of these men and women became the focus of cults. Evidence for these cults may be seen in the reverence paid to their relics by aristocrats, local governors, and emperors; the active proselytizing by preachers; the appearance of miracles at assemblies of the faithful; and even, in the case of the sixth-century auto-cremator Sengyai for example, the existence of independent biographies and popular songs.[6] Some later self-immolators had their cults recognized by the state and were in time officially enfeoffed as local deities. Clearly these monks were celebrated as homegrown bodhisattvas.

In the preceding chapters I have been at pains to stress the variety of meanings of self-immolation. It could be an heroic act that saved humans or other beings or one predicated on an imitation and emulation of the bodhisattvas known from canonical literature. Sometimes a successful act of self-immolation was viewed as equivalent to the attainment of the highest enlightenment; at other times and places it led to rebirth in a Pure Land or in the Heavens. A few self-immolators can be considered almost messianic figures; others defended the *saṃgha* against the depredations of the state or protected the state against internal disorder or foreign invasion. Some monks who gave up their bodies called forth responses that were more local and provided immediate relief from the threats of flood, famine, disease, and drought. Like the teachings of Buddhism themselves, self-immolation was an extremely flexible and adaptable form of expedient means *(upāya)*.

Before we can reassess Chinese Buddhism more generally along the lines suggested by Erik Zürcher in my introduction, it is necessary to pay attention to the complexity of the religious landscape and consider the mass of detail that I have provided in the preceding chapters. But this is only the first stage. If a new history of medieval Chinese Buddhism is to be written it must take into account not only great men and great ideas, but the ways in which these ideas affected the bodies, attitudes, devotions, and practices of believers as well as the very material objects *(stūpas*, stelae, and images) and places (sacred mountains and holy sites) among which these people lived.

The physical practices of Chinese Buddhists may be said to represent the performative aspect of the religion. The practices produced distinctive material results: They changed the shape of the body by burning or cutting off fingers or arms; they etched the teachings into the skin by branding the torso, arm, or head. They produced relics, mummies, and indestructible tongues. Self-immolators affected the lives of witnesses as they saved humans and animals, cured diseases, or converted people to a vegetarian diet. Self-immolators were said to have preserved the *saṃgha* in times of persecution, averted disasters at the close of a *kalpa*, ended warfare, brought rain in times of drought, and turned back floods. Thus their acts were not simply a departure from the world, but an active involvement in it. Although these may have been the acts of extraordinary individuals, I hope that I have shown that they were not completely misguided or deluded. In fact, I would suggest that they were as solidly grounded in scripture and doctrine as any other Buddhist practice in China, and for the most part were understood as part of a wider project designed to make ordinary humans into the heroic and benevolent bodhisattvas celebrated in the literature of the Mahāyāna.

The study of self-immolation is not an artificial and arbitrary creation of modern scholarship, designed to focus on the sensational or grotesque side of Buddhism in China. As I have tried to show throughout, from Baochang's first collection onwards, self-immolation was always considered a valid Buddhist practice. It was not pushed to the margins by Chinese Buddhist authors but was taken seriously as part of the path to buddhahood itself. If we refuse to take self-immolation equally seriously, I believe that we do the tradition, and its heroes, a great disservice.

Appendix 1

Major Collections of Biographies of Self-Immolators

Mingseng zhuan

1. Sengqun 僧群 of Huoshan 霍山 in Luojiang 羅江, Jin 晉 dynasty (265–420)*
2. Tancheng 曇稱 of Hebei 河北, Jin dynasty*[1]
3. Sengzhou 僧周 of Hanshan 寒山 near Chang'an 長安, (Liu-)Song 劉宋 dynasty (420–479)*[2]
4. Faying 法迎 of Gaochang 高昌, (Liu-)Song dynasty*[3]
5. Sengfu 僧富 of Tingwei si 廷尉寺 in Wei commandery 魏郡, (Liu-)Song dynasty*[4]
6. Fayu 法羽, pseudo-Qin 僞秦 dynasty (394–415)*
7. Huishao 惠紹 of Zhaoti si 招提寺 in Linchuan 臨川, (Liu-)Song dynasty*
8. Sengyu 僧瑜 of Lushan 廬山 in Xunyang 尋陽, (Liu-)Song dynasty*
9. Huiyi 惠益 of Zhulin si 竹林寺 in the North, (Liu-)Song dynasty*
10. Daohai 道海 of Jiangling 江陵, (Liu-)Song dynasty*[5]
11. Sengqing 僧慶 of Yixing si 義興寺 in Chengdu 城都, (Liu-)Song dynasty*
12. Sengsheng 僧生 of Sanbao si 三寶寺 in Chengdu, (Liu-)Song dynasty*[6]
13. Hongji 弘濟 of Wudan si 武擔寺 in Chengdu, (Liu-)Song dynasty
14. Daofa 道法 of Xiangji si 香積寺 in Chengdu, (Liu-)Song dynasty*[7]
15. Sengye 僧業 of Cishi si 慈氏寺 in Xinping 欣平, (Liu-)Song dynasty
16. Faguang 法光 of Jicheng si 記城寺 in Longxi 壟西 Qi 齊 dynasty (479–502)*
17. Tanhong 曇弘 of Xianshan si 仙山寺 in Jiaozhou 交洲, Qi dynasty*
18. Fazhu 法紵 of Jingang si 金剛寺, Qi dynasty
19. Hongyuan 弘願 of Jianyuan si 建元寺 in Jinshou 晉壽, (Liu-)Song dynasty

Note: Monks marked with an asterisk have biographies in the *Gaoseng zhuan*.[8]

Three of the above works are preserved in the *Meisōdenshō*: The biographies of Daohai, Daofa, and Sengye, which presumably Shūshō copied because he was not already familiar with them from the *Gaoseng zhuan*.[9] In addition, there are some brief notes towards the end of the text that pertain to Huishao, Daohai, Daofa, and Faguang.[10]

Biqiuni zhuan

1. Shanmiao 善妙 (fl. fifth century) of Shu 蜀 commandery (*Biqiuni zhuan* 2, T 50.2063.939b14–c5)

Account: Shanmiao's secular surname was Ouyang 歐陽, and she became a nun in her childhood. Her younger sister, a widow, and her sister's child lived with her. She wove a length of cloth, purchased oil, and set fire to herself at midnight on the eighth day of the fourth month. She urged the other nuns to work hard to escape *saṃsāra* and said that although she had abandoned her body as an offering to the buddhas in twenty-seven previous lives, only now would she attain the "first fruit."

Translation: Tsai 1994, 51–53.

2. Daozong 道綜 (d. 463) of Sanceng si 三層寺 in Jiangling 江陵 (*Biqiuni zhuan* 2, T 50.2063.940c10–17)

Account: Daozong's family origins are unknown. She burned herself publicly on the night of Daming 大明 7.3.15 (April 18, 463), chanting steadily. The scholar Liu Qiu 劉虯 (438–495) composed a eulogy in verse.

Translation: Tsai 1994, 60.

3. Huiyao 慧耀 (d. 477) of Yongkang si 永康寺 in Shu 蜀 (*Biqiuni zhuan* 2, T 50.2063.941b13–c2)

Account: Huiyao's secular name was Zhou 周 and she was from Xiping 西平.[11] She became a nun in childhood and vowed to burn her body. At the end of the Taishi 泰始 reign period (465–471), the governor Liu Liang 劉亮 (d. 472) gave his permission. Huiyao wished to burn herself on top of a pagoda belonging to Madam Wang 王, the concubine of Zhao Chusi 趙處思 (d.u.). At midnight on the fifteenth day of the first month Huiyao and her disciples arrived. But a letter came from Liu saying her convent was in danger of committing a major offence. Huiyao returned to the convent, where she abstained from cereals and drank oil until 477, when she finally burned herself while reciting scriptures. Before she died she told the nuns that she would leave two pints of bones.

Just over a month before Huiyao burned herself, a monk from Vārāṇasī arrived with a silver vase, which was later used to hold the one-fifth of a pint of *śarīra* produced from Huiyao's bones.

Translation: Tsai 1994, 65–66.

4, 5, 6. Tanjian 曇簡 (d. 493), Jinggui 淨珪 (d. 493), and Tanyong 曇勇 (d. 501), all of Fayin si 法音寺 (*Biqiuni zhuan* 3, T 50.2063.943b29–c23 and 944b17–23)

Account: Tanjian's secular name was Zhang 張 and she was from Qinghe 清河.[12] She was an accomplished meditator and was respected by both religious and laity. She donated her convent to a monk called Huiming 慧明 (d.u.) and built a thatched hermitage on Bai shan. She gathered firewood, saying that she was going to carry out a meritorious act. On the night of Jianwu 建武 1.2.8 (March

11, 493), she mounted a pile of firewood and burned her body. When the local villagers arrived, she was already dead. They built a tomb for her remains.

Jinggui, whose secular name was Zhou 周, was a native of Jiankang. She lived at Fayin si with Tanjian. She understood both scriptures and Vinaya and was a skilled meditator but neglected her body and often looked emaciated. When Tanjian left for Bai shan, Jinggui went with her, and when Tanjian burned her body, she did the same. Her *śarīra* were gathered up and entombed.

Tanyong was Tanjian's elder sister. Like Tanjian and Jinggui she was a meditator and a strict observer of the Vinaya. In 493 she moved to Bai shan with the other two nuns. On the night of Yongyuan 永元 3.2.15 (March 19, 501), she piled up firewood and burned herself in front of witnesses. Her remains were interred.

Translation: Tsai 1994, 79–81; 84–85.

Gaoseng zhuan

1. The Jin 晉 monk Sengqun 僧群 (fl. ca. 404) of Huo shan 霍山 (*GSZ* 12, T 50.2059.404a2–15)

Note: There is an entry on Sengqun in the miracle-story collection *Mingxiang ji* 冥詳記 (Signs from the Unseen Realm), by Wang Yan 王琰 (b. ca. 454, fl. late fifth–early sixth century).[13] The *Gaoseng zhuan* biography mostly reproduces this account verbatim.[14] See also the biography of Sengqun in the *Shimen zijing lu* 釋門自鏡錄 (A Record of Those to Be Mirrored by the Disciples of Śākya), a compilation attributed to Huaixin 懷信 (d.u.), T 51.2083.813c13–21.[15]

Account: Sengqun's native place and dates are unknown. He practiced "keeping the precepts, eating vegetarian food, and chanting the *sūtra*s." He lived on Huo shan in Luojiang district. Sengqun drank magic water from a spring and was never hungry. One day a duck with a broken wing blocked his way to the spring. Unwilling to push the duck aside, he was unable to drink the magic water and died at the age of 140. When young, Sengqun had broken the wing of a duck, so this incident was a repayment of that karmic debt.

2. The Song 宋 monk Tancheng 曇稱 (d. after 420) of Jia shan 駕山 in Pengcheng 彭城 (*GSZ* 12, T 50.2059.404a16–28)

Note: Tancheng's biography is also included in the *Mingseng zhuan*.

Account: Tancheng was from Hebei 河北.[16] About 419 he met an impoverished elderly couple in Pengcheng. He became their slave, and when they died, he hired himself out as a servant to pay for their memorial services. Around 420 a man-eating tiger was active below Jia shan. Tancheng offered his body to save the villagers. The tiger ate everything but his head, which was enshrined in a *stūpa*. The tiger attacks ceased.

3. The Song monk Fajin 法進 (a.k.a. Daojin 道進, d. 444) of Gaochang 高昌 (*GSZ* 12, T 50.2059.404a29–b21)

Note: Fajin's biography appears under the name Faying 法迎 in the *Mingseng zhuan.*

Account: Fajin/Daojin was a disciple of the translator Dharmakṣema. His secular surname was Tang 唐 and he was from Zhangyi 張掖 in Liangzhou 涼州.[17] His patron was Juqu Mengxun 沮渠蒙遜 (r. 401–433) of the Northern Liang 北涼 (397–440). Juqu Jinghuan 璟環 (d.u.) consulted Daojin but ignored the monk's advice concerning his plan to capture Gaochang 高昌. When Anzhou 安周 (?– 460) succeeded to the throne, there was a famine. Daojin offered his own flesh to the starving people and Anzhou opened the granaries. Daojin was cremated but his tongue remained intact. A pagoda and stele were erected for him.

Appended: A brief entry on Daojin's disciple Sengzun 僧遵 (d.u.).

4. The Song monk Sengfu 僧富 (d. after 385) of Yanwei si 延尉寺 in Wei commandery (Wei jun 魏郡) (*GSZ* 12, T 50.2059.404b22–c10)[18]

Account: Sengfu's secular surname was Shan 山 and he was originally from Gaoyang高陽.[19] His father was the magistrate of Lantian藍田, but he died and left Sengfu an orphan.[20] Sengfu knew Yang Yong 楊邕 (d.u.), general of the guards (*weijiangjun*衛將軍) under the Qin 秦 and the literatus Xi Zuochi 習鑿齒 (?–383). He became a disciple of Daoan 道安 (312–385) and later became a recluse at Tingwei monastery. Some bandits kidnapped a young child, planning to use his heart and liver as a sacrifice. Sengfu sliced open his torso, offering his five viscera as ransom. The bandits fled and the monk's wound was stitched up by a passerby. The precise circumstances of Sengfu's death are unknown.

5. The pseudo-Qin 僞秦 monk Fayu 法羽 (ca. 352–396) of Puban 蒲坂 (*GSZ* 12, T 50.2059.404c11–18)

Account: Fayu was a native of Jizhou 冀州 and became a monk at fifteen *sui.*[21] He practiced austerities and cultivated *dhūta.* He wanted "to follow the traces of the Medicine King and to burn his body in homage to the Buddha." Around 396, in Puban, Fayu informed the prince of Jin 晉, Yao Xu 姚緒 (fl. late tenth century), of his intention. He swallowed chips of incense, wrapped his body in cloth, and recited "The Chapter on Abandoning the Body." At the end of his recitation he set fire to himself. He was forty-five years old.

Translation: Gernet 1960, 531.

6. The Song monk Huishao 慧紹 (424–451) of Zhaoti si 招提寺 in Linchuan 臨川 (*GSZ* 12, T 50.2059.404c19–405a7)[22]

Account: Huishao's family is unknown. He refused to eat fish or meat as a child. At eight *sui* he became a disciple of Sengyao 僧要 (d.u.). Huishao practiced austerities and followed Sengyao to Zhaoti si, where he planned to burn his body. In 451 he hired some people to cut firewood, which he stacked up in the Dongshan 東山 grottoes, then opened a niche in the pile large enough for his own body. Sengyao begged him not to go through with his plan. Huishao held a ceremony for the eight precepts on Dongshan, drawing large crowds and donations. He lit the fire, entered the niche, and began to recite the "Original Acts of the Medicine King." A star descended into the smoke and rose back into the sky. As Huishao had predicted, a firmiana tree grew in the spot where he burned himself.

Translation: Gernet 1960, 532.

7. The Song monk Sengyu 僧瑜 (412–455) of Zhaoyin si 招隱寺 on Lu shan 廬山 (*GSZ* 12, T 50.2059.405a8–b1)

Note: Sengyu's biography is also found in the *Mingxiang ji,* 510, with some minor elisions.

Account: Sengyu's secular surname was Zhou 周. He was from Yuhang 餘杭 in Wuxing 吳興, and became a monk at the age of twenty.[23] In 438, together with Tanwen 曇溫 (d.u.), Huiguang 慧光 (d.u.), and others, he built a hermitage on the southern range of Lu shan. On Xiaojian 孝建 2.6.3 of the Song (July 3, 455), he burned himself while reciting the chapter on the Medicine King. Witnesses saw a purple vapor in the sky. He was forty-four. Fourteen days later a firmiana tree with two entwined trunks sprang up in Sengyu's cell. Some said it was the twin *śāla* trees that had been present at the Buddha's *parinirvāṇa*. Zhang Bian 張辯 (fl. mid-fifth century), then governor of Pingnan 平南, witnessed the events and composed the biography and a verse eulogy (*zan* 贊). The eulogy is reproduced at the end of the *Gaoseng zhuan* biography.

Translation: Gernet 1960, 532–533.

8. The Song monk Huiyi 慧益 (d. 463) of Zhulin si 竹林寺 in the capital (*GSZ* 12, T50.2059.405b2–c1)

Note: See also the biography of Fajing 法鏡 (437–500), one of the twenty monks ordained as a result of Huiyi's auto-cremation.[24]

Account: Huiyi was from Guangling 廣陵.[25] During the Xiaojian 孝建 period (454–456) he resided at Zhulin si. He practiced austerities and vowed to burn his body. In 460 he abstained from cereals and ate only sesame and wheat. Two years later Huiyi began to consume only oil of thyme and sometimes pills made of incense. Xiaowu 孝武 (r. 454–464) sent his chief minister, Liu Yigong 劉義恭, prince of Jiangxia 江夏 (413–465), to reason with him.

On Daming 大明 7.8.4 (May 11, 463) Huiyi set up a cauldron full of oil on Zhong shan 鐘山. The emperor followed him there with a large retinue. In the cauldron, the monk lay on a bed wrapped in cloth with a long, oil-soaked cap on his head. He asked the emperor to allow twenty people to join the *saṃgha*.

Huiyi lit the cap, chanting the chapter on the Medicine King. The next morning the emperor heard the sound of pipes and smelled a strange perfume. In the night he dreamed of Huiyi and the next day he held an ordination ceremony for the twenty novices. Yaowang si 藥王寺 (Medicine King monastery) was later built at the site of the auto-cremation.

Translation: Gernet 1960, 533–535.

9. The Song monk Sengqing 僧慶 (437–459) of Wudan si 武擔寺 in Shu 蜀 (*GSZ* 12, T50.2059.405c2–10)

Account: Sengqing's lay surname was Chen 陳 and he came from Anhan 安漢 in Baxi 巴西.[26] His family were members of the "Way of the Five Pecks of Grain." He became a novice at the age of thirteen *sui* at Yixing si 義興寺. Sengqing gave up three of his fingers and vowed to burn his body. He stopped eating grains and consumed only incense and oil. On Daming 3.2.8 (March 27, 459), west of Wudan si, facing an image of Vimalakīrti, he burned his body. The prefect Zhang Yue 張悅 (fl. mid-fifth century), among others, was present. Witnesses saw something like a dragon leap out of the pyre and into the sky. Sengqing was twenty-three. The governor of Tianshui 天水, Pei Fangming 裴方明 (fl. mid-fifth century), had his ashes gathered and erected a *stūpa*.

Translation: Gernet 1960, 535–536.

10. The Qi 齊 monk Faguang 法光 (447–487) of Longxi 隴西 (*GSZ* 12, T50.2059.405c11–18)

Account: Faguang, from Longxi in Qinzhou 秦州, became a monk at the age of twenty-nine.[27] He practiced *dhūta*, did not wear silk, avoided grains, and ate only pine needles. He vowed to burn his body and then ate pine resin and drank oil. On Yongming 永明 5.10.20 (November 21, 487), within Jicheng si 記城寺 in Longxi, Faguang piled up firewood and burned himself. He was forty-one.

Appended: Facun 法存 burned himself around the end of the Yongming reign period (483–493) in Shifeng 始豐 county.[28] The prefect of the commandery, Xiao Mian 蕭緬 (456–491), sent the *śramaṇa* Huishen 慧深 (d.u.) to erect a *stūpa* for his ashes.

Translation: Gernet 1960, 536.

11. The Qi monk Tanhong 曇弘 (ca. 400–455) of Xianshan 仙山 in Jiaozhi 交趾 (*GSZ* 12, T 50.2059.405c19–28)

Account: Tanhong was from Huanglong 黃龍.[29] During the Yongchu 永初 period of the Song (420–422), he wandered south to Tai si 臺寺. Later he went to

Xianshan si in Jiaozhi. He recited the *Wuliangshou jing* and the *Guan wuliangshou jing* and vowed to be reborn in the Pure Land. One day in 455 Tanhong gathered up firewood on the mountain and set fire to himself in secret. His disciples rescued him. About a month later he again attempted to burn himself. When the villagers reached him he was already dead, so they added more firewood. They saw his golden body heading west, riding a golden deer. A pagoda was erected for his ashes and bones.[30]

Translation: Gernet 1960, 536.

Xu gaoseng zhuan

1. The Southern Qi 南齊 *śramaṇa* Shi Faning 釋法凝 (fl. ca. 482–493) of Huizhou si 會州寺 in Shu 蜀 (*XGSZ* 27, T50.2060.678a27–b13)

Note: This biography was probably not added to the *Xu gaoseng zhuan* until the tenth century. (See Ibuki 1990, 62–68.)

Account: Faning was from Huizhou 會州 and his secular name was Pang 龐.[31] Qi Wudi 武帝 (482–493) dreamed of a mountain called Qi. He had a temple built, monks ordained, and granted land for their use. Faning was the first of these monks. He was an ascetic and expert in *dhyāna*. He once went into *dhyāna* for a month and refused food thereafter. Although he later resumed eating, he reduced his diet. At the age of seventy, Faning set fire to a finger in front of a Buddha image. The flames spread to his body for seven days and nights. Onlookers wailed, beat themselves, and made prostrations. The monk left only a pile of ashes, which were enshrined in a *stūpa*. At the time of the biography only his hermitage remained.

2. The Zhou 周 *śramaṇa* Shi Sengyai 釋僧崖 (488?–562) of Yibu 益部 (*XGSZ* 27, T 50.2060.678b14–680b22)

There are five additional sources for the life of Sengyai:

1. *Fayuan zhulin* 96, T 53.2122.993a–994c; only minor textual variants from the *Xu gaoseng zhuan* biography.
2. Biography of Shi Sengan (*Shi Sengan zhuan* 釋僧岸傳) in the *Hongzan fahua zhuan*, T 51.2067.25a–b. A note in the text confirms that "Sengan" is a copyist's error for "Sengyai."
3. Biography of Sengyai in the *Wangsheng xifang jingtu ruiying zhuan* 往生西方淨土瑞應傳 (Accounts of Auspicious Responses of Those Who Were Reborn in the Western Pure Land) by Wennian 文念 (d.u.) and Shaokang 少康 (d. 805), T 51.2070.104b–c.

4. Biography of the Bodhisattva Sengyai (*Sengyai pusa zhuan* 僧崖菩薩傳) in
   one fascicle by the *śramaṇa* Wangming 亡名 (or 忘名) (516–after 567).[32]
   This was an independently circulating biography that is no longer extant.
5. A text called "The Bodhisattva Sengyai Appears in the World in Order to
   Make the Scriptures" (*Sengyai pusa chushi wei zaojing ben* 僧崖菩薩出世爲造
   經本). This is mentioned in the biography of the popular preacher Baotuan 寶彖 (512–561) as having been composed by him (*XGSZ* 8, 50.2060.
   487a11–12). It is no longer extant. On the basis of this text, a song (*qu* 曲)
   was composed, which was very popular in Jiannan 劍南, Sichuan.

Account: Sengyai's secular surname was Mou 牟. He was a descendent of the
Rang 獽 people, who had been forcibly resettled in the mountains and valleys of
Jinyuan金淵in Guanghan廣漢, Sichuan, in the early fifth century.[33] He was a serious child who expressed an early disgust for his body and a desire to burn it. He
joined the army but renounced hunting and tried to convert his fellows.

He became a follower of *dhyāna* master Xi 悉禪師 (d.u.). One day Xi was suffering from the cold and ordered Sengyai to lay a fire, but he made it too close to
his master. Xi challenged him to stick his finger in the fire, which he did. On another occasion the other disciples pushed him into a burning brazier. He laughed
and showed no sign of pain whatsoever. Xi ordained him, personally shaving off
his hair. Then Xi and the disciples all paid homage to him. Sengyai was a monk
for thirty years and remained of sound mind and body even in his seventies.

In the sixth month of Wucheng 武成 1 of the Zhou (July 20–August 18, 559),
at the head of the road west of the ramparts of Yizhou 益州, Sengyai burned his
fingers as he publicly preached the *dharma*. At that time the people commonly
proclaimed him "Bodhisattva Sengyai." *Dharma* master Dui 兌 (d.u.) from Xiaoai
si孝愛寺brought his disciples to pay homage and made Sengyi a gift of his robe.[34]

Later Sengyai announced his intention to burn himself. On the palm of his
burnt arm, the five stumps of bone unexpectedly grew back to a length of three
inches, as white as white jade or snow. When told that the monks and nuns intended to worship his relics in a *stūpa* after his death, Sengyai bit off the bones,
spat them out, and handed them to the assembly, saying, "This should do for a
stūpa!"

On the fourteenth day of the seventh month (September 1, 559), suddenly
there were loud noises as if the earth were shaking and the sky splitting open. In
the sky, some people saw images of dogs, sheep, dragons, serpents, and military
weapons. Sengyai told them not to worry but to prepare the offerings for his self-
immolation. *Dhyāna* master Dao 導 (d.u.) from Xiaoai si bestowed his six-*pāramitā*
khakkara and even his purple cape (*zipi* 紫被) on Sengyai to carry as he entered
the fire.[35] Sengyuan 僧淵 (519–602) sent a patchwork *kāṣāya* for Sengyai to wear.[36]

At first it was not known that these two worthies had given gifts, so huge was the pile of donations, but the next morning Sengyai asked for these objects by name.

By then over one hundred thousand weeping people had assembled around Sengyai's chariot. He preached the *dharma* to the crowd. From time to time he raised his eyes and gazed at the pyre and smiled joyously to himself. Then he lay down on his right side [as if] asleep and not breathing. He looked just like a wooden statue.

Earlier a tall, multistoried structure had been made of wood. On the top was a small chamber constructed of dried hemp soaked in oil. Sengyai circumambulated it three times then climbed to the top. Looking down at his audience he told them that "one heart would remain." No one was willing to light the fire so Sengyai had to do it himself. When the fire had burned out, his heart remained, still red and moist. It was burned again along with his liver, intestines, spleen, and stomach with forty cartloads of fuel. This time only the heart remained in its original condition. *Dharma* master Dui 兌 had it interred beneath a *stūpa* at Baoyuan si 寶園寺.[37]

There were many miracles associated with Sengyai, before and after his death. Once he read the mind of a woman who wished to donate a hairpin but feared her husband's wrath. Foyu 佛與 (d.u.) from Xiaoai si was a monk who enjoyed eating meat and drinking alcohol. As he followed Sengyai's carriage he made a vow to give these up. When he returned to the monastery he saw a golden-colored man who spoke to him about his vow in a mellifluous and elegant voice. When the man disappeared, Foyu circumambulated the *stūpa,* chanting. A voice spoke out of thin air encouraging him to keep to the vegetarian diet.

When Sengyai first mounted the firewood structure, Sengyu 僧育 (d.u.) saw from the gate of Da Jianchang si 大建昌寺 flames that were four or five *zhang* high and three or four *zhang* across. On the day of the auto-cremation, Baohai 寶海 (474–after 559) and *dharma* master Pu 普法師 (d.u.) engaged Sengyai in a long doctrinal debate.[38] Sengyai told his attendant, Zhiyan 智炎 (d.u.), that he should worship sick people because they might be buddhas and sages in disguise.

As Sengyai was about to light the fire strange signs (parasols, monks, flowers, and so on) were observed in the sky. After his death, people in Pixian 郫縣 saw the monk riding a carriage in the sky.[39] At Lingguo si 靈果寺 in Tongzhou 潼州, Huice 慧策 (Huirong 慧榮, d.u.) held a great vegetarian feast.[40] People observed a large black cloud that obscured the sun, dragons and a rain of flowers, banners, and fragrant smoke.

At Ajianizha (Akaniṣṭha) si 阿迦膩吒寺, an ailing monk called Huisheng 慧勝 (d.u.) saw Sengyai in a dream. Sengyai cured him by burning incense and sandalwood around him and revealed that his true name was Bodhisattva Brilliant All-Shining Precious Matrix (Guangming bianzhao baozang pusa 光明遍照寶藏菩

薩). When Huisheng later held a service for Sengyai, people saw heavenly flowers
falling from the sky. In Chengdu, Wang Senggui's 王僧貴 (d.u.) household had
given up meat. When they were discussing giving up vegetarianism, they were visited by a mysterious monk who warned them not to eat meat.

About eight months after the burning, a member of the Rang tribe called
Mou Nandang 牟難當 (d.u.) went hunting. He saw Sengyai riding a big blue deer.
Sengyai told him to renounce hunting. Sengyai's nephew also encountered him
in the mountains.

3. The Zhou recluse (*yi*逸) *śramaṇa* Shi Puyuan 釋普圓 (fl. ca. 560) of Yongzhou 雍州 (*XGSZ* 27, T 50.2060.680b23–c10)

Account: Puyuan's family background is unknown. He was active around central Shaanxi. He practiced *dhūta,* recited the *Huayan jing,* and sat in *samādhi* for
days. He practiced meditation in cemeteries and one night he frightened off a
ghost. One day an evil person begged Puyuan for his head. He was about to chop
it off, but the person begged for his eyes instead. Puyuan gouged them out.
When the person demanded his hand, Puyuan lashed his wrist to a tree and cut
off his arm. He died by the Fan vale 樊川, south of Chang'an. Local villagers divided his body into many pieces and built a pagoda for each.

4. The Sui 隋 *śramaṇa* Shi Puji 釋普濟 (d. 581) of Zhongnan shan 終南山
(*XGSZ* 27, T 50.2060.680c11–681a8)

Account: Puji was from the northern mountains of Yongzhou.[41] His master
was Puyuan (see above). He lived alone in the forest, cultivated *dhyāna,* and favored the *Huayan jing.* During the persecution of Buddhism by Zhou Wudi, he
went to live on Zhongnan shan. Puji vowed that if Buddhism were allowed to
flourish, he would relinquish his body. Under Sui Wendi, Buddhism was restored
and, in front of a large crowd, Puji threw himself off the western cliffs of the Tan 炭
valley. A white pagoda was erected for him on a high peak.

Appended: Another monk also called Puji was a contemporary of Daoxuan
and a very popular preacher in Chang'an. The biography of the Tang Puji is
nearly twice as long as that of his Sui namesake.

5. The Sui *śramaṇa* Shi Puan 釋普安 (530–609), who was a recluse to the
south of the capital suburbs (*XGSZ* 27, T 50.2060.681a9–682b4)[42]

Note: Puan's *Xu gaoseng zhuan* biography is reproduced (almost verbatim)
in the *Huayan jing zhuanji* 華嚴經傳記 (Biographies and Records of the *Huayan
jing*), T 51.2073.167c–168c.

Account: Puan was one of Puyuan's disciples. His secular name was Guo 郭
and he was from Jingyang 涇陽 in Jingzhao 京兆.[43] He also studied under Jing'ai.

He practiced asceticism, memorization, chanting (especially the *Huayan jing*), and *dhyāna*. During the persecution of Zhou Wudi, he found shelter for Jingyuan 靜淵 (544–611) and thirty other monks in the Zhongnan mountains. He was bitten by mosquitoes and gadflies and offered himself to wild dogs and tigers. He begged for food and clothing for the other monks and attributed his narrow escapes from capture to the *Huayan jing*. Under the Sui, Puan continued to face potential misfortunes, which were all averted by the *sūtra*. Once he attempted to buy three pigs to save them from slaughter. A young child clad in a sheepskin miraculously appeared to help Puan, who pulled out a knife and sliced the flesh of his thigh. The pigs were released and circumambulated Puan three times.

In 588 Puan was appointed mentor to the crown prince. He resided at Jingfa 靜法 monastery, founded by Sui Wendi's older sister, but he preferred to sleep in the mountains. At the age of eighty he died at Jingfa si, on Daye 大業 5.11.5 (December 6, 609). A pagoda was raised for his remains on Zhongnan shan near Zhixiang si 至相寺.

6. The Sui *śramaṇa* Shi Dazhi 釋大志 (567–609) of Lu shan 盧山 in Jiujiang 九江 (*XGSZ* 27, T 50.2060.682b5–c11)

Note: Biographies of Dazhi that essentially reproduce the *Xu gaoseng zhuan* version are found in the *Hongzan fahua zhuan* 弘贊法華傳 (Biographies that Broadly Extol the *Lotus Sūtra*), T 51.2067.25c–26c; the *Fahua jing chuanji* 法華經傳記 (Accounts of the Transmission of the *Lotus Sūtra*), T 51.2068.93c–94a (minus Daoxuan's own observations at the end of the *Xu gaoseng zhuan* biography); and the *Shenseng zhuan* 神僧傳 (Biographies of Divine Monks), T 50.984a–b (slightly abbreviated). Brief accounts of the Daye purge and Dazhi's reaction to it appear in the *Fozu tongji* 佛祖統紀 (A Comprehensive Record of the Buddhas and Patriarchs) 39, T 49.2035.362a5–11 and 54, T 49.2035.471a27–29. See also *Fozu tongji* 9, T 49.2035.198b19–c4, and the brief notice in Hurvitz 1962, 177.

Account: Dazhi was a disciple of Tiantai Zhiyi. He came from Shanyin 山陰 in Kuaiji 會稽 and his family name was Gu 顧. After his initial training on Tiantai shan, he moved to Fengding si 峰頂寺 on Mount Lu in 590, where he recited the *Lotus Sūtra* and tried to offer his body to tigers. He established Jingguan 靜觀 monastery on Mount Lianhua 蓮花山 and spent seven years there. Later he moved to Fulin si 福林寺. In 609 Sui Yangdi tried to limit the number of monks and nuns. Dazhi went to Luoyang and offered to burn one arm on Mount Song 嵩岳 in exchange for the protection of the *saṃgha*. He fasted for three days and, in front of a large crowd, he used a red-hot piece of iron to burn his arm. He peeled off the flesh with a knife then wrapped the bones in a cloth soaked in wax and burned them. He died seven days later at the age of forty-three.

Daoxuan appends his own opinions on Dazhi's talent and physical beauty.

He reports that Dazhi was still commemorated by the monks at Lu shan, who read the text of his vow once a year.

7. The Tang *śramaṇa* Shi Zhiming 釋智命 (?–619) of the pseudo-Zheng 僞鄭 (*XGSZ* 27, T 50.2060.682c12–683a24)

Note: Jiu Tang shu 舊唐書 50/2140 mentions Zheng Ting. See also Wang Shichong's 王世充 (d. 621) biography in *Xin Tang shu* 85/2695 and *Zizhi tongjian* 188/5903–5904.

Account: Zhiming's secular name was Zheng Ting 鄭頲, and he was from Rongyang 榮陽.[44] Sometime between 586 and 604 he was "commandant of plumed cavalry" (*yujiwei* 羽騎尉).[45] He resigned, attended Buddhist lectures, and eventually took up farming in Ningzhou 寧州 (present-day Gansu). In 605 or 606 Yang Su 楊素 (d. 606) brought him back into government service.[46] He served Sui Yangdi's eldest son, Yuande 元德 (Prince Yang Zhao 楊昭太子, 579–606), and was promoted to secretary to the heir apparent (*zhongshe ren* 中舍人). When Yuande died in 606, Zheng wandered around listening to lectures on the *Sanlun* 三論 and the *Lotus Sūtra*. After the death of Sui Yangdi in 617, Yang Tong 楊侗 (d. 618) was enthroned as Sui Gongdi 恭帝 by the general Wang Shichong. Zheng held the position of censor-in-chief and went on to serve Wang's Zheng 鄭 dynasty (618–621).

Zheng repeatedly asked to be allowed to become a monk but was denied permission. After reciting the *Lotus Sūtra,* he and his wife gave each other the tonsure. Wang Shichong lost his temper and ordered him to be executed. Zheng begged the executioner to dispatch him quickly before he could be pardoned and released. Before he was killed he composed a death verse. His wife became a *bhikṣuṇī* and in Daoxuan's day she resided at Luozhou si 洛州寺.

8. The Tang *śramaṇa* Xuanlan 玄覽 (613?–644) of Hongfu si 弘福寺 in the capital (*XGSZ* 27, T 50.2060.683a25–b19)

Note: Xuanlan died in 644 just before the first draft of the *Xu gaoseng zhuan* was completed.

Account: Xuanlan's surname was Li 李, and he was from Fangzi 房子 in Zhaozhou 趙州.[47] He was adopted by his uncle, the commandant of Wanquan 萬泉 in Puzhou 蒲州.[48] At thirteen he left home and became a disciple of *dhyāna* master Chao 超禪師 in Fenzhou 汾州.[49] His uncle brought him home, but let him go when Xuanlan explained that although his body belonged to his uncle, his mind belonged to the buddhas.

At the beginning of the Zhenguan 貞觀 (627–649) period, Xuanlan went to Chang'an to receive ordination. In 644 he took off his clothes and left them in a bundle with his fellow monks at Hongfu si. He threw himself in the Wei 渭 river, but a crowd pulled him out. Xuanlan explained that if they stopped him it would be bad for his *karma* and theirs. He threw himself in again, and three days later his corpse surfaced. Some villagers pulled it out and erected a pagoda for him. Meanwhile his fellow monks opened the bundle of clothes and saw the vow Xuanlan had left behind. They went to the place of his death to investigate what had happened.

9. The Tang *śramaṇa* Shi Fakuang 釋法曠 (?-633) of Hongshan si 弘善寺 in the capital (*XGSZ* 27, T 50.2060.683b20-c17)

Account: Fakuang's surname was Luo 駱, and he was from Xianyang 咸陽 in Yongzhou.[50] He studied Confucianism in his youth but converted when he heard a disciple of Daoan, Master Rong 榮師 (d.u.) of Hongshan si, lecture on the *Da zhidu lun*. Fakuang's mastery of this text later made his own teachings popular in the capital. He was also skilled in recitation and had considerable knowledge of scripture, learning the *Wuliangshou jing* in a single day. On Zhenguan 貞觀 7.2.21 (April 5, 633), he entered Zhongnan shan. There he took off his robes, hung them on a tree, and cut his throat with a knife. Six months later, after an extended search, his friends found his "Eulogy on Discarding the Body."

Appended: A nameless monk from Dasheng si 大乘寺 in Fenzhou 汾州.[51] The biography was probably added long after 645.[52] The monk detested *saṃsāra*. He restricted his diet and ate incense, and his self-immolation was a public affair with flowers and incense, banners and parasols. He jumped from Zixiaxue 子夏學 peak on Xi shan 西山, facing west.[53] The crowd of religious chanted, "Excellent (*shanzai* 善哉)!" When the monk reached the ground he got up and sat upright, but he was dead by the time the crowd reached him.

10. The Tang *śramaṇa* Shi Huitong 釋會通 (d. 649) of Baolin 豹林 valley on Zhongnan shan (*XGSZ* 27, T 50.2060.683c18-684a19)

Note: Appended are three biographies that do not appear to have formed part of the original *Xu gaoseng zhuan*.[54] Huitong's biography was added after the date of the preface (645).

Account: Huitong was from near the Yusu 御宿 river in Wannian 萬年, Yong-zhou.[55] He led a secluded and ascetic lifestyle in the Baolin valley on Zhongnan shan. He read the *Lotus Sūtra* and was inspired by the Medicine King. One night in 649, he stacked up firewood and made a niche within. He chanted as far as the Medicine King chapter before ordering the fire to be lit. In the southwest, a great white light appeared, which flowed into the mass of flames, and Huitong fell on his back. By dawn both his body and the fire were burnt out. The witnesses raised a white pagoda for his remains. Daoxuan reports that the inscription was still there in his day.

Appended: (1) Two nuns, who were sisters, at the beginning of the Zhenguan reign period (627–649) in Jingzhou 荆州 .[56] They recited the *Lotus Sūtra* and loathed their bodies. They restricted their food and clothing, consumed fragrant oils, and abstained from grain. Later they ate only incense and honey. After widely announcing their intention to burn their bodies, on the night of Zhenguan 3.2.8 (March 8, 629), they set up two high seats on Jingzhou's main road. They wrapped their bodies in waxed cloth up to the crown of the head. In front of a large crowd, they recited the *Lotus* and set fire to each other. At daybreak their bodies were still intact, but then the fires both simultaneously flared up again. The bones were smashed but two tongues remained intact. The witnesses raised a high *stūpa* for them.

Appended: (2) Recently, west of the walls of Bingzhou并州, a student (*shusheng* 書生) aged about twenty-four or twenty-five recited the *Lotus Sūtra* and vowed to burn his body in homage. He made a basket from bundles of dried mugwort stems and in the middle of the night he set fire to it and burned himself. When people came to save him, he was already dead, so they added more fuel to the fire.

Appended: (3) A contemporary account of the teaching of Shandao 善導 (613–681) that seems to have been added at a fairly late date. In Xihe 西河 Shandao encountered the followers of Daochuo 道綽 (562–645), who practiced only reciting the name of the Buddha Amitābha. In Chang'an, he promoted this teaching and copied out several tens of thousands of scrolls of the *Amituo jing*阿彌陀經 (*Sukhāvatī*[*amṛta*] *vyūha*, T 366). When Shandao was preaching at Guangming si 光明寺, someone asked him if he would definitely be reborn in the Pure Land if he were to chant the name of Amitābha. Shandao said he would. This person then chanted "Namu Amituofo" incessantly, climbed to the top of a willow tree, threw himself off, and died. The matter was reported to the Department of State Affairs.

Translation: Gernet 1960, 546.

11. The Tang *śramaṇa* Ācārya Shao (Shao sheli) 紹闍梨 (fl. ca. 605) of Zizhou 梓州 (*XGSZ* 27, T 50.2060.684a20–b3)

Note: This biography was probably not added until after the tenth century; see Ibuki 1990, 62–68.

Account: Ācārya Shao was from Xuanwu 玄武 in Zizhou 梓州 .[57] His secular name was Pu 蒲. Once, before he became a monk, he tried to feed himself to snakes. As a monk he practiced only recitation and circumambulation. At the beginning of the Daye period (605–617), the snakes in Ruzhou汝州became extraordinarily ferocious and attacked people.[58] When Shao arrived he set up a thatched canopy and drove them away. At the age of 109 he became ill and told his disciples to expose his corpse as a donation to snakes and birds. When birds and beasts did not attack it after a month, they interred it.

12. The Tang *śramaṇa* Shi Daoxiu 釋道休 (d. 629) of Fuyuan si 福緣寺 in Xinfeng 新豐, Yongzhou (*XGSZ* 27, T 50.2060.684b4–c3)[59]

Account: Daoxiu lived not far from Chang'an. He was an ascetic and meditator who would sit for seven days. Then he would come off the mountain to beg for food and preach. One day in the summer of 629, he did not appear at the expected time. The villagers went to his meditation hut to look for him and found him dead. They kept guard for three nights before they realized he was truly deceased. Daoxiu's body did not rot, so they left it there and closed up his hut against vermin.

In early winter 630 Daoxuan went to see the mummy. People living north of the mountain had installed his body in a hut. Although Daoxiu's skin had turned leathery and his bones had fused together, his facial expression and posture had not changed. The villagers had added lacquer-soaked cloth to the surface of his body. Daoxuan reports that in life Daoxiu used only three robes and sometimes sat naked in winter.

Song gaoseng zhuan

1. The Tang monk Sengzang 僧藏 (d.u.) from Fenzhou 汾州 (*SGSZ* 23, T 50.2061.855a23–b10)[60]

Account: Sengzang's secular name, the name of his monastery, the name of his master, and the date of his death are not reported. He was extremely humble; if monks or laypeople bowed to him, he would bow and run away. He stripped off his robes in the summer and offered his body to insects. He died peacefully, sitting upright with his palms together, reciting the name of Amitābha.

2. The Tang monk Zhengshou 正壽 (d. ca. 710) from Shanguang si 山光寺 in Handong 漢東 (*SGSZ* 23, T 50.2061.855b11–c7)

Account: Zhengshou's background is unknown, but he was a disciple of the Chan master Zao 慥 of Nanta 南塔 (si 寺). Later he became a recluse at a mountain monastery in Suibu 隨部. Li Chongfu 李重福, prince of Qiao 譙王 (680–710), was the prefect of Junzhou 均州. Li became a patron of Master Zao for whom he constructed the *shengzang* 生藏 (living repository) pagoda. When Zao named Zhengshou as his succesor, the prince ordered him to come to meet him. First, Zhengshou asked Zao's permission to test the pagoda. He entered it and died sitting upright. His body did not decay, and he became known as "the Upādhyāya who tested the pagoda." Li constructed another pagoda for Zao.

Appended comment: Zanning discusses the implications of Zhengshou preceding his master into *nirvāṇa*.

3. The Tang monk Wuran 無染 (d. ca. 836–840) of Shanzhu geyuan 善住閣院 on Wutai shan 五臺山 (*SGSZ* 23, T 50.2061.855c9–856b2)

Note: See also *Guang qingliang zhuan* 廣清涼傳 (Extensive Records of Cool-and-Clear [Wutai shan]), T 51.2099.1116a23–c16.

Account: Wuran's family name and native place are unknown. He was trained on Zhongtiao shan 中條山, where he lectured on the Four-Part Vinaya, the *Nirvāṇa Sūtra,* and some Yogācāra treatises.[61] He constantly recited the *Huayan jing.* In 791 he arrived on Wutai shan, where he actively sought an encounter with Mañjuśrī. Over twenty years or so he made more than seventy-two complete circuits of the mountain. One day he saw a monastery that housed tens of thousands of Indian monks and Mañjuśrī himself. Mañjuśrī told him that he should support the community on the mountain and not abandon his body in vain. Wuran organized donations for vegetarian feasts. To record every one million monks fed, he burned one finger. Eventually he burned off all ten.

During the Kaicheng 開成 period (836–840), at the age of seventy-four and after fifty-five years as a monk, Wuran said farewell to his companions. The layman Zhao Hua 趙華 (d.u.) carried waxed cloth, hemp, and oil to the summit of the central terrace, where Wuran ordered him to wrap his body in the cloth. He promised that if he attained awakening, he would deliver Zhao. Contrary to his wishes, Wuran's disciples gathered his relics and placed them in a pagoda on the south side of Fanxian shan 梵仙山. The pagoda was still there in Zanning's day.

Translation: Partly translated in Kieschnick 1997, 37–38.

4. The Tang monk Dinglan 定蘭 (d. 852) of Fugan si 福感寺 in Chengdu prefecture 成都府 (*SGSZ* 23, T 50.2061.856b3–23)

Account: Dinglan's secular name was Yang 楊, and he was a native of Chengdu. He was a butcher, but he repented of his transgressions. His mother and father had died young, and he had no money to pay for ancestral rituals. One year he stripped naked and entered Qingcheng shan 青城山. He allowed mosquitoes to bite at him to repay the compassion of his parents. He also copied *sūtra*s in his own blood, burned off his arm, tore off his ears, and gouged out his eyes and fed them to birds and animals. A stranger appeared who replaced Dinglan's eyes.

In 849 Xuanzong 宣宗 (r. 846–859) invited Dinglan to court with his disciple Youyuan 有緣 (835–907). In 852 Dinglan vowed to burn his shoulder and subsequently died. The emperor bestowed on him the posthumous name Juexing 覺性 and had the pagoda Wuzhen 悟真 built; a cult was still based there in Zanning's day.

5. The Tang monk Hongxiu 鴻休 (d. 880 or 881) of Jianfu si 建福寺 on Huangbo shan 黃檗山 in Fuzhou 福州 (*SGSZ* 23, T 50.2061.856b24–c8)

Account: Hongxiu's origins are unknown, but he lived and taught on Huangbo shan. He was beheaded by Huang Chao rebels. When they saw no blood, the rebels fell back and confessed their transgressions. Hongxiu's disciple Jingxian 景先 cremated his corpse and placed the relics in a bag. A layperson stole them, but Jingxian retrieved them with help from a fortune-teller and enshrined them. The Chan monk Qinghuo 清豁 (?–976) composed a eulogy.

6. The Tang monk Quanhuo 全豁 (828–887) from Yantou yuan 巖頭院 in Ezhou 鄂州 (*SGSZ* 23, T 50.2061.856c10–26)[62]

Note: Biographies in the *Jingde chuandeng lu* 景德傳燈錄 (Jingde Era [1004–1016] Records of the Transmission of the Lamp) 16, T 51.2076.326a10–327a10, and the *Longxing fojiao biannian tonglun* 隆興佛教編年通論 (Longxing Era [1163–1164] Comprehensive Discussion and Chronology of Buddhism), compiled by Zuxiu 祖琇 (d. after 1164), 28, *XZJ* 130.340a b.

Account: Quanhuo's secular name was Ke 柯, and he was from Quanzhou 泉州 in Fujian. His tonsure master was Master Yi 誼公 (d.u.) of Qingyuan 清源, and he received full ordination from Yuanzhao 圓照 (727–809) of Ximing si 西明寺, Chang'an.[63] He studied at Baoshou si 保壽寺 and later with the Chan master Deshan Xuanjian 德山宣鑑 (782–865) in Wuling 武陵.[64] Sometime during the period 885–888 rebels came to loot the monastery at Tangnian shan 唐年山.[65] Quanhuo refused to give them anything and they killed him. On May 4, 887, his disciples buried him temporarily; later they burned his remains and obtained forty-nine grains of *śarīra*. The emperor Xizong bestowed on him a posthumous name. Xuantai 玄泰 of Nanyue (d. after 901) composed the stele inscription for his *stūpa*.

Appended comment: Zanning discusses the above two biographies and compares Buddhist self-immolation with Taoist "sword liberation."

7. The Tang monk Yuanhui 元慧 (819–896) of Fakongwang si 法空王寺 in Jiaxing 嘉興, Wujun 吳郡 (*SGSZ* 23, T 50.2061.857a5–23)[66]

Note: Zanning refers to an independently circulating biography.

Account: Yuanhui was a member of a distinguished branch of the Lu 陸 family and a descendent of Lu Ji 陸機 (261–303).[67] He was the second son of Lu Dan 陸丹 (d.u.), administrative supervisor (*jucao* 糾曹) of Wenzhou 溫州.[68] In 837, at the age of eighteen, he became a disciple of Qingjin 清進 (d.u.) at Fakongwang si. In 841 Yuanhui took the precepts at Hengyang 恒陽 and travelled to Wutai shan.[69] In 842 he returned to Jianxing si 建興寺 at Jiahe 嘉禾 (Jiaxing). He maintained the "Three Whites" (*sanbai* 三白), recited the mantras of the five divisions of the Diamond Realm, and burned incense on his arm. During the Huichang 會昌 persecution (845–847), he was forced to return to lay life. In 853 Fakongwang si was rebuilt, and Yuanhui burned incense on his arm in homage to the Buddha's tooth at Bao'en shan si 報恩山寺. Then he crossed the stone bridge at Tiantai shan. During the Xiantong 咸通 period (860–873), at Chongzhen si 重真寺 in Fengxiang鳳翔, he burned off his left thumb in front of the Buddha's finger relic while reciting the *Lotus Sūtra*. The thumb grew back in less than a month. He died on Qianning 乾寧 3.9.28 (November 7, 896); his disciple, Duansu 端肅 (d.u.), and others erected a memorial stele and buried him in Wugui 吳會.[70] He was known as the "Upādhyāya of the Three Whites" (*sanbai heshang* 三白和尚).

Appended comment: Zanning addresses the miraculous regrowth of Yuanhui's thumb and the meaning of the term "Three Whites."

8. The Tang Master Bundle of Grass (Shucao shi 束草師, d. before 853) of Puti si 菩提寺 in the capital (*SGSZ* 23, T 50.2061.857b2–13)

Note: See the *Sita ji* 寺塔記 (Record of Monasteries and Stūpas) 1/17 (Soper 1960, 29), and the *Taiping guangji* 太平廣記 (Extensive Accounts of the Taiping Era) 98/653.

Account: A monk arrived suddenly at Puti si in the Pingkang 平康 quarter of Chang'an. No one knew where he was from or his name. He always carried a bundle of straw and sat in the corridors of the veranda. When the other monks urged him to move into proper accommodation, he took offense. He used his bundle of straw to set fire to himself and the next morning only ashes and cinders remained. His incineration was attributed to *samādhi* fire. Laypeople made an image of the monk out of his ashes and worshipped it at the side of the Buddha hall.

Appended comment: Zanning discusses the *samādhi* of the fire realm.

9. The Tang forest dweller (*lanruo*蘭若; Skt. *āranyaka*) Xingming 行明 (fl. ca. 900) of Nanyue 南嶽 (*SGSZ* 23, T 50.2061.857b19–c11)

Account: Xingming's secular name was Lu魯, and he was from Changzhou長洲 in Wujun 吳郡.[71] He travelled extensively and worshipped bodhisattvas on Wutai shan and Emei shan 峨眉山. He ended up at Qibaotai si 七寶台寺 (Monastery of the Terrace of the Seven Precious Materials) on the Zhurong 祝融 peak of Nanyue, where he became friends with Xuantai.[72] He rejected the examples of Sengyai and Qu Yuan 屈原 (d. ca. 315 BCE) but wished to emulate Prince Mahāsattva and fed himself to tigers. Xuantai burned his remains and collected the *śarīra*. He composed a eulogy for his friend.

Appended comment: Zanning discusses Xingming's perfection of *dāna*.

10. The Jin 晉 (936–946) monk Xichen 息塵 (875?–937?) of Sanxue yuan 三學院 in Yonghe 永和, Taiyuan 太原 (*SGSZ* 23, T 50.2061.857c14–858b1)

Account: Xichen was the son of a merchant called Yang 楊 from Bingzhou 并州.[73] His mother had an auspicious dream before his birth. He left home at twelve, studied the *Vimalakīrtinirdeśa,* and observed the Vinaya. At Chongfu si 崇福寺 he was a disciple of *dharma* master Gan 感 (d.u.).[74] Wu Huangdi 武皇帝 (Li Keyong 李克用, 856–908), father of the first emperor of the Later Tang) invited him to stay in the Jingtu yuan 淨土院 (Pure Land Cloister) at Da'an si 大安寺.[75] Xichen tried to give his body to wild dogs and tigers but failed. He also fed his body to gnats. At Xianyan si 仙巖寺, after repeatedly reading the canon, he held a vegetarian banquet and burned off a finger.[76] Every month he fed himself to water creatures in a river or pond. He bought caged birds and beasts and set them free, gave food to prisoners, helped the poor, and occasionally gave a banner or a parasol to local *stūpa*s.

In 931 he established the Sanxue yuan 三學院 behind the Da Anguo si 大安國寺. After prostrating to every character of the *Huayan jing* and the *Da Foming jing* 大佛名經 (Great Sūtra of the Names of the Buddha, T 14.441), he burned off another finger. Jin Gaozu 晉高祖 (r. 936–942) bestowed on him the imperial purple robe.

In front of the Buddha's middle finger bone at Famen si 法門寺 in Fengxiang 鳳翔 prefecture, Xichen burned off another finger. He died at Tianzhu si 天柱寺 at the age of sixty-three, after forty-four years as a monk. His disciples cremated him and obtained several hundred relics. Jin Gaozu had them interred in the mountains west of the Jin river, where a small *stūpa* still existed in Zanning's time.

Appended comment: Zanning discusses the variety and diversity of Xichen's practices.

Translation: Partly translated in Rhie 1977, 72–77.

11. The Jin monk Toyuk 道育 (Chn. Daoyu, 858?–938) of Pingtian si 平田寺 on Tiantai shan (*SGSZ* 23, T 50.2061.858b2–25)

Account: Toyuk was from Silla, and his family name is unknown. In 892 he went to Mount Tiantai and stayed for the rest of his life. He carried only a single bowl for food. During the day he performed menial tasks in the monastery. He always wore a thick robe, but every summer and autumn he would expose his chest, back, and legs to insects. The only thing he ever said was "Yiyi!" He spontaneously exuded multicolored, pearl-like *śarīra.* He was more than eighty years old when he died in 938, and after his cremation countless *śarīra* were found. Zanning met him in 935. He reports that a group of tigers once came to sniff Toyuk but did not eat him.

12. The Jin monk Jingchao 景超 (d. ca. 936–943) from Xiangji hermitage 香積庵 on Lu shan in Jiangzhou 江州 (*SGSZ* 23, T 50.2061.858b26–c11)

Account: Jingchao's native place is unknown. On Lu shan he made a full prostration to each character in the *Huayan jing.* After two rounds of recitation he burned a finger and then paid homage to the *Lotus Sūtra* in the same manner. He spontaneously exuded many *śarīra,* which people collected. Sometime during the Tianfu 天福 period (936–943) he died, and his remains were interred in a pagoda that was still a place of pilgrimage in Zanning's time.

Appended comment: Zanning discusses whether the burning of fingers was a true imitation of scriptural models. He compares the biographies in his collection to accounts of upright officials in the dynastic histories.

13. The Jin monk Zhitong 志通 (d. after 939) from Famen si in Fengxiang fu 鳳翔府 (*SGSZ* 23, T 50.2061.858c12–859a19)

Note: See also *Fozu tongji* 27, T 49.2035.276c16–23; *Jingtu wangsheng zhuan* 淨土往生傳 (Biographies of Those Who Attained Deliverance in the Pure Land) 2, T 51.2071.125b8–c6; *Wangsheng ji* 往生集 (Collection on Attaining Deliverance) 1, T 51.2072.132b22–c5.

Account: Zhitong's secular name was Zhang 張, and he was the son of a well-known family from Youfufeng 右扶風.[77] During the Later Tang (923–936) in Luoyang he met the Tripiṭaka master Furiluo 縛日囉 (Śrīvajra).[78] When Zhitong left to visit the mountains of Tiantai and Luofu 羅浮, his master encouraged him to take some Indian texts with him. King Wenmu 文穆 (Qian Yuanguan 錢元瓘, 887–941; r. 932–941) of Wu-Yue invited him to court and installed him at the Zhenshenta si 真身塔寺 (True Body Stūpa Monastery). Zhitong later went to Tiantai shan and stayed at Zhiyi's former monastery. After reading the *Xifang jingtu lingrui zhuan* 西方淨土靈瑞傳 (Accounts of Numinous Signs of the Western Pure Land), he took up Pure Land practices.

Zhitong threw himself off a rock called "the Beckoning Hand" (*zhaoshou shi* 招手石), which was associated with a legend told of Zhiyi. He first landed in a tree, so he jumped again. He fell onto some grass, where he lay unconscious. The other monks thought that he must have been eaten by tigers. They consulted a spirit medium, who told them that a deity in golden armor was aiding him.

Zhitong later went to Fahua shan 法華山 in Yuezhou 越州, where he cultivated Pure Land practices. His body spontaneously produced *śarīra,* and he died sitting on his meditation seat. When he was cremated a five-colored cloud of smoke covered the crown of his head and there was a remarkable fragrance.

Appended comment: Zanning compares Zhitong's story with some other examples of divine providence from the scriptures and earlier biographies.

14. The Jin monk Daozhou 道舟 (864–941) of Yongfu si 永福寺 in Lingwu 靈武 on the northern frontier (*shuofang* 朔方) (*SGSZ* 23, T 50.2061.859a21–b12)

Account: Daozhou's secular name was Guan 管, and he was from Huile 迴樂 on the northern frontier.[79] As a child, he recited the *Shijing* 詩經 (Book of Odes) and the *Shangshu* 尚書 (Book of Documents). He became a novice and was later ordained at the Kongque wang yuan 孔雀王院 (Queen Māyūrī Cloister) of Long-xing si 龍興寺. He had Yongxing si 永興寺 built but did not take charge of it. Some time between 918 and 929 he said farewell to the military governor of Ling[wu], Han Zhu 韓洙 (?–929), and entered the Baicao 白草 valley of Helan shan 賀蘭山, where dried-up springs gushed forth again and numinous serpents swam in the streams.[80] Later Daozhou climbed Fa tai 法臺, where he preached to large crowds. He painted in his own blood an image of Guanyin. He ended a drought by fast-ing. In 882 he cut off his left forearm below the *stūpa* at Nianding yuan 念定院 and burned it in homage to Guanyin, making a vow for peace. He cut off his left ear to pray for rain and repeatedly fasted to pray for snow. On Tianfu 天福 6 (*xinchou* 辛丑).2.6 (March 6, 941), he died seated in the lotus position at the age of seventy-eight. His remains did not decay, and his disciples added some lacquered cloth. During the Jianlong 建隆 period (960–963), Guo Zhongshu 郭忠恕 (?–977) com-posed a stele inscription for him.

15. The Han 漢 (947–950) monk Hongzhen 洪真 (fl. ca. 947–950) of Guang'ai si 廣愛寺 in Luojing 洛京 (Luoyang) (*SGSZ* 23, T 50.2061.859b13–25)

Account: Hongzhen's surname was Chunyu 淳于, and he was from Suanzao 酸棗 in Huazhou 滑州.[81] His master taught him the *Lotus Sūtra;* when he had recited it about ten thousand times, he asked the emperor for permission to burn his body but was refused. Hongzhen gave away his belongings and vowed to end his life that year. He died sitting upright without any sign of illness, and when his body was cremated only the tongue remained. Zanning reports that in his own day Hongzhen was still revered.

16. The Zhou 周 (951–960) monk Huiming 慧明 (d. ca. 954–959) of Baoen si 報恩寺 in Qiantang 錢塘 (*SGSZ* 23, T 50.2061.859b26–c11)

Note: See also *Jingde chuandeng lu* 25, T 51.2076.410b13–c24.

Account: Huiming's surname was Jiang 蔣, and he was from Qiantang.[82] He travelled throughout Fujian and Yue 越 and attained awakening under the Chan master Fayan Wenyi 法眼文益 (885–958).[83] At Baisha 白沙 on Tiantai shan he taught in the styles of the Chan masters Xuefeng Yicun 雪峰義存 (822–908) and Zhang-qing Huileng 長慶慧稜 (854–932).[84] Later he inherited the teaching of Xuansha Shibei 玄沙師備 (835–908).[85] King Zhongyi of Wu-Yue founded the Da Baoen si 大報恩寺 for him and gave him the title Chan Master Yuantong Puzhao 圓通普照禪師 (Perfect Understanding and Universal Radiance). Huiming died sometime dur-ing the Xiande 顯德 reign period (954–959). At his disciple Yongan's 永安 (d.u.) re-quest he was cremated and left behind five-colored *śarīra*. Huiming had burned his finger to honor Mañjuśrī on Mount Tiantai and later burned three more fingers.

17. The Zhou monk Pujing 普靜 (887–955) of Ciyun si 慈雲寺 in Jinzhou 晉州 (*SGSZ* 23, T 50.2061.859c12–29)

Note: See the long inscription on which the biography is based in the *Shanyou shike congbian* 山右石刻叢編 10, *Shike shiliao xinbian* 石刻史料新編 (New Edition of Historical Materials Inscribed on Stone), vol. 20, 15155a–15156b.

Account: Pujing's surname was Ru 茹, and he was from Hongdong 洪洞 in Jinzhou 晉州.[86] He became a novice under Huicheng 惠澄 (d.u.), who taught him to recite *sūtra*s and spells. At Famen si he paid homage to the relics of the Buddha. He travelled and lectured extensively throughout Henan and Anhui and went on to Kaifeng 開封. In 943 he returned to his home village, where he fasted and vowed to sacrifice one thousand bodies to attain true awakening quickly. In 955 the Buddha relics were invited to Ciyun monastery. Pujing told Lord Yang 楊 (probably Yang Tingzhang 楊廷璋 912–971), the metropolitan governor (*zhoumu* 州牧), that he intended to burn his body and Yang agreed. At the *stūpa,* on the eighth day of the fourth month (May 2, 955), in front of a large audience he entered a firewood hut and set it alight. He was sixty-nine. His disciples gathered his remaining ashes and paid homage to them.

18. The Song monk Shouxian 守賢 (ca. 890–ca. 968) of Dasheng si 大聖寺 in Hengyang 衡陽 (*SGSZ* 23, T 50.2061.860a1–12)

Note: See also *Tiansheng guangdeng lu* 天聖廣燈錄 20 (*XZJ* 135.399b–c) and *Wudeng huiyuan* 五燈會元 15 (*XZJ* 138.288d).

Account: Shouxian's surname was Qiu 丘, and he was from Yongchun 永春 in Quanzhou 泉州.[87] He was tonsured at Jixiang yuan 吉祥院. He attained awakening under the Chan master Yunmen 雲門 (864–949) and later went to Hengyang.[88] Shouxian did not wear silk; he wore only trousers made of coarse cloth, which he never changed. One day during the Gande 乾德 period (963–968) on Nanyao shan 南窯山, he gave himself to a hungry tiger. All that remained were his two legs encased in his trousers, which his disciples cremated and from which they obtained countless *śarīra*. He was seventy-four years old. Zanning reports that in his day Shouxian's remains were still enshrined in a small pagoda.

19. The Song monk Shiyun 師蘊 (ca. 893–973) of Bore si 般若寺 on Tiantai shan (*SGSZ* 23, T 50.2061.860a13–b6)

Account: Shiyun was from Jinhua 金華 in Zhejiang. During the Longde 龍德 period of the later Liang (921–923), he travelled all over China. Later he returned to Deshao's 德韶 (891–972) community, where he was in great demand for his jokes.[89] He chanted *sūtra*s, memorized *dhāraṇī*s, and could explain many texts. He said that he planned to throw himself off the stone bridge on Yanzuo peak 宴坐峰, but his friends talked him out of it.

In 973 he died sitting upright without any illness. His body was kept for four-teen days in very hot weather, but it showed no signs of corruption. When he was cremated the monks recovered his unburnt tongue and other *śarīra* from the ashes. After they burned the tongue it took the shape of a lotus. They interred it in a small pagoda. Later a skeptic burned it dozens of times over. Shiyun appeared to be over eighty years old when he died.

20. The Song monk Shaoyan 紹巖 (d. 971) of Zhenshen baota si 真身寶塔寺 in Hangzhou 杭州 (*SGSZ* 23, T 50.2061.860b7–29)

Account: Shaoyan's family name was Liu 劉, and he was from Yongzhou 雍州. At seven *sui* he became a novice under the Chan master Gaoan 高安.[90] At eighteen he was ordained by the Vinaya master Huaihui 懷暉.[91] He studied under Fayan Wenyi along with Deshao. Finally he resided at Shuixin si 水心寺 by Qiantang lake 錢塘湖, where he constantly recited the *Lotus*. Lotus flowers bloomed miraculously in the courtyard.

In 961 he vowed to imitate the Medicine King and burn his body. But the king of Wu-Yue, Zhongyi, would not allow him. Shaoyan threw himself in the Caoe river 曹娥江, but a passing fisherman pulled him out.

Shaoyan lived at Fahua shan 法華山 in Yue until he was ordered by edict to move to Hangta si 杭塔寺, where the Shangfang jingyuan 上方淨院 was constructed for him. In Kaibao 開寶 4 (971), he fell ill but refused medicine. At the age of seventy-three, after fifty-five years as a monk, he died seated upright in the lotus position. After a state-sponsored funeral he was cremated on Longjing shan 龍井山. His disciples collected *śarīra* and enshrined them in the portrait hall. Sun Chengyou 孫承祐 (936–985), military commissioner of the Daning army (*Daning jun jiedushi* 大寧軍節度使) with the posthumous rank of grand preceptor (*zeng taishi* 贈太師), composed a stele relating these events.[92]

21. The Song monk Wennian 文輦 (895–978) of Tiantai shan (*SGSZ* 23, T 50.2061.860c1–28)

Account: Wennian was from Pingyang 平陽 in Yongjia 永嘉 commandery (Zhejiang). He was trained in Jinhua 金華.[93] On Mount Jinyun 縉雲 he attained awakening under the Chan master Mingzhao 明昭 (d.u.). Next he followed Deshao for thirty years. To evaluate the words of his teachers against those of the Buddha, he read the whole canon three times over.

In 978, at the age of eighty-four, he made a "Buddha *stūpa*" of sandalwood, entered it, and sat with his legs crossed. He set fire to himself, reciting *sūtra*s as he burned. He left countless *śarīra*, which were enshrined in a small pagoda.

Appended comment: Zanning tackles the issue of whether or not self-immolation is permitted for monks.

22. The Song monk Huaide 懷德 (d. 983) of Puzhaowang si 普照王寺 in Linhuai 臨淮 (*SGSZ* 23, T 50.2061.860c29–861a12)

Huaide was originally from Jiangnan 江南 and became a novice in his youth.
He was ordained because of his ability to recite the *Lotus*. At Sishang 泗上 he
paid obeisance to the image of Sengqie 僧伽 (d. 710). At the same time Song
Taizong 太宗, (r. 976–997) had sent the eunuch of high rank Li Shenfu 李神福
(947–1010) to honor Sengqie's image. The *śarīra* that were miraculously produced by this ritual were buried deep under the foundations of a new pagoda,
where Huaide vowed to burn his body. First he gave away his robes, his bag, and
so on. On Taiping xingguo 太平興國 8.4.8 (May 22, 983), dressed in paper
clothes, he covered his body in oil and wax. Holding in his hands two candles,
he climbed into the pyre and set fire to it. The onlookers wept as he recited
sūtras and burned. Many *śarīra* were collected from the ashes. This was reported
to the emperor.

Fayuan zhulin

1. Ning Fengzi 甯封子 of the time of the Yellow Emperor (*Fayuan zhulin* 96,
T 53.2122.992a1–5)
Note: See *Liexian zhuan* 列仙傳, *DZ* 294 1.1b; translated in Campany 1996,
218. Compare with the translation in Kaltenmark 1987, 43–47.
Account: Legend has it that Fengzi was the Yellow Emperor's master potter.
Someone came to visit him who could cause his palm to burst into flames and
emit five-colored smoke. This person taught the art to Fengzi, who then started a
fire and burned himself: He ascended and descended following the smoke from
the fire. When the remaining ashes were examined, his bones were found among
them and were buried on a mountain north of Ning, hence his name, Master of
the Tumulus at Ning.

2. The Song *śramaṇa* Shi Huishao 釋慧紹 (*Fayuan zhulin* 96, T
53.2122.992a6–22)
Note: See the *Gaoseng zhuan* biography.

3. The Song *śramaṇa* Shi Sengyu 釋僧瑜 (*Fayuan zhulin* 96, T 53.2122.992a23–
b16)
Note: See the *Gaoseng zhuan* biography.

4. The Song *śramaṇa* Shi Huiyi 釋慧益 (*Fayuan zhulin* 96, T 53.2122.992b17–
c15)
Note: See the *Gaoseng zhuan* biography.

5. The Liang *śramaṇa* Shi Daodu 釋道度 (*Fayuan zhulin* 96, T 53.2122.992c16-993a5).

Note: See the funerary inscription for Daodu, "Liang Xiaozhuangyansi Daodu Chanshi bei" 梁小莊嚴寺道度禪師碑, composed by Xiao Gang 蕭綱 (503–551), later Liang Jianwendi 梁簡文帝 (r. 549–551), collected in *Sŏkwŏn salin* 釋苑詞林 (A Forest of Words from Śākya's Garden), fasc. 193, *Han'guk Pulgyo chŏnsŏ* 韓國佛教 全書 (Complete Works of Korean Buddhism), vol. 4, pp. 660–662. In the *Gaoseng zhuan* (13, T 50.2059.412c27), we find mentioned a monk called Daodu who donated seven *kāṣāya*s to help defray the cost of casting a Buddha image at the lesser Zhuangyan si 小莊嚴寺 . This is very probably the same Daodu. A fuller account of Daodu's contribution to the construction of this important monastery is found in the *Fayuan zhulin* (64, T 53. 2122.772b29–c7), quoting *Liangjing siji* 梁京寺記 (Record of Monasteries in the Liang Capital).[94]

Daoshi says that the *Fayuan zhulin* entry is based on the *Liang gaoseng zhuan,* but the extant version does not contain an entry for Daodu.

Account: Daodu was a *dhyāna* master at the lesser Zhuangyan si during the Putong years of the Liang (520–526). Although Liang Wudi told him to think of the body as a poisonous tree, to expose the corpse as a donation for birds and beasts, and that cremation was inappropriate because of the eighty thousand worms in the body, Daodu piled up firewood and gradually restricted his diet. On Putong 7.11.3 (December 22, 526), the monastery bell started ringing; it rang again on December 27th. Daodu ceased eating and drank only a pint of water per day from the bathing bucket.

On January 13, 527, the monks saw light and vapor emitting from the bucket. On the morning of January 17th they saw a purple glow radiating from a niche in the meditation hall. Towards evening a large flock of birds suddenly appeared on a single tree and then all flew off to the west. That night multicolored rays of light lit up the monastery and a fire started to burn on the summit of the mountain. The monks found Daodu in the fire with his hands together. He was sixty-six. The prince of Wuling interred the remains beneath a pagoda. Later, people heard the sound of a stone chime on the mountaintop and an old, dead tree came back to life.

6. The Zhou *śramaṇa* Shi Sengyai 釋僧崖 (*Fayuan zhulin* 96, T 53.2122.993a6-994c3)

Note: See the *Xu gaoseng zhuan* biography.

7. The Zhou *śramaṇa* Shi Jing'ai 釋靜藹 (*Fayuan zhulin* 96, T 53.2122.994c4-995c8)

Note: See Jing'ai's biography in the *Xu gaoseng zhuan,* which appears in the "defenders of the *dharma*" (*hufa* 護法) section, T 50.2060.625c-628a; discussed in Teiser 1988b, 437–439, and Jan Yün-hua 1965, 252–253. A biography also appears in the *Da Tang neidian lu* 大唐內典錄 (Great Tang Catalogue of Volumes of the Inner [Teaching]), compiled by Daoxuan, T 55.2149.27c, 331c; the *Wangsheng xifang jingtu ruiying zhuan* 往生西方淨土瑞應傳 (Biographies of Auspicious Responses of Those Who Were Reborn in the Western Pure Land) by Wennian 文念 (d.u.) and Shaokang 少康 (d. 805), T 51.2070.104c; the *Fozu tongji,* T 49.2035.358c; and the *Fozu lidai tongzai* 佛祖歷代通載 (Comprehensive History of the Buddhas and Patriarchs), compiled by Nianchang念常 (d. 1341), T 49.2036.557c–558a.

Account: As a boy Jing'ai was inspired to leave home by the pictures of the hells that he saw at a local monastery. He had a distinguished monastic career, studying and lecturing on major texts. He tried to dissuade Zhou Wudi from proscribing Buddhism but failed and retreated to Zhongnan shan. Convinced that the *dharma* was beyond rescue, he eviscerated himself, hanging his entrails on the surrounding trees. Finally, using his own blood, he composed a lengthy series of verses on his self-immolation (preserved in the biography). The preface explains that Jing'ai gave up his body for three reasons: The many misfortunes suffered by the body, his inability to protect the *dharma,* and his desire to see the Buddha and the sages of the past.

8. The Sui *śramaṇa* Shi Dazhi 釋大志 (*Fayuan zhulin* 96, T 53.2122.995c9–27)
Note: See the *Xu gaoseng zhuan* biography.

9. The Tang *śramaṇa* Shi Huitong 釋會通 (*Fayuan zhulin* 96, T 53.2122.995c28–996b8)
Note: See the *Xu gaoseng zhuan* biography.

Shishi liutie

Shishi liutie 釋氏六帖 (The Buddhists' Six Documents), compiled by Yichu 義楚 (fl. mid-tenth century), 944–954.[95] The section is entitled *Juanshen wei fa* 捐身爲法 (Donating the Body for the *Dharma*) and includes biographies taken from the self-immolation sections of the *Gaoseng zhuan* and the *Xu Gaoseng zhuan,* followed by biographies of defenders of the *dharma* from Daoxuan's collection.

1. Sengqun 僧群 injures a duck (*Shishi liutie* 12, 257)
2. Tanhong 曇稱 becomes a slave (*Shishi liutie* 12, 257)
3. Fajin 法進 donates his body (*Shishi liutie* 12, 257)
4. Sengfu 僧富 cuts himself up (*Shishi liutie* 12, 258)
5. Fayu's 法羽 bravery (*Shishi liutie* 12, 258)
6. Huishao 惠紹 causes a firmiana to grow (*Shishi liutie* 12, 258)
7. The double firmiana of Sengyu 僧瑜 (*Shishi liutie* 12, 258)
8. Huiyi 惠益 the Medicine King (*Shishi liutie* 12, 258)

9. Sengqing 僧慶 is like a dragon (*Shishi liutie* 12, 258)

10. Faxian 法仙 eats pine needles (*Shishi liutie* 12, 258)[96]

11. Tanhong's 曇弘 golden deer (*Shishi liutie* 12, 258)

12. Fakuang 法曠 burns his body (*Shishi liutie* 12, 258)

13. Sengyai 僧崖 withstands fire (*Shishi liutie* 12, 258)

14. Bingyuan 並圓 gives away his arm (*Shishi liutie* 12, 259)[97]

15. Puji 普濟 eats grass (*Shishi liutie* 12, 259)

16. Puan 普安 gives away his body (*Shishi liutie* 12, 259)

17. Dazhi 大志 burns his arm (*Shishi liutie* 12, 259)

18. Zhiming's 知命 personal salvation (*Shishi liutie* 12, 259)

19. Xuanlan 玄覽 leaves a text behind (*Shishi liutie* 12, 259)

20. Fakuang 法曠 piles up grass (*Shishi liutie* 12, 259)

21. Shao 紹 feeds a tiger and it leaves (*Shishi liutie* 12, 259)[98]

22. Shitong 食通 recites the scriptures (*Shishi liutie* 12, 259)[99]

23. Shandao's 善導 *nianfo* 念佛 (*Shishi liutie* 12, 259)[100]

24. Daoxiu's 道休 seven days (*Shishi liutie* 12, 259)

25. Jing'ai 靜藹 pulls out his heart (*Shishi liutie* 12, 260)

Liuxue seng zhuan

Liuxue seng zhuan 六學僧傳 (Biographies of Monks by the Six Categories of Specialization), compiled by Tane 曇噩, 1366, *XZJ* 133.210–334. The section is entitled *Yishenke* 遺身科 and contains twenty-five main biographies, all drawn from earlier *Gaoseng zhuan* accounts.

1. Sengqun 僧群 of the Jin (*Liuxue seng zhuan* 9, *XZJ* 133.293b–c)

2. Tancheng 曇稱 of the Song (*Liuxue seng zhuan* 9, *XZJ* 133.293c)

3. Fajin 法進 of the Song (*Liuxue seng zhuan* 9, *XZJ* 133.293c–d)

4. Sengfu 僧富 of the Song (*Liuxue seng zhuan* 9, *XZJ* 133.293d)

5. Fayu 法羽 of the Song (*Liuxue seng zhuan* 9, *XZJ* 133.293d–294a)

6. Huishao 慧紹 of the Song (*Liuxue seng zhuan* 9, *XZJ* 133.294a)

7. Sengyu 僧瑜 of the Song (*Liuxue seng zhuan* 9, *XZJ* 133.294a)

8. Sengqing 僧慶 of the Song (*Liuxue seng zhuan* 9, *XZJ* 133.294a–b)

9. Huiyi 慧益 of the Song (*Liuxue seng zhuan* 9, *XZJ* 133.294b)

10. Tanhong 曇弘 of the Song (*Liuxue seng zhuan* 9, *XZJ* 133.294b)

11. Faguang 法光 of the Qi (*Liuxue seng zhuan* 9, *XZJ* 133.294c)

12. Faning 法凝 of the Qi (*Liuxue seng zhuan* 9, *XZJ* 133.294c)

13. Puyuan 普圓 of the Qi (*Liuxue seng zhuan* 9, *XZJ* 133.294c–d)

14. Puji 普濟 of the Sui (*Liuxue seng zhuan* 9, *XZJ* 133.294d)

15. Fakuang 法曠 of the Tang (*Liuxue seng zhuan* 9, *XZJ* 133.294d–295a)

16. A nameless Tang monk of Fenzhou 汾州 (*Liuxue seng zhuan* 9, *XZJ* 133.294d–295a)

17. Huitong 會通 of the Tang (*Liuxue seng zhuan* 9, *XZJ* 133.294d–295a–b)

18. Xuanlan 玄覽 of the Tang (*Liuxue seng zhuan* 9, *XZJ* 133.295b–c)

19. Master "Bundle of Grass" (Shucao shi 束草師) of the Tang (*Liuxue seng zhuan* 9, *XZJ* 133.295b–c)

20. Wuran 無染 of the Tang (*Liuxue seng zhuan* 9, *XZJ* 133.295c–d)

21. Xingming 行明 of the Tang (*Liuxue seng zhuan* 9, *XZJ* 133.295d–296a)

22. Pujing 普靜 of the Zhou (*Liuxue seng zhuan* 9, *XZJ* 133.296a)

23. Shouxian 守賢 of the Song (*Liuxue seng zhuan* 9, *XZJ* 133.296a–b)

24. Wennian 文輦 of the Song (*Liuxue seng zhuan* 9, *XZJ* 133.296b)

25. Huaide 懷德 of the Song (*Liuxue seng zhuan* 9, *XZJ* 133.296b)

Bu xu gaoseng zhuan

1. Yu Mituo 喻彌陀 of the Song; appended, Jingzhen 淨真 (*Bu xu gaoseng zhuan* 19, 160d–161a)

Account: Sijing 思淨 (before 1070–1137) was the son of a Mr. Yu 喻 from Qiantang 錢塘. Because of his skill in painting Amitābha, Yang Wuwei 楊無爲 named him Yu Mituo.[101] Sijing also carved an image of Maitreya. He provided shelter and fed nearly three million monks over the span of less than twenty years. He expanded his dwelling into a monastery. He went to the stronghold of some rebels and offered himself in lieu of the inhabitants of the entire city. The rebels were so shocked they reduced their attacks and many lives were saved. In the winter of 1137, Sijing passed away with his legs crossed. Zhang Wugou 張無垢 (d.u.) composed an inscription for his *stūpa*.

Appended: When Jingzhen arrived in Qiantang in Hangzhou he found that the Yangzi river had burst its banks. He wrote to the military commissioner Zhao Duanming 趙端明 (Zhao Yuhuan 趙與懽, *jinshi* 1214), announcing his intention to visit the palace of the *nāga* to persuade him to stop the flood.[102] Jingzhen threw himself into the sea, returning briefly three days later to report the success of his mission. The emperor bestowed on him the title *huguo fashi* 護國法師 (Dharma Master Protector of the State) and set up a memorial to him in Huiling 會靈.

2. The Transformation Monk (Huaseng 化僧); appended, Jixiang 吉祥 and Ciji 慈濟 (*Bu xu gaoseng zhuan* 19, 161a–b)

Account: The Transformation Monk's name is unknown. He frequented the marketplaces of Pi 郫 and Fan 繁 in Sichuan.[103] At dawn on Chongning 崇寧 5.12.2 (December 28, 1106), he came into the city to beg for food. After noon he suddenly put his clothes in a bag, begged for some soup, straightened his robes, and sat cross-legged. Before the soup arrived he announced his imminent death. His body was returned to a valley north of Pi and enshrined, and his mummy was still there in Minghe's day. At the end of the biography is an account by the local literatus Yang Tianhui 楊天惠 (doctoral candidate, 1080).

Appended: (1) Jixiang knew all the fish in the fishpond in front of his monastery by name and preached to them.

Appended: (2) Ciji died standing up on a steep rock on Qingdian shan 青顛山, located northeast of Erhai 洱海 lake (Yunnan). He had performed prostrations there every day.

3. The Chan master Faqing 法慶 of Dajue si 大覺寺 in Xianping 咸平 prefecture (*Bu xu gaoseng zhuan* 19, 161b–c)

Account: Faqing's master was Foguo Weibo 佛國惟白 (fl. 1101). Faqing's disciple was impressed by a tale about Chan masters of the past, so Faqing told him that he would return from death if his disciple called his name, thus proving that such feats were still possible. Faqing foretold the time of his death, composed a verse, and gave away his possessions. On Huangtong 皇統 3.5.5 (June 19, 1143), he died sitting upright. His disciple shouted, and he returned briefly for a final exchange and to compose a farewell verse.

4. The two masters Jueqing 覺慶 and Delin 德林 of the Yuan 元 (*Bu xu gaoseng zhuan* 19, 161c–d)

Account: (1) Jueqing stressed the merits of practices such as surfacing roads, digging wells, donating hot water, running tea stalls, and providing acupuncture and medicine. During the Zhizheng 至正 period (1341–1367), Jueqing went to Yunjian 雲間 (Songjiang 松江, Jiangsu). He set his date of death as the twenty-third day of the first month and wrote letters of farewell to his friends. Two days later he died. His body was still sweating and he looked as if he were still alive ten days later. A layman called Chen Yuanjian 陳源堅 (d.u.) donated his house as a chapel to enshrine his mummy.

Account: (2) Delin was a native of Dongou 東甌 who resided at Zheze si 柘澤寺 in Shanghai during the Zhizheng period.[104] One day he asked for a coffin and announced that he would burn his body on the first day of the ninth month. His request was ignored. On the appointed day he traded his bag and bowl for some firewood. Fire spontaneously rose from his body. Witnesses feared that his autocremation would bring bad fortune to the locale, but Delin reassured them that the rain would wash away all traces of his act.

5. The Monk Who Shed His Soul (Luopo seng 落魄僧) of the Ming; appended, Xuemei 雪梅 (*Bu xu gaoseng zhuan* 19, 161d–162b)

Note: A shorter version also appears in the *Jiansheng yewen* 翦勝野聞, attributed to Xu Zhenqing 徐禎卿 (1479–1511), *Guang Baichuan xuehai* 廣百川學海, vol. 2, 743–744.[105] A brief biography of Yonglong 永隆 (1359–1392) appears in the *Mingshi chaolüe* 明史鈔略, SBCK edition, fasc. 3, 88, p. 7b; and in Zha Jizuo's 查繼佐 *Zuiwei lu* 罪惟錄, SBCK edition, fasc. 26, p. 4a.

Account: Yonglong 永隆 (1359–1392) was the son of a Mr. Shi 施 from Gusu 姑蘇 in Jiangsu. He became a novice at twenty and took the tonsure at Chongfu si 崇福寺 on Yin shan 尹山.[106] A god told him that the monastery had been founded during the Tianjian 天監 era (502–519) of the Liang dynasty but had burned down towards the end of the Yuan (1206–1347). The god promised to protect him if he rebuilt the monastery. When Yonglong copied the *Lotus* and the *Huayan jing* in his own blood, *śarīra* were produced from the brush. During the reconstruction, a change in the wind direction saved the boats ferrying timber from being blown out to sea. The timber dealers donated a large Buddha image to show their thanks. The great hall was completed in 1391.

In 1392 Yonglong took his disciples to Nanjing to be ordained. Ming Taizu suspected deception and sent his bodyguard to arrest the novices. Yonglong offered to burn his body in exchange for their release. He composed a verse and wrote on a stick of incense, which he said could be used to pray for rain. When he burned himself there was an unusual fragrance and flocks of cranes flew overhead. Many *śarīra* were produced. The novices were pardoned and ordained. Later there was a drought and Taizu ordered his officials to use the incense. In response to the heavy rain that fell, Taizu composed a poem on "the monk who shed his soul." Yonglong's disciples interred his remains beneath a *stūpa* on Yin shan.

Appended: Xuemei was an unconventional monk-poet. One day, when he was walking around in the marketplace, some children sang, "Old Xuemei! If you won't go home right now, when do you want to go home?" He answered, "Going home, going home," and then died.

6. Zuyu 祖遇 of the Ming (*Bu xu gaoseng zhuan* 19, 162b–c)

Zuyu (1445–1484) practiced meditation in the Falin caverns 法琳洞 in Yuanan 遠安 (Hubei), where he fasted for long periods. In 1479 the vice-commissioner of education, Xue Gang 薛綱 (*jinshi* 1464), met him. On a return visit in 1482 Xue noticed that a rockfall had nearly smashed Zuyu's hut; he scolded the monk for staying there. In 1484 Zuyu was crushed by a landslide and died at the age of forty.

Appended: Minghe adds a comment to this biography.

7. Shanxin 善信 and Dayun 大雲 (*Bu xu gaoseng zhuan* 19, 162c–d)

Note: Compare Shanxin's biography in the *Xin xu gaoseng zhuan* and the

Gujin tushu jicheng 古今圖書集成 (Synthesis of Books and Illustrations Past and Present), vol. 50, 61745c. This account of his life was drawn from the local gazetteer *Songjiang fuzhi* 松江府志 (Gazetteer of Songjiang Province).

Account: (1) Shanxin (*zi* Wuyi 無疑, No Doubt, d.u.) was the son of a Mr. Wu 吳 from Jiading 嘉定 in Suzhou. He became a monk at the age of twenty-nine and, being illiterate, he only practiced meditation. He awakened under the Chan master Wanfeng 萬峰 (d.u.). Later he appeared to be slightly ill and asked to be put in his coffin. His body spontaneously combusted. A verse eulogy is appended to the biography.

Appended comment: "This was surely a case of someone who attained awakening and who was eager to enter *nirvāṇa.*"

Account: (2) Dayun began his career at Jixiang si 吉祥寺 in Beijing, where his fellow disciple was a monk called Daji 大極 (d.u.). In the Jiajing 嘉靖 reign period (1522–1566), Dayun lived at Guangde si 廣德寺, where two monks continually squabbled. Dayun told them how Daji had died vowing to be reborn in the Pure Land. Then he sat down and died in exactly the same manner.

8. Guangyu 廣玉 and Ningyi 寧義 (*Bu xu gaoseng zhuan* 19, 162d–163a)

Account: (1) Guangyu (*zi* Wuxia 無瑕, d. 1584) was a native of Honglian chi 紅蓮池 in Sichuan and had been a scholar in secular life. He founded a monastery called Leiyin si 雷音寺 (Sound of Thunder) on the peak of Jiufeng shan 九峰山. In 1584 he announced that he would depart on the seventh day of the third month and ceased drinking water. On the day of his death, he bathed and ascended the lecturer's seat. The sky clouded over and there was a clap of thunder as he died. His corpse was placed in a coffin; three months later he looked as if he were still alive. His disciples placed his lacquered body inside a pagoda on the peak's summit.

Account: (2) Ningyi (d. 1583) first lived on Sandui shan 三堆山 and later travelled to other places. He was an ascetic who ate only vegetables and beans. In 1583 he stacked up firewood and burned himself.

9. Yetai 夜臺 and Qiuyue 秋月 (*Bu xu gaoseng zhuan* 19, 163a–c)

Account: Yetai (d. 1610) was a native of Western Shu, and in his youth he practiced gymnastics and dietetics. He was tonsured on Emei shan and visited the major Buddhist mountain sites. Because he roamed Wutai shan by night he was known as "Yetai" (Night Terraces). Among his many adventures, he met a tiger and tried to feed it with his own body; he frightened off a bandit; and he froze to death in a deep snowbank. Some monks rescued him and thawed him out with hot water. On the mountain Yetai saw lights, wild animals, and ghosts. He also saw Mañjuśrī, who sometimes appeared as an old *bhikṣu* or as a beautiful woman holding a baby in her arms.

In 1603 Yetai came to the capital, where the empress dowager Cisheng 慈聖 (1546–1614) patronized him. He held large assemblies of monks at Tayuan si 塔院 and Longquan si 龍泉寺. He had two bells cast for Emei shan and Wutai shan and obtained from the court two Buddhist canons for Putuo 普陀山 shan and Emei shan. On Jiuhua shan 九華山 he established a ritual space for the water-land assembly (*shuilu hui* 水陸會). He donated money and food to hermitages and poor monks.

One day in Guangling 廣陵 Yetai suddenly fell ill, and a layman cut off his finger to make a soup to cure him. When the monk recovered he bought a large boat and placed a "water-land" image in it. On December 9, 1610, Yetai, a single disciple, and two merchants set sail. Yetai jumped into the sea, saying that he was imitating the Bodhisattva Jietuo. Chen Jiru 陳繼儒 (1558–1639), a well-known local poet and painter, composed a written record of this occurrence.[107]

Qiuyue was an old monk who had spent his whole career on Xuanmu shan 玄墓山 in Suzhou. He upheld the precepts, practiced prostration and recitation, and drank tea. In 1621, as he was sailing along the coast, he suddenly stood up in the prow of the boat and performed prostrations, calling the name of the Buddha. Then he jumped into the waves. As Qiuyue sank between the waves, he still had his palms together, calling the name of the Buddha.

Xin xu gaoseng zhuan siji

1. The Southern Song *śramaṇa* Shi Dehui 釋德輝 (1141–1204) of Jingci si 淨慈寺 in Lin'an 臨安 (*Xin xu gaoseng zhuan* 39, 1191)
Account: Dehui died when his monastery caught fire. His death verse is reproduced in the biography. His monastery had burned down once before in 1127, when it was part of a defensive line against the Jurchen invaders. It was rebuilt by Gaozong 高宗 (r. 1127–1162) of the Southern Song.

2. The Southern Song *śramaṇa* Shi Miaopu 釋妙普 of Qinglong an 青龍庵 in Huating 華亭 (*Xin xu gaoseng zhuan* 39, 1191–1194)
Account: Miaopu (*hao* Xingkong 性空, d. 1142) was a native of Hanzhou 漢州 and lived in Huating.[108] He was a Chan monk and a disciple of Sixin 死心 (1043–1114) of Mount Huanglong 黃龍 in Jiangxi. He admired the "the Boatman Ācārya" (Chuanzi *heshang* 船子和尚), a Tang Chan master who had also lived in Huating. Miaopu lived on the banks of the Xiu river 秀水 and composed song lyrics. Towards the end of the Northern Song, rebels passed through the town of Wuzhen 烏鎮. Miaopu composed his funerary memorial and invited them to behead him. They let him go and spared the townspeople.

In the winter of 1142, Miaopu constructed a large basin with holes and exchanged verses with a colleague on Mount Xuedou 雪竇 about his plan to drown himself.[109] He also left behind a death verse. He sat cross-legged in the basin and played his flute as he sank beneath the waves. Three days later his disciples found his body on the sand, sitting upright. Five days later they cremated him and obtained *śarīra* as big as beans. Two cranes flew continually over his pyre. His remains were interred in a pagoda at Qinglong an.

Translation: Partly translated in Demiéville 1984, 71–74.

3. The Yuan *śramaṇa* Shi Delin 釋德林 of Zheze si 柘澤寺 in Shanghai (*Xin xu gaoseng zhuan* 39, 1195)

Note: See the *Bu xu gaoseng zhuan* biography.

4. The Ming *śramaṇa* Shi Mingxing 釋明星 (ca. 1478–1568) of Bolin si 柏林寺 in Changsha 長沙; appended, the "Maṇḍala Worthy" (Mantuluo zunzhe 曼荼羅尊 者, fl. ca. 1573–1620); Canling 參靈 (d. 1644) (*Xin xu gaoseng zhuan* 39, 1195–1198)

Account: Mingxing was a native of Changsha and was born with an unusually shaped body. As a novice at Bolin si he fed a beggar and was expelled. This beggar taught him how to pray for clear skies or rain. In 1568 there was a severe drought. Mingxing vowed that if it did not rain in three days he would burn his body. A local official built an altar, put firewood on top, and ordered him to climb it. After three days there was no sign of rain and the official ordered that the fire be lit. When the fire was a few feet from the altar, the wind picked up and rain fell. Mingxing died and was cremated the following year. A monastery was founded to commemorate his offering, and many high-ranking officials came to the monastery to pray for rain in times of drought.

Appended: (1) The Maṇḍala Worthy was the son of a Mr. Zhou 周 from Changsha, and his personal name was Fu 福. People called him Zhou the Transcendent (Zhou xian 周仙) or Master Zhou, the True Man (Zhou gong zhenren 周公真人). He observed the Vinaya and practiced austerities. He also read Mahāyāna *sūtra*s, *dhāraṇī*s, and the esoteric sections of the canon. He built a hermitage below Heimi feng 黑糜峰 with a *maṇḍala* where he cultivated esoteric practices for several decades. One day Fu announced that he would "bathe in fire." He stacked up firewood, bathed and changed his clothes, and sat cross-legged on top. His disciples were all too afraid to light the fire. As Fu held the wooden fish and chanted spells, the pyre spontaneously burst into flames. Later when the villagers prayed for rain, they just called out his name. In the rain could be heard the sounds of the wooden fish and chanted spells.

Appended: (2) Canling also came from Changsha. His secular surname was Qu 瞿 and he was known as Qu Heshang 瞿和尚 (Upādhyāya Qu). In local gazetteers his name was later miswritten as Canling 餐苓 (eating numinous fungus). He became a novice at the old Huashan si 古華山寺, where he prayed to Guanyin. He liked esoteric *sūtra*s and travelled to Western Shu to learn *mudrā*s. He brought back the *Mahāyoga tantra,* which he studied intently. Canling was a hermit on Jilong shan 集龍山 in Hunan for more than forty years. Around 1644 he stacked up firewood on the banks of the Baisha river, lit the fire, and recited the *Mahāyoga tantra.* Accompanied by great gusts of wind and peals of thunder, his body was transformed before the eyes of the crowd. In the eighth month of the same year, a monastery was founded to commemorate him. The monks there made offerings to an image of him. People prayed in times of drought, flood, or epidemic and always obtained a response. In 1867 the locals requested that Canling receive imperial recognition. The emperor gave him the title "True Man All-Encompassing Protector" (Puhu zhenren 溥護真人).

5. The Ming *śramaṇa* Shi Shanxin 釋善信 of Shishui an 施水庵 in Shanghai (*Xin xu gaoseng zhuan* 39, 1198–1199)

Note: Compare with Shanxin's biography in the *Bu xu gaoseng zhuan.*

Account: Shanxin was a practitioner of *nianfo* and was awakened through reading *sūtra*s and *śāstra*s at Fangshui an 放水庵 in Shanghai under his master Zhide 智德 (d.u.). He was bathed, placed in his coffin, and burned by a spontaneous blaze. His fellow monks erected a pagoda for him and painted his image.

6. The Ming *śramaṇa* Shi Puzhao 釋普照 (fl. 1522–1566) of Baohua shan si 寶華山寺 in Jinling 金陵 (*Xin xu gaoseng zhuan* 39, 1199)

Account: Puzhao's native place and his family are unknown. He lived on the site of the medieval wonder worker Baozhi 寶志 (418–514). When tigers tried to climb into the cave, Puzhao cut off his arm and gave it to them, and they left.

7. The *Ming śramaṇa* Shi Mingxiu 釋明秀 (d.u.) of Jingmen 荆門 (*Xin xu gaoseng zhuan* 39, 1199–1200)

Account: Mingxiu was a native of Tianchuan 天川 in Yubi 宇碧. After forty years in Jingmen, one day he bathed, did obeisance to the Buddha, and announced that he was "going to the West." Sitting cross-legged on his mat, fire shot out from within him as he chanted the name of the Buddha. Unbeknownst to the witnesses, the mat was actually placed on top of a large stack of firewood that was already ablaze.

8. The Ming *śramaṇa* Shi Kangzhai 釋康齋 (fl. ca. 1628–1644) of Liwu shan 栗塢山 in Fuyang 富陽; appended, the *bhikṣuṇī* of Guihua 歸化 (*Xin xu gaoseng zhuan* 39, 1200–1202)

Account: Kangzhai was a solitary meditator with no known monastic affiliation. One day he announced his departure and begged for a bundle of firewood.

He stacked it up and sat on top, covering his head in an oil-soaked turban. He spat out "*samādhi* fire" but was unable to ignite his body because of the rising *qi* from a pregnant woman in the audience. Once she left he was able to burn himself. His disciples placed his remains in his cave.

Appended: In 1644 an unnamed nun of Guihua 歸化 in Fujian gathered firewood, stacked it up like a tower, and sat on top, chanting the name of the Buddha. Later, people founded a nunnery and erected a pagoda in her honor. Poets composed many verses about her. The biography contains four examples of these verses.

9. The Ming *śramaṇa* Shi Langran 釋郎然 (d.u.) of Linting an 林亭庵 in Jizhou 薊州 (*Xin xu gaoseng zhuan* 39, 1202–1203)

Account: Langran was a native of Baodi 寶坻, and lived in a small hermitage.[110] Although he was stupid, he was honest and respected by the locals. He was taught a method of *nianfo* by an old monk on Pan shan 盤山 in Hubei. After practicing it for three years, an internal fire burned him but left his body intact. His skin looked like old copper and made a sound when struck. Zhuoan Zhipu 拙庵智朴 (fl. 1671) composed a poem about him that is preserved in the biography.

10. The Qing *śramaṇa* Shi Xinggao 釋行杲 of Li'an si 理安寺 in Hangzhou (*Xin xu gaoseng zhuan* 40, 1207–1208)

Account: Xinggao was a disciple of Cangxue 蒼雪 (d.u.) and later inherited the *dharma* of the Chan master Ruoan Tongwen 箬庵通問 (1608–1645).[111] In early 1678 he went to Helin 鶴林 to bid farewell to Tianshu Zhi 天樹植.[112] He asked that his bones be thrown into the river. On the twenty-fourth day of that month a fire broke out in the neighboring hermitage and his attendant urged him to flee. But Xinggao would not leave, and they both died. Xinggao's bones were scattered by his disciples, and he left behind a record of his sayings in one fascicle.

11. The Qing *śramaṇa* Shi Hairun 釋海潤 (d. 1690) of Huashan 華山 in Jiangning 江甯; appended, a monk of Changjing 長涇; a monk of Luoshu 羅墅 (*Xin xu gaoseng zhuan* 40, 1208–1209)

Account: Hairun (*zi* Xiyi 西一) was a native of Shanyang 山陽 in Shaanxi. He arrived on Huashan in 1690 saying that he had come on a matter of life and death that would take place at noon on the first day of the fourth month. On that day, people saw a fire on the summit of the mountain. On Guiren peak 貴人峰 they found Hairun sitting cross-legged with fire rushing out of his eyes, ears, mouth, and nose. His body remained upright even after the fire had burned out.

Appended: (1) An unnamed monk of Changjing was dull and stupid and practiced only *nianfo*. One day he suddenly announced that he had to leave the next

day. At noon he sat cross-legged on a seat; fire shot out of his mouth and incinerated him.

Appended: (2) An unnamed monk of Luoshu whose secular surname was
Zhou practiced *nianfo* single-mindedly. He gave away his bowl and begged for a
bundle of firewood, which he stacked up. In front of a large audience fire shot out
of his mouth and burned his body. The local population founded the Hermitage
of the Transformed Body (Huashen an 化身庵) and erected a pagoda for him.

12. The Qing *śramaṇa* Shi Wuming 釋無名 (ca. 1590–1674) of Jingmen 荊門
(*Xin xu gaoseng zhuan* 40, 1209–1210)

Account: Wuming (No Name) was a promoter of social projects such as the
Wanshan 萬善 bridge. In 1674 he stacked up firewood south of the city walls and
sat on top, holding the wooden fish. After he had the pyre lit he predicted that
in forty years time the foundations of the bridge would have to be repaired. The
day after his death someone saw him in the mountains. In 1714 the official Song
Sisheng 宋思聖 (d.u.) arrived and noticed that the bridge was listing slightly. He
paid for its repair.

13. The Qing *śramaṇa* Shi Danyuan 釋淡遠 (d.u.) of Falun si 法輪寺 in
Hengyang衡陽; appended, Xiangying香英 (*Xin xu gaoseng zhuan* 40, 1210–1212)

Account: Danyuan was responsible for three miracles. First, he predicted the
death of a student who had been freed from jail by a divine monk. Second, during an epidemic he got people to burn incense and pray to the Buddha. People
saw a divine monk circumambulating them and were quickly cured. Third,
Danyuan's monastery had a problem with deer and rabbits eating the plants in
the garden, so he prayed to the mountain god. The next day dozens of dead animals lay outside the fence. Danyuan protested that the god had gone too far and
the animals came back to life. He foretold the day of his death and stacked up
firewood and burned himself. He left a large number of relics, and someone saw
him that same day at the Zhushi 朱石 ford.

Appended: Xiangying lived in a hermitage on Mount Yan 燕 in Hebei. He did
not allow his disciples to engage in agriculture. His disciples wanted to plant
black sesame on some fallow land outside the monastery to supply oil for lamps.
Although the sesame was harvested and the oil pressed and stored, it splashed
out of the jars and was lost.

One day Xiangying gathered the assembly and sat cross-legged, holding his
bowl. Using incense he set fire to his toes. The fire burned up to his abdomen
while he continued to recite and chant. When it reached his chest he died. That
same day someone met him and asked him where he was going. He replied, "To
the Western lands." One of his disciples went to find him and arrived just as his

remains were about to be placed in a pagoda. He realized that his master had died precisely at the moment when the layman had met him on the road.

14. The Qing *śramaṇa* Shi Zhian 釋止安 (d. 1740) of Yunlin si 雲林寺 in Hangzhou (*Xin xu gaoseng zhuan* 40, 1212–1213)

Account: Zhian practiced austerities but lived in a poor, dilapidated monastery that was always short of food. On June 26, 1740, he burned himself, vowing that the buildings should be lofty and bright and the monastery kitchen full of food.

15. The Qing *śramaṇa* Shi Zhaizi 釋齋子 (d.u.) of Zhusheng si 祝聖寺 on Nanyue; appended, Huiming 慧明 (*Xin xu gaoseng zhuan* 40, 1213)

Account: Zhaizi led an austere life and never spoke or smiled. He begged every day for a single bowl of rice. One day he visited Tiefo si 鐵佛寺, where someone had left out some lumber. He set fire to it while sitting cross-legged within the pyre, beating the wooden fish, and chanting the name of the Buddha.

Appended: Every day Huiming ate bitter herbs and always talked about being unborn. One day he built a coffin and stacked up firewood. He washed himself, entered the coffin, and burned himself.

16. The Qing *śramaṇa* Shi Liaoan 釋了庵 (fl. Qianlong period 1736–1795) of Jin shan si 金山寺 in Jiangnan 江南; appended, the "Spinner Monk" (Luosi seng 絡絲僧) (*Xin xu gaoseng zhuan* 40, 1213–1215)

Note: This biography also appears in the *Jingtu shengxian lu* 淨土聖賢錄 (Records of the Sages and Worthies of the Pure Land), compiled at the end of Daoguang 道光 era (1821–1850), 6, *XZJ* 135.281c–282a.

Account: Liaoan visited masters at many famous mountain sites. When not travelling, he went into deep seclusion. On Mount Han'gao 漢泉 in Hubei, a layman donated a park. After practicing there for some years, Liaoan fell ill and wanted to return to Jiangnan. When he had spent some time in the meditation hall of Jinshan si, his health improved and he moved to Jiangning 江寧, where he resided in the city monastery. One day he stacked up firewood in front of the courtyard and sat on top of it. Repeatedly chanting the name of the Buddha, he ordered the monks to light the fire, but none of them obeyed. Then the distant smell of a burning candle reached his nose. Liaoan exhaled and fire shot straight out of his nose, igniting the pyre. He had instructed his disciples to grind his bones to powder and throw them into the river to feed the insects and fish.

Appended: The "Spinner Monk" had been a spinner before he left home. He lived alone in a derelict hermitage, only chanting the name of the Buddha; he could not support himself so he had to spin in exchange for food. One day he appeared at the house of the layman Wu Xiling 吳西泠 (Wu Shuxu 吳樹虛, fl. eighteenth century) and tried to sell him a basket full of useless scraps of paper. The monk explained that he needed to buy a load of firewood so he could "return to the West." The layman agreed to pay for it. When he arrived at the monk's hermitage, he found him sitting on top of a pile of blazing firewood. As he raised his hand to wave goodbye, he wiped his face, revealing its golden color. There was a crowd of several hundred witnesses.

17. The Qing *śramaṇa* Shi Chengyuan 釋成淵 (d. 1746) of Shangfang Huanglong an 上方黃龍庵 on Fang shan 房山 (*Xin xu gaoseng zhuan* 40, 1216–1218)

Account: Chengyuan (*zi* Shuiyue 水月, surname Hu 胡) was a native of Longnan 龍南 in Jiangxi. In his youth he became a novice at Donghua shan 東華山 under Huijing 慧敬 (d.u.). He travelled extensively, studying with a succession of masters. At Tiantai shan, he obtained the *dharma* at Guangrun si 廣潤寺 from the "Elder of Jingtang" 鏡堂長老 and awoke to the meaning of the *Laṅkāvatāra sūtra*.[113] Chengyuan spent thirteen years lecturing before bidding his disciples farewell and heading north in 1736. When he was invited to take charge of Huanglong si, he was already seventy years old. He dwelt on Mount Fang for seven years as a recluse. On September 29, 1746, during the mid-autumn festival, people were gazing at the full moon when Chenyuan disappeared, leaving a single gourd and basket in his room. He also left a farewell verse.

The next year his body was discovered sitting upright, perched on top of Cuiwei 翠微 peak. The villagers burned his body there and interred his remains beneath a pagoda. A layman called Fang Zun 方嶟 (d.u.) recorded this incident for the local gazetteer.

18. The Qing *śramaṇa* Shi Xingcan 釋性參 (1742–1818, *zi* Xinheng 心恒) of Ciyun si 慈雲寺 in Yichang 宜昌 (*Xin xu gaoseng zhuan* 40, 1218–1220)

Account: Xingcan's secular surname was Liu 劉, and he was a native of Jianli 監利.[114] When he was forty, both his parents died. He took the tonsure at Yuquan si 玉泉寺 in Dangyang 當陽 under Jingran 靜然 (*zi* Xianyuan 顯遠).[115] Xingcan travelled around Hubei performing austerities, teaching, and converting, and opened up the three public monasteries (*congshe* 叢社): Rulai 如來, Yanqing 廷慶, and Shuiyue 水月. Then he returned to Yichang and dwelt at Ciyun si for several years before he left for Wannian si 萬年寺. There he taught the virtue of the precepts and recited the *Diamond Sūtra*.

One day, at the age of seventy-six, Xingcan told his disciples that he was about to depart for the West. He ordered them to stack up firewood, and on August 16, 1818, he climbed on top and recited a *gāthā*. Flames shot out from within him and consumed him in front of over one thousand witnesses. Seven grains of *śarīra* were interred under seven pagodas in front of the monastery.

19. The Qing *śramaṇa* Shi Xingkong 釋性空 (d. 1807) of Zisheng si 資聖寺 in Jingzhou 荆州 (*Xin xu gaoseng zhuan* 40, 1220)

Account: Xingkong recited the *Huayan jing* continuously for several decades. One day, in the *dingmao* 丁卯 year of the Jiaqing 嘉慶 period (1807), he stacked up firewood and burned himself. Amid the flames appeared the image of an arhat. There was an unusual fragrance that did not disperse for three days.

20. The Qing *śramaṇa* Shi Changhui 釋常慧 (1845–1914) of Tianning si 天寧寺 in Changzhou 常州; appended, the "Man of the Way," Xianghuo 香火道人 (*Xin xu gaoseng zhuan* 40, 1220–1222)

Account: Changhui was a native of Huo shan 霍山 , and in his youth he became a novice at Jingdu si 淨度寺 on Jiuhua shan.[116] He was ordained in 1875 and in 1891 went to Tianning si in Changzhou, where he took up Pure Land practices. In 1906 he moved to Putong yuan 普同院 , where he kept watch over a monk in sealed retreat who was reciting the *Lotus Sūtra*. Inspired by the Medicine King, Changhui made a vow to give up his body to save the world. In 1911 he wanted to burn himself to stop all killing in the world. On May 11, 1914, he burned himself. He had a disciple whom he had asked to light the fire, but on the day he failed to arrive. The witnesses made donations and erected a pagoda with an inscription.

Appended: Xianghuo was the son of a Mr. Zhu 朱 of Danyang 丹陽 in Jiangsu and served at Changguo si 昌國寺. He was dedicated to *nianfo*. One day he announced that he had to "transform and depart" and asked for a bundle of firewood. Someone laughed at him and offered to set fire to the pyre for him. On the appointed day, surrounded by onlookers, Xianghuo sat calmly on top of the stack of firewood. No one was willing to light the fire, so he did it himself. As the head monk of Changguo si rushed up, Xianghuo's heart flew out of the fire. When the fire was extinguished, the heart was seen to be undamaged and was later gilded. While Xianghuo was burning, people elsewhere saw him in the clouds, beating the wooden fish as he headed west.

21. The Qing *śramaṇa* Shi Zhenyuan 釋真源 (1846–1900) of Longan si 隆安寺 in Yanjing 燕京 (*Xin xu gaoseng zhuan* 40, 1223–1224)

Account: Zhenyuan (*zi* Chongshou 崇壽, surname Wang 王) was a native of Daxing 大興 near Beijing. He suffered many childhood illnesses and swore to devote himself to praying to the Buddha. He studied the Vinaya and in his later years concentrated on Pure Land practice. During the Boxer Rebellion of 1900, foreign armies entered the capital and burned monastic buildings, including Longan si. Zhenyuan remained alone in the monastery and was burned to death.

Hongzan fahua zhuan

1. The Song monk Shi Huishao 釋慧紹 of Zhaoti si 招提寺 (*Hongzan fahua zhuan* 5, T 51.2067.23c17–24a4)

2. The Song monk Shi Sengyu 釋僧瑜 of Lu shan 廬山 (*Hongzan fahua zhuan* 5, T 51.2067.24a5–28)

3. The Song monk Shi Huiyi 釋慧益 of Zhulin si 竹林寺 (*Hongzan fahua zhuan* 5, T 51.2067.24a29–b26)

4. The Liang monk Shi Sengming 釋僧明 of Shimen si 石門寺 (*Hongzan fahua zhuan* 5, T 51.2067.24b27–c12)

Account: Sengming's family name is unknown. He lived on Shimen shan in Zhaoyi xian 招義縣, Hao zhou 濠州, where he constructed a heavenly palace and made an image of Maitreya.[117] When he recited the *Lotus Sūtra,* he always heard the sound of fingers snapping and a voice saying "Excellent!" During the Tianjian period, he asked Liang Wudi for permission to burn his body. Wudi approved and Sengming burned himself on the rock in front of the Maitreya palace.

Sengming's body was completely reduced to ashes except for one finger-nail. The ground surrounding the site of the auto-cremation sank and formed a pond. Two or three days later, flowers bloomed in it, and all those who drank the water were cured of disease. Some people gathered up the monk's ashes and made them into an image; they also carved a smaller wooden image. They burned the nail relic again and smeared the ashes on the wooden image. It began moving and wherever it went, flowers bloomed as large as trees. An inscription on a pagoda recorded all this in detail.

Appended: A layman from Pinglu 平陸 district in Jiaozhou 交州 chanted the *Lotus* and wanted to imitate the Medicine King.[118] Where he burned himself the earth swelled up in the shape of a human body. His father dug up the mound and within it found a golden statue as big as a man. He wanted to raise it so that it stood upright, but it suddenly disappeared.

5. The Liang monk Shi Daodu 釋道度 of Ruona shan 若那山 (*Hongzan fahua zhuan* 5, T 51.2067.24c14–25a21)

Note: See references under the entry for Daodu in the *Fayuan zhulin* above. The monastic affiliation of Heling si 何令寺 is erroneous and appears to be a mis-reading by Huixiang of his source. The inscription reads 還指寺北，何公禪室之基 ("he then pointed to a place to the north of the monastery where was laid the foundation of the meditation room built by [or for] the Venerable He"). Huixiang has wrongly read or misconstrued 何公禪室 as 何令寺.[119]

Account: Daodu was a native of Pingyang 平陽, and his surname was Liu 劉.[120]
He arrived in the state of Liang in 502 and stayed at Dinglin si 定林寺 on Zhong
shan 鐘山, where he practiced *dhyāna.* He numbered Liang Wudi's stepbrothers,
Prince Anchengkang 安成康 of the Liang and Prince Poyang Zhonglie 鄱陽忠烈,
among his disciples.[121] In 518 he personally made one hundred copies of the *Lotus Sūtra* and recited the chapter on the Medicine King day and night. He met the
emperor at the Juedian 覺殿 (Awakening Hall) of Hualin si 花林寺, where he explained his plan to burn his body.[122] In return he received an edict encouraging
him to expose his corpse instead.

Daodu replied that he could not change his mind but he intended to obey
Wudi's command. In 526 he moved to Heling si on Ruona shan in Dongzhou 東州,
where he lived in a meditation chamber in the cliffs. He piled up a storied structure
of firewood and gradually reduced his intake of food. On Putong 7.11.3 (December
22, 526), the monastery bell started to ring; it rang again on the eighth day of that
month (December 27th). On the twenty-third day (January 11, 527), Daodu invited
a hundred monks to a ceremony on the mountain. More than 300 religious and laypeople came and more than 170 received the bodhisattva precepts from him.

The account of Daodu's self-immolation follows that of the *Fayuan zhulin,*
but the biography also contains details of his transmission of a contact relic to a
disciple and the text of an edict extolling his actions.

6. The Zhou monk Shi Sengyai 釋僧崖 of Dasheng si 大乘寺 in Yizhou 益州
(*Hongzan fahua zhuan* 5, T 51.2067.25a22–b19)

7. The Sui monk Shi Fachong 釋法充 of Huacheng si 化城寺 on Lu shan
(*Hongzan fahua zhuan* 5, T 51.2067.25b20–c3)
Note: Compare with Fachong's biography in the section on "defenders of
the *dharma*" in the *Xu gaoseng zhuan,* T 50.2060.559c.
Account: Fachong's surname was Bi 畢, and he was a native of Jiujiang 九江.[123]
He recited the *Lotus* constantly and repaired monastic buildings. At Huacheng si
on Mount Lu's Banding 半頂 (Half Summit), he practiced meditation. Fachong
disapproved of the activities of some of the monks there. In particular he was always lecturing them about women in the monastery. He threw himself from the
summit of Xianglu peak 香爐峰, vowing to smash his body and bones to be reborn
in the Pure Land. In midair his body righted itself and he floated gently to earth,
landing in a deep valley. When one of the monks peered over the precipice, he
heard a voice from hundreds of feet below. Fachong was still chanting the *Lotus.*
After they brought him back to the monastery, the bad monks gave up consorting
with women. When Fachong eventually died in 600, his body did not smell or de-
compose even in the hot weather.

8. The Sui monk Shi Dazhi 釋大志 of Fengding si 峰頂寺 on Lu shan (*Hongzan fahua zhuan* 5, T 51.2067.25c4–26a9)

9. A man in the household of the regional inspector, the prince of Jiang 刺史 蔣王 , in Ji zhou 箕州 (*Hongzan fahua zhuan* 5, T 51. 2067.26a10–18)

Account: In the household of the regional inspector, the prince of Jiang (Li Yun 李惲, d. 675), in Ji zhou, there was an indentured servant whose personal and family names are unknown. He was devoted to the *Lotus* from the age of eight or nine, and he recited it from memory day and night. His daughter was a concubine of the prince, and she told him of her father's wish to burn his body. The prince gave his permission. The servant went into the mountains, bathed, and purified himself and his altar. A month later his daughter ordered some men to gather up her father's ashes. His body and bones were completely consumed, and all that was found was a tongue, still fresh and moist. The prince's son-in-law Wei Zheng 韋 徵 (d. after 674) saw the tongue and informed the prince. When the prince saw it, he too was impressed. Even several years later the tongue remained unchanged.

10. The Tang *bhikṣuṇī*s of Jingzhou 荆州 who were sisters; appended, the student from Bingzhou 并州 (*Hongzan fahua zhuan* 5, T 51. 2067.26a19–b5)

11. The Tang monk Shi Huitong 釋會通 of Baolin 豹林 valley in Yongzhou 雍 州 (*Hongzan fahua zhuan* 5, T 51. 2067.26b6–13)

12. The Tang monk Shi Tanyou 釋曇猷 of Yueling shan 月嶺山 in Xiangzhou 襄州; appended, Hulun 護論 of Ximing si 西明寺 (*Hongzan fahua zhuan* 5, T 51. 2067.26b14–c11)

Account: Tanyou's family name was Zhang 張, and he was a native of Xuzhou 許州. He became a monk after he conceived a profound disgust for the world. He heard that in Changsha si 長沙寺, there was a miraculous Buddha image that had been made by Aśoka himself and had flown to China.[124] He decided to burn his body in homage to the image just like the Medicine King.

In 666 Tanyou made the vow in front of the image. He heard the sound of fingers snapping in approval. At first it looked as if wet weather would prevent him from carrying out his vow, but on the night of the fifteenth of the second month (March 26, 666), the clouds cleared, revealing the light of a full moon. Tanyou wrapped himself in waxed cloth and set fire to his hands and the crown of his head. He kept his eyes on the image and vowed to see the Buddha Pure and Bright Excellence of Sun and Moon. As the flames finally flared up and consumed him, he could still be heard preaching.

Witnesses asked him to leave behind some sign and in the ashes they found his skull. The local officials arrived at dawn, performed prostrations, and circumambulated the relic. But when they left it suddenly exploded. The dozen or so remaining witnesses prayed for relics and eight grains appeared, rising and sinking in the air. They were interred in the monastery, where the sound of fingers snapping in approval could still be heard.

Appended: When Hulun first began to recite the *Lotus,* he burned one finger at the completion of each fascicle. By the time he had completed reading the *sūtra,* he had burned off eight fingers.

Translations: Stevenson 1995, 435–436, and Shinohara 1992, 169.

Appendix 2

Critical Evaluations of Huijiao, Daoxuan, and Zanning

Huijiao's *Critical Evaluation* (*GSZ* 12, T 50.2059.405c29–406b13)

Whoever possesses form values his body. Whoever thinks and feels treasures his life. For this reason, people eat fat, drink blood, ride sleek horses, and wear fine clothes to make themselves comfortable and feel pleasant.[1] People eat medicinal herbs (朮) and swallow elixirs, guard life (*fangsheng* 防生), and nourish the nature (*yangxing* 養性) to extend their lives. This reaches a point where, out of stinginess, people would not pluck out a single hair even to benefit all under heaven or out of meanness they would not give up a single meal even to ensure [someone else's] survival.[2] This is terrible indeed! But here are people who possessed far-reaching awareness and penetrating vision. They offered themselves to feed others.[3] They innately realized that the three realms are merely a dwelling place during the long night and awakened to the fact that the four forms of birth are dreamlike and illusory spheres (*jing* 境), that the essence (*jing* 精) and the spirit (*shen* 神) move rapidly like the wings of a gnat (*fei* 蜚), and that the physical form and the skeleton are confined like jars of grain.[4] Therefore, they pay not the slightest heed to their bodies, from the crown of the head to the feet.[5] States and cities, wives and children, have been given away as though they were bundles of grass.[6] The present comment concerns these men.

Only for a duck did Sengqun abstain from water and give up his body; Sengfu stopped to help a mere boy, slicing open his own belly so that his life could be saved.[7] Fajin sliced his flesh to feed people, and Tancheng fed himself to a starving tiger. They all excelled in the way of aiding everyone (*jianji zhi dao* 兼濟之道).[8] These are cases of benefiting beings while being oblivious to oneself (*wangwo liwu* 忘我利物). In the past, a prince discarded his body and the merit extended for nine *kalpa*s.[9] [King Śibi] sliced his thigh and exchanged [the flesh] for a bird, astonishing sentient beings throughout the trichiliochosm.[10] People like this [that is, bodhisattvas] have already become transcendent and have reached the ultimate.

Next then are [the cases of] Fayu up to Tanhong. They all reduced their bodies to ashes, discarding that which is treasured and loved. Some did it as a heartfelt aspiration for the Pure Land (Anyang 安養); for others it was due to a vow to be reborn in Tuṣita heaven (Zhizu 知足).[11] Thus a double firmiana appeared

within a cell or a single star appeared in the sky.[12] These auspicious omens were
brilliant and outstanding and appeared time after time.[13] But the teachings of the
sage are not all the same; there are indeed differences between what is permitted
and what is forbidden. If one performs great expedients for the good of sentient
beings, acts in accordance with the times, and demonstrates a myriad of benefits
[in the world], then [such actions] are not prohibited by the teachings. As the
scripture says, "If you can burn a finger of your hand or a toe, this greatly exceeds
the gifts of whole states and walled cities."[14] But, for ordinary monks who have left
home, it is fundamental that they attract sentient beings with their awe-inspiring
deportment (*weiyi* 威儀); if they damage the body they destroy the marks (*xiang* 相;
Skt. *lakṣaṇa*) of a field of merit (*futian* 福田; Skt. *puṇyakṣetra*).[15]

Investigating this in order to discuss it, one finds that there are advantages
and disadvantages. The advantages lie in being oblivious to the self (*wangshen* 忘
身); the disadvantages lie in breaking the precepts. This is why Nāgārjuna says,
"Bodhisattvas who are new to practice are not able to practice fully all the perfections (*du* 度; Skt. *pāramitā*s) simultaneously."[16] Some fulfilled the perfection of
charity (*tan* 檀; Skt. *dāna*) but went against filiality (*xiao* 孝), such as the prince
who gave himself to the tiger. Some fulfilled the perfection of wisdom but went
against compassion, such as those who required others to give up food and so
on.[17] These all come from practices that are not yet completely perfected, so they
are all unbalanced.

Also the Buddha has said, "The body has eighty thousand worms, which
share the same *qi* 氣 as the human being. When a person's life is over, the worms
all die along with it."[18] This is why, after the death of an arhat, the Buddha permitted the burning of the body. But now we have people who burn themselves when
they are not yet dead, and in some cases there may be a disadvantage as far as the
life of the worms is concerned. In speaking of this, some might say, "If arhats are
worthy of entering flames, what is so unusual about an ordinary person doing
likewise?" Others might say, "Those who enter flames have previously cast away
their lives, and using their spiritual and intellectual powers, only then do they
burn themselves." This being so, bodhisattvas who have attained the stage of the
clan (*xingdi* 性地; Skt. *gotrabhūmi*) also have not yet escaped receiving a physical
body as karmic retribution.[19] Some on occasion cast their bodies into a mass of
flames. Others on occasion split up their bodies and divided them among
people.[20] So we should know that in the discussion on killing worms, our investigation has not been completely detailed.[21]

Now the three poisons and the four inverted views are the root of *saṃsāra*,
while the seven factors of enlightenment and the eightfold path are the necessary
way to true *nirvāṇa*.[22] Surely it is not the case that it is necessary to burn the body
to escape suffering? But if [bodhisattvas] are at the stage close to [the perfection

of] forbearance (*ren* 忍), then they condescend to mingle their traces with ordinary people. Some on occasion have cast away their bodies for the benefit of beings. Then the words of my discussion do not apply to them. But when it comes to followers who are ordinary people, because their study has not been extensive, ultimately they have not realized that one should spend one's whole life in practicing the Way. Why have they thrown away their bodies and lives? Some wished to be famous for a moment, others that their fame might be transmitted for ten thousand generations. But at the point when the fire reached the firewood, remorse and fear [within their minds] began to reinforce each other. As they had broadly publicized [their intention to burn themselves], they were ashamed of compromising their integrity, and they had to resolve to go through with their auto-cremation, vainly inflicting ten thousand sufferings on themselves. These cases are not discussed under the rubric of *yishen*.

The eulogy (*zan* 贊) says:[23]

> If a person can stiffen his will (*zhi* 志), then metal and stone cannot be considered hard.[24]
> Melting away what others consider important, they sacrificed it for that precious city,
> With its luxuriant vegetation and aromatic firmiana trees, and its fine floating purple buildings.
> Mounting the smoke with glittering colors, spitting out tallies and bearing auspicious omens.
> They remain noble for a thousand years, their reputation is transmitted for ten thousand generations.

Daoxuan's *Critical Evaluation* (*XGSZ* 27, T 50.2060.684c4–685c8)

I have heard that to treat life lightly and to die while upholding one's principles has been difficult since antiquity. But to make a temporary escape and have no shame about it is easy even now. In the biographies of men of purpose and men of consistent character, those people with moral integrity are listed and extolled. In the *Classics* words to describe greater or lesser accomplishment are recorded. They serve as a warning to those of ordinary ability while also functioning as positive examples to those who are spiritually advanced. Only the Way is honored, only Virtue gives birth to things. Therefore [self-immolators] are able to be oblivious to both success and failure and to dispense with both right and wrong. They have directly realized the origin of *saṃsāra* and understood the types and modes of deluded thought. These enlightened people have understood the body as a provisional construct: Like dust it has no nature of its own. They have recognized that life is like a flowing stream; it arises and decays by virtue of the mind. Beginning from this [body], all things have but an illusory existence. How can one have wisdom and yet believe that it is possible to preserve them forever? This being so, then when one is alive and attached to the world, when one has not yet escaped from bondage, one should depend on a great cause and use it to purify the confusion of the mind.

Some battered themselves so as to increase their suffering and shame. Some constrained themselves to serve the enslaved and oppressed. Some burned themselves to remove the source of desire. Some gouged themselves to exhaust the roots of delusion. Wrapping up the body to make a torch, they transcended the path of delusion. Burning the arm to make light, they set forth the repayment of virtue from time to time. As for the signs of those who hung lamps [on themselves] or inserted iron [hooks into their bodies], their traces are as [numerous as trees in] a forest; and the precedents of the ability to make [the body] into a mountain of flesh or a sea of milk (*ruhai* 乳海) are well known from earlier texts.[25] They all removed the major root of the inverted view of belief in a self and showed the disgusting nature of the destructible physical body. They traded that rotten dwelling, which is destined to die, for the adamantine *dharmakāya* (*fashen* 法身). Is this not what the *sūtra*s say? These are certainly words of the utmost significance. Now if one values life as a treasure, then the body (*xing* 形) is the most valuable thing, but when one investigates this, it is life (*ming* 命) that is fundamental. Surely it is not the case that the great sages established their teachings on the basis of something false? Therefore, the most honorable Medicine King burned his body, which was a consequence of his comprehensive vow, but when ordinary people below burned themselves in admiration, how could they avoid losing their true mind?

However, when Sengyai put his body right into a fierce blaze, the sound of his recitation did not waver. Dazhi severed his arm with red-hot iron, yet his spiritual constancy was renewed. Xuanlan sacrificed his life in midstream; although he was pulled out, he went back in and drowned. Fa'an [法安, should be read as Puan 普安] gave up his body to bonds and fetters; when he was released he turned himself in again. So we know that what integrity they had could not be snatched away, and what they put into practice could not be concealed. These are certainly things that ought to be praised; they are certainly acts that are difficult to perform. Also there were those who pulled out their intestines and hung them on trees, and those who sliced their flesh in the forest. They lifted up their faces and approached the naked blade, taking the ignominy and humiliation with a smile. This is all just the same as in the *jātaka*s and is also worthy of admiration.[26] Thus arhats (*siguo* 四果) and bodhisattvas (*zhengshi* 正士) incinerated their bodies to escape their critics. Eight thousand people received confirmation [of their future buddhahood], protected the *dharma,* and escaped this corrupt world (*renjie* 忍界).[27] By what power did some ascend to a high place? By means of what faculty were the others able to cast off suffering? Was it not the case that because they cherished a peaceful [mind] and broadly saved people, their practice transcended the distinction between self and others? They regarded form and marks as just accumulated dust and realized that life is like a candle in the wind so that they were able to follow in the footsteps of the former sages. Through their sincerity they became exemplars (*zong* 宗) on whom [those who live during the times of] the semblance and degenerate *dharma* (*xiangmo* 像末) can rely.[28]

Someone asks, "Now if one hates life, one ought to dig out the seed that causes rebirth. Surely by cutting off the fruit of suffering, one cannot pull up the root of the arising of phenomena [that leads to suffering]? I have not yet heard the meaning of this. Please explain it for me." The argument that is put forward indeed has continuing implications. Moreover, arising and causation stretch in an unbroken line, like a range of mountains that mutually support each other. The self is a basis for what has arisen, just as the smoke depends on the pyre.[29] Because what matters most in life is one's body, one applies the remedy in accordance with what is perceived to be the most valuable. It is like when one is sick in the secular world, methods for curing [the sickness] are to be considered in accordance with [the symptoms] of the physical body. Therefore, burning or drowning are meant to awaken one to greed or anger, and humility is meant to attack stupidity and arrogance. This practice is worthy of admiration, as when one practices quiet contemplation (*jingguan* 靜觀) yet still allows the mind to follow forms. This way is worthy of praise and is not unlike identifying being with emptiness. If one is deluded as to the traces [of this practice] and declares, "I can do this!" doing so just complicates the basis of illusion and increases the amount of suffering. Thus to uphold a single stanza of a *sūtra* is superior to abandoning many bodies.[30] This common saying is only directed towards people such as these. More troubling are those who are not able to practice what they hear, which just increases their constant bondage [of *saṃsāra*]. It would be better for them to cast off limbs or fingers to drive away feelings of attachment. The holy teachings are all-embracing, their meaning includes knowing one's limits; if one's allotted powers are weak, how can one dare to think of emulating [the sages]?[31]

Some gave a groan of pain as they approached the end, others went for death enthusiastically. When we look back at earlier biographies, which period does not have them? Also there were some who were ignorant of the traces of the teachings and were afflicted by sexual desire; fearing that their names might be excluded from the eminent places of the records, they cut off their sexual organs to be like eunuchs. These people mistook arrogance and their own absurd ideas as virtues, and they brought disgrace on the *saṃgha.* Of course, there is profound meaning in the holy teachings. This is really due to the fact that what brings about one's desire to love is deluded. If people realized their delusion, there would be no attachment. Not knowing that they should turn back and regulate the mind within, instead these people deludedly cut at their external form. Therefore, although they cut off their limbs, their defiled attachment keeps on increasing. It becomes a deep hindrance to the Way and makes manifest many difficulties with the precepts. [This practice] should be added to offenses entailing expulsion (*binzui* 擯罪; Skt. *pārājika*). How can one dare to rely on it to produce merit?

Also there are those who, at the point of death, leave instructions to expose their bones in the forest. Some [ask to be] sunk in turbid streams, greatly aiding birds and fish. Some have their virtue recorded with deep tombs, high mounds, or glorious steles. Some are placed in caves high in the cliffs, looking out over the wise in the distance. Some have their whole bodies transformed by fire and do not do damage to the spirit, which was originally born with [the body]. Some have their bones pulverized and images made of the paste; their bodies are displayed and worshipped respectfully. [On the other hand, there are those who] bore holes in the skin, cut off the nose, cut off the feet, and say this is "casting off the troubles of the world."[32] They gouge out eyes and discard limbs to destroy desire.[33] Those who take this path are very numerous, and so I have given an account of them. Those who have their corpses exposed in the forest undergrowth can reduce or eliminate thoughts that are shallow and base. Birds and beasts eat their fill, the dead and the living both prosper because of [these corpses]. The advantage of this practice lies in the mutual complementariness [between the dead human beings and the living animals]; however, this practice falls short of performing the principle of universal deliverance (*jianji* 兼濟). Where there are worms and maggots, they squirm around outside the flesh. Then birds peck and swallow voraciously. Wasting away in the wilds, it is a sight that arouses one's feelings of compassion and pity.

Hence there are four types of funerals in the Western Regions: cremation (*huozang* 火葬), when [the body] is burned with firewood; water burial (*shuizang* 水葬), when [the body] is sunk in deep rivers; earth burial (*tuzang* 土葬), when [the body] is buried by the side of cliffs; and forest burial (*linzang* 林葬), when [the body] is abandoned in the wilderness. Kings of the *dharma* (*fawang* 法王; Skt. *dharmarāja*) and wheel-turning kings (*lunwang* 輪王; Skt. *cakravartin*) all depended on fire sacrifice [cremation].[34] The secular world esteemed this constant practice so that other [forms of funerals] were rarely practiced. As for what was transmitted to Xia in the east (*dongxia* 東夏, that is, China), only forest and earth [burials] were heard of.[35] There were scarcely any traces in the world of the two techniques of water and fire. So coffins were made of earthenware at the time of

Yu虞, and this was the beginning of the abandoning of forest [burial] and cremation (*xinzang*薪葬).³⁶ The founder of the Xia (*Xia hou*夏后) and the sagely Zhou
(*sheng Zhou* 聖周) continued this practice of using earthenware coffins.³⁷ The
people of the Yin 殷 dynasty used wooden inner and outer coffins with [the body]
wrapped up.³⁸ In middle antiquity (*zhonggu* 中古), civilization flourished, and government was formed on the basis of benevolent education.³⁹ Although burial was
promoted, only a few actually practiced it. So they covered up bones and interred
corpses, they lowered coffins into graves and buried them. In upper antiquity
(*shanggu* 上古), "they had graves (*mu* 墓) but not grave mounds (*fen* 墳)," and the
practice had not yet reached the masses.⁴⁰ After He Xu 赫胥 was buried in Lu
Ling 盧陵, there started to appear a tumulus (*ling*陵) that was based on [the appearance of] a mountain.⁴¹ In lower antiquity (*xiagu* 下古), this was passed down,
and everyone practiced earth burial. There was much confusion and [there are
parts that are] hard to chronicle, and therefore I have omitted them. Now if one
sets up stelae to record actions and makes an account of words, this guides the
pure thread of the actions of later generations. If one teaches widely by setting up
*stūpa*s, this sets forth the fine merits of the virtuous of former times. What is set
forth in the *Āgama*s then grows greater in the world. As for burying corpses by the
side of *stūpa*s, it was established far away and then spread to the border regions;
the serious adoption of [the practice of making] paste from the bones was actually empty understanding and fawning imitation.⁴²

There are also those who are determined to cut themselves off from the human realm and go into the deep forest while still alive. They widely announce
[their intention] to the fourfold *saṃgha* in the hope that people will beg them to
stay many times over. They lose the intention [of actually going] but enjoy doing
this with enthusiasm. Religious and laity eulogize them. Followers mutually encourage each other, but this leads to their mutual remorse and sadness.

Releasing the body among crags and gullies is an offense according to the Vinaya, and one should be expelled from the assembly [for doing so].⁴³ But if we
discuss the intention, then one has thus produced a great sacrifice. As for other
cases in which people cut off their flesh as surplus, although they accord with the
ultimate teaching, yet their minds contain impurities and many defiled [desires]
to remain in the world. It is necessary to be able to be unrestrained and unat-
tached, to open up and transform delusion. Therefore, details [of these cases]
are not given in this critical evaluation.

It is fitting to rely on the enlightened and sagacious. There are many cases in
the world of the false practice of abstention from grain (*duanli*斷粒); refining the
body (*lianxing*練形) in the expectation of a feathery transformation (*yuhua*羽化);
and eating drugs to escape from the heavy corpse.⁴⁴ Some inhale and exhale dew;
some breathe *yin* and *yang*; some have recourse to drugs to lead a long life; some

cultivate their *qi* to last as long as heaven and earth; some extend their lives to maintain themselves for Maitreya (*ci shi* 慈氏, literally, "Mr. Compassion"); some seek heterodox arts out of fear of death. Examples of these things are very numerous: How could people have time to hear all of them? These are things that the former sages have closed off and later worthies have renounced, yet people spare no energy in pursuit of them, following the corrupt practices of the time. They pick up a hoe and go to the hills and peaks, seeking the restorative *qi* of the five kinds of numinous fungus (*wu zhi* 五芝); they shoulder a spade and go to the valleys in search of the brilliant glow of the eight types of mineral (*ba shi* 八石).[45] They employ a left-hand [heterodox] path to honor themselves and consider using excessive sacrifices (*yinci* 淫祀) as their ultimate purpose. They follow completely the lesser and stupid methods and have not yet escaped from the limits of life. They have vainly affiliated themselves with Buddhism and wasted their whole lives. What a great pity! We should know that there is a fixed length for the great period between birth and death; so the first fruits [of *karma*] may be measured, but the remainder cannot yet be discussed. Yet they suddenly attempt to assess the way of the sages with an ordinary mind, thus comprehensively forming the obstacle of ignorance.[46] We should know why this does not work. Instead others use exertion in cemeteries (*hanlin* 寒林, literally, "cold forests") employing ordinary understanding so as to realize [the principle of] impermanence.[47] They give up their lives but end up continuing the great teachings so that people are led to the Way. The marks of the intact body and the broken body, the means of provisional practice and true practice, are the signs that make known the manifest and miraculous transformation and the great way through which one approaches the great sages. Some are as pure as ice but still have attachments, as is shown by their extravagant funerals.[48] Those who empty their minds and are attached to nothing live and die wherever things lead them. I have not discussed this path exhaustively, and this is certainly only an abbreviated discussion.

Zanning's *Critical Evaluation* (*SGSZ* 23, T 50.2061.861a12–862a12)

All those who are trapped in the bondage of the world are possessed of a self. Those who have life, which is floating and transient, are continually reborn into bodies that are possessed of form. All of them value themselves while treating others lightly, taking for themselves while leaving little for others. But the stingier they are, the meaner they become. They are like the black dragon (*lilong* 驪龍) who jealously guards his pearl, or the black ox (*liniu* 犛牛) who begrudges his tail, or the peacock who is possessive about his multicolored feathers, or the musk deer who protects his fragrant gland.[49] There are examples of this in the rules of the Confucians (*rushi* 儒氏) and the Confucian classics. Regarding their own bodies, [Confucians] claim, "One should not dare to harm the skin and hair one inherits from one's mother and father. One should always know how to protect them carefully."[50] There are those who so esteem this example they are not seen by their students for three years. In another example, the teacher sits alone and does not come down into the hall.

But here [in these cases of self-immolation], because their minds roam beyond the ordinary world, the teaching is liberated from constraints. Some were able to attain great merit and could not be hindered by small faults. They "promised their friends that they would die for them," and they "were willing to sacrifice themselves for the sake of humaneness."[51] They gradually came into accord with the unhindered and so approached enlightenment.

There are cases [in history] of people who rejected ritual and music, who were contemptuous of loyalty and trust.[52] There were those who rejected the good and great and drank the pure and harmonious; then there are the cases of "washing one's ears and saying farewell to glory" and of "clutching a rock and drowning in the water."[53] These are all completely contradictory to the Confucian model, but they are quite close to the Buddhist model.

The Buddha discarded his body for the sake of beings. He threw away his life to benefit the living. Compared with those who would not even pluck out a hair from their leg to benefit others, they are as different as summer and winter.[54] Compared with those who jealously guard the body inherited from their parents, they are as distinct as [the two stars] *shen* 參 and *chen* 辰.[55] In this way one can verify whether a teaching is profound or shallow, and whether a practice is right or wrong. An analogy would be: The more money one lends out, the more interest one receives.

When our world-honored one was at the stage prior to enlightenment, at first he merely reduced his speech and later he was able to be liberated from the body. As for carriages and clothes, he outdid [Zilu 子路], who was willing to share his carriages and clothes until they were worn out.[56] As for elephants and horses he was more generous than those who just lent them out. He gave up his fertile land, and he did not take the territory bestowed on him. He treated them as if he were brushing off dust; he gave them up as if slipping off a pair of sandals. And now we have examples of people smearing their skin and serving it as a meal [to insects], gouging out their eyes to satisfy those who asked for them.[57] Some burned their fingers like lamps, some chopped up their bodies into a hundred slices. Some saved gaunt and hungry tigers or proselytized to mighty fish.

Thus running before the *kalpa*s they came before Maitreya [like the Buddha], and by attaining Buddhahood early they enjoyed the status of Śākyamuni. They practiced all these—beginning by [giving away] external wealth and ending by [giving away] inner wealth. When they reached the point of bringing the wholesome roots to fruition, they transformed something that was hard to give away into something easy to give away. Now if one stops at external wealth because one finds it difficult to give away, then it is because one finds external wealth difficult to give away that one is an ordinary person. But if one donates one's inner wealth and finds it easy to abandon, then it is because it is easy to abandon that one is a bodhisattva. One should know that the buddhas of the three time periods all extol this method. This is true and real cultivation; it is the foremost form of charity.

Surely we have seen the Bodhisattva Sengyai 僧崖 calmly and carefully mounting the wooden tower or the Man of the Way Dazhi 大志, magnanimous and splendid, burning his wrist bone?[58] The people watching them had troubled expressions, but they themselves looked as if they found it easy. [This is because] they had already done this in their past lives. They made these donations again in this life. After repeated donations, they regarded the seven treasures (*qibao* 七寶) as less valuable; after repeated emptying, the three wheels transcend the [worldly] tracks.[59] Riding [the three wheels] to cross [*saṃsāra*] is called "true deliverance" (*zhengui* 真歸). They attained adamantine bodies and left behind jade grains of relics as a response.[60]

In this present record, there are (Seng 僧)zang 藏, who, in the blazing heat, stripped off and fed himself to mosquitoes and midges; and (Zheng 正)shou 壽, who tested the *stūpa*—when seated within he passed away perfectly. Dinglan 定蘭 affected the Heavenly King, who returned his eyes. Hongxiu 鴻休 drove off powerful bandits by repaying his past karmic hatred. (Xing 行)ming 明 fed himself to wild animals, thus destroying meanness. (Jing 景)chao 超 burned a lamp by igniting his finger. In addition, there are cases of the tongue not being consumed, of bodies drowning but not sinking, of people entering *stūpa*s made of firewood and burning of their own accord, and of people revealing their naked bodies in order to be bitten. These are all as virtuous as the cases above if we remember that *karma* has different results, according to its causes.

One should know that the body is a phantom. With a phantom body, what is there to depend on? One realizes that matter is like a bubble, the form of which arises only temporarily. The phantom is created by the mind; it is a provisional and false construct. When the bubble bursts, the water clears, floating and sinking in mutual coexistence. This is why the great sages [bodhisattvas] think in terms of numbers of lives, whereas those of the lesser vehicle nurture their lives until they reach extinction. They value making the basis of suffering subside, and they think of removing the inverted view of a "self." This cannot be called seeing the body as only a husk or contemplating it as dust and ashes.

An analogy [to this idea] is someone who devotes himself to study in a grass hut and attaches a bowstring to a pile of earth. He is recruited for "taking the path of ascending the clouds," he is sought out for his "military merit beyond the boundary." Consequently [the ruler] bestows on him a single house as a dwelling and attaches eight halberds to the gate. Then he becomes an honorable *shi* 士 and harvests the benefits of being enfeoffed as a feudal lord. Those who exchange a bag for feeding cattle for the weapons of Nārāyaṇa are just the same as this.[61]

Someone asks, "Using this teaching to proselytize China, is it not what Han *libu* 韓吏部 (Han Yu) thought was a calamity? Originally there were only two heterodoxies [non-Confucian teachings], those of Yangzi and Mozi.[62] Now in addition there is Buddhism! By applying oneself to these odd and extreme practices, the harm is very severe." I reply, "If one is truly discussing benevolence and righteousness, then one excludes the Way and its virtue from the discussion. When one speaks correctly of suffering and emptiness, then it is right to be sparing in mention of loyalty and trust. But to return to the example used by Han Yu: Truly if one sits in a well and looks at the sky, one does not yet to see the whole sky."[63] A major tenet of Confucius' teaching is "I do not yet know about the living, how can I know about the dead."[64] And Zhuangzi says, "It toils me with life and rests me with death."[65] In view of [Zhuangzi] drumming on a pot and singing—one might get the impression that he probably knew what is not subject to death.[66] These two teachings do not discuss the fact that when a person dies, his spirit is not destroyed but goes on to receive retribution in accordance with his wholesome and unwholesome actions; therefore, there is good or bad that derives from the karmic cause. It was by this means that they [the self-immolators] changed coarse into fine and exchanged the weak for the strong. They sell the fragile forms of the aramanthus and in exchange receive the fine clothing of flower hairpins. Thus they perfumed the seeds that gave rise to their manifested actions.[67] Each rebirth is better than their former rebirths, each reward is more powerful than their earlier rewards. By gouging out their fleshly eyes, they acquired the eyes of a buddha; they slice up an ordinary body and so trade it for a golden one. [One might compare it with] the seed of the ficus, which is very small yet [the tree when it is grown] can provide shade for many carriages. These are true statements and not untrustworthy words.[68] The bodhisattvas benefit others and are worthy of emulation.

Someone asks, "Now as for this practice of burning, good people will not be in any doubt about it. But there are bad people who have become accustomed to stabbing and slicing, and they will say the pain of it is just a trifle. Having [seen people] receive the 'lingering death' (*lingchi* 陵遲) punishment, they will say that this burning and roasting is just a stage act. Some occasionally did it by copying others, while others committed it by force to deceive the world. What good roots do such examples plant? It is just seeking out pain and suffering for oneself."

I reply, "Although stupid people will take pleasure in bearing [pain], evil people are able to stand much injury. If they ever experience burning and feed themselves to insects or animals, driven by their shallow sincerity, they will mysteriously summon a good karmic reward and have a good cause planted. By means of a drifting mind, one may attain a drifting reward. [For example,] there was once a girl who playfully threw on a *kāṣāya* and a brahman who got drunk and put on a *dharma* robe.[69] From the coming together of these various causes, they attained complete and final enlightenment."

Someone asks, "In Yijing's records and translations he repeatedly stresses that one must not do such burning. This person had personally visited the Western Regions, he was fully familiar with what is permitted there, and there was nothing he did not know about the teachings. [According to him,] it is not permitted to cause injury. What about that?" I reply, "This is the restrictive teaching of the *Āgama*s. How could it obstruct or damage the teaching of the Mahāyāna? If someone abandons their inner wealth, they will certainly perfect *dānapāramitā*. This is why the *Zhuangyan lun* 莊嚴論 (*Mahāyānasūtrālaṃkāra*) says, 'If one is able to give away one's body and life, then this is an exceedingly rare marvel, and one perfects the *dānapāramitā* of a bodhisattva.'"[70] Thus we know that even after the four cakravartin kings had left the world during the time when one could only practice the ten good actions, if the Way still prevails in the world, there will be enough good people under the reign of Yao 堯, and if filiality is upheld, the Zeng 曾 family will give birth to honorable sons.[71]

In the fourth year of our Sagely Emperor (979), people of the Liang-Zhe 兩 浙 area submitted [to the court] a reliquary made by King Aśoka for the *śarīra* of Śākyamuni Buddha.[72] At first it was worshipped in the Zifu hall 滋福殿, and later it was invited to enter the inner chapel, where it repeatedly manifested marvelous signs. On the fifteenth day of the second month of the eighth year (April 1, 983), by edict it was placed in a wooden *stūpa,* which was nearly one thousand *chi* 尺 in height, at Kaibao si 開寶寺. The reliquary was first interred in a deep brick shaft, and on that day it issued a divine radiance, which spread out, lighting up both sky and land. At that time, among the crowd of religious and laity there were those who scorched the crowns of their heads and their fingers, and those who burned sticks of incense [on their skin]. The court bestowed different awards on them. If it were not for the bodhisattvas of great equanimity and heavenly kings of great good fortune, how could one be able to exhort or force ordinary people to give away the treasure of their own bodies?

Right here in this land the conch-shaped topknot *(uṣṇīṣa)* is seen, and the precious treasures are complete, and we also realize that at this moment Vulture Peak is pure and so our region is transformed.[73] In the historical works composed by Fan Yun 范雲 (461–503), he records a number of auspicious omens.[74] In the texts compiled by Wang Shao 王劭 (d.u.), he records the inhumation [of relics] in *stūpa*s in a number of prefectures.[75] The Sui distributed relics, and the Tang interred the True Body. To compare [these earlier cases] with the relic veneration in our dynasty is like comparing the dimensions of a patch of field with those of Mount Iron Ring [that is, Sumeru]. What this compilation records is the attainment and transmission of expounding the *dharma*. These people who were able to bear what is hard to bear, although they are gone they still exist. Those who received a body by giving away a body, although they died, they still live. One depicts the five fungi before plants and trees, one arranges the four auspicious omens before fish hairs.[76] It is as the *Shijing* 詩經 says: "Take your pattern from King Wen, and the myriad regions will have confidence in you."[77]

Notes

Introduction

1. For this account of Daodu's 道度 (462–527) self-immolation I follow the funerary inscription "Liang Xiaozhuangyan si Daodu Chanshi bei" 梁小莊嚴寺 道度禪師碑, composed by Xiao Gang 蕭綱 (503–551)—who later became the Liang emperor Jianwendi 梁簡文帝 (r. 549 551)—and preserved in the Korean epigraphical collection *Sŏkwŏn salin* 釋苑詞林 (A Forest of Words from Śākya's Garden), fasc. 193, *Han'guk Pulgyo chŏnsŏ* 韓國佛教全書 (Complete Works of Korean Buddhism), vol. 4, 660–662. See also the biographies of Daodu in *Hongzan fahua zhuan* 弘贊法華傳 (Biographies Which Broadly Extol the *Lotus*) 5, T 51.2067.24c14–25a21; and *Fayuan zhulin* 法苑珠林 (A Grove of Pearls in a Dharma Garden) 96, T 53.2122.992c16–993a5.

2. The prince of Wuling mentioned in the inscription was probably the emperor Liang Wudi's 梁武帝 (r. 502–549) eighth son, Xiao Ji 蕭紀 (508–553). See his biography in *Liang shu* 梁書 (Book of the Liang) 55/825–828. *Liang shu* 3/68 says that the prince of Wuling was appointed governor of Eastern Yangzhou in the sixth month of Putong 5 (July 17–August 14, 524).

3. Prip-Møller 1967, 178.

4. Pingyang is located in present-day Linfen 臨汾, Shanxi.

5. See his biography in *Han shu* 漢書 (Book of the [Former] Han) 44/2157.

6. The Chinese way of reckoning age *(sui)* holds that a person is one year old at birth. Thus twenty *sui* equals nineteen years old. This Bhadra can very likely be identified with the Buddha-bhadra who was the teacher of Sengchou 僧稠 (480–560). See Chen Jinhua 2002a, 152, n. 9. The inscription offers Chengwang si 城王寺 as the name of the monastery. No monastery of that name is known to me, and I suspect that Fawang si 法王寺, a famous monastery on Song shan 嵩山 is intended. My thanks to Chen Jinhua for suggesting this reading.

7. Zhong shan (Bell mountain) is now known as Zijin shan 紫金山. It stood northeast of the Liang capital, Jiankang 健康, close to the Yangzi river.

8. Prince Anchengkang was Liang Wudi's father's seventh son, Xiao Xiu 蕭秀 (475–518). See *Liang shu* 22/341.

9. Daodu took these copies, plus five hundred fascicles of the *Nirvāṇa Sūtra*

and Liang Wudi's commentary on the *Mahāprajñāpāramitā sūtra* (which the emperor had bestowed on him) to the North, where he proselytized until some time before Putong 4 (523), when he returned to Jiankang.

10. The chapel is referred to in the inscription as Hualin Dengjue dian 花林 等覺殿 , that is to say, the building called the "Hall of Equality" (Dengjue dian 等 覺殿) in the Hualin 華林 palace garden—as seen, for example, in the biography of Huijue 慧覺 (450–535) in *XGSZ* 12, T 50.2060.469b, translated by Andreas Janousch (Janousch 1999, 114). Chen Jinhua discusses this building in his study of the Buddhist Palace Chapel in the time of Liang Wudi (forthcoming).

11. *Han'guk Pulgyo chŏnsŏ*, vol. 4, 661b.

12. *Han'guk Pulgyo chŏnsŏ*, vol. 4, 661c; *Hongzan fahua zhuan* 5, T 51.2067.24 c21–24.

13. Ohnuma 1997 and 1998.

14. See Ohnuma 1997, 84–92.

15. Ohnuma 1997, 85.

16. On this practice, see the study by Liu Shufen (1998), later published in English as Liu 2000.

17. See, for example, *Shisong lü* 十誦律 (Ten Recitation Vinaya), T 23.1435. 284a–b. On Buddhist attitudes to cremation, see the article "Dabi" in *Hōbōgirin* 6, 803–815. Phyllis Granoff (1992) discusses the issue of killing parasites in the cremation process.

18. On Wudi's Buddhist persona see Janousch 1999 and Chen Jinhua's forthcoming article "*Pañcavārṣika* Assemblies in Liang Wudi's (r. 502–549) Buddhist Palace Chapel."

19. The most comprehensive discussion of *ganying* is now found in Sharf 2002, 77–133.

20. Sharf 2002, 83.

21. Gernet 1960, Jan 1965, Benn 1998. Gernet's article prompted Jean Filliozat to publish a study of auto-cremation in Indian sources (Filliozat 1963). Orzech (1994) and Raveri (1992) have both offered more theoretical reflections on the materials studied by Jan and Gernet. Studies of suicide in Buddhism that discuss self-immolation include La Vallée Poussin 1919 and Lamotte 1965 (later translated into English as Lamotte 1987). Robert Lingat (1965) wrote briefly about self-immolation in Thailand.

22. Funayama 2002. The work of Nabata (1931) was apparently not followed up by many other scholars. Mizuo 1963 is only one page long. Okamoto 1974 is rather introductory. Myōjin Hiroshi's two short articles (1985 and 1996) present much interesting material not covered in this book. Naitō 1986 examines auto-cremation and related practices in Japan.

23. See Lin 2001, for example; also Cai 1996, 85–88, on self-immolation by nuns. Yan (1999, 147–159) offers some interesting insights into the connections between self-immolation and esoteric Buddhism in China. Zhang Yong (2000, esp., 341–350) discusses self-immolation in the context of the sixth-century cult leader Mahāsattva Fu 傅大士.

24. Cf. King 2000, 148, n. 6. King opts to use the term "to refer to religiously motivated self-sacrifice by means of burning oneself to death."

25. See Funayama 2002, 349–348 [sic].

26. The fullest discussion of the variety of meanings of sheshen may be found in Funayama 2002, esp. 351–346.

27. See the examples of this usage cited by Funayama (2002, 348–347).

28. See Funayama 2002, 321–320; Gernet 1995, 243–245.

29. The best-known Indian auto-cremators, in the West at any rate, are the gymnosophist Kalanos, who burned himself in the time of Alexander the Great (356–323 BCE), and a śramaṇa called Khegas of the Augustan era. Both acts were recorded by the geographer and historian Strabo (64/63 BCE–ca. 21 CE). See Filliozat 1963, 35. On the practice of sati (widow burning) in India, see Weinberger-Thomas 1999.

30. See Benn 1998.

31. Lin (2001, 73–74) discusses types of ascetic practices attributed to non-Buddhists in Indian Buddhist scriptures known in China.

32. To mention but three significant works on aspects of Sinification: Buswell 1990, Gregory 1991, and Sharf 2002.

33. Zürcher 1982a, 161–162.

34. On this point, see Shinohara 1988, 122. On the importance of epigraphical sources for the study of Chinese Buddhism in general, see the work of Yagi Sentai (1981, 1982, 1983). More recently, note the important collection of Ding Mingyi (1998).

35. The canon in question is the Taishō shinshū daizōkyō 大正新脩大藏經.

36. See, for example, Jan 1965, 265.

37. Buswell (1992, 198) reports that auto-cremation is "exceedingly rare" in contemporary Korea, but many monks burn their fingers (195–197). As for contemporary finger burning in China, Raoul Birnbaum has shared his knowledge on this topic with me over the last few years.

38. T 53.2122.994c–995c and T 50.2060.625c–627b, respectively.

39. For example, a record of miracles associated with the Renshou 仁壽 relic distribution campaign (601–604) briefly mentions a boy who recited the Lotus Sūtra and burned himself to death. See Guang Hongming ji 廣弘明集 (Extended Collection for Propagating and Elucidating Buddhism) 17, T 52.2103.215c. My thanks to Chen Jinhua for this reference.

40. *Da zhidu lun* T 1509.25.149b; translated in Lamotte 1944–1981, vol. 2, 712–713.

41. See translations of these stories, references to their sources in various canonical languages, iconography, and secondary scholarship in Lamotte 1944–1981, vol. 2, 713–723.

42. See Howard 2001.

43. This facet of Fu's career is discussed in Hsiao 1995. In Chinese, see Zhang Yong 2000.

44. *Siming zunzhe jiaoxing lu* 四明尊者教行錄 (Record of the Teaching and Practices of the Venerable Siming), T 46.1937.898a–901a.

45. See, for example, the biography of Lang Yuling 郎餘令 (d.u.) in *Jiu Tang shu* 舊唐書 (Old Book of the Tang) 189/4961–4962, and *Xin Tang shu* 新唐書 (New Book of the Tang) 199/5659–5660. When Lang was the administrative supervisor in Youzhou 幽州, his subordinates wished to see an itinerant monk burn himself to death. Lang insisted it was a trick and that it would be depraved to go and witness it. He took the monk in for questioning and extracted a confession from him. The biography of Zhang Yan 張淹 (?–466) in *Nan shi* 南史 (History of the Southern Dynasties) 32/833 and *Song shu* 宋書 (Book of the Song) 46/1400 says that when he was the governor of Dongyang 東陽, he forced his subordinates to burn their arms to glorify the Buddha and made common people bow before the Buddha thousands of times to atone for their crimes. Zhu Shouchang 朱壽昌 (d. after 1070), whose biography is found in the exemplars of filiality section of *Song shi* 宋史 (History of the Song) 456/1304–1305, lost his mother and in his search for her branded his arm, burned the crown of his head, and drew blood to copy Buddhist scriptures.

46. See *Shangshu gushi* 尚書故實 (Stories Told by Minister [Zhang]), 1:12; summarized in MacGowan 1889, 9–10, but the source is uncited.

47. See Morrell 1985, 279–280.

Chapter 1 "Mounting the Smoke with Glittering Colors"

1. See the remarks of Koichi Shinohara in the opening pages of Shinohara 1988. For Indian Buddhist hagiography, which focused on a relatively small number of holy figures, see the study by Ray (1994). A bibliographic summary of some representative earlier works on the subject may be found in note 7, page 11, of Ray's book, to which should now be added Schober 1997. There is nothing comparable to the *Gaoseng zhuan* genre in Indian or Tibetan Buddhist materials.

2. These dates for Baochang, usually given as "fl. 519," were suggested to me by Chen Jinhua (personal communication, April 14, 2001).

3. Cao Shibang (1995) has suggested that the compiler of *Biqiuni zhuan* may

in fact have been an unknown nun rather than Baochang. His argument is intriguing, if not fully convincing.

4. See Wright 1954, 395–397.

5. The influence of Peter Brown's work on the Christian holy men of Late Antiquity on recent scholarship dealing with medieval China has been so marked that this idea hardly needs to be restated, but see, for example, Shinohara 1994.

6. Zürcher 1982a, 165.

7. *XZJ* 134.8a–b.

8. Baochang's biography may be found in *XGSZ* 1, T 50.2060.426b–427c. On the compilation of the *Mingseng zhuan,* see Wright 1954, 409, n. 2. Note also the work of Kasuga (1935).

9. These other collections are surveyed in Makita 1989a, 5–15, and Wright 1954, 412–424.

10. *XZJ* 134.1a–17c.

11. We may note that the *Mingseng zhuan* is still mentioned in the monograph on literature in the *Jiu Tang shu* 舊唐書 46/2000, so it probably did not drop out of circulation all that quickly. Note also the presence there of a text called *Mingseng lu* 名僧錄 (Record of Famous Monks).

12. Huijiao's borrowing from Baochang was noted by Wright (1954, 408–412), but Shinohara (1994) argues with some justification that both Wright and Makita (1989a) have underestimated the importance of Baochang's work as the first comprehensive collection of biographies of Chinese monks.

13. See Makita 1989a, 39–41, where the *Mingseng zhuan*'s headings are conveniently laid out.

14. The formal organization of the *Gaoseng zhuan,* and in particular the grouping of biographies by the activities of monks, is discussed by Wright (1954, 390), who draws attention to secular antecedents for this in the work of the historians Sima Qian 司馬遷 (ca. 145–86 BCE), Ban Gu 班固 (32–92), and the contemporary example of the *Zhongchen zhuan* 忠臣傳 (Biographies of Loyal Officials) by the prince of Xiangdong 湘東王—that is, Xiao Yi 蕭繹 (508–554), the future Liang Yuandi 元帝 (r. 552–554).

15. See the study and translation by Tsai 1994, also Georgieva 1996 and Zhang 1999. Self-immolation by nuns is also discussed briefly in Cai 1996, 85–88. On biographies of East Asian female practitioners in general, see Kleine 1998.

16. Makita (1989a, 39–41) compares Baochang's rubrics with those employed by Huijiao. See Shinohara 1994, 484–485, on the "homogenizing effect" of the ten categories. Although the relevant section in the *Gaoseng zhuan* is entitled *wangshen* 亡身 in the body of the text as we now have it, Huijiao refers to it in his preface by the same title it had in his predecessor's collection, namely *yishen.* (See Wright 1954, 405.) Makita briefly introduces Huijiao's use of the

category *wangshen* but does not offer much insight as to why Huijiao selected it (Makita 1989a, 46–47).

17. On the compilation of the *Gaoseng zhuan*, see Wright 1954. For a more recent discussion of the date of compilation, see Makita 1989a, which dates it to 531 (519 being the latest date mentioned in the text). The life of Huijiao is examined in detail by Makita (1989a, 1–5) and by Wright (1954, 395–400). On the life and work of Huijiao, see also Zheng 1986.

18. *GSZ* 14, T 50.2059.419a. See Shinohara 1994, 483; Kieschnick 1997, 4; and Wright 1954, 408.

19. The early eighth-century catalogue *Kaiyuan shijiao lu* 開元釋教錄 (Record of Buddhist Teachings [Compiled during] the Kaiyuan Period), compiled by Zhisheng 智昇 (fl. 669–740) and completed in 730, remarks on the noncanonical status of the *Mingseng zhuan*, T 55.2154.538a. See Makita 1989a, 66, n. 1, for other early Chinese Buddhist biographical material listed in the monograph on literature in the *Sui shu* 隋書 (Book of the Sui).

20. *XGSZ* 1, T 50.2060.425a. See Wright 1954, 394, citing the research of Yamazaki Hiroshi 山崎宏, which reveals that of 151 monks whose biographies specify a geographical location, 121 are from this region of China.

21. *GSZ* T 50.2059.419a3–11; translation by Wright (1954, 406) with adaptations.

22. T 16.663.354a19–356c18.

23. See, for example, the following Chinese translations:

1. *Liudu ji jing* 六度集經 (Sūtra of the Collection of Six Pāramitās) 1 (no. 4), T 3.152.2b; translated in Chavannes 1910, vol. 1, 15–17.
2. *Pusa benxing jing* 菩薩本行經 (Sūtra of the Original Acts of the Bodhisattva) 3, T 3.155.119a.
3. *Pusa bensheng man lun* 菩薩本生鬘論 (*Jātakamālā*) 1, T 3.160.332b–333b.
4. *[Foshuo] Pusa toushen yi ehu qita yinyuan jing* [佛說] 菩薩投身飴餓虎起塔因緣經 (*Vyāghrījātaka*, Sūtra of the Causes and Conditions of the Erection of the Stūpa for the Bodhisattva Who Gave Away His Body to Feed the Hungry Tigress), T 3.170.424b–428a.
5. *Xianyu jing* 賢愚經 (Sūtra of the Wise and Foolish) 1 (no. 2), T 4.202.352b–353b.
6. *Jinguangming zuisheng wang jing* 金光明最勝王經 (Sūtra of Golden Light) 10, T 16.665.450c–456c.

See Lamotte 1944–1981, vol. 1, 143, n.1, for Sanskrit sources and iconography.

24. See, for example, Karetzky 2000, esp. 75–90; Rhie 1999, 38, 46.

25. Hammond 1991, 87.

26. Hammond 1991, 88.

27. See the examples in Hammond 1991 89, n. 10.

28. The use by local magistrates of prayers and petitions to local gods, who were often thought to control tigers, is noted in Hammond 1991. Encounters between officials and supernatural forces were a staple of anecdotal literature in traditional China. A study of this trope as it appears in the Song is offered in Boltz 1993. A Buddhist example may be found in a story told of the third patriarch of the Chan school, Sengcan 僧粲 (d.u.) in *Lidai fabao ji* 歷代法寶記 (Records of the Jewel of the Dharma through the Ages), T 51.2075.181b27–28. I am indebted to Chen Jinhua for this reference.

29. *GSZ* 12, T 50.2059.404a16–28. Pengcheng, present-day Tongshan 銅山 county in Jiangsu, was one of the earliest centers of Buddhist activity in China (see Zürcher 1959, 26–28).

30. *GSZ* 12, T 50.2059.404a24–25.

31. T 3.170.424b–428a. See above, n. 23, item 4, for details of this text.

32. See Ohnuma 1997.

33. *GSZ* 12, 50.2059.404a29–b21.

34. Juqu Mengxun and his descendants were devout Buddhists (see Hurvitz 1956, 57, n. 1, and the sources cited therein). Mengxun's biography is in *Wei shu* 99/2203. He could be rather capricious in his affections and is largely remembered in Buddhist history for having ordered the assassination of Dharmakṣema (see *GSZ* 2, T 50.2059.326c).

35. I presume that "Jinghuan" does not refer to Mengxun's successor, Mao-qian 茂虔 (d.u.), whose belief in Buddhism is also attested in the biography of Buddhavarman (Futuobamo 浮陀跋摩, *GSZ* 2, T 50.2059.339a20–24), because by this time Maoqian had been captured by the Northern Wei 北魏 emperor Tuoba Tao 拓跋燾 (r. 424–452) after an attack on the Northern Liang in 439 (see Molè 1970, 93, n. 95). It could refer to (or be another name of) Wuhui 無諱 (d.u.), one of Maoqian's younger brothers. Wuhui succeeded Maoqian as the leader of the Northern Liang forces that survived the 439 attack (see *Song shu* 98/2416, *Wei shu* 99/2209, and *Bei shi* 北史 [History of the Northern Dynasties] 93/3085). Funayama (1995, 20) suggests that "Jinghuan" is a conflation or confusion of the names of Mengxun's two sons, Maoqian and Wuhui.

36. Gaochang is Karakhoja, located near present-day Turfan in Eastern Xinjiang.

37. *GSZ* 12, T 50.2059.404b3–4.

38. See Jia 1995. Jia suggests that the monk mentioned in an important contemporary inscription as the instigator of many political initiatives under the Liang is none other than Daojin.

39. Juqu's successors were also devout Buddhists, as is evidenced by the

inscription *Juqu Anzhou zaosi gongde bei* 沮渠安周造寺功德碑 (Stele on the Merits of Juqu Anzhou's Construction of Monasteries), written by Xiahou Can 夏侯粲 [?–after 445] in 445 and noted in Hurvitz 1956, 58, n. 1. On this important epigraphic source, see Jia 1995, Rong 1998, and the studies quoted therein. Anzhou's biography is in *Wei shu* 99/2205; his reign is also described in *Song shu* 98/2417–2418.

40. The triple refuge refers to laypeople taking refuge in the Three Jewels of Buddha, Dharma, and Saṃgha.

41. *Shewei* is one Chinese Buddhist rendering of the Sanskrit *dhyāpayati*. On this and other terms for cremation, see the entry on "Dabi" in *Hōbōgirin* 6, 573–585.

42. On Dharmakṣema and his career, see Chen Jinhua 2004.

43. See Yamada 1989 and Chapter 2.

44. On cannibalism in China see, for example, des Rotours 1963 and 1968, and the rather uncritical historical survey by Chong (1990). Note also Raimund Kolb's (1996) long review of Chong's work, which contains much valuable supplementary material.

45. See Michihata 1979b and Durt 1998.

46. See Durt 1998 and the many references cited therein. I hope to return in a later study to the relationship between slicing the thigh to make medicine (as recommended in Indian Vinaya texts) to feed hungry beings in the *jātaka*s and *avadāna*s and its later appearance as a mark of filiality in non-Buddhist Chinese biographies. In the meantime, note the brief remarks in Michihata 1968, 82.

47. *GSZ* 12, T 50.2059.404b22–c10.

48. Wei commandery is in present-day Henan.

49. On the belief in the use of the heart and liver of adolescents to prepare elixirs in a somewhat later period, see Barrett 2004. On the use of human parts in Chinese medicine more generally, see Cooper and Sivin 1973. On blood sacrifice in China, see Kleeman 1994. On the later phenomenon of "killing people to serve demons" (*sharen jigui* 殺人祭鬼), see Eberhard 1968, 170–183.

50. The five viscera are the liver, heart, spleen, lungs, and urino-genital system.

51. Chinese wound medicine in premodern times remains somewhat mysterious, known only through scattered references such as this. See, for example, the biography of the physician Hua Tuo 華佗 (d. 208) in *Sanguo zhi* 三國志 (Records of the Three Kingdoms) 29/799–803, translated in DeWoskin 1983, 140–153, which mentions abdominal suturing (141). On Hua Tuo see Chen Yinque 1977, 1119–1122, and Mair 1994, 688, n. 1. On abdominal suturing in East Asia, see Okano 2000. It is possible that suturing wounds was one of several Indian medical practices associated with this semilegendary physician. Dr. Christine Salazar of the University of Cambridge informs me that there are Greek and Roman descriptions of abdominal sutures from the first and second

centuries CE, and it seems the technique was frequently successful. See her book, Salazar 2000.

52. *GSZ* 12, T 50.2059.404a2–15. Other sources for Sengqun's life are discussed in Appendix 1. Huo shan can be identified with Huotong shan 霍童山 (also called Zhiti shan 支提山), close to present-day Ningde 寧德 city in Fujian. It was associated with both Buddhism and Taoism from quite early on. See Schipper 2002 (in Chinese) for the significance of this mountain in the Taoist tradition.

53. Jin'an was near the present-day city of Fuzhou in Fujian. Tao Kui lacks a biography but is mentioned in *Wei shu* 96/2109, where his title at the time was *shangshu* 尚書 (imperial secretary). The *Taishō* edition reads Jinshou 晉守, but the Zhonghua shuju edition provides an alternate reading of Jin'an 晉安; see *Gaoseng zhuan* (Zhonghua shuju edition), 446. This reading is confirmed in the *Fayuan zhulin*, T 53.2122.764c7.

54. Sengqun's biography appears in the Tang Buddhist compendium *Fayuan zhulin* 63, T 53.2122.764c, in the section on karmic debts rather than self-immolation.

55. This point is made more generally in the entry on "Daijuku" in *Hōbōgirin* 7, 803–815.

56. On abstention from grain, see Lévi 1983; Campany 2002, 22–24; and Campany 2005.

57. *DZ* 388 3.22a, translated in Kohn 1993, 150. On this text as a whole, see Yamada Toshiaki 1989 and the studies noted by him in note 2 on page 99.

58. See also Benn 2000.

59. Sengqun's biography is drawn from the *Mingxiang ji* 冥詳記 (Signs from the Unseen Realm) by Wang Yan 王琰 (b. ca. 454, fl. late fifth–early sixth centuries). See *Mingxiang ji*, 457.

60. See the examples in Chapter 6. Huisi 慧思 (515–577) provides another, more famous, example of a Buddhist monk who was reputed to have used Taoist alchemical techniques to extend his life. See Magnin 1979, especially 21–23, and the scholarship cited by Chen Jinhua (2002a, 201 n. 65).

61. *GSZ* 12, T 50.2059.404c11–18.

62. See Filliozat 1963, 49, n. 52, for a rather caustic observation on Gernet's rendering of the term (Gernet 1960, 531). On the specific practices of *dhūta*, for which a number of different lists are given in the sources, see *Bukkyō dai jiten*, 2335a, and the well-documented survey by Ray 1994, 293–323.

63. See the remarks of Lin Huisheng on auto-cremation as *dhūta* in Lin 2001, 73–74. See Kieschnick 1997, 34–35, for a discussion of *dhūta* practitioners in *Gaoseng zhuan* literature as a whole.

64. *GSZ* 12, T 50.2059.404c14

65. Yao Xu was a paternal uncle of the Tibetan ruler Yao Xing 姚興 (366–416), known as the emperor Wenhuan huangdi 文桓皇帝 of the Later Qin 後秦, which ruled North China in 384–417; see *Jin shu* 117–118/2975–3006.

66. For *xie* 屑 (chips), the Three editions and the Palace edition read *you* 油 (oil), which is equally plausible and accords with other examples of the use of oil; see T 50.2059.404n26. The reference to the *sheshen pin* is slightly problematic. Gernet (1960, 531, n. 6) understands this as an explicit reference to a chapter by that name in the *Sūtra of Golden Light* (T 16.663.354a). Because this translation seems to have been made by Dharmakṣema between 414 and 421 (and probably in fact was not started before 420; see Chen Jinhua 2004), the date of the translation could only just be reconciled with the date of Fayu's auto-cremation if it fell in the latter part of the Qin (384–417)—as Gernet admits. Filliozat (1963, 49, n. 52) speculates that Fayu may have known an earlier translation or the Sanskrit version of the text. But there is, in fact, no indication in his biography that Fayu was familiar with any Indic languages, and Dharmakṣema's is the first recorded translation. What seems to rule out Dharmakṣema's translation entirely is the fact that, according to *Zizhi tongjian* 資治通鑑 (Comprehensive Mirror for the Aid of Government) 108/3436, Yao Xu was the military commander in Puban 蒲圻 (an error for 蒲坂) in or soon after 396. In addition, the content of this particular chapter, which recounts the famous sacrifice of the Bodhisattva to a starving tigress, is perhaps slightly at odds with Fayu's method of self-immolation. See Gernet 1960, 542, n. 1, for a synopsis of the text in question. My own feeling is that, on the grounds of date and context, *sheshen pin* may be a reference to "The Original Acts of the Medicine King" in the *Lotus Sūtra*. Alternatively, it could be a simple error or have been inserted into the text at some later date.

67. Zürcher 1982a, 163.

68. The Dong shan referred to here is presumably not the mountain of that name near present-day Fuzhou, but a mountain in or close to Yangzhou.

69. *Kan* originally designated the niche for an image. By the tenth century it had come to mean "coffin," perhaps partly by association with auto-cremators, in whose biographies the term is often used, as here, to designate the space within the pyre. For a Song dynasty definition of the term, see *Shishi yaolan* 釋氏要覽 (Essential Readings for Buddhists) compiled by Daocheng 道誠 (fl. 1017), T 54.2127.307c2–7.

70. The eight precepts commonly taken by laypeople are not to kill; not to take things; not to engage in ignoble (sexual) conduct; not to lie; not to drink alcohol; not to indulge in cosmetics or jewelry, dancing or music; not to sleep on fine beds; and not to eat after noon. See *Da zhidu lun* T 25.1509.159b19–c19, translated in Lamotte 1944–1981, vol. 2, 826–828. For a survey of ceremonies for bestowing the eight precepts in medieval China, see Funayama 1995, 54–56.

71. Fascicle 6 in Kumārajīva's translation of the *Lotus, Miaofa lianhua jing* 妙法蓮花經, *Saddharmapuṇḍarīka,* T 9.262.52a–55a; fascicle 9 in Dharmarakṣa's *Zheng fahua jing* 正法花經, *Saddharmapuṇḍarīka,* T 9.263.125a–127a. On the contents of this chapter, see Chapter 2.

72. As Gernet points out (1960, 532, n. 2), Kumārajīva's translation of the *Lotus* contains the phrase *yixin qiufo* 一心求佛 ("seek the Buddha with a unified mind"), T 9.262.53a25. Dharmarakṣa's version contains the phrases *yong yixin gu wuyou kuhuan* 用一心故無有苦患 ("employ the one mind and there will be no suffering"), T 9.263.125b25, and *dang yixin si* 當一心思 ("one ought to think with a unified mind"), T 9.263.125c25.

73. *GSZ* 12, T 50.2059.405a8–b1; translated in Gernet 1960, 532–533.

74. Lu shan, between Jiujiang 九江 and Xingzi 星子 in northern Jiangxi, was already an important Buddhist site by this time. See, for example, Zurcher 1959, 208–209.

75. Full dates are given as follows: reign period, year, month, day. Xiaojian 2.6.3 is the third day of the sixth lunar month of the second year of the Xiaojian reign period.

76. Purple vapor (*ziqi* 紫氣) was considered an auspicious sign in medieval China. It was noted, for example, when Laozi 老子 disappeared to the West, according to Sima Zhen's 司馬貞 (early eighth century) commentary on his biography in *Shiji* 史記 (Records of the Historian), which quotes from the *Liexian zhuan* 列仙傳 (Arrayed Biographies of Transcendents). See *Shiji* 63/2141, n. 2. This passage no longer appears in the received text of the *Liexian zhuan.*

77. *GSZ* 12, T50.2059.405a13–21.

78. *GSZ* 12, T50.2059.405b2–c1; translated in Gernet 1960, 533–535. On Zhulin si, see Chen Jinhua 2004, 241–242, n. 65.

79. Gernet (1960, 533, n. 2) suspects that *mai* 麥 (barley or wheat) was written in error for the name of some oleaginous plant. Sesame, along with pine resin and needles, is recommended as a wondrous foodstuff in many medieval Taoist texts; see, for example, *Taishang lingbao wufuxu* (*DZ* 388, 2.1a; Kohn 1993, 150).

80. The Three editions and the Palace edition read 酥油 (butter) for 蘇油 (oil of thyme). See T 50.2059.405n.13.

81. Liu Yigong was the fifth son of the emperor Song Wudi 宋武帝 (r. 421–422). His biography is in *Song shu* 61/1640–1653.

82. Huiyi's auto-cremation, like many others, seems to have taken place at night.

83. *GSZ* 12, T 50.2059.405b23–27.

84. See Strong 2004, 98–123, and the accounts of André Bareau (Bareau 1963 and 1975).

85. Strong 2004, 100–110; Bareau 1975, 155.

86. See BBC News, "New light on human torch mystery." According to the BBC

web page: "BBC 1's *QED*—which brought together the world's top fire experts—looked at cases of spontaneous human combustion from around the world. And the programme discovered that the so-called wick-effect, in which a body is devoured by flames from its own body fat, is behind the mystery. Using a dead pig wrapped in cloth, they simulated a human body being burned over a long period and the charred effect was the same as in so-called spontaneous human combustion."

87. Canonical accounts of bodhisattvas who made torches of their bodies are discussed in Chapter 2.

88. Strong 2004, 106.

89. See John Strong's synopsis of the various arguments (2004, 106–110).

90. On this collection, see Campany 2002.

91. See, for example, *Taishang lingbao wufuxu, DZ* 388, 2.2b–3a, which describes how to make pills out of the "five wonder plants" (pine resin, sesame, pepper, ginger, calamus); translation in Kohn 1993, 152–153.

92. *Miaofa lianhua jing,* T 9.262.53b; Hurvitz 1976, 295.

93. *Miaofa lianhua jing,* T 9.262.53b. The translation is from Hurvitz 1976, 294–295; I have omitted his notes.

94. *SZ* 12, T50.2059.405c2–10; translated in Gernet 1960, 535–536. "Way of the Five Pecks of Grain" was another (somewhat derogatory) name for "Way of the Celestial Masters" (Tianshi dao 天師道), founded in Sichuan after Zhang Daoling 張道陵 (a.k.a. Zhang Ling 張陵, 34–156) received a revelation from Laozi in 142. See Robinet 1997, 55–56.

95. Shu refers here to present-day Chengdu 成都, Sichuan. The biography of Daowang 道汪 (d. 465) records that in late 464 or 465 he became the abbot of Wudan si. He had been active in Chengdu for some time before becoming abbot, and it is likely that he knew Sengqing. See *GSZ* 7, T 50.2059.371c.

96. Zhang Yue's appointment as prefect of Yizhou in 456 is noted in *Song shu* 6/119. See also *Song shu* 84/2131. He was also a patron of Daowang, *GSZ* 7, T 50.2059.371c18–20.

97. Tianshui is present-day Tianshui county in Gansu. Pei Fangming has a biography in *Song shu* 45/1382–1384.

98. Other examples of auto-cremation in front of images are discussed in later chapters. See also the case explored in detail in Shinohara 1998a.

99. Translated in Gernet 1960, 536.

100. On the ascetic practice of avoiding silk, see Kieschnick 1999.

101. *GSZ* 12, T 50.2059.405c12–17.

102. Shifeng is present-day Tiantai 天臺 in Zhejiang.

103. *GSZ* 12, T 50.2059.405c17–18. Xiao Mian was a nephew of the Qi emperor Gaodi 高帝 (r. 479–482). His biography is in *Nan Qi shu* 南齊書 (Book of the Southern Qi) 45/794–795. The monk Huishen is not known from other sources.

104. *GSZ* 12, T 50.2059.405c19–28; translated in Gernet 1960, 536. Jiaozhi is the present-day Tonkin region in North Vietnam.

105. *Guan wuliangshou jing* is an apocryphon; see Fujita 1990.

106. *Biqiuni zhuan* 2, T 50.2063.939b14–c5, translated in Tsai 1994, 51–53.

107. *Biqiuni zhuan* 2, T 50.2063.940c10–17, translated in Tsai 1994, 60.

108. See Tsai 1994, 135, n. 113. Liu has biographies in *Nan Qi shu* 54/937 and *Nan shi* 50/1248–1254.

109. *Biqiuni zhuan* 2, T 50.2063.941b13–c2, translated in Tsai 1994, 65–66.

110. Liu Liang has biographies in *Song shu* 45/1377 and *Nan shi* 17/479.

111. Presumably these must have been recremated because two *sheng* of bones are said to have produced just under one-fifth *sheng* of relics. See Tsai 1994, 65–66.

112. *Biqiuni zhuan* 3, T 50.2063.943b29–c13, translated in Tsai 1994, 79–80; T 50.2063.943c14–23, translated in Tsai 1994, 80–81; T 50.2063.944b17–23, translated in Tsai 1994, 84–85.

113. Bai shan presumably refers to the mountain of that name close to the capital, Jiankang.

114. The text says the eighteenth night, but the eighth, which is a more auspicious date, seems more likely. The day commemorates the Buddha's *parinirvāṇa* and is also the day when Jinggui chose to cremate herself. See Tsai 1994, 141, n. 56. There are further problems with the date not mentioned by Tsai. The Jianwu reign period was inaugurated at the beginning of the tenth month, so technically speaking there can have been no eighth day of the second month of Jianwu 1. This date probably refers to Yongmong 永明 11.2.8. When emperor Wudi 武帝 (r. 482–493) of the Southern Qi died, the Yongming era (482–493 [Yongming 1–11]) ended in the seventh month and the new reign name Longchang 隆昌 was adopted. Longchang was then replaced in the tenth month by Yanxing 嚴興, which was in turn followed by Jianwu 建武 when emperor Mingdi 明帝 (r. 494–498) assumed the throne. In cases such as this, when more than one reign name was employed in a single year, the year in question was generally referred to by the last reign name granted. Although, strictly speaking, the eighth day of the second month of this year fell under Yongming 11, it is still referred to in this source as Jianwu 1.2.8. My thanks to Chen Jinhua for clarifying this issue.

115. T 50.2063.943c9–13, translation from Tsai 1994, 79–80 with some adaptations.

116. Bynum 1987.

117. Tsai 1994, 85.

118. *Firmiana simplex* (Chinese parasol tree) is a member of the cacao, or chocolate, family (*Sterculiaceae*) of the order Malvales. Native to Asia, it grows to a height of 12 meters (40 feet) with deciduous leaves up to 30 centimeters (12 inches) across and small greenish white flowers that are borne in clusters. Note

that the *wutong* is not a paulownia, although it has frequently been misidentified as such. See Needham 1996, 593–595.

119. *GSZ* 12, T 2059.50.405a6.

120. *Zhuangzi* 17, *Zhuangzi yinde* 莊子引得 *(A Concordance to Chuang Tzu)*, p. 45, l. 86.

121. *GSZ* 12, T 50.2059.405a13–24.

122. Cole 1999, 36.

123. Lippiello 2001, 69–70; 111–112. The quotation is from an image of intertwined trees on the ceiling of the Wu Liang shrine. See Wu Hung 1989, 240.

124. *GSZ* 12, T 50.2059.405c26–28.

125. The white deer, on the other hand, was a well-known auspicious sign. See Lippiello 2001, 98–102.

126. Wu is present-day Suzhou; Pingnan was a commandery in Liangzhou 梁州. Zhang Bian has a brief biography in *Song shu* 53/1515. His connections with Buddhism are discussed in Tang 1997, 307–308.

127. Sengyu had a separate biography written by Zhang Bian, of which only this eulogy remains; see Wright 1954, 426. Another eulogy by Zhang Bian, again part of what was once a separate biography for the exegete Tanjian 曇鑒 (d.u.), may be found in *GSZ* 7, T 50.2059.370a. The eulogy is not preserved in the *Mingxiang ji* version of Sengyu's biography as reconstructed from the *Fayuan zhulin*. See *Mingxiang ji*, 510; *Fayuan zhulin* 63, T 53.2122.770a20–b8.

128. *GSZ* 12, T 50.2059.505b.

129. *GSZ* 13, T 51.2059.417b24.

130. *GSZ* 12, T 50.2059.405b27–c1.

131. *GSZ* 12, T 50.2059.405c29–406b13; translated in full in Appendix 2.

132. See Wright 1954, 390–391, on the secular antecedents to the critical evaluation. See *Meisōdenshō, XZJ* 134.8d–9a, for a critical evaluation preserved from the *Mingseng zhuan.*

133. A good introduction to the range of techniques employed for longevity in medieval China may be found in Kohn and Sakade 1989.

134. King Śibi is discussed in Chapter 2.

135. On the spontaneous combustion of arhats, see Wilson 2003.

136. That is, if one is determined one can break even metal and stone.

137. *GSZ* 12, T50.2059.406b11–13.

Chapter 2 The *Lotus Sūtra*, Auto-Cremation, and the Indestructible Tongue

1. See the remarks of George Tanabe on this feature in Tanabe and Tanabe 1989, 2.

2. Pulleyblank 1960, 99.

3. The scholarship on the structure and formation of the *Lotus* is discussed in Abbott 1986, 45–49.

4. T 9.262.5b-10b; Hurvitz 1976, 22–47.

5. T 9.262.19a-20a; Hurvitz 1976, 101–119.

6. T 9.262.19b12-14; Hurvitz 1976, 102.

7. On medieval practices inspired by and dedicated to the *Lotus,* see Michihata 1980.

8. Hsin-ju Liu 1988, 96.

9. For example, T 9.262.30c19, 45b15, 53b12, 59b22; Hurvitz 1976, 175, 183, 252, 328.

10. T 9.262.4b9-10; Hurvitz 1976, 15.

11. T 9.262.35c; Hurvitz 1976, 200–201.

12. See, for example, Hsin-Ju Liu 1988, 97, and passim; Nakamura 1980, 186–187, and the scholarship cited therein.

13. Wang 2005.

14. Wang 2005, xv.

15. Following the Kumārajīva version of the *Lotus Sūtra, Miaofa lianhua jing* 妙法蓮花經 7, T 9.262.53a–55a; translated in Hurvitz 1976, 291–302.

16. *Miaofa lianhua jing* 7, T 9.262.53b; Hurvitz 1976, 295.

17. See Durt 1999.

18. *Miaofa lianhua jing* 7, T 9.262.53b22–25; translation in Hurvitz 1976, 295, except for the last line, which is not translated.

19. *Miaofa lianhua jing* 7, T 9.262.53c25–26; translation in Hurvitz 1976, 297.

20. *Miaofa lianhua jing* 7, T 9.262.54a5–7; translation in Hurvitz 1976, 297–298.

21. The magical return of King Śibi's eyes is discussed in Chapter 3.

22. *Miaofa lianhua jing* 7, T 9.262.54a11–16; translation in Hurvitz 1976, 298.

23. See Zürcher 1959, 65–70.

24. See Tsukamoto 1985, 221–223. His argument is based on early mentions of the *Lotus* in the *Gaoseng zhuan* and the *Biqiuni zhuan.*

25. Taken from the catalogue for the exhibition "The *Lotus Sūtra* and Its World, Buddhist Manuscripts of the Great Silk Road."

26. See the examples given from epigraphic and textual sources in Suwa 1997c, 322–323.

27. See Jan 1977.

28. See *Chu sanzang ji ji* 出三藏記集 (Collection of Records Concerning the Translation of the Three Storehouses) 10, T 55.2145.90c11.

29. For an overview of some of the major Chinese commentaries, see Kanno 1994.

30. See Gjertson 1989, 41.

31. T 34.1718.114c27. See also Zhanran's 湛然 (711–782) *Fahua wenju ji* 法華文句記 (Records of the Textual Commentary on the *Lotus Sūtra,* T 34. 1719.312c1). On the *Fahua wenju,* see the study by Hirai Shun'ei (1985). Compare the slightly longer account of Man's self-immolation in the *Fahua jing chuanji* 法華經傳記 (Accounts of the Transmission of the *Lotus Sūtra*) 2, T 51.2068.56c7–13.

32. *XZJ* 134.416c–d; preface dated 1198, *XZJ* 134.408–448. Zongxiao was a major ideologue of Southern Song Tiantai. In addition to this work, he compiled an important Pure Land anthology, the *Lebang wenlei* 樂邦文類 (Compendium of the Land of Bliss), and an account of the Tiantai patriarch Zhili, the *Siming Zunzhe jiaoxing lu.*

33. See Hurvitz 1962, 109.

34. *Miaofa lianhua jing shu* 妙法蓮華經疏 (Commentary on the *Lotus Sūtra*), *XZJ* 150.411d; translation from Kim 1990, 324, with some modifications.

35. See Kim 1990, 202, 276, and 290.

36. See *Fahua yishu* 法華義疏 (Commentary on the Meaning of the *Lotus*), T 34.1721.620c26–28).

37. Filliozat 1963.

38. On Prince Moonlight in medieval China, see the well-known article by Erik Zürcher (1982b). As Zürcher shows (pp. 22–33), the popularity of this savior derived not from *Samādhirāja* itself but from earlier texts.

39. Compare Filliozat's translation from the Sanskrit and Tibetan in Filliozat 1963, 23–27.

40. For a summary of Yijing's argument against self-immolation, see Chapter 4.

41. Yamada 1989, 110.

42. T 4.208.533b–c. Compare the translation by Chavannes (1910, vol. 1, 85–86) of the same story in the *Liudu ji jing,* T 3.152.14c–15a.

43. T 25.1509.130c9–19; Lamotte 1944–1981, vol. 1, 579–580.

44. Translated and discussed in Strong 1992, 207–208. Strong notes a similar version of this account that stars Upagupta rather than King Aśoka.

45. Saddhatissa 1975, 63.

46. See Campany 1993 and the scholarship noted therein; Strickmann 1996, 136–140; and the extensive monograph by Yü Chün-fang (2001).

47. Campany 1993, 244.

48. Note, for example, the chapter entitled "Praesentia" in Brown 1981, 86–105.

49. Campany 1993, 255.

50. *Miaofa lianhua jing,* T 9.262.56c20–22; Hurvitz 1976, 56. Stories about believers released from imprisonment by calling on Guanyin are discussed in Campany 1991.

51. Suwa 1997b. See also Suwa 1997c and 1997d for further research on this topic.

52. See the discussion in Chapter 1.

53. Farmer 1992, 26–27.

54. *Miaofa lianhua jing* 6, T 9.262.49b15–22; translated in Hurvitz 1976, 273.

55. Suwa 1997b, 323.

56. See Lu Xun, 1967, 541. This collection contains a number of stories about the unburned tongue. On the collection and its author, see Campany 1996, 90.

57. See, for example, *Shimen zijing lu* 釋門自鏡錄 (A Record of Those to Be Mirrored by the Disciples of Śākya, compilation attributed to Huaixin 懷信) 1, T 51.2083.805c17–19.

58. T 25.1509.127a. My translation follows the French translation of Lamotte 1944–1981, vol.1, 556.

59. See Suwa 1997b, 321, which draws on the biographies of Kumārajīva in the *Chu sanzang jiji* and the *Gaoseng zhuan*.

60. Note the allusion to this case in Daochuo's 道綽 (562–645) *Anle ji* 安樂集 (Pure Land Collection), T 47.1958.18b1–3; see Young 2000, 41.

61. On some of these texts, see Matoba 1982, 1984, 1986.

62. T 51.2067. On Huixiang's identity and the texts attributed to him see Ibuki 1987 and Chen Yuan 1999, 78–79, nn. 67 and 68.

63. Haozhou is present-day Fengyang 鳳陽 county in Anhui.

64. The account of Sengming's consulting Liang Wudi seems to contradict what we learned about Wudi's opposition to auto-cremation from the biography of the Liang monk Daodu in the Introduction.

65. *Hongzan fahua zhuan* 5, T 51.2067.24c3–9

66. See Rockhill, Leumann, and Nanjio 1972, 118.

67. Soymié 1961.

68. The most interesting study of this is the late Michel Strickmann's chapter "L'icone animée" in Strickmann 1996, 165–211. On miracles attributed to Buddhist images in China, see Soper and Ōmura 1959, 243–252. Some Tang accounts of Buddhist images that came to life were the subject of a penetrating study by Glen Dudbridge (1998).

69. Jiaozhou is present-day Cangwu 蒼梧 county in Guangxi.

70. Hurvitz 1976, 225–236.

71. T 51.2067.26b; Stevenson 1995, 435–436, and Shinohara 1992, 169.

72. On the Aśokan image, see Shinohara 1991, 213–215.

73. On the term *buqu*, see Hucker 1985, 391. Daoxuan also provides a definition of the term as it relates to monastic dependents; see his *Liangchu qingzhong yi* 量處輕重儀 (Procedures for Measuring and Handling Light and Heavy Property) 1, T 45.1895.845b14–17. According to Daoxuan, the status of a personal retainer was midway between a domestic servant and a slave. On Li Yun's faith in Buddhism

and the career of another of his concubines who became a nun, see Chen Jinhua 2002c, esp. 56–58.

Chapter 3 *Saṃgha* and the State

1. The fullest study of Daoxuan's life and works is Fujiyoshi 2002.

2. A discussion of these textual problems may be found in Ibuki 1990; see also Fujiyoshi 2002, 245–298.

3. The early Tang was of course a great period of secular history writing, and Daoxuan's work was in a sense part of the spirit of the age. On official history writing, see Twitchett 1992. For unofficial histories of earlier dynasties produced in the Sui and early Tang, the tables in Shi Guodeng 1992, 34–36, give some idea of the number of historians working in this period.

4. Daoxuan drew on four types of material for his collection: (1) oral information from travellers and informants, (2) his own personal experiences and investigations, (3) religious and secular historical documents, and (4) funerary inscriptions. These sources are surveyed in Shi 1992, 51–91.

5. *XGSZ* 27, T 50.2060.683a25–b19. Hongfu si was later known as Xingfu si 興福寺. It was endowed by the emperor Taizong in 634 in memory of his mother, Empress Taimu 太穆. See Xiong 2000, 259; Wright 1973, 256–258; Ono 1989, vol. 1, 388–390, vol. 2, 129–136.

6. Connections with Zhongnan shan are noted throughout Fujiyoshi 2002.

7. Fujiyoshi 2002, 101. On Taizong and Buddhism, see Weinstein 1987, 7–11, and Wright 1973. On the relationship of Daoxuan's contemporary Xuanzang 玄奘 (602–664) with Taizong, see Jan 1990, 13–41.

8. On Zhou Wudi's suppression of Buddhism, see Nomura 1968.

9. *XGSZ* 27, T 50.2060.680b23–c10. Chen Jinhua (2002a, 202–203) discusses another of Puyuan's disciples.

10. It is interesting to note that Zhongnan shan was the home of many *Huayan jing* devotees in the sixth and seventh centuries, including Sun Simo 孫思邈 (alternative reading, Sun Simiao), (581–682), the noted Chinese medical writer whose connections with Buddhism and in particular the *Huayan jing* have been studied by Sakade 1992. Note also that Sun Simo and Daoxuan were friends. See *SGSZ* 6, T 50.2061.790c; Shi Guodeng 1992, 17–18.

11. See Kieschnick's comments on this episode (1997, 46).

12. Camporesi 1988, esp. 1–46.

13. *Xianshou* is the name of a bodhisattva and a *parivarta* in the *Huayan jing* (*Da Fangguangfo huayan jing* 大方廣佛華嚴經 [Buddhabhadra's version] 6, T 9.278 432c–441b; *Da Fangguangfo huayan jing* [Śikṣānanda's version] 14, T 10.279.72a–80c). It was the Huayan patriarch Fazang's epithet, and he explained how he

understood the term *xianshou* in his *Huayan jing tanxuan ji* 華嚴經探玄記 (Investigating the Mysteries of *Huayan jing*) 4, T 35.1733.186b21–26.

14. *XGSZ* 27, T 50.2060.680c16–20.

15. On the Sui patronage of Buddhism, see, most recently, Chen Jinhua 2002a. The extensive literature on this topic (nearly all of it in Japanese) is surveyed in Chen's first footnote, 1–2. Kimura Kiyotaka (1977, 57–58) briefly discusses Puji's mention of *xianshou guo*.

16. *XGSZ* 27, T 50.2060.681a9–682b4.

17. Jingyuan's biography is in *XGSZ* 11, T 50.2060.511b–512a.

18. *XGSZ* 27, T 50.2060.681a16–21.

19. See Ohnuma 1997, 269.

20. *XGSZ* 27, T 50.2060.681a28–b2. Wudi released him on the grounds that, although his policy had driven monks out of the cities, he did not wish to have them driven out of the mountains as well.

21. *XGSZ* 27, T 50.2060.681b10.

22. *XGSZ* 27, T 50.2060.682a23–27.

23. *XGSZ* 27, T 50.2060.683b20–c17.

24. This is exactly the same place where Puji died after leaping from a cliff.

25. *XGSZ* 27, T 50.2060.683c5–11.

26. *XGSZ* 27, T 50.2060.683c19–26.

27. *XGSZ* 27, T 50.2060.683c22–26. This mention of an inscription usually means that the biography was based on it. We may invoke here Arthur Wright's comment on Huijiao's use of inscriptions in the *Gaoseng zhuan:* "We are perhaps safe in assuming that as a general rule, when he mentions the existence of a memorial inscription as a biographical fact, he had access to the data it contained" (Wright 1954, 427); also quoted in Shinohara 1988, 194, n. 1. Given the location it is likely that Daoxuan actually saw this inscription, as indeed he may have seen others on Zhongnan shan.

28. *XGSZ* 27, T 50.2060.682b5–c11.

29. On this monk, see the study by Hurvitz 1962 and Chen Jinhua 1999a. There is extensive Japanese scholarship on Zhiyi, but note most importantly the work of Satō Tetsuei (1961 and 1981).

30. Mount Lu, twenty *li* north of present-day Nankang 南康 in Jiangxi, had by this time long been an important Buddhist site.

31. On this policy, see *Fozu tongji* 54, T 49.2035.471a27–29. Zhipan 志磐 (d. after 1269), the compiler, believes that Yangdi's policy was reversed because of Dazhi's death. Daoxuan, on the other hand, in his *Ji shenzhou sanbao gantong lu* 集神州三寶感通錄 (Record of Miraculous Responses to the Three Jewels in China), indicates that the policy was still enforced (see T 52.2106.406b21). I have been unable to confirm this action by Yangdi in any official historical source.

32. Song yue 嵩岳, the Central Marchmount, was just south of Luoyang.

33. *Zhai* 齋 in this context means a vegetarian banquet. This was, and continues to be, a standard way for laypeople to donate to the *saṃgha*. The seven assemblies are traditionally given as (1) *bhikṣu* (*biqiu* 比丘), fully ordained monks; (2) *bhik-ṣuṇī* (*biqiuni* 比丘尼), fully ordained nuns; (3) *śikṣamāṇā* (*shichamona* 式叉摩那), nuns preparing for full ordination who follow six more rules than the novices; (4) *śrāmaṇera* (*shami* 沙彌), male novices; (5) *śrāmaṇerikā* (*shamini* 沙彌尼), female novices; (6) *upāsaka* (*youposai* 優婆塞), laymen who take the five precepts; and (7) *upāsikā* (*youpoyi* 優婆夷), laywomen who take the five precepts. The category *śikṣamāṇā* seems not to have been commonly instituted in Chinese Buddhism and was replaced by other categories such as *tongxing* 童行 (monastic laborer).

34. *XGSZ* 27, T 50.2060.682b17–c2.

35. *XGSZ* 27, T 50.2060.682c4

36. Reading 尼僧 (nuns and monks) for 見僧 (seeing monks).

37. *XGSZ* 27, T 50.2060.682c7–11.

38. *XGSZ* 27, T 50.2060.682c12–683a24.

39. Note the policy Daoxuan adopts for including the biography of Wei Yuansong 衛元嵩 (fl. ca. 567), who was originally a monk but returned to lay life and turned against his former religion, as discussed in Yu Jiaxi 1977, 238.

40. On Wang Shichong's short-lived dynasty, see Wechsler 1976, 166–167. Hu Sanxing's 胡三省 (1230–1302) annotation to the *Zizhi tongjian* (188/5903–5904) says that Zheng Ting was serving Li Mi 李密 (582–618), another contender for power, before he was captured by Wang Shichong.

41. See Tonami 1990 (in English).

42. Li Shimin refers to him as a "murderous bastard" in his instructions to the chief monk of Shaolin monastery; see Tonami 1990, 11.

43. *Vaipulya* ("extended") in this sense refers to Mahāyāna *sūtra*s.

44. A *khakkara* is a monk's staff.

45. *XGSZ* 27, T 50.2060.682c27–683a12.

46. See *Jiu Tang shu* 50/2140, where the case of Zheng Ting is mentioned in a discussion of appropriate punishments conducted in the early years of the reign of Taizong. At the time Taizong remarked that Wang Shichong killed Zheng Ting and only then felt remorse. See also *Xin Tang Shu* 46/1409, which says this discussion took place in the fifth year of Taizong's reign, 631. *Zizhi tongjian* 193/6931 says more specifically that the conversation took place in the eighth month of that year but elides Taizong's remarks on Wang Shichong. Wang Shichong's biography in the *Xin Tang Shu* also says that he had Zheng Ting executed and later felt remorse; see 85/2695.

47. See Tonami 1999, 55, and n. 38 in particular for Li Shimin's distress at the parlous state of Buddhism in Luoyang after his defeat of Wang Shichong.

48. In other words, we have no firm date for this event; we know only that it happened before Wang's defeat.

49. *Zizhi tongjian* 188/5903–5904.

50. *XGSZ* 27, T 50.2060.683a14–19. Jizang's biography is in *XGSZ* 11, T 50.2060.513c–515a.

51. On the death verse in general, see Demiéville 1984. Another early poem composed by a self-immolator is the thirty-verse *gāthā* composed by Jing'ai; see the entry on this monk in Appendix 1 for details.

52. This is the *Prajñāpāramitā sūtra.*

53. The poem is also preserved in the *Quan Tang shi* 全唐詩 (Complete Tang Poetry) 733/8382; compare the translation in Demiéville 1984, 25. On some famous poems composed before execution in early medieval China, see Wu Fusheng 2003.

54. *XGSZ* 27, T 50.2060.683a20–24.

55. Sengyai's biography is so long and complex that I have prepared a separate study of it, "Written in Flames: Self-immolation in Sixth-century Sichuan," Benn 2006.

56. Teiser 1988a.

57. *XGSZ* 27, T 50.2060.679a11–14. The term *xie dashengjing jiao* 寫大乘經教 is hard to understand here. In literary Chinese *xie* usually means "to copy" or "to scribe," but Chinese texts do not normally speak of "copying the teachings" in quite this manner. From the title of the popular account of Sengyai (*Sengyai pusa chushi wei zaojing ben,* The Bodhisattva Sengyai Appears in the World to Make the Scriptures), it seems as if Sengyai's actions were credited with the creation or copying of scriptures (see Appendix 1 for details). This suggests that the donations raised at his auto-cremation may have been used to copy *sūtra*s, but this is not made explicit in the *Xu gaoseng zhuan* account.

58. My account of Fu Xi and his followers draws on the study of Bea-hui Hsiao (1995), which includes a full translation of Xu Ling's 徐陵 (507–583) memorial inscription for Fu in the *Shanhui dashi yulu* 善慧大師語錄 (Recorded Sayings of the Great Master Shanhui), *XZJ* 120.1–55.

59. *XZJ* 120.4b; Hsiao 1995, 103. On Hou Jing see, most recently, Pearce 2000.

60. Hsiao 1995, 103.

61. *XZJ* 120.4c–d; Hsiao 1995, 104.

62. *XZJ* 120.4c; Hsiao 1995, 105.

63. See Shaffer (1997, 827–828), who detects a systematic collapse that affected trade across much of Eurasia in the mid-sixth century. Note the remarks of T. H. Barrett on Shaffer's research and the impact of the sixth-century crisis on Chinese religion in Barrett 2001, 5–7.

64. Keys 1999.

65. See Hubbard 2001, esp. 117–119.

66. *XGSZ* 27, T 50.2060.680a1–3.

67. See Appendix 1.

68. See Ohnuma 1997 and 1998.

69. *Liudu ji jing*, T 3.152.2b–c; translated in Chavannes 1910, vol. 1, 17–19.

70. *Da Tang Xiyou ji* 大唐西域記 (Great Tang Records of the Western Regions) 10, T 51.2087.929a–c; Beal 1969, 212–214. This episode does not appear in earlier Chinese accounts of the life of Nāgārjuna; see Young 2000.

71. See Lamotte 1944–1981, vol. 1, 255–260; Parlier 1991.

72. Fasc. 12, T 4.201.321–323; translated in Huber 1908, 330–341.

73. *XGSZ* 27, T 50.2060.5679a18–21.

74. The Wei river was actually some distance to the northeast of Tang Chang'an. See Xiong 2000, map 1.2.

75. *Wu* 五 (five) in the received text must, I think, be understood as 吾 (a personal pronoun).

76. *XGSZ* 27, T 50.2060.683b8–10.

77. *XGSZ* 27, T 50.2060.683b14–18. *Mingxue* 名學 (famous scholars) is probably written in error here for *tongxue* 同學 (fellow disciples). I have amended the translation accordingly. If we preserve the received text, this sentence might be translated as "After reading the text he left, famous scholars went to investigate [the place where he had died]."

78. Translated in Chavannes 1910, vol. 1, 11, 226–227.

79. There are two extant Chinese translations: *Beihua jing* 悲華經, translated by Dharmakṣema, T 3.157; and *Dasheng bei fentuoli jing* 大乘悲分陀利經, translator unknown, T 3.158. For this story, see *Dasheng bei fentuoli jing* T 3.158.382a; Yamada 1989, 108–115. It also appears in the compendium by Baochang (completed in 516 CE) *Jinglü yixiang* 經律異相 (The Sūtras and Vinayas Considered in Their Particularities, T 53.2121.57a1–b6).

80. Jingzhou is present-day Jiangling 江陵 county in Hubei 湖北.

81. *XGSZ* 27, T 50.2060.683c26–684a7; see Georgieva 1996, 57–58.

82. Gernet 1960, 557.

83. *XGSZ* 27, T 50.2060.684b4–c3; see Gernet 1960, 556–557. Xinfeng was northeast of present-day Lintong 臨潼 county in Shaanxi.

84. Other examples of Daoxuan writing in the first person are cited and discussed in Shi Guodeng 1992, 51–63.

85. *XGSZ* 27, T 50.2060.684b15–18. On the practice of adding lacquered cloth to the body, see Foulk and Sharf 1994, 166–167; and Demiéville 1973, 414–415.

86. The life and work of Shandao is discussed in Pas 1987.

87. See Ibuki 1990, 62, fig. 1.

88. Xihe is equivalent to present-day Taiyuan 太原 prefecture in Shanxi. Daochuo has a biography in *XGSZ* 20, T 50.2060.593c11–594b1.

89. The monastery Guangming si in the Huaiyuan ward 懷遠坊 of Chang'an was founded in 584 by Sui Wendi. It was renamed Dayun si 大雲寺 by Empress Wu in 690 as part of her legitimation campaign, which made use of the *Dayun jing*. See Xiong 2000, 306, and more pertinently Forte 1976, 76, and the sources cited in n. 21, which reveal that the monastery was probably not named Dayunjing si 大雲經寺 as Xiong thinks.

90. *XGSZ* 27, T 50.2060.684a11–19; compare the translation in Gernet 1960, 546.

91. T 83.158b3–8; Pas 1987, 69–70.

92. Pas 1987, 70, and 83, n. 14.

93. *XGSZ* 684c4–685c8 A full translation appears in Appendix 2.

94. On this history, see Cole 1996, Ebrey 1990, and Liu Shufen 1998 (in Chinese) and 2000 (in English).

95. T 24.1451.220c21–221a6. My thanks to Shayne Clarke for reminding me of this reference.

96. Self-castration was not unknown in medieval Chinese Buddhism. Guangyi 光儀 (?–735) was a son of the prince of Langye 瑯琊 (d.u.) who became a monk to escape the retribution of Empress Wu (*SGSZ* 26, T 50.2061.873a–c). He castrated himself to avoid the clutches of his cousin; see Cao Shibang 1981. This and other cases of self-castration in China and Japan are also discussed in Faure 1998, 34–37.

Chapter 4 Is Self-Immolation a "Good Practice"?

1. T 53.2122.269a7–b15.

2. These biographies and their sources are discussed in Appendix 1.

3. *Fayuan zhulin* 96, T 53.2122.989c6–27.

4. *Zhuangzi* 32, *Zhuangzi yinde* p. 98, ll. 47–48; Graham 1989, 125.

5. The references are to Prince Mahāsattva and King Śibi. By giving himself to the hungry tigress Śākyamuni was able to attain Buddhahood nine *kalpas* before the Bodhisattva Maitreya. Compare La Vallée Poussin 1929 for other explanations of how Śākyamuni overtook his fellow student.

6. *Fayuan zhulin* 96, T 53.2122.989c24–27. The white oxcart here stands for the Mahāyāna, and the precious raft for the means by which humans are saved or ferried to the other shore—in other words, liberation.

7. The *Lotus* is quoted in the *Fayuan zhulin* 96, T 53.2122.991a22–b25.

8. Respectively, *Jinguangming jing*, T 16.663.335–357 (4 fascicles in 8 chapters); *Hebu jinguangming jing* 合部金光明經, T 16.664.359–402 (8 fascicles); and

Jinguangming zuisheng wang jing 金光明最勝王經, T 16.665.16.403–457 (10 fascicles in 31 chapters). Baogui's is not really an independent translation but a patchwork of translations by Dharmakṣema, Pararmārtha, and Yaśogupta.

9. *Fayuan zhulin* 96, T 53.2122.991b26–c7. The quotation from *Questions of Mañjuśrī* comes from T 14.468.503a12-23; some lines have been elided in Daoshi's citation.

10. *Fayuan zhulin* 96, T 53.2122.991c7–10.

11. Many of these stories are analyzed very thoroughly in Ohnuma 1997 and 1998.

12. Hubert Durt unravels some of these legends in Durt 1998. See also Lamotte 1944–1981, vol. 1, 144, n. 3, for sources in Sanskrit and Chinese.

13. *Liudu ji jing,* T 3.152.17a–b; translated in Chavannes 1910, vol. 1, 101–104.

14. T 3.152.32c; translated in Chavannes 1910, vol. 1, 220–224.

15. T 4.203.464b; translated in Chavannes 1910, vol. 3, 29, and Willemen 1994, 85–86.

16. See Chapter 3.

17. The story is discussed in Ohnuma 1997, 260. Literary and artistic accounts of King Padmaka are collected in Lamotte 1944–1981, vol. 5, 2298–3000.

18. See, for example, the summary of the contents of the *Tonggui ji* by Morimoto Shinjun 森本真順 in *Bussho kaisetsu dai jiten* 仏書解説大辭典 (Encyclopedia of Buddhist Literature with Explanations), vol. 10, 300d–302a. This assessment of Yanshou as the creator of a Chan–Pure Land synthesis is now also to be found in English-language scholarship (see Shih 1992, which includes a translation of the first fascicle of the text). Welter 1993 seeks to adjust the balance and present the work of Yanshou in its full complexity. Huang Yi-hsun (2001) in a recent dissertation also argues against the view that Yanshou was a promoter of the so-called "dual practice of *nianfo* (intoning the Buddha's name) and meditation." In her opinion, Yanshou placed much more emphasis on meditation.

19. T 48.2017.969b–c, 971a–972a, and 972c, respectively.

20. This text is usually referred to in English as the *Record of the Source Mirror,* but this is not how Yanshou actually intended the title to be understood (see the preface, especially T 48.2016.415a18–19). I have not had an opportunity to study Yanshou's references to self-immolation in this voluminous work. However, *Guanxin xuanshu* 觀心玄樞 (Profound Pivot of the Contemplation of the Mind), which is generally taken as a synopsis of the *Zongjing lu* does discuss self-immolation in connection with *baoen* 報恩 (repaying the kindness [of the Buddha]). Huang Yi-hsun (2001, 397–400) translates the relevant passages. In these sections Yanshou does sound a rather more cautious note about the power of the practice.

21. See the list of sources for the study of Yanshou's biography in Welter 1993, 42–43. On the biography of Yanshou, see Welter 1993, 53–95, and Welter 1988.

22. Zanning lived on Mount Tiantai and at least moved in the same circles as Yanshou, even if the two were not personally acquainted. Daoyuan remains an obscure figure but is said to have studied under Tiantai Deshao 天臺德韶 (891–972), who was also Yanshou's master. See Welter 1993, 96, n. 1.

23. Yanshou's biography is in *SGSZ* T 50.2061.887a–b. See Welter 1993, 55–57, 193–194.

24. *Jingde chuandeng lu* 26, T 51.2076.421c–422a; translated in Chang 1982, 250–253, and Welter 1993, 194–198.

25. Welter 1993, 121–122.

26. See *Fahua xuanyi* 法華玄義 (Mysterious Meaning of the *Lotus*), T 33.1716.805c; Welter 1993, 131–132.

27. Welter 1993, 155–156; *Tonggui ji*, T 48.2017.970c.

28. Welter 1993, 155. The concept of self-immolation as a form of *dānapāramitā* is already implicit in the *Lotus Sūtra;* see Filliozat 1963, 30–31.

29. Note, for example, Zanning's remarks in *SGSZ* T 50.2061.710a and 857c8–11, and Jan Yün-hua 1965, 263–264. See Chapter 5 for a fuller discussion of the issue.

30. T 48.2017.969b26–c19. Because this section of the text is crucial for understanding Yanshou's point of view, I have given a full translation at the end of this chapter.

31. See *Pusajie yishu* 菩薩戒義疏 (Commentary on the Meaning of the Bodhisattva Precepts), recorded by Guanding on the basis of Zhiyi's teachings, T 40. 1811.576b6.

32. *Tonggui ji*, T 48.2017.969c2–4.

33. Fazang, *Fanwang jing pusa jie benshu* 梵網經菩薩戒本疏 (Root Commentary on the Bodhisattva Precepts of the *Book of Brahmā's Net*), T 40.1813.641b–c; compare Iishii 1996, 332–360.

34. If one plans to commit a *pārājika* or *saṃghāvaśeṣa* offense but does not do so, or if one plans to commit such an offense and fails, it is a *sthūlātyaya* offense. See the entry "Chūranja" in *Hōbōgirin*, vol. 5, 507a–522a. *Duṣkṛta* is the lightest type of offense in the Vinaya. The offender is required only to confess to a single good monk or nun.

35. Zanning's comment appended to the biography of Wennian, *SGSZ* T 50.2061.860c23–28. See Chapter 5 for the context of his remarks.

36. See Groner 1984, 190. Tiantai Zhanran should not be confused with either of the two other monks named Zhanran active around the same time; see Chen Jinhua 1999b.

37. Kieschnick 1997, 63.

38. On the audience for the *Song gaoseng zhuan,* see Dalia 1987.

39. See Benn 1998, 312–316.

40. *Gandhakuṭī* (*xiangtai* 香臺, perfume chamber) was the cell reserved in a monastery as the residence of the Buddha; it later designated the building housing the image of the Buddha. In either case, the grass growing in or around such a chamber would belong to the Buddha. Early epigraphical evidence for this term is discussed in Schopen 1997, 268–271.

41. T 54.2125.231a28-b11; compare Takakusu 1896, 195.

42. T 54.2125.231b14–17; Takakusu 1896, 196.

43. T 54.2125.231b23–24; Takakusu 1896, 197.

44. T 54.2125.231b25–26; Takakusu 1896, 197.

45. T 54.2125.231b26–28; Takakusu 1896, 197.

46. T 54.2125.231c3–4; Takakusu 1896, 197–198.

47. T 54.2125.231c10–12; Takakusu 1896, 198.

48. T 54.2125.231c–233c; Takakusu 1896, 198–215.

49. *XZJ* 149.396b–397b. This episode is discussed in Chen Jinhua's forthcoming monograph on Fazang. My thanks to the author for pointing out this reference.

50. See Welter 1993, 117.

51. See the official accounts in the *Wudai huiyao* 五代會要 (Essentials of the Five Dynasties) 16, the *Jiu Wudai shi* 115, and the *Xin Wudai shi* 新五代史 (New History of the Five Dynasties) 12. But see Welter 1993, 25, n. 6, on the reliability of these figures. The main points of Shizong's edict are summarized in Shih 1992, 86–87.

52. *Wudai huiyao* 12/202. See also *Zizhi tongjian* 292/9527.

53. *Zongjing lu,* T 48.2106.415a; *Jingde chuandeng lu,* T 51.2076.422a; translated in Chang 1982, 253.

54. *Chuan shou pusa jie wen* 傳受菩薩戒文 (Text on Transmission of the Bodhisattva Precepts) in one fascicle and the *Shou pusa jie yi* 受菩薩戒儀 (Etiquette for the Transmission of the Bodhisattva Precepts) also in one fascicle are listed in the *Zhijue chanshi zixing lu* 智覺禪師自行錄 (Record of the Personal Conduct of the Chan Master Zhijue [Yongming Yanshou]), *XZJ* 111.83d. The surviving text is *Shou pusa jie fa, XZJ* 105.8c–11d, which could of course be one of the above-mentioned texts under a different title. See Jan Yün-hua 1991, 303.

55. *XZJ* 105.8c3–4.

56. *Zongjing lu,* T 48.2106.675c11–21; see Jan Yün-hua 1991, 302.

57. Jan Yün-hua 1991.

58. Section 35, T 48.2017.969c20–970a22. On these ascetics see, for example, Jizang's commentary on the *Vimalakīrtinirdeśa* (*Weimo jing yishu* 維摩經義疏), T 38.1781.941b3, and the *Daban niepan jing* 大般涅槃經 (*Mahāparinirvāṇa*

sūtra), T 12.374.406a27. An interesting story in which the auto-cremation of Ni-granthas is foiled by the Buddha's use of the fire *samādhi* may be found in *Za baozang jing* 雜寶藏經, T 4.203.488b1–29.

59. See *Da zhidu lun* 88, T25 1509.682a1–5; *Da zhidu lun* has . . . *famen* 法門 (*dharma* access) rather than . . . *dao* 道. The same distinction is made twice in Yanshou's *Zongjing lu*, again drawing on the *Da zhidu lun;* see *Zongjing lu* 4, T 48.2016. 434c4–8 and 15, T 48.2016.496b9–12.

60. T 48.2017.970a2–4.

61. The Heaven of Extensive Rewards is the third of the eight heavens included at the level of the fourth *dhyāna* of the realm of form.

62. T 34.1719.354c.

63. See T 14.468.503a17 for the source of Yanshou's quotation.

64. Section 36, T 48.2017.970a23–b14.

65. T 10.279.309a16–17.

66. Section 37, T 48.2017.970b15–25.

67. Section 38, T 48.2107.970b26–971a12.

68. *Da zhidu lun* 11, T 25.1509.140a–b. I follow here the translation of Lamotte 1944–1981, vol. 2, 658–659, although it seems to omit some phrases from the Chinese.

69. T 48.2017.970c14–17.

70. T 9.262.54a11–16; translation in Hurvitz 1976, 298.

71. T 9.262.3a14–15; translation in Hurvitz 1976, 7.

72. Section 39, T 48 2107.971a13–972a21.

73. See references to Jing'ai in Chapter 3 and the entry in Appendix 1.

74. See Appendix 1 for a synopsis of Sengyai's biography.

75. T 48.2017.971b7–12. See the references to *dharma* master Man in Chapter 2. Note, however, that the self-immolator of that name mentioned by Zhanran who burned himself in Changsha was a Liang-dynasty monk. There was no Tiantai institution in the Liang. Either these were two different self-immolators called Man or Yanshou misidentified Man as a Tiantai follower and a *dhyāna* master. For the auto-cremation of Jingbian in Guanding's biography of Zhiyi, see *Sui Tiantai Zhizhe dashi biezhuan* 隋天台智者大師別傳 (Separate Biography of the Great Master Zhizhe of Mount Tiantai, Sui Dynasty), T 50.2050.197c4–5. On this important disciple of Zhiyi, see Sekiguchi 1961, 62–74, and Penkower 2000, 284, n. 87. I am not altogether convinced by Sekiguchi's attempt to identify Jingbian as a monk called Huibian 慧辨 of Changgan si 長干寺. Fu and his disciples are discussed in Chapter 3.

76. T 25.1509.114b16–18; Lamotte 1944–1981, vol. 1, 452.

77. T 25.1509.480c22–481a2. Unfortunately Lamotte's translation of the *Da zhidu lun* did not reach this point.

78. T 14.467.491a17–20. The title of the *sūtra* appears in Yanshou's work as *Lengjia shanding jing* 楞伽山頂經.

79. T 48.2017.972a16–20.

80. Section 40, T 48.2017.972a22–c17.

81. T 19.945.132c10–13; translated in Luk 1966, 156. On the composition of this *sūtra* in medieval China, see Benn, forthcoming.

82. The *Wusheng yi* does not seem to have survived, but a text of that name appears in either one or two fascicles in several catalogues of works brought back from China by Japanese monks such as Saichō 最澄 (767–822) and Enchin 圓珍 (814–891). See, for example, T 55.2160.1059b16, T 55.2170.1093c21, T 55.2172.100c21, T 55.2173.1106b17. Judging by where it appears in these catalogues, it may well have been a Chan text. It was certainly a favorite work of Yanshou's; he quotes from it repeatedly in his *Zongjing lu*. See, for example, T 48.2016.438b23, 441b16, 459c10, 474a21, and so forth.

83. On this trope in Indian accounts of the "gift of the body," see Ohnuma 1998.

84. Section 41, T 48 2107.972c18–23.

85. This seems to be a paraphrase of the *Dasheng xiuxing pusa xingmen zhujing yaoji* 大乘修行菩薩行門諸經要集 (Collection of Essentials from the Sūtras on the Accesses to Practice of the Bodhisattvas Who Cultivate the Mahāyāna), T17.847.939a25.

86. Shaoyan's biography is in *SGSZ* T 50.2061.860b.

87. See De Groot 1893, 50–51. The text has been altered so that the sense of the precept has been changed. In the original it is clear that one teaches "Bodhisattvas new to practice," but in the *Tonggui ji* the text reads as if one should be teaching tigers, wolves, lions, and so forth. Compare Welter's translation in 1993, 219.

88. *Mamai* 馬麥 (Skt. *yava-taṇḍula*) or, literally, "horse wheat." Contrary to Welter 1993, 219, n. 4, the reference is in fact to an incident that occurred when King Agnidatta invited the Buddha to spend the summer retreat in Verañjā. There was a famine, so the Buddha and 500 *bhikṣus* survived on horse fodder for three months. See *Shanjianlü piposha* 善見律毗婆沙 (*Samantapāsādikā*), T 24.1462.706a–707a; translated in Bapat and Hirakawa 1970, 128.

Chapter 5 Local Heroes in a Fragmenting Empire

1. Koichi Shinohara (1998b) has made some interesting observations on the growth of indigenous relics with reference to Chan biographies.

2. The best study of Wu-Yue and Buddhism remains Chavannes 1916. There is a good, brief account of Wu-Yue, including a description of the ruler's religious

activities, in Worthy 1983. I have not yet seen the recent proceedings of a conference on Buddhism in Wu-Yue published by the *Hangzhou foxue yuan* in 2004.

3. The original title was prefixed with the character *da* 大 for "Great Song"; see Chen Yuan 1999, 29. On Zanning and the *Song gaoseng zhuan,* see Dalia 1987. See also Welter 1995 and 1999, and Makita 1984. For Zanning's dates, see Chou 1945, 248, n. 27.

4. See Welter 1999 passim for various anecdotes concerning Zanning's erudition and wit.

5. I discuss some obvious discrepancies in biographies related to the translation and transmission of the *Śūraṃgama sūtra* in Benn, forthcoming. See also Cao 1999.

6. *SGSZ* 23, T 50.2061.855b11–c7. Zao is unknown from other sources. A Nanta (si) is also mentioned in *SGSZ* 13, T 50.2061.787b17, in a much later biography. This monastery was at Yang shan 仰山, Shouchun 壽春 (in present-day Shou 壽 county, Anhui), so it is probably not the same Nanta mentioned here, which was located in Xiangzhou 相州 (present-day Anyang, Hebei).

7. Present-day Sui 隨 county of Dean 德安 municipality in Hubei.

8. Li Chongfu was enfeoffed as the prince of Qiao in 704; see his biography in *Jiu Tang shu* 86/2835–2837 and *Xin Tang shu* 81/3594. He later led an uprising in Luoyang against Ruizong 睿宗 (r. 710–712), which was suppressed without too much trouble, whereupon he committed suicide. See *Zizhi tongjian* 209/6653–6654 and 210/6654–6655; *Jiu Tang shu* 86/2835–2837; *Xin Tang shu* 81/3594–3595. See also Twitchett 1994, 24, n. 76. Fitzgerald 1968, 170, presents some suggestions as to why he was referred to as Zhongzong's "second son," which technically he was not. Zanning (or another intermediary biographer) appears to have borrowed heavily from the *Jiu Tang shu*'s source, although he has recast the story to suggest that Li Chongfu would have been better off following his more Buddhist inclinations than throw in his lot with the instigator of the rebellion, Zhang Lingjun 張靈均 (d.u.), whose name at least suggests a Taoist background. Junzhou is present-day Jun 均 county in Hubei.

9. It seems that the pagoda was designed as a place for Master Zao to die; otherwise why would it be built while he was still alive? See some similar examples of pagodas as places to die in Kosugi 1993, 287–291.

10. *SGSZ* 23, T 50.2061.855b25–c1.

11. "Traps" or "cages" (*fanlong* 樊籠) is used here metaphorically for the snares of *karma.* See, for a scriptural example of this usage, *Dabaoji jing* 大寶積經 (*Mahāratnakūṭa*) 92, T 11.310.526c22.

12. The reference is to the first line of the *Xunzi* 荀子 (*Xunzi zhuzi suoyin* 荀子逐字索引, p. 1, l. 1): "Blue comes from the indigo plant but is bluer than the plant itself." This is obviously a reference to Zhengshou being more advanced than his teacher.

13. *SGSZ* 23, T 50.2061.855c2–7. The phrase "a thousand *li* in a single day" was a common saying in literary Chinese. It occurs, for example, in the *Lüshi Chunqiu* 呂氏春秋 (Mr. Lü's Spring and Autumn Annals) 25.4 (*Lüshi chunqiu zhuzi suoyin* 呂氏春秋逐字索引, p. 163, l. 6).

14. For Indian examples, see Ray 1994, 58, 108, 116, 130, 227.

15. *SGSZ* 23, T 50.2061.855c9–856b2. See also *Guang qingliang zhuan* 廣清涼傳 (Extensive Records of Cool-and-Clear [i.e.,Wutai shan]) 2, T 51.2099.1116a23–c16.

16. On Mañjuśrī and Wutai shan, see Lamotte 1975 and Birnbaum 1983, 1984, 1986, 1989–1990. On Buddhapālita, see his biography in *SGSZ* 2, T 50.2061.717c15–718b7; Lamotte 1975, 86–88; Birnbaum 1983, 10. Chen Jinhua discusses the Buddhapālita legend in the context of Empress Wu's connections with Mount Wutai in Chen 2002d, 103–110.

17. Fusheng tian 福生天 *(Puṇyaprasava)* is one of the heavens in the fourth *dhyāna* realm. See *Fanyi mingyi ji* 翻譯名義集 (Collection of Terms and Their Meanings from the Translations), T 54.2131.1075c15. Perhaps the name of the monastery is intended to suggest that it is one of the heavens.

18. *SGSZ* 23, T 50.2061.855a23–b10.

19. *SGSZ* 23, T 50.2061.855b4–6.

20. The Bodhisattva Never-Disparaging (Changbuqing pusa 常不輕菩薩, Sadāparibhūta) bowed to everyone he met, telling them all that they would become buddhas. Although constantly abused, he never grew angry. See Hurvitz 1976, 279–285; *Miaofa lianhua jing* 6, T 9.262.50b–51c.

21. *SGSZ* 23, T 50.2061.856b3–23.

22. Northwest of present-day Chengdu city, Sichuan. Qingcheng was a mountain with strong Taoist associations and counted as one of the Taoist marchmounts.

23. The term *qulao* is used to refer to the efforts made by one's parents in raising a child. See *Maoshi* 毛詩 32 and 202 (*Maoshi zhuzi suoyin* 毛詩逐字索引, p. 15, l. 6; p. 97, l. 28); Legge 1991, vol. 4, pt. 1, 50; vol. 4, pt. 2, 350.

24. On Ding Lan, the exemplar of filiality in the Han, see Wu Hung 1989, 282–285, and Knapp 2004; in later Buddhist sources, see Cole 1998, 121–124.

25. See the biography of Wu Meng in *Jin shu* 95/2842–2843.

26. *SGSZ* 23, T 50.2061.858b2–25.

27. Zanning would then have been a novice of sixteen. See Chou 1945, 248, and Dalia 1987, 154.

28. On the widespread and significant practice of blood writing, see Kieschnick 2000.

29. *SGSZ* 23, T 50.2061.856b15–16. This King of the Southern Heavens seems to be one of the deities with whom Daoxuan was in contact. See *Daoxuan*

lüshi gantong lu 道宣律師感通錄 (Vinaya Master Daoxuan's Record of Miraculous Responses), T 52.2107.435c.

30. There are many versions of this story; see Ohnuma 1997, 269.

31. Other stories about the donation of the eyes by the Bodhisattva are related in the *Karuṇāpuṇḍarīka*. See Yamada 1989, 106, 113.

32. *SGSZ* 23, T 50.2061.857b19–c11.

33. Biographies in *SGSZ* 17, T 50.2061.818 a4–18; *Jingde chuandeng lu* 16, T 51.2076.330c13–331a1; *Wudeng huiyuan* 五燈會元 (Essentials of the Five Records of the Transmission of the Flame) 6, *XZJ* 138.100a–b. Xuantai was frequently asked to write epitaphs for monks, including Yuanzhi 圓智 (769–835) (*SGSZ* 11, T 50.2061.776a1–12), his teacher Qingzhu 慶諸 (807–888) (*SGSZ* 12, T 50.2061.780c15–781a7), and the patriarch of the Caodong 曹洞 lineage, Caoshan Benji 曹山本寂 (840–901) (*SGSZ* 13, T50.2061.786b17–c3), in addition to the two self immolators Xingming and Quanhuo. My thanks to Chen Jinhua for supplying additional information on Xuantai.

34. The reference is to the minister of King Qingxiang of Chu 楚頃襄王 (r. 298–363 BCE), who, after losing his position at court due to intrigue, drowned himself in the Miluo 汨羅 river while clutching a large stone to his bosom. See his biography in *Shiji* 史記 (Records of the Historian), 84/2481–2491, translated in Watson 1961, 499–508. See also the preface to *Wen xuan* 文選 (Selections of Literature), translated in Knechtges 1982, 77, and Declercq 1998, 381.

35. Prince Mahāsattva fed himself to a hungry tigress; see the sources discussed in Chapter 1. This act of sacrifice meant that the prince leapfrogged over many *kalpa*s of training as a bodhisattva, thus overtaking the future Buddha Maitreya.

36. The quote is from the *Wenzi* 文子, which attributes it to Laozi, although no such phrase is found in the received version of the *Daode jing*. See *Tongxuan zhen jing* 通玄真經 (True Scripture of Communion with Mystery), *DZ* 746, 11.5b.

37. *SGSZ* 23, T 50.2061.857b27–c11.

38. *SGSZ* 23, T 50.2061.860a1–12.

39. It is worth noting in passing that the term used here (*yiti* 遺體) must refer to cremated remains, although the term generally denotes the (uncremated) corpse.

40. See his biography in *SGSZ* 12, T 50.2061.781c7–26.

41. *SGSZ* 23, T 50.2061.856b23.

42. On the Huichang persecution, see Weinstein 1987, 114–136.

43. *Pusa shanjie jing* 菩薩善戒經 (The Wholesome Precepts of the Bodhisattva), T 30.1582, 1583.

44. *SGSZ* 23, T 50.2061.856b24–c8. On the Huang Chao rebellion, see Levy 1955; Somers 1979, 720–747, 756–762. The rebellion lasted for nine years (875–

884) and devastated virtually the whole of China. Fujian fell into the hands of the
rebels in 877 (see *Jiu Tang shu* 9/268, *Xin Tang shu* 19/703). This date does not
quite square with the time frame of 880–881 offered in the biography. The rebels
captured Luoyang in the eleventh month of 880 and Chang'an in the fifth
month of the following year. The effect of the rebellion on Buddhism was severe;
see Weinstein 1987, 147–150.

45. Levy 1955, 3.

46. *SGSZ* 23, T 50.2061.856c10–26.

47. *Jingde Chuandeng lu* 16, T 51.2076.326a10–327a10. See Shinohara
1998b, 319. Juefan Huihong 覺範惠洪 (1071–1128) later criticized Zanning for
placing this eminent Chan master in the self-immolation section; see *Linjian lu*
林間錄 (Record of Linjian) 1, *XZJ* 148.294b. I am indebted to George Keyworth
for this reference. See also Kieschnick 1997, 13.

48. The "problems" referred to here amounted to nothing less than the complete breakdown of Tang imperial rule and the devastating wars between rival
warlords of the time. See Somers 1979, 766–789.

49. *Xiongdi* 兄弟 (brother) seems to be used here in the sense of a lay sup-
porter of a Chan community. The term is attested in the sense of co-religionist in,
for example, the *Jingde chuandeng lu* 10, T 51.2076.276b. It could, however, mean
Tian Yong *and* his brother. I have so far been unable to identify this person.

50. T 50.2061.856c19–27.

51. See the biography of An Shigao in *GSZ* 1, T 50.2059.323a–324b, translated in Robert Shih 1968, 4–12. For a fuller study of this man and his descen-
dents, see the fascinating study by Forte 1995.

52. *Jianjie* is perhaps equivalent to the type of transformation known as
bingjie 兵解 (martial liberation or liberation by the blade) discussed in Campany
2002, 59.

53. *SGSZ* 23, T 50.2061.856c28–857a4.

54. On *liuli* (derived ultimately perhaps from the Sanskrit *vaiḍūrya*), see
Pelliot 1912, 446. The term might also mean "glass" by this time; see Schafer
1963, 235–237.

55. *SGSZ* 23, T 50.2061.858b26–c11.

56. *SGSZ* 23, T 50.2061.858c12–859a19.

57. *SGSZ* 23, T 50.2061.860c29–861a12.

58. On Sengqie, see Makita 1957, 1–30; Barrett 2005. Extracts from his *Song
gaoseng zhuan* biography appear in Xu 1998, 397–399. Note also the cogent remarks of Lothar von Falkenhausen (1998, esp. 414–418) in response to Xu's work.

59. Li Shenfu's biography is in *Song shi* 466/13605–13610.

60. *SGSZ* 23, T 50.2061.861a10–12.

61. *SGSZ* 23, T 50.2061.857a5–23. The Three Whites are usually explained as

the three white foods (milk, curds, and white rice) recommended for esoteric practitioners in texts such as the *Dayun jing qiyu tanfa* 大雲經祈雨壇法 T 19.990, and the *Shiyi mian shenzhou xin jing* 十一面神咒心經 (Heart Sūtra of the Holy Dhāraṇī of Eleven-faced [Guanyin]), T 20.1071. Zanning, however, was obviously familiar with a different list; see his appended comment later in this chapter. On the practice of burning incense on the body, see Benn 1998.

62. For the history of the Buddha's tooth relic in China, see the entry "Butsuge" in *Hōbōgirin*, vol. 3, 203–205; and Chen Yuan 1981. The complex history of Bao'en monastery is recounted in the *Wujun tujing xuji* 吳郡圖經續記 (The Illustrated Guide to Wujun, Continued Records), 3 fascs., completed in 1134 by Zhu Changwen 朱長文 (?–1099?), 31–33.

63. The stone bridge on Mount Tiantai is a natural phenomenon: a very narrow rock formation with a large boulder covered in slippery green moss blocking easy passage across it. It is twenty feet thick but only four or five inches across in places. Only very advanced practitioners were supposed to be able to cross it. The first reference is in *GSZ* 2, 50.2059.395c–396a, the biography of Tanyou 曇猷 (d.u.) (see also *Fayuan zhulin* T 53.2122.594c). According to an ancient tradition, beyond the bridge were beautiful temples where those who attained awakening resided. Tanyou could not cross it at first, but after fasting he went through the boulder and met the monks who lived on the other side. They told him he would return in ten years. As he left, he saw the boulder had closed up again. See Fong 1958, esp. 13–17.

64. Chongzhen si was better known at the time as Famen si 法門寺, west of Chang'an. The finger relic was brought to Chang'an by Yizong in the third month of 873 and returned to Famen si/Zhongzhen si in the twelfth month. See *Jiu Tang shu* 19a/683; *Longxing Fojiao biannian tonglun* 隆興佛教編年通論 (Longxing Era [1163–1164] Comprehensive Discussion and Chronology of Buddhism, compiled by Zuxiu 祖琇 [d. after 1164], 1164), *XZJ* 130.348a; *Zizhi tongjian* 252/8165; *Cefu yuangui* 冊府元龜 (The Primal Tortoise, Document Treasury), 52/11a–b; *Fozu tongji* T 49.2035.389a; Weinstein 1987, 146. The best study of Famen si and its relic is Chen Jingfu 1990; see also Huang Chi-chiang 1998.

65. *SGSZ* 23, T 50.2061.857a16–19.

66. *SGSZ* 23, T 50.2061.857a23–29.

67. This probably refers to Yang Tingzhang 楊廷璋 (912–971); his biography is in *Song shi* 255/8903–8905. According to the *Jiu Wudai shi* 114/1514–1515, he was appointed prefect of Jinzhou 晉州 on Xiande 1.3 *gengzi* 庚子 (possibly May 954; the date is problematic because there was no *gengzi* day in the third month that year). It is quite likely that Yang would still have been in this position a year later in 955. My thanks to Chen Jinhua for helping me to identify this figure.

68. Guangsheng si is in Zhaocheng 趙城 county in Shanxi.

69. *SGSZ* 23, T 50.2061.859c21–29.

70. *SGSZ* 23, T 50.2061.857b2–13. Puti si was founded in 582, closed in 845 (at the start of the Huichang persecution), and renamed Baotang si 保唐寺 in 846. See Xiong 2000, 273, 304.

71. See Best 1991, 185–189, for canonical references to this *samādhi*.

72. *SGSZ* 23, T 50.2061.857b6–13.

73. See *Pusa cong doushutian jiang shenmutai shuo guangpu jing* 菩薩從兜術天降神母胎說廣普經 (Extensive Universal Sūtra Spoken by the Bodhisattva upon Descending from Tuṣita Heaven into the Womb of the Holy Mother) T 12.384. 1036c.

74. *Shangshu* 43 (*Shangshu zhuzi suoyin* 尚書逐字索引, p. 40, l. 2); compare the translation in Legge 1991, vol. 3, pt. 5, 471. Zanning has omitted the character *huo* 或 in the quotation.

75. *SGSZ* 23, T 50.2061.857b14–18.

76. *SGSZ* 23, 857c14–858b1.

77. *SGSZ* 23, T 50.2061.858a1–3. This monastery was located thirty *li* southwest of Taiyuan 太原.

78. On the *Da Foming jing*, see Kuo 1995. Actually the two texts mentioned here only add up to 110 fascicles: The *Huayan jing* is 80 fascicles and the long version of the *Da Foming jing* is 30.

79. *SGSZ* 23, T 50.2061.858a12–13.

80. *SGSZ* 23, T 50.2061.858a13–16.

81. *SGSZ* 23, T 50.2061.858a16–18.

82. *SGSZ* 23, T 50.2061.858a19–25.

83. *SGSZ* 23, T 50.2061.858b26–c11.

84. *SGSZ* 23, T51.2060.858c7–11.

85. *SGSZ* 23, T 50.2061.858c12–859a19.

86. See Zhiyi's biography, *XGSZ* T 50.2060.564c, and the earliest source for Zhiyi's life, *Sui Tiantai Zhizhe dashi biezhuan* 隋天台智者大師別傳 (Separate Biography of the Great Master Zhizhe of Mount Tiantai, Sui Dynasty), T 50.2050.191b, 193a. See Shinohara 1992, 118–120; 132, n. 13, for additional sources and discussion.

87. *SGSZ* 23, T 51.2061.859a8–13.

88. The text reads Fahua chuan 川; I presume that a mountain is meant rather than a river. Fahua shan is twenty-five *li* southwest of Shaoxing 紹興 county in Zhejiang.

89. Bakkula was a major disciple of the Buddha and famous for his longevity. He survived five assassination attempts. See *Da zhidu lun* 24, T 25.1509.238a, and Lamotte 1944–1981, vol. 3, 1530, and especially the sources noted by the author on pp. 1386–1387.

90. See his biography in *XGSZ* 16, T 50.2061.559c3–17.

91. *SGSZ* 23, T 50.2061.859a17–20.

92. *SGSZ* 23, T 50.2061.859b13–25.

93. *SGSZ* 23, T 50.2061.859a21–b12.

94. The reference is, of course, to the terrible upheavals of the Huang Chao rebellion; see *Zizhi tongjian* 255/8261–8268 and Somers 1979, esp. 756–762.

95. Here *liulei* 留累 is probably a mistake for *zhulei* 囑累, the passing on of deathbed instructions.

96. This procedure has already been mentioned in Chapter 3.

97. Guo Zhongshu's biography is in *Song shi* 宋史 442/13087–13088.

98. *SGSZ* 23, T 50.2061.859b2–12.

99. Faure 1993, 23.

100. *Jingde chuandeng lu* 22, T 51.2076.384a27–b23.

101. *SGSZ* 23, T 50.2061.859b26–c11. See also *Jingde chuandeng lu* 25, T 51.2076.410b13–c24.

102. *SGSZ* 23, T 50.2061.860a13–b6. Deshao, a disciple of Fayan Wenyi, was a major figure in the mature Chan tradition of the tenth century. Among many others he taught Yongming Yanshou and Daoyuan, the compiler of the *Jingde chuandeng lu*. See his biographies in *SGSZ* 13, T50.2061.789a20–b10, and *Jingde chuandeng lu* 25, T 51.2076.407b–410a.

103. "Holy seat" is a polite reference to the monk's body.

104. *SGSZ* 23, T 50.2061.860a26–b6.

105. *SGSZ* 23, T 50.2061.860c1–28.

106. A saying of Mingzhao's is preserved in the *Congrong lu* 從容錄 (*Wansong laoren pingchang Tiantongjue heshang Songgu congrong an lu* 萬松老人評唱天童覺和尚頌古從容庵錄 [The Record of the Conggu Hermitage: Old Man Wansong's (Xingxiu 行秀, d. after 1246) Commentary on *Songgu* by Ācārya (Zheng)jue 正覺 (d. after 1157) of Tiantong (si)]), T 48.2004.283b20–21.

107. A *ticou* is an elaborate wooden chamber used in royal funerals in early China. The term refers to the peculiar construction method, in which the walls were built from pieces of wood arranged so that the sides showing the year-rings faced outwards. My thanks to Lothar von Falkenhausen for clarifying this point for me.

108. *SGSZ* 23, T 50.2061.860c13–22.

109. Daoxuan comments on the number of monks attached to the Da Chanding si 大禪定寺 who died sitting upright in his critical evaluation on the practitioners of *dhyāna* in the *Xu gaoseng zhuan*. See Chen Jinhua, in preparation.

110. I owe this observation to remarks made by Raoul Birnbaum at the conference "Body, Form and Practice in East Asian Buddhism" held at Lewis and Clark College, Portland, Oregon, April 24,1999.

111. *SGSZ* 23, T 50.2061.859b13-25, 860a13–b6.

112. *SGSZ* 23, T 50.2061.860b7-29.

113. See the following examples from the *Ji Shenzhou sanbao gantong lu*. A person who initially failed to see the relic burned one of his fingers, and the relic then appeared. This seems to imply that the obstructions of his bad *karma* were such that they could be removed only temporarily by the offering of a finger; T 52.2106. 406c19–24, compare Daoshi's remarks on burning the head or finger to see the Buddha in the *Fayuan zhulin* 38, T 53.2122.586b10–13. Zhicong 智琮 (d. after 662) placed charcoal on his arm and burned incense on it, which brought forth light from the relic. See T 52.2106.407a4–9 and *Fayuan zhulin* 38, T 53.2122.586b25–29. My thanks to Chen Jinhua for bringing these examples to my attention.

114. The major sources on Xu You are discussed in Declercq 1998, 393–396.

115. *Shiji* 84/2490–2491; translated in Hawkes 1985, 59–60.

116. See, for example, Gernet 1996, 324–326.

117. On the various forms of the path *(mārga)* in Buddhism, see Buswell and Gimello 1992.

118. *Han Changli wenji jiaozhu* 韓昌黎文集校注 (The Collected Prose of Han Yu, Collated and Annotated) 615. See Dubs 1946, 11–12, and Hartman 1986, 84–86; 135; 139–140; 158; 251; 258; 304, n. 166; 325, n. 58.

119. For accounts relating to 819, see *Tang Huiyao* 47/838; *Jiu Tang shu* 15/466, 160/4198; Hartman 1986, 84–85. For 873, see the biography of Li Wei in *Xin Tang shu* 181/5354. For a broader account of the imperial veneration of Buddha relics in the Tang, see Huang Chi-chiang 1998.

120. Yamada 1989, 114.

121. The interment of the relic is well documented in Song sources; see Huang Chi-chiang 1994, 160.

Chapter 6 One Thousand Years of Self-Immolation

1. References are to the paginated edition of 1923, reprinted several times, most recently in the *Dazang jing bubian* 大藏經補編 (Buddhist Canon: Supplementary Sections), vol. 27, 301–310. Four pages of the original are reproduced on each page of this reprint.

2. See Hasebe 1993, 447–448 for a discussion of the title of this work.

3. See Hasebe's assessment (1993, 447–454) of the value of the *Bu xu gaoseng zhuan.*

4. Demiéville 1984.

5. On Daojie, see Yu Lingbo 1995, 39–42. Yu Qian (also known as Yu Meian 喻昧庵) remains rather an obscure figure in the history of modern Chinese Buddhism.

6. The sources are explained in the introductory matter (*juanshou* 卷首), which unfortunately does not appear to be reproduced in any of the paginated printings of the collection but may be found in the string-bound first edition (n.p., n.d.). I consulted the edition found in the Harvard-Yenjing Library. This edition has been reprinted in the *Gaoseng zhuan heji* 高僧傳合集 (Combined Collection of Eminent Monks), 775–959. The sources used are listed on pp. 775a–776a.

7. See *Bukkyō dai jiten*, vol. 8, 144d.

8. *Fahua jing xianying lu* 2, *XZJ* 134.438d–439a.

9. The eight classes of deities including *deva*s and *nāga*s usually present at the preaching of Mahāyāna *sūtra*s are *deva* (*tian* 天), *nāga* (*long* 龍), *yakṣa* (*yecha* 夜叉), *gandharva* (*qiantapo* 乾闥婆), *asura* (*axiuluo* 阿修羅), *garuda* (*jialouluo* 伽樓羅), *kimnara* (*jinnaluo* 緊那羅), and *mahoraga* (*mohouluojia* 摩睺羅伽).

10. The "two sages" referred to here are Song Huizong 宋徽宗 (r. 1110–1125), the retired emperor, and his son Qinzong 欽宗 (r. 1125–1127). Both had been captured and were being held by the Jin.

11. *Fahua jing xianying lu* 2, *XZJ* 134.438d–439a.

12. This is probably Guo Hao 郭浩 (1087–1145). See his biography in *Song shi* 367/11440–11442.

13. *Fahua jing xianying lu* 2, *XZJ* 134.439a.

14. *Xin xu gaoseng zhuan* 39, 1201–1202. Guihua is present-day Guihua county in Fujian.

15. The allusion is to *Zhuangzi* 3, *Zhuangzi yinde*, p. 8, l. 19. Graham 1989, 65 reads: "If the meaning is confined to what is deemed the 'firewood,' as the fire passes on from one piece to the next we do not know it is the 'cinders.'"

16. *Xin xu gaoseng zhuan* 39, 1201.

17. "The true person without rank" is the famous formulation of the Chan master Linji Yixuan 臨濟義玄 (d. 866). See the discussion of the phrase in Faure 1993, 261–263.

18. *Xin xu gaoseng zhuan* 40, 1220–1222. Changzhou is in present-day Jiangsu.

19. Jiuhua shan is in present-day Qingyang 青陽 county in Anhui.

20. The practice of sealed retreat in the late Qing is discussed in Goossaert 2002.

21. *Xin xu gaoseng zhuan* 40, 1221.

22. *Xin xu gaoseng zhuan* 40, 1222. Di was a renowned scholar and constitutionalist of the time.

23. *Xin xu gaoseng zhuan* 40, 1209–1210.

24. *Lian*, literally "incorruptible," was a government subsidy paid to officials in an attempt to discourage corruption.

25. *Xin xu gaoseng zhuan* 40, 1212–1213.

26. *Xin xu gaoseng zhuan* 40, 1212.

27. Changing patterns of patronage in the Ming are discussed in Brook 1993. On the state of some monasteries in the Ming and Qing, see T'ien 1990.

28. *Xin xu gaoseng zhuan* 40, 1213.

29. *Xin xu gaoseng zhuan* 40, 1220.

30. *Xin xu gaoseng zhuan* 40, 1214–1215.

31. Wu was the author of a number of gazetteers of Buddhist monasteries including the *Wulin da zhaoqing lüsi zhi* 武林大昭慶律寺志 (Gazetteer of the Great Zhaoqing Vinaya Monastery in Wulin).

32. *Xin xu gaoseng zhuan* 40, 1215.

33. *Xin xu gaoseng zhuan* 40, 1211–1212.

34. *Bu xu gaoseng zhuan* 19, 161d–162b.

35. On Ming policy towards Buddhism, and especially the regulation of ordination summarized here, see Yü Chün-fang 1981, 155–162, and the scholarship cited therein. For a broader survey of Buddhism under the Ming, see Yü Chün-fang 1998.

36. Yonglong's biography gives the date of 1392, but this is hard to confirm in other sources.

37. Something similar happened in 1407; see Yü Chün-fang 1981, 158. In 1395 Taizu defrocked all monks who failed a national examination; see *Da Ming huidian* 大明會典 (Complete Regulations of the Great Ming), 104.4a, b.

38. This was just outside the Zhonghua 中華 gate of Nanjing. It was so named because a rain of flowers fell there in the time of Liang Wudi.

39. I have been unable to verify the existence of this poem in other sources.

40. Yin shan is fifty *li* north of Hang 杭 county in Hangzhou.

41. A shorter version of the story does appear in Xu Zhenqing's 徐禎卿 (1479–1511) *Jiansheng yewen*翦勝野聞. See *Guang Baichuan xuehai*廣百川學海, vol. 2, 743–744. If this text was indeed by Xu Zhenqing, it is certainly earlier than Minghe's version, but the attribution to Xu may be spurious (see *Siku quanshu zongmu tiyao* 四庫全書總目提要 [General Catalogue of the *Complete Books in Four Treasuries* with Descriptive Notes], 1220). Brief biographies of Yonglong that recount the same events also appear in the *Mingshi chaolüe*明史鈔略 (Draft Outline of the History of the Ming), Sibu congkan edition, fasc. 3, 88, p. 7b; and Zha Ji-zuo's 查繼佐 (1601–1676) *Zuiwei lu* 罪惟錄 (Record of Reflections on Transgressions), Sibu congkan edition, fasc. 26, p. 4a.

42. See Benn 1998.

43. *Xin xu gaoseng zhuan* 39, 1195–1196.

44. *Xin xu gaoseng zhuan* 39, 1196–1197.

45. *Xin xu gaoseng zhuan* 39, 1197.

46. *Xin xu gaoseng zhuan* 39, 1197–1198.

47. *Bu xu gaoseng zhuan* 20, *XZJ* 134.162d–163a.

48. *Bu xu gaoseng zhuan* 20, *XZJ* 134.161d. Dongou is ten *li* east of Tiantai county in Zhejiang. Shanghai during the Yuan was a district of Songjiang 松江 prefecture and not the major city that it is today.

49. Here I think we must understand *kan* in the sense of "coffin" rather than "niche" as in the earlier biographies.

50. *Xin xu gaoseng zhan* 39, 1198–1199.

51. *Xin xu gaoseng zhuan* 39, 1199–1200.

52. *Xin xu gaoseng zhuan* 39, 1200–1202.

53. For an excellent discussion of Boxer incendiary magic and female pollution, including earlier examples of such beliefs, see Cohen 1997, 119–145.

54. See the examples cited in Cohen 1997, 131–132.

55. *Xin xu gaoseng zhuan* 39, 1202–1203.

56. See his biography in *Xin xu gaoseng zhuan* 39, 1813–1814; for further sources, see Hasebe 1979, 71, entry no. 959.

57. *Xin xu gaoseng zhuan* 40, 1208.

58. *Xin xu gaoseng zhuan* 40, 1209. Changjing was sixty *li* east of present-day Jiangyin 江陰 county in Jiangsu.

59. On this theme, see Yoshikawa 1992.

60. *Xin xu gaoseng zhuan* 40, 1209.

61. *Xin xu gaoseng zhuan* 40, 1213–1215.

62. *Xin xu gaoseng zhuan* 40, 1218–1220.

63. Although the "numinous tower" (*lingtai* 靈臺) may allude ultimately to the tower from which the Zhou kings communicated with heaven and celebrated in the poem of the same title in the *Shi jing*, the term was frequently used in Chan sources to refer to the mind.

64. *Xin xu gaoseng zhuan* 40, 1219.

65. See Wilson 2003 and Benn, forthcoming.

66. *Bu xu gaoseng zhuan* 20, *XZJ* 134.161a–b. Pi is present-day Pi county in Sichuan, and Fan is northeast of present-day Xinfan 新繁 county.

67. The allusion is to a well-known story from the *Lüshi chunqiu* 呂氏春秋 (Spring and Autumn Annals of Mr. Lu). A man loses a sword in a river. He cuts a notch in the side of his boat to mark where it fell so he can find it again.

68. *Bu xu gaoseng zhuan* 20, *XZJ* 134.161a–b.

69. *Bu xu gaoseng zhuan* 20, *XZJ* 134.161b–c.

70. *Dongshan wuben dashi yulu* 洞山悟本大師語錄 (Recorded Sayings of the Great Master Wuben of Dongshan), T 47.1986. The story referred to here concerns Dongshan Liangjie 洞山良介 (807–869), whose disciples wept as their master was about to die. He suddenly opened his eyes and told them, "Those who have left home should not be attached to external things. This is true cultivation. Alive, they should work hard, in death they should rest. Why should there be any

grief?" He ordered the head monk to prepare vegetarian feasts for the monks. But his disciples still grieved for him. After dinner on the seventh day he told them, "When monks act they should not be heedless. What a noise and fuss you made when I first intended to depart." On the eighth day, he died, sitting upright. See *Jingde chuandeng lu* 15, T 51.2078.23b, and Chang 1982, 70.

71. *Bu xu gaoseng zhuan* 20, *XZJ* 134.161b–c.

72. *Bu xu gaoseg zhuan* 20, *XZJ* 134.162c–d.

73. *Bu xu gaoseng zhuan* 20, *XZJ* 134.162d.

74. *Bu xu gaoseng zhuan* 20, *XZJ* 134.161c–d.

75. Such practices are discussed in Barend ter Haar's study (1999) of the White Lotus movement.

76. *Bu xu gaoseng zhuan* 20, *XZJ* 134.160d. See also Huang Qijiang 1996, 18.

77. A painting attributed to Sijing is still extant in Japan. See Shimada 1961.

78. *Bu xu gaoseng zhuan* 20, *XZJ* 134.160d.

79. *Bu xu gaoseng zhuan* 20, *XZJ* 134.160d-161a.

80. Zhao Yuhuan was a member of the Song royal family; see his biography in *Song shi* 413/12402–12407. People also called him Zhao Fozi 趙佛子, either for his benevolence or because of his faith in Buddhism.

81. I have been unable to identify Huiling.

82. *Xin xu gaoseng zhuan* 39, 1191–1194. See also Demiéville 1984, 71–74. Huating is near present-day Shanghai.

83. Wuzhen is near present-day Wuxing in Zhejiang. Formerly a solider in Xiuzhou 秀州, Xu Ming rebelled on Jianyan 2.5.2 (*yiyou* 己酉) (June 1, 1128) and was captured and executed by Song forces less than six weeks later on Jianyan 2.6.12 (*yichou* 乙丑) (July 12, 1128). See *Song shi* 25/456; also mentioned in 247/8764; 367/11434; 369/11470, 11477–11478; 370/11503.

84. Close to present-day Ningbo, on the coast of Zhejiang.

85. *Xin xu gaoseng zhuan* 39, 1193–1194.

86. Note again the importance of correct posture at the moment of death.

87. See *Jingde chuandeng lu*, T 51.2076.315b19–28, which describes how the Boatman Ācārya disappeared into oblivion while sailing. My thanks to Chen Jinhua for pointing out this reference, which Demiéville appears to have missed.

88. *Xin xu gaoseng zhuan* 39, 1194.

89. Z*hiyin* 知音 "to know music" also means "to know the truth."

90. *Xin xu gaoseng zhuan* 39, 1194. *San chang* 散場 is a theatrical term for the end of a scene.

91. *Bu xu gaoseng zhuan* 20, *XZJ* 134.163a–c.

92. On Cisheng, see *Dictionary of Ming Biography,* 856–859. On her support for Buddhism, see Chen Yunü 1997.

93. The biography presumably refers to the two monasteries on Wutai shan.

On the dragon-flower assemblies, see the biography of Wuran discussed in Chapter 3.

94. The water-land assembly was a large-scale esoteric ritual conducted for all the dead on water or land. It became popular in the Song and was conducted for the royal families of the Yuan and Ming. It continues to be performed today. See Makita 1989b and, more briefly, the entry by Daniel Stevenson and Marsha Weidner in Weidner 1994, 280–282, and the sources cited therein.

95. On the term *daoren* as used by lay Buddhists in the Song and later, see ter Haar 1999, 27, and passim. We noted the use of human flesh as medicine in Chapter 1. By the Ming, this act was commonly associated with filial devotion to one's aged parents.

96. See the examples of such water-land paintings in Weidner 1994.

97. Here Jietuo might perhaps indicate the Buddha's disciple Adhimukta, but I must confess that this particular story is not known to me. There is a story about a monk of that name in the *Huayan jing zhuanji*, T 51.2073.169a–c, but there are no instructions about dividing the body in that account.

98. *Bu xu gaoseng zhuan* 20, *XZJ* 134.163b.

99. See his biography in *Ming shi* 298/7631–7632.

100. *Bu xu gaoseng zhuan* 20, *XZJ* 134.163c.

101. *Bu xu gaoseng zhuan* 20, *XZJ* 134.163c.

Conclusion

1. See Benn 1998, 311, for examples.

2. The possibility that the pseudo-*Śūraṃgama sutra* was composed in part to trump Yijing's charges is discussed in Benn 1998 and Benn, forthcoming.

3. We saw a hint of this in the passages cited by Yanshou concerning the Nigranthas.

4. Zhuhong alludes to the following incident. The Tang Huayan master Zongmi became entangled in a lawsuit when one of his lectures caused a member of his audience, Taigong 泰恭 (?–811+), to cut off his arm. Zongmi wrote approvingly of the incident in a letter to Chengguan ("Guifeng Dinghui Chanshi yaobing Qingliang Guoshi shu" 圭峰定慧禪師遙秉清涼國師書, T 39.1795.577b26–28). Chengguan was more cautious in his reply and requested Zongmi not to encourage such practices. This exchange is discussed most fully in Chen Jinhua's forthcoming monograph on Fazang. I am indebted to the author for sharing a draft of that work with me.

5. *Dazang jing bubian* 大藏經補編 (Great [Buddhist] Canon: Supplementary Section), 23.291a–b. Wenling refers to Jiehuan 戒環 (d.u.), a Song commentator on the *Lotus Sūtra*. I have not traced the source of the quotation.

6. See the entry on Sengyai in Appendix 1 for details.

Appendix 1 Major Collections of Biographies of Self-Immolators

1. The *Gaoseng zhuan* dates this monk to the Song dynasty.

2. Sengzhou's biography does not appear in the self-immolation section of the *Gaoseng zhuan* but rather among the "practitioners of *dhyāna*" (*xichan* 習禪) — although Sengzhou certainly came to a fiery end. See *GSZ* 11, T 50.2059. 398b13–c5.

3. Faying appears in the *Gaoseng zhuan* under one of his alternative names, Fajin 法進.

4. The *Gaoseng zhuan* gives Yanwei si 延尉寺 as the name of the monastery. Tingwei si seems more likely given that *tingwei* (chamberlain for law enforcement) was a court rank (see Hucker 1985, 512). The monastery may have been converted from the residence of a lay donor who held this rank.

5. Daohai does not appear in the self-immolation section of the *Gaoseng zhuan,* but his name appears with a number of his colleagues who vowed to be reborn in the Pure Land in a short appendix to the biography of his contemporary, the exegete Tanjian 曇鑒. See *GSZ* 7, T 50.2059.370a16.

6. Sengsheng's biography appears in the "scriptural recitation" (*jingsong* 經誦) section of the *Gaoseng zhuan.* Although he did ask to be cremated after his death, there is no indication in this biography that he was a self-immolator per se. See *GSZ* 12, T 50.2059.406c27–407a5 and 409a16.

7. Daofa's biography appears in the *Gaoseng zhuan* section "Practitioners of *dhyāna*" and records his habit of stripping before an image of Maitreya and allowing mosquitoes to feed on his body; *GSZ* 11, T 50.2059.399b6–14 and 400c7.

8. See also the table comparing *Gaoseng zhuan* biographies of self-immolators with *Mingseng zhuan* biographies in Makita 1989a, 33.

9. *XZJ* 134.12c–d.

10. *XZJ* 134.16c–d. These look like personal notes that Shūshō took to remind himself of certain miraculous or unusual occurrences in the biographies he had read.

11. South of present-day Chengdu, Sichuan.

12. Present-day Qinghe county in Hebei.

13. *Mingxiang ji,* 457. For a brief introduction to this collection, see Campany 1996, 82–83; note also Gjertson 1981, 293–294.

14. On Huijiao's use of the *Mingxiang ji,* see Campany 1996, 83, n. 190; Wright 1954, 418.

15. Ibuki (1987) argues that Huaixin should be identified with Huixiang 慧祥 (?–706+), the author of the *Hongzan fahua zhuan.*

16. Hebei indicates the region north of the Huanghe 黃河 river, not the modern-day province of Hebei.

17. Northwest of present-day Zhangyi 張掖 county in Gansu.

18. Yanwei si should be read as Tingwei si 廷尉寺; see above note 4.

19. Gaoyang is in present-day Shandong 山東.

20. Lantian was southwest of Chang'an 長安.

21. Northeast of present-day Lucheng 潞城 county in Shanxi 山西.

22. Linchuan was a commandery in Yangzhou 揚州 and was located just west of present-day Linchuan. Zhaoti si is not known from other sources.

23. Yuhang was a district of Wuxing, present-day Hangzhou 杭州 in Zhejiang 浙江. See the map in Zürcher 1959, 115.

24. *GSZ* T 51.2059.417b24.

25. Near present-day Yangzhou 揚州 in Jiangsu.

26. North of present-day Nanchong 南充 county in Sichuan.

27. Close to present-day Longxi in Gansu.

28. Shifeng is present-day Tiantai 天臺 in Zhejiang.

29. Huanglong is in present-day Chaoyang 朝陽, Liaoning 遼寧.

30. *GSZ* 12, T 50.2059.405c26–28.

31. Huizhou is present-day Jingyuan 靖遠 county in Gansu.

32. There is some confusion over the correct orthography for Wangming's name. In the *Xu gaoseng zhuan* biography of Sengyai (*XGSZ* 27, T 50.2060.680b22) and in the *Lidai sanbao ji* 12, T 49.2034.101a19, it appears as 忘名, but as 亡名 in the *Da Tang neidian lu* 大唐內典錄 (Great Tang Record of Buddhist Scriptures) 5, T 55.2149.272b16, and in the *Xu gaoseng zhuan* biography of the man himself (*XGSZ* 7, T 50.2060.481b–482b).

33. Guanghan is present-day Guanghan county in Sichuan.

34. This is presumably the same *dharma* master Dui who was Wangming's master. See T 50.2060.481b. An account of Xiaoai si may be found in the biography of Zhixuan 智炫 (d. after 581), *XGSZ* 23, T 50.2060.631b–632b. This monastery was so named after Prince Poyang 鄱陽王 (Liang Wudi's younger brother Xiao Hui 蕭恢 [474–524], biography in *Liang shu* 22/350–352) buried his mother there. See Suwa 1997a, 210–211, for an account of Xiao Hui's activities relating to Buddhism in Sichuan. Note that Hui's son Xiao Fan 蕭範 (also Prince Poyang) governed Yizhou from 526–537, (Suwa 1997a, 214–250). Thus the monastery with which Sengyai was associated had close links with the Liang royal family.

35. *Dhyāna* master Dao is not known from other sources. A *khakkara* is a monk's staff with six rings (the "six *pāramitā*s") at the top. These staffs could be extremely ornate and their upper parts made of silver. It is hard to be certain what is meant by the term *zipi*, but presumably it is not the same as the famous "purple robe" first bestowed on eminent monks by Empress Wu. According to

Chen Jinhua, the *pi* 披 of *zipi* 紫披 cannot be understood as a robe. He believes that it was probably no more than a piece of cloth that a monk wore over one shoulder; this is currently known as a *pijian* 披肩; see Forte 2003, 146, n. 3.

36. Sengyuan has a biography in T 50.2060.574b. He was a major figure in the Buddhism of Shu at this time and was later a resident of the Da Zhihu si 大陟岵寺 in Chang'an.

37. Mentioned in *XGSZ*, 13.531a, and *SGSZ*, 14.793a, as being in Chengdu.

38. Baohai has a biography in *XGSZ* 9, T 50.2060.492b–c. The *Foguang da cidian* 佛光大辭典 (Encyclopedic Dictionary of the Buddha Light) 6751c gives his dates as 474–553, making it hard to place him at Sengyai's auto-cremation in 559. However, I believe this rests on an ambiguous reading in his biography. *Shi nian bashi* 時年八十 could mean that he was eighty when Shu was annexed by the Northern Zhou in 553, or it may be the start of a new sentence: "In the year that he was eighty . . . ." My thanks to Chen Jinhua for pointing out the ambiguity involved here.

39. Present-day Pixian, northwest of Chengdu.

40. Tongzhou is a Western Wei name for present-day Mianyang 綿陽 in Sichuan. It is not to be confused with the town of the same name in Shaanxi.

41. Yongzhou occupied the northern part of present-day Shanxi and the greater portion of the area northwest of Gansu.

42. Note the variant title of the biography in the Yuan and Ming editions, T 50.2060.678 n. 13, n. 14. The title of his biography gives no monastic affiliation, which is very unusual in Daoxuan's collection.

43. Jingyang is thirty *li* southeast of present-day Jingyang county in Shanxi.

44. Rongyang is southeast of present-day Huichang 會昌 county in Jiangxi 江西. But perhaps Xingyang 滎陽 (in present-day Henan) should be read here rather than Rongyang 滎陽? The biography says that Zheng was from a powerful and famous clan. The Xingyang Zheng were just such a clan; we know nothing of any significant Zheng from Rongyang. Because of their similar orthography Rongyang and Xingyang are easily confused; see, for example, *XGSZ* T 50.2060.625c15 and 644b28.

45. This was the lowest of eight commandant titles conferred on inactive officials (*sanguan* 散官) ranked 9b. The title was established in 586 and discontinued after 604. See Hucker 1985, 588; *Lidai zhiguan biao* 歷代職官表 (Historical Tables of Official Posts), 65/1249a.

46. Yang Su's biography is in *Sui shu* 隋書 (Book of the Sui), 48/1288–1296.

47. I follow the Three editions here in reading "Zhao" for "Sui," T 50.2060.683 n. 5. Fangzi is fifteen *li* southwest of present-day Gaoyi 高邑 county in Hebei 河北. Zhaozhou is ten *li* east of Longping 隆平 county in Hebei.

48. Puzhou is twenty-five *li* east of Gaoyang 高陽 county in Hebei. I have not been able to identify the location of Wanquan.

49. Fenzhou is present-day Fenzhou prefecture in Shanxi. Chao is most likely Zhichao 志超 (571–641); his biography is in *XGSZ* 12, T 50.2060.591c26–592c20.

50. Twenty *li* east of present-day Xianyang county in Shaanxi.

51. Fenzhou is present-day Fenzhou district in Shanxi.

52. See Ibuki 1990, 62, fig. 1, for the late addition of this biography.

53. The mountain is southwest of present-day Taiyuan 太原 in Shanxi.

54. See Ibuki 1990, 62, fig.1.

55. North of Lintong 臨潼 county in Shaanxi.

56. Jingzhou is present-day Jiangling 江陵 county in Hubei 湖北.

57. Xuanwu is southeast of present-day Zhongjiang 中江 county. Zizhou is present-day Santai 三台 county in Sichuan.

58. Ruzhou is present-day Linru 臨汝 county in Henan.

59. See Gernet 1960, 556–557.

60. Fenzhou is present-day Fenzhou prefecture in Shanxi.

61. Zhongtiao shan is in present-day Yongji 永濟 county in Shanxi.

62. Ezhou is present-day Jiangnan.

63. Yuanzhao has a biography in *SGSZ* 15, T 50.2061.804b8–805c5. For his birth and death dates, see Fang 1991, 75. On Ximing si, see Xiong 2000, 262–265.

64. Baoshou si was a very large imperially supported monastery; see Xiong 2000, 276, n. 221, and p. 317.

65. In Wuchang 武昌, Hubei.

66. Jiaxing is south of present-day Jiaxing city in Zhejiang.

67. See his biography in *Jin shu* 54/1467–1481.

68. Here *jiucao* is an alternative name for the title *lushi canjunshi* 錄事參軍事, an administrative supervisor found on the staff of a prefecture; see Hucker 1985, 323. Wenzhou is present-day Wenzhou city in Zhejiang.

69. Present-day Quyang 曲陽 in Hebei.

70. Common late-Tang name for Pingjiang fu 平江府, present-day Jiangsu and Suzhou.

71. Wujun is in present-day Wu 吳 county, Jiangsu, so here Changzhou probably refers to Changzhou yuan 長洲苑 in that same county.

72. The same monk who had composed the stele inscription for Quanhuo.

73. Bingzhou is southwest of present-day Taiyuan 太原 city in Shanxi.

74. Chongfu si was a large and important monastery five *li* south of Taiyuan. I have not been able to identify *dharma* master Gan.

75. On Li Keyong, see *Jiu Wudai shi* 舊五代史 (Old History of the Five Dynasties), 25/331–346.

76. This monastery was located thirty *li* southwest of Taiyuan.

77. Youfufeng is thirty *li* east of Guanzhong 關中 county in Shaanxi.

78. A monk of this name seems to have been in Koryŏ in 938; see Kamata 1996, 39.

79. South of present-day Lingwu 靈武 county in Ningxia 寧夏.

80. Han Xun 韓遜 was the military commander of Lingwu at the time. Appointed in 918, he died in 929; see *Jiu Wudai shi* 132/1745. Helan shan is a range of mountains west of Ningxia 寧夏 county in present-day Gansu.

81. Fifteen *li* north of present-day Yanjin 延津 county in Henan.

82. Present-day Qiantang in Hangzhou.

83. Biographies in the *Song gaoseng zhuan* 13, T 50.2061.50.780c14–781b8, and the *Jingde Chuandeng lu* 24, T 51.2076.398b2–400a11.

84. Yicun has biographies in the *Song gaoseng zhuan* 12, T 50.2061.781c28–782c17; the *Chodang chip* 祖堂集 (Patriarchs' Hall Collection) 7 (as reproduced in vol. 3 of *Sodōshū sakuin* 祖堂集索引 by Yanagida Seizan 柳田聖山, p. 1688, sec. 99); and the *Jingde chuandeng lu* 16, T 51.2076.327a10–328b13. Huileng's are in the *Chodang chip* 10 (1668, secs. 66–67); the *Song gaoseng zhuan* 13, T 50.2061.787a4–17, and the *Jingde chuandeng lu* 18, T 51.2076.347b16–348c3.

85. Biographies in the *Song gaoseng zhuan* 13, T 50.2061.785c18–786a8; the *Chodang chip* 10, (1673, sec. 37); and the *Jingde Chuandeng lu* 18, T 51.2076. 343c27–347b15.

86. Hongdong is in present-day Shanxi.

87. Yongchun is in present-day Fujian.

88. On Yunmen, see Sørensen 1988 and App 1994.

89. Deshao, a disciple of Fayan Wenyi, was a major figure in the mature Chan tradition of the tenth century. See his biographies in the *Song gaoseng zhuan* 13, T 50.2061.789a20–b10; and the *Jingde chuandeng lu* 25, T 51.2076.407b–410a.

90. This may be Gaoan Benren 高安本仁 (d.u.). See *Chodang chip* 12, (1681, secs. 145–146).

91. Evidently this is not the Tang Chan master of that name, who died in 815; see his biography in the *Song gaoseng zhuan* 10, T 50.2061.767c26–768a12. I have not been able to identify this Huaihui.

92. Sun has a biography in the *Song shi* 480/13916–13917. See Chavannes 1916, 216. A native of Qiantang, Sun was notorious for his fabulous wealth, which he spent on precious rocks and elaborate miniature landscapes; see Stein 1990, 37–39.

93. Present-day Jinhua county in Zhejiang.

94. *Liangjing siji* is no longer extant. On the text, see Suwa 1997a, 137–147.

95. References are to the Zhejiang chubanshe edition of 1990.

96. This is actually the biography of Faguang 法光.

97. This is actually the biography of Puyuan 普圓.

98. This account has Shao feeding tigers rather than snakes as in the *Xu gaoseng zhuan* version.

99. This is actually the biography of Huitong 會通 from the *Xu gaoseng zhuan*.

100. This account is rather different from the one preserved in the *Xu gaoseng zhuan*.

101. Yang Wuwei is most likely a reference to Yang Jie 楊傑 (ca. 921–ca. 1090); his biography is in *Song shi* 443/13102–13103. Yang, a well-known author of the time, took the style name Wuwei zi (Master Non-Action) after his native place (in present-day Anqing 安慶, Anhui). On Yang Jie, see Huang Qijiang 2003.

102. Zhao Yuhuan's biography is in *Song shi* 413/12402–12407.

103. Pi is present-day Pi county in Sichuan; Fan is northeast of present-day Xinfan 新繁 county.

104. Dongou is ten *li* east of Tiantai county in Zhejiang. Shanghai in the Yuan was a district of Songjiang 松江 prefecture and not the major city that it is today.

105. See *Siku quanshu zongmu tiyao* 四庫全書總目提要 (General Catalogue of the *Complete Books in Four Treasuries* with descriptive notes), 1220, for doubts concerning the attributed authorship.

106. Yin shan is fifty *li* north of Hang 杭 county in Hangzhou.

107. See Chen's biography in *Ming shi* 298/7631–7632.

108. Hanchuan 漢川 is close to present-day Hankou 漢口 in Hebei. Huating is near Shanghai.

109. Close to present-day Ningbo, on the coast of Zhejiang.

110. Baodi is southeast of present-day Beijing.

111. See Hasebe 1979, 34, entry no. 334, for sources.

112. According to Hasebe 1979, 60, entry no. 771, this monk died in 1671.

113. We may tentatively identify this monk as Jingtang Qing 清 (d.u.); see Hasebe 1979, 102, entry no. 1551.

114. Jianli is present-day Jianli county in Hubei.

115. Dangyang is 140 *li* north of present-day Yichang in Hubei.

116. Note that this Huo shan is in Anhui and distinct from the mountain of the same name in Ningde, Fujian.

117. Present-day Fengyang 鳳陽 county in Anhui.

118. Jiaozhou is present-day Cangwu 蒼梧 county in Guangxi.

119. My thanks to Chen Jinhua for pointing to the source of Huixiang's error.

120. Pingyang is located in present-day Linfen 臨汾, Shanxi.

121. Prince Anchengkang was Liang Wudi's father's seventh son, Xiao Xiu 蕭秀 (475–518); see *Liang shu* 22/341. Prince Poyang Zhonglie was his ninth son, Xiao Hui 蕭恢 (474–524); see his biography in *Liang shu* 22/350–352.

122. Juedian and Hualin si are also misreadings by Huixiang of his source. See Introduction, n. 10.

123. Present-day Jiujiang city in Jiangxi.

124. See Shinohara 1991.

Appendix 2 *Critical Evaluations* of Huijiao, Daoxuan, and Zanning

1. "Riding sleek horses and wearing fine clothes" alludes to the *Lunyu* (Analects), *Yongye*雍也 6.4 (*Lunyu zhuzi suoyin*論語逐字索引 *A Concordance to the Lunyu*, p. 12, l. 14): "The Master said, 'When Chi was proceeding to Qi he had fat horses to his carriage and wore light furs. I have heard that a superior man helps the distressed but does not add to the wealth of the rich.'" The translation is from Legge 1991, vol. 1, 185–186.

2. "Pluck out a single hair" is from the *Mencius* 13.26 (*Mengzi zhuzi suoyin*孟子逐字索引 *A Concordance to the Mengzi*, p. 70, l. 4): "Mencius said, 'The principle of the philosopher Yang was—"Each one for himself." Though he might have benefited the whole kingdom by plucking out a single hair, he would not have done it.'" The translation is from Legge 1970, 464.

3. I have emended *zhan* 瞻 (look up at) and translated it here as *shan* 贍 (offer).

4. It is possible that *gu*榖 (grains) is an error for *ke* 殼 (shell), thus "the outer shell of a jar" rather than "jars of grain." The three realms (*sanjie* 三界) are the realm of desire (*yujie* 欲界), the realm of form (*sejie* 色界), and the realm of formlessness (*wusejie* 無色界). The "long night" (*zhangye* 長夜) refers to saṃsāra. The four forms of birth (*sisheng* 四生) are *taisheng* 胎生 *(jarāyu-ja),* or birth from the womb (humans, animals); *luansheng*卵生 *(aṇḍa-ja),* or birth from the egg (birds); *shisheng* 濕生 *(saṃsveda-ja),* or birth from moisture (insects); and *huasheng* 化生 *(upapādu-ja),* or birth by transformation (those who dwell in the heavens and hells).

5. The allusion is again to the *Mencius,* continuing from the passage in note 2 above: "The philosopher Mo loves all equally. If by rubbing smooth his whole body from the crown to the heel, he could have benefited the kingdom, he would have done it" (Legge 1970, 464–465). According to Mencius, both Yangzi and Mozi went too far—one because of selfishness, the other indiscriminate love—but Huijiao appears to side with Mozi here. My thanks to Chen Jinhua for pointing out where Huijiao's sympathies lay in this case.

6. The allusion is to the *Lotus Sūtra* (T 9.262.53b), which extols self-immolation thus: "Even if one were to give realms and walled cities, wives and children, they would still be no match for it. Good man, this is called the prime gift. Among the various gifts, it is the most honourable, the supreme. For it constitutes an offering of Dharma to the thus come ones" (Hurvitz 1976, 295). On the offering of children by Prince Viśvantara/Sudāna in the Chinese tradition, see Durt 1999.

7. I follow the Yuan and Ming editions here in reading *zhi* 止 (stop) for *xin* 心 (mind); see *GSZ* 12, T 50.2059.406n. 7.

8. This is another reference to the *Mencius* (13.9): "When the men of antiq-

uity realized their wishes, benefits were conferred on them by the people. If they did not realize their wishes, they cultivated their personal character, and became illustrious in the world. If poor they attended to their own virtue in solitude; if advanced to dignity they made the whole kingdom virtuous as well" (Legge 1970, 453).

9. This is a reference to the Buddha in a former life, when as Prince Mahāsattva, son of King Mahāratha, he offered his body to a tigress. This popular *jātaka* as it appears in the *Sūtra of Golden Light* is discussed above. His self-sacrifice accelerated his bodhisattva career, shortening it by nine *kalpas*.

10. The reference is to the *jātaka* of King Śibi, who gave his flesh in exchange for a pigeon. See Lamotte 1944–1981, vol. 1, 143, n. 1, for sources and Ohnuma 1998 for a discussion of the story.

11. Anyang is one of the Chinese names used for Sukhāvatī, the Pure Land of Amitābha. Zhizu, usually rendered as "Doushuai tian" 兜率天, is Tuṣita Heaven, fourth of the six heavens in the realm of desire and the place whence the future Buddha Maitreya will descend. Although technically not a Pure Land, a number of medieval Chinese Buddhists vowed to be reborn there. See, for example, the biography of Daoan, *GSZ* 6, T 50.2059.358c21.

12. The text reads *guan* 館 (mansion) rather than the Chinese for "star" here.

13. The double firmiana and the appearance of a star refer to the biographies of Sengyu and Huishao, respectively.

14. *Lotus Sūtra,* T 9.262.54a13–14.

15. A field of merit is an object or person to whom one should direct religious practice to accumulate merit. The most important are the Three Jewels of Buddha, Dharma, and Saṃgha. The body of a monk as a field of merit is obviously intended here.

16. This appears to be a paraphrase of the *Da zhidu lun,* T 25.1509.179c25-26: 若新行菩薩。則不能一世一時遍行五波羅蜜. See Lamotte 1944–1981, vol. 2, 979.

17. I suspect that there is a reference here to a *jātaka* to parallel that of Prince Mahāsattva but so far the allusion escapes me.

18. This is perhaps a paraphrase of the *Shisong lü* 十誦律, T 23.1435.284a–b. See also the article "Dabi" in *Hōbōgirin* 6, 803–815.

19. During the second stage of the bodhisattva career, in which the practitioner determines his future path, he performs the practices of the *śrāvaka,* the *pratyekabuddha,* or the bodhisattva. Texts in which this stage appears are discussed in Hirakawa and Groner 1990, 305–306.

20. I follow the Three editions and the Palace edition here in reading *ti* 體 for *hai* 骸 (skeleton), T 50.2059.406 n. 14.

21. I follow the Three editions and the Palace edition here in reading *mo* 莫 for *jing* 竟 , T 50.2059.406 n. 16.

22. The three poisons are greed, hatred, and delusion. The four inverted views are that existence is permanent, joyful, possessed of a self, and pure. The seven factors of enlightenment are: *zefa* 擇法, correctly evaluating the teaching; *jingjin* 精進, making effort at practice; *xi* 喜, rejoicing in the truth; *qing'an* 輕安, attainment of pliancy; *nian* 念, keeping proper awareness in meditation; *ding* 定, concentration; and *xingshe* 行捨, detachment of all thoughts from external things. The eightfold path consists of: right view, right thought, right speech, right action, right livelihood, right effort, right mindfulness, and right concentration.

23. Like the *lun,* the *zan* (historical judgments in verse that appear appended to eight of the ten *lun* in the *Gaoseng zhuan*) derive from the conventions of earlier secular historiography. Fan Ye 范曄 (398–445) first gave these verses the name *zan* and added them to the end of his critical evaluations in the *Hou Han shu* 後漢書 (History of the Later Han). See Wright 1954, 391.

24. That is, if one is determined one can break even metal and stone.

25. On the story of the mountain of flesh, see the references from the *Karuṇāpuṇḍarīka* given in Chapter 2. I am not sure what *avadāna* or *jātaka* story Daoxuan has in mind when he refers to the "sea of milk." A reference to the Buddha's body as a sea of milk is found in the *Jinse tongzi yinyuan jing* 金色童子因緣經 (Sūtra of the Causes and Conditions of the Golden Lad) 10, T 14.550.887a12.

26. *Benji* 本紀 (basic annals) is a Chinese historiographical term for a chronological account of a ruler and his government, the first section of any dynastic history. It seems out of place here; from the context I suspect that it may be an error for *benji* 本記, often used for the "biography" of the Buddha (see, for example, the titles of T 184, 185, 188, 196, 199) and as a cognate term for *benyuan* 本緣, which can mean *jātaka.*

27. Here *renjie* stands for *suopo jie* 娑婆界, or Sahā world, the corrupt world in which we live.

28. Or possibly *xiangmo* means "the end of the semblance *dharma.*"

29. Reading *gou* 搆 here as *gou* 構 (stacked-up firewood).

30. The reference is to the *Lotus Sūtra,* where the claim that it is better to uphold even a single stanza of the *Lotus* appears immediately after the account of the Medicine King's auto-cremation (T 9.262.54a11–16, translation in Hurvitz 1976, 298).

31. *Siqi* 思齊 here alludes to the *Lunyu* 4.17: 見賢思齊焉，見不賢而內自省也。*Lunyu zhuzi suoyin,* p. 8, l.12: "When we see men of worth, we should think of equalling them; when we see men of a contrary character, we should turn inwards and examine ourselves" (Legge 1991, vol. 1, 170).

32. Cutting off the nose and cutting off the feet were forms of punishment in China; they should be understood as pejorative references when discussing extreme ascetic acts.

33. I read 支 here as 肢, following the Three editions and the Palace edition.

34. "King of the *dharma*" is an epithet of the Buddha, but it may also mean a king who is devout and protects and encourages the *dharma*. A *cakravartin* is an enlightened ruler of the world who turns the *dharma* wheel.

35. Terms used for "China" in Chinese Buddhist texts merit a study of their own.

36. "Yu" here refers to the legendary emperor Shun舜, whose personal name was Youyu 有虞. This and following references to burial practices in antiquity allude to the *Li ji* 禮記 3.2 (*Liji zhuzi suoyin* 禮記逐字索引, p. 12, ll. 3–4).

37. *Xia hou* refers to the founder of the Xia dynasty (traditional dates 2205–1786 BCE), King Yu 禹 (r. 2205–2197 BCE); the Zhou dynasty's dates are 1122–249 BCE.

38. Yin was the first reign title of the Shang 商 dynasty (1766–1122 BCE).

39. The references to upper, middle, and lower antiquity are common in Tang writing, although there seems to be no consensus as to the precise periods meant. Certainly lower antiquity referred to the writer's own time. Middle antiquity usually meant the Spring and Autumn Period and the Han and upper antiquity to the period before that.

40. Daoxuan quotes the *Li ji* 3.6 here: 古也墓而不墳 (*Liji zhuzi suoyin*, p. 11, ll. 18–19).

41. The connection between He Xu (who appears in *Zhuangzi* 9 as a sage whose subjects are ignorant of both sages and politics) and tumuli baffles me.

42. On burial by the side of *stūpas* in India, see Schopen 1987. The reference to a paste made of bones refers to the practice of grinding up leftover bones and adding them to flour to make dough balls for birds and animals to eat. It also refers to the making of images and miniature *stūpas* out of bone paste, which we have seen elsewhere in the biographical accounts.

43. *Chu* 初 seems to be an error here for the homophone 出.

44. Daoxuan refers here to Taoist practices, although as we have seen, abstention from grain was also practiced by fifth-century Buddhists.

45. These references are to vegetable and mineral elixirs.

46. I follow the Three editions and the Palace edition here in reading *dao* 道 for *lü* 慮 (T 50.2060.685n30).

47. The reference here is to meditation on the corpse.

48. I follow the Song and the Palace editions in reading *bing* 冰 for *shui* 水 (T 50.2060.685n31). *Houzang* 厚葬 may allude to the *Lunyu* 11.11, where Confucius objects to the extravagant funeral of Yan Yuan 顏淵 (*Lunyu zhuzi suoyin*, p. 27, ll. 8–9); see Legge 1991, vol. 1, 240.

49. The *lilong* appears in the *Zhuangzi* 32, *Zhuangzi yinde* 莊子引得, *A Concordance to Chuang Tzu*, p. 90, ll. 44–45. The *liniu* appears in the *Shanhai jing* 山海經

(Classic of Mountains and Seas) 4, *Shanhaijing zhuzi suoyin; Mutianzi zhuan zhuzi suoyin; Yandanzi zhuzi suoyin* 山海經逐字索引; 穆天子傳逐字索引; 燕丹子逐字索引 *Concordances to the Shanhaijing, Mutianzizhuan, Yandanzi,* p. 23, l.14. The peacock appears in the *Shuoyuan* 說苑 (Garden of Speech) 17.51; see *Shuoyuan zhuzi suoyin* 說苑逐字索引 *A Concordance to the Shuoyuan,* p.149, l. 23. The allusion to the musk deer remains obscure.

50. I have emended *ji* 飢 (hunger) to *ji* 肌 (flesh). For the classic statement of this idea, see the opening lines of the *Xiao jing* 孝經 (Classic of Filiality), *Erya zhuzi suoyin; Xiaojing zhuzi suoyin* 爾雅逐字索引; 孝經逐字索引 *Concordances to Erya, Xiaojing,* p.1, l. 5; Legge 1899, 466.

51. The first of these alludes to the *Liji* 2, *Liji zhuzi suoyin,* p. 2, ll. 13–14; the second to the *Lunyu* 15.9, *Lunyu zhuzi suoyin,* p. 42, l. 21; Legge 1991, vol. 1, 297.

52. The allusion is to the *Laozi* 38.

53. "Those who rejected the good and great" alludes to Sima Qian's comments on Taoism; see *Shiji* 3289. The case of "washing one's ears" refers to that of Xu You 許由; the drowned man is Qu Yuan.

54. The allusion is to the philosopher Yang; see note 2 above.

55. *Shen* (Orion) and *chen* (Venus) never appear together in the sky at the same time.

56. The allusion is to the *Lunyu* 5.26. See *Lunyu zhuzi suoyin,* p. 11, ll. 18–20; Legge 1991, vol. 1, 182.

57. Here I read *mu* 目 (eyes) for *zi* 自 (self).

58. See Chapter 3.

59. The seven treasures, or seven precious materials, are usually given in Buddhist sources as gold, silver, lapis lazuli, crystal, pearl, red coral, and ammonite, agate, or coral. See the discussion of this list in Hsin-ju Liu 1988, 92–94. *Sanlun* 三輪 probably stands for the three marks of existence, although it is not entirely clear which "three wheels" are implied here.

60. Here *duodu* 馱都 *(dhātu)* is meant in the sense of *sheli (śarīra),* or relic.

61. Nārāyaṇa is one of the names of the god Viṣṇu.

62. Here Zanning alludes to the *Mengzi* 6.9 (*Mengzi zhuzi suoyin,* p. 43, l. 30–35); Legge 1970, 282–284. In this passage Confucius complains at length about the teachings of Yangzi and Mozi. Mencius foresees disaster if their teachings are not stopped and Confucius' teachings are not promoted.

63. This metaphor appears in Han Yu's famous essay, *Yuan dao* 原道 (Origins of the Moral Way). See *Han Changli wenji jiaozhu* 韓昌藜文集校注 (Complete Prose of Han Changli [Han Yu], Collated and Annotated), 13.

64. *Lunyu* 11.12, *Lunyu zhuzi suoyin,* p. 27, l. 13; Legge 1991, vol. 1, 241.

65. *Zhuangzi* 6, *Zhuangzi yinde,* p. 16, l. 24; p. 17, l. 57; Graham 1989, 88.

66. The reference is to Zhuangzi's apparently bizarre actions after the death of his wife, see Graham 1989, 122.

67. X*ianxing* 現行 here refers to the appearance of things in their manifest aspect as they emerge from the seeds (which have been "perfumed" by previous actions) in the *ālayavijñāna* (storehouse consciousness).

68. Here *shiyan* 食言 means "false or untrustworthy words."

69. The girl was the future nun Utpalavarṇā. In her *jātaka* she tells of how in a previous life she was a comedian and put on a nun's robe in jest. As a consequence she became a *bhikṣuṇī* at the time of the Buddha Kāśyapa. See *Da zhidu lun* 13, T 25.1509.161b, translated in Lamotte 1944–1981, 844–846. My thanks to Hubert Durt for identifying this reference. I have not yet traced the parallel story of the brahman.

70. This is a paraphrase of the passage in T 31.1604.650a. The passage concerning Yijing's objections is translated in Kieschnick 1997, 45; my translation essentially follows his.

71. The reference is to Zeng Can 曾參, the disciple of Confucius particularly known for his filiality.

72. Liang-Zhe refers to the kingdom of Wu-Yue.

73. The *uṣṇīṣa* of the Buddha was often considered invisible, so here Zanning is drawing attention to the particular good fortune of China. See the discussion of the various interpretations of this particular mark of the Buddha in Lopez 2005, esp. 20-23.

74. See his biography in *Nan shi* 57/1415–1420.

75. On Wang Shao and his collection *Sheli ganying ji* 舍利感應記 (Record of Numinous Responses to Relics), which details the miracles that occurred during the Renshou relic distribution campaign, see Chen Jinhua 2002a, 52–53.

76. In other words there is a hierarchy to the natural order. In the Buddhist order of things, bodhisattvas are exemplars like the five types of fungus and the four auspicious things.

77. *Maoshi* 235 (*Maoshi zhuzi suoyin*, p. 117, ll. 12–13); Legge 1991, vol. 4, 431. King Wen is the ideal model, like the Buddha.

Bibliography

Translations of Chinese and Japanese titles have been supplied by the author in parentheses in roman script with no quotation marks. Secondary literature in Chinese and Japanese with English titles is indicated in italics for books and within quotation marks for articles.

Dictionaries

Bukkyō dai jiten 仏教大辭典 (Encyclopedia of Buddhism). Mochizuki Shinkō 望月信亨. Revised edition. 10 vols. Kyoto: Sekai Seiten Kankō Kyōkai, 1954–1963.

Bussho kaisetsu dai jiten 仏書解説大辭典 (Encyclopedia of Buddhist Literature with Explanations). Ono Genmyō 小野玄妙, ed. 15 vols. Tokyo: Daitō Shuppan, 1933–1936, 1974, 1988.

Dictionary of Ming Biography, 1368–1644. L. Carrington Goodrich, ed.; Chaoying Fang, assoc. ed. The Ming Biographical History Project of the Association for Asian Studies. 2 vols. New York: Columbia University Press, 1976.

Foguang da cidian 佛光大辭典 (Encyclopedic Dictionary of the Buddha Light). Xingyun 星雲, ed. 8 vols. Kaohsiung: Foguang chubanshe, 1988.

Hōbōgirin 法寶義林. *Hōbōgirin: Dictionnaire encyclopédique du Bouddhisme d'après les sources Chinoises et Japonaises*: fascicles 1 (1929), 2 (1930), 3 (1937), 4 (1967), 5 (1979), 6 (1983), 7 (1994), 8 (2003). Tokyo: Maison Franco-Japonaise.

Primary Sources

Chen shu 陳書 (History of the Chen). Yao Silian 姚思廉 (557–637), comp. Beijing: Zhonghua shuju, 1972.

Chodang chip 祖堂集 (Patriarchs' Hall Collection). Reproduced in vol. 3 of *Sodōshū sakuin* 祖堂集索引 by Yanagida Seizan 柳田聖山. Kyoto: Kyoto Daigaku Jinbun Kagaku Kenkyūjo, 1980–1984.

Dai Nihon Bukkyō zensho 大日本佛教全書 (Complete Buddhist Works of Japan). Suzuki Gakujutsu Zaidan 鈴木学術財団, ed. Revised Edition. 100 vols. Tokyo: Kōdansha, 1970–1973.

Da Ming huidian 大明會典 (Complete Regulations of the Great Ming). 1587. Reprint, Taipei: Dongnan shubaoshe, 1963.

Daozang [*Zhengtong daozang* 正統道藏, 1445]. Includes the *Wanli xu daozang* 萬曆 續道藏, 1607. 1,120 vols. Shanghai: Commercial Press, 1923–1926. Reprint, 60 vols., Taipei: Yiwen Yinshuguan, 1962.

Dazang jing bubian 大藏經補編 (Great [Buddhist] Canon: Supplementary Section). Lan Jifu 藍吉富, ed. Taipei: Xinwenfeng, 1984–1986.

Erya zhuzi suoyin; Xiaojing zhuzi suoyin 爾雅逐字索引；孝經逐字索引 *Concordances to Erya, Xiaojing*. Institute of Chinese Studies, Ancient Chinese Texts Concordances Series, Philosophical Works, nos. 16–17. Hong Kong: Shangwu yinshu guan, 1995.

Gaoseng zhuan 高僧傳 (Biographies of Eminent Monks). Huijiao 慧皎 (497–554). Beijing: Zhonghua shuju, 1996.

Gaoseng zhuan heji 高僧傳合集 (Combined Collection of Eminent Monks). Shanghai: Shanghai guji chubanshe, 1995.

Guang baichuan xuehai 廣百川學海 (A Sea of Learning from One Hundred Broad Rivers). Feng Kebin 馮可賓 (fl. 1630), comp. Taipei: Xinxing shuju, 1970.

Gujin tushu jicheng 古今圖書集成 (Synthesis of Illustrations and Books Past and Present). 10,000 *juan*. Chen Menglei 陳夢雷, Jiang Tingxi 蔣廷錫 et al., comps. Palace edition, 1726. Reprint, 82 vols., Chengdu: Zhonghua shuju and Bashu shushe, 1985.

Han Changli wenji jiaozhu 韓昌黎文集校注 (Complete Prose of Han Changli [Han Yu], Collated and Annotated). Ma Qichang 馬其昶, ed. Shanghai: Gudian wenxue chubanshe, 1986.

Han'guk Pulgyo chŏnsŏ 韓國佛教全書 (Complete Works of Korean Buddhism). Tongguk taehakkyo pulchŏn kanhaeng wiwŏnhoe nae Han'guk Pulgyo chŏnsŏ pyŏnch'an wiwŏn 東國大學校佛典刊行委員會內韓國佛教全書編纂委員, ed. 12 vols. Seoul: Tongguk Taehakkyo Ch'ulpansa, 1979.

Han shu 漢書 (Book of the [Former] Han). 120 *juan*, compiled in 58–76. Ban Gu 班固 (32–92), comp. Bcijing: Zhonghua shuju, 1962.

Hou Han shu 後漢書 (Book of the Later Han). 120 *juan*. Fan Ye 范曄 (398–445), comp. Beijing: Zhonghua shuju, 1965.

Jin shu 晉書 (Book of the Jin). 130 *juan*, decreed in 644, compiled in 646–648. Fang Xuanling 房玄齡 (578–648) et al., comps. Beijing: Zhonghua shuju, 1974.

Jiu Tang shu 舊唐書 (Old Book of the Tang). 200 *juan*, completed in 945. Liu Xu 劉昫 (887–946). Beijing: Zhonghua shuju, 1975.

Jiu Wudai shi 舊五代史 (Old History of the Five Dynasties). 150 *juan*, completed in 973. Xue Juzheng 薛居正 (912–981). Beijing: Zhonghua shuju, 1976.

Lidai zhiguan biao 歷代職官表 (Historical Tables of Official Posts). Ji Yun 紀昀 (1724–1805). 2 vols. Reprint, Shanghai: Shanghai guji chubanshe, 1989.

Liji zhuzi suoyin 禮記逐字索引 *A Concordance to the* Liji. Institute of Chinese Studies Ancient Chinese Text Concordance Series, Classical Works, no. 2. Hong Kong: Shangwu yinshu guan, 1992.

Lunyu zhuzi suoyin 論語逐字索引 *A Concordance to the* Lunyu. Institute of Chinese Studies Ancient Chinese Text Concordance Series, Classical Works, no. 14. Hong Kong: Shangwu yinshu guan, 1995.

Lüshi chunqiu zhuzi suoyin 呂氏春秋逐字索引 *A Concordance to the* Lüshichunqiu. Institute of Chinese Studies Ancient Chinese Text Concordance Series, Philosophical Works, no. 12. Hong Kong: Shangwu yinshu guan, 1994.

Maoshi zhuzi suoyin 毛詩逐字索引 *A Concordance to the* Maoshi. Institute of Chinese Studies Ancient Chinese Text Concordance Series, Classical Works, no. 10. Hong Kong: Shangwu yinshu guan, 1995.

Mengzi zhuzi suoyin 孟子逐字索引 *A Concordance to the* Mengzi. He Zhihua 何志華 , ed. Chinese University of Hong Kong Institute of Chinese Studies Ancient Chinese Text Concordance Series, Classical Works, no. 15. Hong Kong, Shangwu yinshu guan, 1995.

Mingxiang ji 冥詳記 (Signs from the Unseen Realm). Wang Yan 王琰 (b. ca. 454, fl. late fifth–early sixth centuries). In *Guxiaoshuo gouchen* 古小說勾沈, compiled by Lu Xun 魯迅 (1881–1936), 449–534. Hong Kong: Xinyi chubanshe, 1967.

Nan Qi shu 南齊書 (Book of the Southern Qi). 59 *juan*. Xiao Zixian 蕭子顯 (489–537), comp. Beijing: Zhonghua shuju, 1972.

Nan shi 南史 (History of the Southern Dynasties). Li Yanshou 李延壽 (seventh century). Beijing: Zhonghua shu, 1975.

Quan Tang shi 全唐詩 (Complete Tang Poetry). 900 *juan*. Peng Dingqiu 彭定求 (1645–1719) et al., comps. Printed by Cao Yin 曹寅 (1658–1712), imperial preface of 1707. Beijing: Zhonghua shuju, 1960.

Sanguo zhi 三國志 (Records of the Three Kingdoms). 65 fascicles, compiled in 285–297. Chen Shou 陳壽 (233–297), comp. 5 vols. Beijing: Zhonghua Shuju, 1962.

Shangshu gushi 尚書故實 (Stories Told by Minister [Zhang]). 1 *juan*. Li Chuo 李綽 (ninth century). In *Congshu jicheng* 叢書集成, series 1, vol. 2,739. Shanghai: Shangwu yinshu guan, 1935.

Shangshu zhuzi suoyin 尚書逐字索引 *A Concordance to the* Shangshu. He Zhihua 何志華 , ed. Institute of Chinese Studies Ancient Chinese Text Concordance Series, Classical Works, no. 9. Hong Kong: Shangwu yinshu guan, 1995.

Shanhaijing zhuzi suoyin; Mutianzi zhuan zhuzi suoyin; Yandanzi zhuzi suoyin 山海經逐字索引; 穆天子傳逐字索引; 燕丹子逐字索引 *Concordances to the Shanhaijing, Mutianzizhuan, Yandanzi*. Institute of Chinese Studies Ancient Chinese Text Concordance Series, Historical Works, nos. 9–10; Philosphical Works, no. 11. Hong Kong: Shangwu yinshu guan, 1994.

Shi ji 史記 (Records of the Historian). 130 *juan.* Sima Qian 司馬遷 (145–86 BCE) and Sima Tan 司馬談 (180–110? BCE). Beijing: Zhonghua shuju, 1959.

Shike shiliao xinbian 石刻史料新編 (New Edition of Historical Materials Inscribed on Stone). 90 vols. Taipei: Xinwenfeng, 1977–1986.

Shishi liutie 釋氏六帖 (The Buddhists' Six Documents). Compiled in 944–954. Yi-chu 義楚 (fl. tenth century), comp. Typeset edition, reprinting the 1944 Pu-hui Canon edition of Shanghai, itself based on the Japanese woodblock edition of 1669. Hangzhou: Zhejiang guji chubanshe, 1990.

Shuoyuan zhuzi suoyin 說苑逐字索引 *A Concordance to the* Shuoyuan. D. C. Lau, ed. Institute of Chinese Studies Ancient Chinese Text Concordance Series, Classical Works, no. 8. Hong Kong: Shangwu yinshu guan, 1992.

Siku quanshu zongmu tiyao 四庫全書總目提要 (General Catalogue of the *Complete Books in Four Treasuries* with Descriptive Notes). Compiled in 1798. Ji Yun 紀昀 et al., comps. Beijing: Zhonghua shuju, 1997.

Sita ji 寺塔記 (Record of Monasteries and Stūpas). 2 *juan,* compiled in 843–853. Duan Chengshi 段成式 (803?–863), comp. Beijing: Renmin meishu chubanshe, 1964.

Song shi 宋史 (History of the Song Dynasty). 496 *juan,* completed in 1345. Tuo Tuo 脫脫 (1313–1355) et al. Beijing: Zhonghua shuju, 1977.

Song shu 宋書 (Book of the Song). 100 *juan.* Shen Yue 沈約 (441–513). Beijing: Zhonghua shuju, 1974.

Sui shu 隋書 (Book of the Sui). 85 *juan,* compiled in 636–656. Wei Zheng 魏徵 (580–643) et al., comps. Beijing: Zhonghua shuju, 1973.

Taiping guangji 太平廣記 (Extensive Records of the Taiping Era). 500 *juan,* compiled in 977–978. Li Fang 李昉 (925–996) et al., comps. Beijing: Zhonghua shuju, 1961.

Taiping yulan 太平御覽 (Imperial Readings of the Taiping Era). Completed in 983. Li Fang 李昉 (925–996). Edited by Wang Yunwu 王雲五. 1935. Reprint, Taipei: Yangwu yinshuguan, 1980.

Taishō shinshū daizōkyō 大正新脩大藏經 (Great [Buddhist] Canon, Newly Compiled in the Taishō Era). Takakusu Junjirō 高楠順次郎 et al., eds. 100 vols. Tokyo: Taishō Issaikyō Kankōkai, 1924–1932.

Wang Youcheng jijian zhu 王右丞集箋注 (Collected Works of Wang Youcheng [Wang Wei], Collated and Annotated). Zhao Diancheng 趙殿成, ed. Beijing: Zhonghua shuju, 1962.

Wenyuan yinghua 文苑英華 (Beautiful Flowers from the Garden of Literature), 1,000 *juan,* compiled in 982–987. Li Fang 李昉 (925–996) et al., comps. Beijing: Zhonghua shuju, 1966.

Wujun tujing xuji 吳郡圖經續記 (The Illustrated Guide to Wujun, Continued

Records). 3 *juan,* completed in 1134. Zhu Changwen 朱長文 (?–1099?).
Nanjing: Jiangsu guji chubanshe, 1999.

Wu zazu 五雜俎 (Five-Part Miscellany). 16 *juan,* completed in 1616. Xie Zhaozhe
謝肇淛 (1567–1624). 2 vols. Beijing: Zhonghua shuju, 1959.

Xin Tang shu 新唐書 (New Book of the Tang). 225 *juan,* compiled in 1043–1060.
Ouyang Xiu 歐陽修 (1007–1072), Song Qi 宋祁 (998–1061), et al., comps.
Beijing: Zhonghua shuju, 1974.

Xin Wudai shi 新五代史 (New History of the Five Dynasties). 74 *juan.* Ouyang
Xiu 歐陽修 (1007–1072). Beijing: Zhonghua shuju, 1974.

Xunzi zhuzi suoyin 荀子逐字索引 *A Concordance to the* Xunzi. Institute of Chinese
Studies Ancient Chinese Text Concordance Series, Philosophical Works,
no. 26. Hong Kong: Shangwu yinshu guan, 1996.

Xu wenxian tongkao 續文獻通考 (Continuation of *Wenxian tongkao* [General History of Institutions and Critical Examination of Documents and Studies]).
Completed in 1586. Wang Qi 王圻 (*jinshi* 1565), comp. Wanli woodblock
edition. Reprint, Taipei: Wenhai chuban she, 1979.

Xuzang jing 續藏經 (Continued [Buddhist] Canon). Taipei: Xinwenfeng, 1968–
1970. Reprint of *Dai Nihon zokuzōkyō* 大日本續藏經 . 150 vols. Kyoto: Zōkyō
shoin, 1905–1912.

Zhuangzi yinde 莊子引得 *A Concordance to Chuang Tzu.* Harvard-Yenching Institute Sinological Index Series, suppl. 20. Cambridge, Mass.: Harvard University Press, 1956.

Zizhi tongjian 資治通鑑 (Comprehensive Mirror for the Aid of Government). 294
juan. Sima Guang 司馬光 (1019–1086) et al., comps. Presented to the throne
in December 1084. Beijing: Guji chubanshe, 1956; Beijing: Zhonghua
shuju, 1963; Hong Kong: Zhonghua shuju, 1971. This edition includes
Sima Guang's *Zizhi tongjian kaoyi* 資治通鑑考異 and Hu Sanxing's 胡三省
(1230–1302) *Zizhi tongjian* (*yinzhu*) 資治通鑑 (音註).

Secondary Studies in Asian Languages

Cai Hongsheng 蔡鴻生. 1996. *Nigu tan* 尼姑譚 (Nuns' tales). Guangzhou: Zhong-
shan daxue chubanshe.

Cao Shibang (Tso Sze-Bong) 曹仕邦. 1981. "Sengshi suozai Zhongguo shamen
jianshou yinjie de yixie shili 僧史所載中國沙門堅守淫戒的一些實例" (Some
examples recorded in monastic histories of Chinese monks firmly maintaining the precept against sex). *Huagang foxue xuebao* 華岡佛學學報 5: 275–
288.

———. 1995. "Biqiu Shi Baochang shifou 'Biqiuni zhuan' zhuanren de yiwen
比丘釋寶唱是否《比丘尼傳》撰人的疑問" (A question of doubt as to

whether Baochang was the compiler of *Biographies of Bhikṣuṇīs*). In *Fojiao sixiang de chuancheng yu fazhan—Yinshun daoshi jiuzhi huadan zhushou wenji* 佛教思想的傳承與發展 — 印順導師九秩華誕祝壽文集 (Transmission and development of Buddhist thought: A festschrift for Master Yinshun's ninetieth birthday), compiled by Shi Hengqing 釋恆清, 455–466. Taipei: Dongda tushu gongsi.

———. 1999. "*Song gaoseng zhuan:* Feng huangming xiuzhuan de sengtu lei-zhuan宋高僧傳: 奉皇命修撰的僧徒類傳" (*Song gaoseng zhuan:* Categorized biographies of monks compiled on imperial command). In his *Zhongguo fojiao shixue-shi—Dong Jin zhi Wudai* 中國佛教史學史 — 東晉至五代 (Histori-cal-bibliographical studies in Chinese Buddhism from the Eastern Jin to the Wudai periods), 131–147. Taipei: Fagu wenhua.

Chen Jingfu 陳景富. 1990. *Famen si shilue* 法門寺史略 (A brief history of Famen si). Xi'an: Shaanxi renmin jiaoyu chubanshe.

Chen Yinque 陳寅恪. 1977. "*Sanguo zhi* Cao Chong Hua Tuo zhuan yu fojiao gushi" 三國志曹沖華佗傳與佛教故事 (Biographies of Cao Chong and Hua Tuo in the *Sanguo zhi* and their relationship with Buddhist legends). In *Chen Yinque xiansheng quan ji* 陳寅恪先生全集 (Collected works of Chen Yinque). Taipei: Jiushi chuban youxiang gongsi.

Chen Yuan 陳垣. 1981. "Faxian foya yinxian ji 法獻佛牙隱現記" (Account of the disappearance and [re-]appearance of the Buddha's tooth [brought to China by] Faxian). In *Chen Yuan shixue lunzhu xuan* 陳垣史學論著選 (A se-lected collection of Chen Yuan's articles on history), edited by Chen Yuesu 陳樂素 and Chen Zhichao 陳智超, 568–570. Shanghai: Shanghai renmin chubanshe.

———. 1999 (1955). *Zhongguo fojiao shiji gailun* 中國佛教史藉概論 (A general dis-cussion of the historical sources of Chinese Buddhism). Shanghai: Shang-hai shudian chubanshe.

Chen Yunü 陳玉女. 1997. "Ming Wanli shiqi Cisheng huangtaihou de chongfo-Jianlun Fo Dao liang shili de duizhi 明萬曆時期慈聖皇太后的崇佛 — 兼論佛、道兩勢力的對峙 " (Empress Cisheng's promotion of Buddhism in the Wanli period of the Ming—also with references to the confrontation be-tween the two forces of Buddhism and Taoism). *Chenggong daxue lishi xue-bao* 成功大學歷史學報 23: 195–245.

Chen Yuzhen陳昱珍. 1992. "Daoshi yu *Fayuan zhulin*道世與《法苑珠林》" (Daoshi and the *Fayuan zhulin*). *Zhonghua foxue xuebao* 中華佛學學報 5: 233–261.

Ding Mingyi 丁明夷. 1998. *Fojiao xinchu beizhi jicui*佛教新出碑志集粹 (Collection of newly excavated Buddhist stele inscriptions). Taipei: Foguang wenhua shi ye youxian gongsi.

Fang Guangchang 方廣錩. 1991. *Fojiao Dazang jing shi: 8–10 shiji* 佛教大藏經史 8–

10世紀 (History of the Buddhist canon: Eighth to tenth centuries). Beijing: Zhongguo shehui kexue chubanshe.

Fujiyoshi Masumi 藤善真澄. 1995. "Ei Gensū den seiritsu kō 衛元嵩傳成立考" (An investigation of the formation of the biography of Wei Yuansong). *Tōyōshi kenkyū* 東洋史研究 54, no. 2: 62–95.

———. 2002. *Dōsen den no kenkyū* 道宣伝の研究 *A study for the life of Dau-Xuan.* Kyoto: Kyōto Daigaku Gakujutsu Shuppankai.

Funayama Tōru 船山徹. 1995. "Rikuchō jidai ni okeru bōsatsukai no juyō katei 六朝時代における菩薩戒の受容過程" (On the acceptance of the bodhisattva precepts during the Six Dynasties period). *Tōhō gakuhō* 東方學報 67: 1–135.

———. 2002. "Shashin no shisō Rikuchō bukkyō shi no ichi danmen 捨身の思想 — 六朝仏教史の一断面" (The concept of "abandoning the body": One aspect of Six Dynasties Buddhist history). *Tōhō gakuhō* 74: 358–311 (reverse pagination).

Hangzhou foxue yuan 杭州佛學院, comp. 2004. *Wu-Yue fojiao xueshu yantaohui lunwen ji* 吳越佛教學術研討會論文集 (Collected papers from the conference on the study of Buddhism in Wu-Yue). Beijing: Zongjiao wenhua chubanshe.

Hasebe Yūkei 長谷部幽蹊. 1979. *Min Shin Bukkyō shi kenkyū josetsu* 明清佛教史研究序説 *Introduction to the historical study of Buddhism in the Ming and Ching dynasties.* Taipei: Xinwenfeng.

———. 1993. *Min Shin Bukkyō kyōdanshi kenkyū* 明清佛教教團史研究 (Studies on the history of the Buddhist orders of the Ming and Qing). Kyoto: Dōhōsha shuppan.

Hirai Shun'ei 平井俊榮. 1985. *Hokke mongu no seiritsu ni kansusru kenkyū* 法華文句の成立に関する研究 (A study of the compilation of the *Textual Commentary on the Lotus*). Tokyo: Shunjūsha.

Huang Qijiang (Huang Chi-chiang) 黃啓江. 1996. "Bei-Song shiqi Liang-Zhe de Mituo xinyang 北宋時期兩浙的彌陀信仰" (Amitābha belief in the Liang-Zhe area during the Northern Song). *Gugong xueshu jikan* 故宮學術季刊 (fall 1996): 1–38.

———. 2003. "Bei-Song jushi Yang Jie yu fojiao—Jianbu Songshi Yang Jie benzhuan zhi que 北宋居士楊傑與佛教—兼補宋史楊傑本傳之缺" (The Northern Song layman Yang Jie and Buddhism: Supplementing deficiencies in Yang Jie's *Song shi* biography). *Hanxue yanjiu* 漢學研究 21, no.1 (series no. 42, June 2003): 253–277.

Ibuki Atsushi 伊吹敦. 1987. "Tō Sō Ejō ni tsuite 唐僧慧祥に就いて" (On the Tang monk Huixiang). *Waseda Daigaku Daigakuin Bungaku Kenkyūka kiyō* 早稲田大学大学院文学研究科紀要 *Bessatsu* 別冊 14, *Tetsugaku shigaku hen* 哲学史学編: 33–45.

———. 1990. "Zoku kōsōden no zōkō ni kansuru kenkyū 續高僧傳の增廣に関する研究 " (Research on the expansion of the *Xu gaoseng zhuan*). *Tōyō no shisō to shūkyō* 東洋の思想と宗教 7: 58–74.

Iishii Kōsei 石井公成. 1996. *Kegon shisō no kenkyū* 華厳思想の研究 *Evolution and metamorphosis of Huayan philosophy in China, Korea and Japan*. Tokyo: Shunjūsha.

Jan Yün-hua (Ran Yunhua) 冉雲華. 1990. "Xuanzang dashi yu Tang Taizong jiqi zhengzhi lixiang tanwei 玄奘大師與唐太宗及其政治理想探微" (An investigation of the great master Xuanzang's relationship with Tang Taizong and his political thought). In his *Zhonghua fojiao wenhua yanjiu lunji* 中華佛教文化研究論集 (Collected essays on Chinese Buddhist culture), 13–41. Taipei: Dongchu chubanshe.

———. 1991. "Yanshou de jielü sixiang chutan 延壽的戒律思想初探 " (A preliminary study of Yanshou's thought on monastic discipline). *Zhonghua foxue xuebao* 4: 297–310.

Jia Yingyi 賈應逸. 1995. "*Juqu Anzhou zaosi gongde bei* yu Bei-Liang Gaochang fojiao 《且渠安周造寺功德碑》与北涼高昌佛教" (*The inscription on the merit of Juqu Anzhou's building of monasteries* and Buddhism in Northern Liang Gaochang). *Xiyu yanjiu* 西域研究 2: 35–42.

Kasuga Reichi 春日禮智. 1935. "Jōdokyō shiryō to shite no *Meisōden* shijishō *Meisōden* yōbunshō narabi ni Miroku nyorai kannōshō daishi shoin no *Meisōden* ni tsuite 浄土教史科としての名僧傳指示抄名僧傳要文抄並に弥勒如来感応抄第四書引の名僧傳に就いて" (Extant sections of the *Mingseng zhuan* as historical materials on Pure Land Buddhism). *Shūkyōgaku kenkyū* 宗教学研究 12: 53–118.

Kimura Kiyotaka 木村清孝. 1977. *Shoki Chūgoku kegon shisō no kenkyū* 初期中國華嚴思想の研究 (A study of early Huayan thought in China). Tokyo: Shunjūsha.

Kosugi Kazuo 小杉 一雄 . 1993 (1937). "Nikushinzō oyobi yuikaizō no kenkyū 肉身像及遺灰像の研究" (Research on flesh-body images and ash icons). In *Nihon, Chūgoku miira shinkō no kenkyū* 日本、中国ミイラ信仰の研究 (Research on mummy beliefs in Japan and China), edited by the Nihon Miira Kenkyū Gurupu 日本ミイラ研究グルプ, 277–310. Tokyo: Heibonsha, 1993. Originally published in *Tōyō gakuhō* 東洋学報 24, no. 3: 93–124.

Lin Huisheng 林惠勝. 2001. "Shaozhi fenshen—Zhongguo zhongshi fahua xinyang zhi yi mian xiang 燒指焚身 — 中國中世法華信仰之一面向" (Burning the fingers and auto-cremation—On one aspect of belief in the *Lotus Sūtra* in medieval China). *Zongjiao yu wenhua xuebao* 宗教與文化學報 1: 57–96.

Liu Shufen 劉淑芬. 1996. "Foding zunsheng tuoluoni jing yu Tangdai zunsheng jingchuang de jianli—jingchuang yanjiu zhi yi 佛頂尊勝陀羅尼經與唐代

尊勝經幢的建立 — 經幢研究之一" (The *Foding zunsheng tuoluoni jing* and the establishment of the *Zunsheng tuoluoni* scripture pillars in the Tang—Research on scripture pillars). *Zhongyang yanjiuyuan lishi yuyan yanjiusuo jikan* 中央研究院歷史語言研究所集刊 67, no. 1: 145–193.

———. 1998. "Linzang—Zhonggu fojiao lushizang yanjiu zhi yi 林葬 — 中古佛教露屍葬研究之一" (Research on forest burial—Medieval Buddhist burial by exposing the corpse). *Dalu zazhi* 大陸雜誌 96, no. 3: 22–136.

Lo Hsiang-lin (Luo Xianglin) 羅香林. 1960. *Tangdai Guangzhou Guangxiao si yu Zhong-Yin jiaotong zhi guanxi* 唐代廣州光孝寺與中印交通之關係 *Kwang-hsiao monastery of Canton during the T'ang with reference to Sino-Indian relations.* Hong Kong: Institute of Chinese Culture.

Lu Xun 魯迅, ed. 1967. *Gu xiaoshuo gouchen* 古小說鉤沈 (Ancient tales rescued from oblivion). Hong Kong: Xinye chubanshe.

Makita Tairyō 牧田諦亮. 1957. *Chūgoku kinsei Bukkyōshi kenkyū* 中国近世佛教史研究 (Research in recent Chinese Buddhist history). Kyoto: Heirakuji Shoten.

———. 1976. *Gikyō kenkyū* 疑經研究 (Studies on suspect scriptures). Kyoto: Kyōto daigaku Jinbun kagaku kenkyūjo.

———. 1984. "Sannei to sono jidai 賛寧とその時代" (Zanning and his times). In his *Chūgoku Bukkyōshi no kenkyū* 中国仏教史の研究 (Research on Chinese Buddhist history), vol. 2, 111–145. Tokyo: Daitō Shuppansha.

———. 1989a. "Kōsōden no seiritsu 高僧傳の成立" (The formation of the *Gaoseng zhuan*). In his *Chūgoku Bukkyōshi no kenkyū* 中国仏教史の研究 (Research on Chinese Buddhist history), vol. 3, 1–71. Tokyo: Daitō Shuppansha. Originally published in two parts in *Tōhō gakuhō* 44 (1973): 101–125 and 48 (1975): 229–259.

———. 1989b. "Suirikue shōkō 水陸會小考" (A brief study of the Water-Land Assembly). In his *Chūgoku Bukkyōshi no kenkyū* 中国仏教史の研究 (Research on Chinese Buddhist history), vol. 2, 213–235. Tokyo: Daitō Shuppansha. Originally published in *Tōhō shūkyō* 12 (July 1980): 14–32.

Matoba Yoshimasa 的場慶雅. 1982. "Chūgoku ni okeru Hokkekyō no shinkō keitai (1)—Hokke Denki 中国における法華経の信仰形態 (1)— 法華伝記" (Forms of faith in the *Lotus Sūtra* as manifested in China (1)—The *Fahua chuanji*). *Indogaku Bukkyōgaku kenkyū* 印度学仏教学研究 31, no. 1: 275–277.

———. 1984. "Chūgoku ni okeru Hokkekyō no shinkō keitai (2)—Hokke Denki to Kōsan Hokke-den ni okeru Hokkekyō no dokuju to reigen setsuwa ni tsuite 中国における法華経の信仰形態 (2)— 法華伝記と弘賛法華傳における法華経の讀誦と霊驗說話について" (Forms of faith in the *Lotus Sūtra* as manifested in China (2)—Recitation of the *Lotus Sūtra* and miracle stories in the *Fahua chuanji* and the *Hongzan fahua zhuan*). *Indogaku Bukkyōgaku kenkyū* 32, no. 2: 375–377.

———. 1986. "Chūgoku ni okeru Hokkekyō no shinkō keitai (3) —Shin, Shin, Sō o chūshin to shite 中国における法華経の信仰形態 (3) —晋秦宋を中心として" (Forms of faith in the *Lotus Sūtra* as manifested in China (3) —Focusing on the Jin, Qin, and Song dynasties). *Indogaku Bukkyōgaku kenkyū* 34, no. 2: 57–59.

Michihata Ryōshū 道端良秀 . 1968. *Bukkyō to Jukyō rinri: Chūgoku Bukkyō ni okeru kō no mondai* 仏教と儒教倫理：中国仏教における孝の問題 (Buddhist and Confucian ethics: The issue of filiality in Chinese Buddhism). Kyoto: Heirakuji shoten.

———. 1979a. *Chūgoku Bukkyō shisōshi no kenkyū : Chūgoku minshū no Bukkyō juyō* 中国仏教思想史の研究：中国民衆の仏教受容 (Studies in the history of Chinese Buddhist thought: The acceptance of Buddhism by the Chinese populace). Kyoto : Heirakuji Shoten.

———. 1979b. "Chūgoku Bukkyō to jikininniku no mondai 中国仏教と食人肉の問題" (The issue of cannibalism and Chinese Buddhism). In Michihata 1979a, 309–325. Originally published in 1964 in *Jikaku Daishi kenkyū* 慈覚大師研究, edited by Fukui Kōjun 福井康順, 391–404. Tokyo: The Association of the Tendai Sect for Buddhist Studies.

———. 1979c. "Chūgoku Bukkyō to jikiniku kinshi no mondai 中国仏教と食肉禁止の問題" (The issue of the restriction on eating meat in Chinese Buddhism). In Michihata 1979a, 271–291. Originally published in 1964 in *Jikaku Daishi kenkyū* 慈覚大師研究 , edited by Fukui Kōjun 福井康順 , 309–325. Tokyo: The Association of the Tendai Sect for Buddhist Studies.

———. 1980. "Chūgoku Bukkyō ni okeru Hokkekyō no shinkō 中國佛教における法華經の信仰" (*Lotus Sūtra* beliefs in Chinese Buddhism). In his *Chūgoku Bukkyō to shakai to no kōshō* 中國佛教と社會との交渉 (Chinese Buddhism and its relation to society), 94–110. Kyoto: Heirakuji shoten.

Mizuo Gensei 水尾現誠. 1963. "Shashin ni tsuite—Ekyō no tachiba 捨身について —慧皎の立場" (On self-immolation: The position of Huijiao). *Indogaku Bukkyōgaku kenkyū* 22: 174–175.

Myōjin Hiroshi 明神洋 . 1985. "Chūgoku Bukkyōto no shōshin to Dōkyō" 中国仏教徒の焼身と道教 (Daoism and the burning of the body by Chinese Buddhists). *Waseda Daigaku Daigakuin Bungaku Kenkyūka kiyō* 早稲田大学大学院文学研究科紀要 *Bessatsu* 別冊 12, *Tetsugaku shigaku hen* 哲学史学編：41–50.

———. 1996. "Chūgoku shakai ni okeru Bukkyō no shashin to heian 中国社会における仏教の捨身と平安 (Buddhist self-immolation and peace in the context of Chinese society). *Nihon Bukkyō gakkai nenpō* 日本仏教学会年報 61: 99–110.

Nabata Ōjun 名畑応順. 1931. "Shina chūsei ni okeru shashin ni tsuite 支那中世に於ける捨身に就いて" (On self-immolation in medieval China). *Ōtani gakuhō* 大谷學報 12, no. 2: 1–43.

Naitō Masatoshi 内藤正敏. 1986. "Shōshin, kajō to dochū nyūjō 焼身火定と土中入定" (Auto-cremation, fire *samādhi*, and subterranean *samādhi*). In *Bukkyō minzokugaku taikei* 仏教民俗学大系 (Outline of studies on Buddhism and folk customs), edited by Hagiwara Tatsuo 萩原龍夫 and Shinno Toshikazu 真野俊和, vol. 2, 129–154. Tokyo: Meicho shuppan.

Nomura Yōshō 野村耀昌. 1968. *Shūbu hōnan no kenkyū* 周武法難の研究 (Research on Zhou Wudi's persecution of Buddhism). Tokyo: Azuma shuppan.

Okamoto Tensei 岡本天晴. 1974. "Rikuchō ni okeru shashin no ichi sokumen 六朝における捨身の一側面" (On one aspect of self-immolation in the Six Dynasties). *Indogaku Bukkyōgaku Kenkyū* 44: 862–868.

Okano Makoto 岡野誠. 2000. "Tō no An Kinzō no kappuku" 唐の安金蔵の割腹 (An Jinzang of the Tang's slicing of the abdomen). *Hōshigaku kenkyūkai kaihō* 法史學研究會會報 5: 33–37.

Ōno Hōdō 大野法道. 1954. *Daijō kaikyō no kenkyū* 大乗戒經の研究 (Research on Mahāyāna precepts *sūtra*s). Tokyo: Risōsha.

Ono Katsutoshi 小野勝年. 1989. *Chūgoku Zui Tō Chōan jiin shiryō shūsei* 中国隋唐長安寺院史料集成 *Compilation of historical records about the temples in Chang'an*. 2 vols. Kyoto: Hōzōkan.

Rong Xinjiang 榮新江. 1998. "*Juqu Anzhou bei* yu Gaochang Da Liang zhengquan" 《且渠安周碑》与高昌大涼政權 (The Juqu Anzhou stele and the great Liang regime). *Yanjing xuebao* 燕京學報, n.s., 5: 65–92.

Satō Tetsuei 佐藤哲英. 1961. *Tendai daishi no kenkyū* 天台大師の研究 (A study of great master Tiantai). Kyoto: Hyakkaen.

———. 1981. *Zoku Tendai daishi no kenkyū* 續天台大師の研究 (A continued study of great master Tiantai). Kyoto: Hyakkaen.

Schipper, Kristopher. 2002. "Diyi dongtian: Mindong Ningde Huotong shan chukao 第一洞天：闽东宁德霍童山初考" (The paramount cavern-heaven: A preliminary investigation of Mount Huotong in Ningde, eastern Min). http://www.xiguan.net/Schipper/009.htm.

Sekiguchi Shindai 関口真大. 1961. *Tendai shōshikan no kenkyū* 天台小止観の研究 (Research on Tiantai's *Lesser Calming and Contemplation*). Tokyo: Sankibō busshorin.

Shengyan 聖嚴. 1988. *Mingmo Zhongguo fojiao zhi yanjiu* 明末中國佛教之研究 (Research on Chinese Buddhism of the late Ming). Taipei: Taiwan xuesheng shuju.

Shi Guodeng 釋果燈. 1992. *Tang Daoxuan* Xu gaoseng zhuan *pipan sixiang chutan* 唐道宣《續高僧傳》批判思想初探 (A preliminary study in evaluating the *Xu gaoseng zhuan* by Daoxuan of the Tang). Taipei: Dongchu chubanshe.

Shimada Shūjirō 島田修二郎. 1961. "Yu Mida Shijō to sono Amida zō 喩彌陀思淨 とその阿彌陀像" "The monk painter Ssu-ching and his painting of Ami-tābha" in *Bukkyō shigaku ronshū: Tsukamoto Hakushi shōju kinen* 佛教史學論集：塚本博士頌壽記念 (Collected essays on the study of Buddhist history: Festschrift for Dr. Tsukamoto), edited by Tsukamoto Hakushi Shōju Kinenkai 塚本博士頌壽記念會, 431–442. Kyoto: Tsukamoto Hakushi Shōju Kinenkai.

Smith, Thomas E. 1998. "Rikuchō ni okeru butsudō ronsō to Ressenden no denshō 六朝における仏道論争と列仙伝の伝承" (Buddho-Taoist debates in the Six Dynasties and the transmission of the *Liexian zhuan*). In *Dōkyō no rekishi to bunka* 道教の歴史と文化 (Taoist history and culture), edited by Yamada Toshiaki 山田利明 and Tanaka Fumio 田中文雄, 145–166. Tokyo: Hirakawa.

Suwa Gijun 諏訪義純. 1997a. *Chūgoku Nanchō Bukkyōshi no kenkyū* 中国南朝仏教史の研究 (Research on Buddhist history of the Southern Dynasties of China). Kyoto: Hōzōkan.

———. 1997b. "Rikuchō kara Zui-Tō jidai ni okeru zetsu fushō no shinkō ni tsuite 六朝から隋唐時代における舌不焼の信仰について" (On belief in the unburned tongue from the Six Dynasties to the Sui and Tang periods). In Suwa 1997a, 303–327. Originally published in 1990 as "Chūgoku bukkyō ni okeru zetsu fushō no shinkō ni tsuite—Rikuchō kara Zui-Tō o chūshin toshite 中国仏教における舌不焼の信仰について—六朝から隋唐を中心として" (On belief in the unburned tongue in Chinese Buddhism, focusing on the Six Dynasties to the Sui and Tang) in *Tōyōgaku ronshū—Satō Kyōgen Hakushi shōju kinen* 東洋学論集—佐藤匡玄博士頌寿記念 (Collected essays on East Asian studies: Festschrift for Satō Kyōgen), edited by Satō Kyōgen Hakushi shōju kinen ronshū kankōkai, 229–256. Kyoto: Hōyō shōten.

———. 1997c. "Tō kara Sō ni okeru zetsu fushō no setsuwa ni tsuite 唐から宋における舌不焼の説話について" (On tales of the unburned tongue from the Tang to the Song). In Suwa 1997a, 328–331. Reprinted from *Aichi gakuin daigaku jinbun bunka kenkyūjo hō* 愛知学院大学人間文化研究所報 20 (December 1994).

———. 1997d. "Waga kuni setsuwa shū ni okeru zetsu fushō jukyō kara dokuro jukyō e no suii—Chūgoku no bukkyō setsuwa o tō shite わが国説話集における舌不焼誦経から髑髏誦経への推移—中国の仏教説話を通して" (The shift from unburned tongues that recite scripture to skulls that recite scripture in Japanese collections of tales—with reference to Chinese Buddhist tales). In Suwa 1997a, 332–348. Originally published in 1996 as "Waga kuni setsuwa shū ni mieru zetsu fushō jukyō kara dokuro jukyō e no suii わが国説話集に見える舌不焼誦経から髑髏誦経への推移" (The shift from unburned tongues that recite scripture to skulls that recite scripture as seen in Japanese collections of tales) in *Hotoke no kyōka—Butsudō gaku* 仏の教化―仏道学 (The teaching of the Buddha: Studies in Buddhist doctrine), 235–256, edited by Ujitani Yūken 宇治谷祐顕. Kyoto: Hōzōkan.

Tang Yongtong 湯用彤. 1997. *Han-Wei liang-Jin Nanbeichao fojiaoshi* 漢魏兩晉南北朝佛教史 (History of Buddhism during the Han, Wei, both Jin dynasties, and period of the Northern and Southern dynasties). Beijing: Beijing Daxue chuban she.

Tonami Mamoru 礪波護. 1999. *Zui-Tō no Bukkyō to Kokka* 隋唐の仏教と国家 (Sui-Tang Buddhism and the state). Tokyo: Chūō kōron sha.

Wang Bangwei 王邦維. 1995. *Nanhai jigui neifa zhuan jiaozhu* 南海寄歸內法傳校注 (An Account of the *Dharma* Sent Back from the Southern Seas, collated and annotated). Beijing: Zhonghua shuju.

Wang Jinglin 王景琳. 1991. *Zhongguo gudai siyuan shenghuo* 中國古代寺院生活 (Life in ancient Chinese monasteries). Xi'an: Xi'an xinhua yinshuachang.

Yagi Sentai 八木宣諦. 1981. "Chūgoku ni okeru Bukkyōsho sekkoku no keishiki ni tsuite 中国における仏教書石刻の形式について" (On the types of stone inscriptions of Buddhist writings in China). *Taishō daigaku sōgō Bukkyō kenkyūjo nenpō* 大正大学総合仏教研究所年報 3: 93–105.

———. 1982. "Sekkoku Bukkyō shiryō kenkyū 石刻仏教資料研究, 1" (A study of sources on Buddhism inscribed on stone, 1). *Taishō daigaku sōgō Bukkyō kenkyūjo nenpō* 大正大学総合仏教研究所年報 4: 65–81.

———. 1983. "Sekkoku Bukkyō shiryō kenkyū 石刻仏教資料研究, 1 (zoku 続)" (A study of sources on Buddhism inscribed on stone, 1 [continued]). *Taishō daigaku sōgō Bukkyō kenkyūjo nenpō* 大正大学総合仏教研究所年報 5: 53–72.

Yamabe Nobuyoshi 山部能宜. 2000. "*Bonmōkyō* ni okeru kōsōgyō no kenkyū 『梵網経』における好相行の研究" (Research on the cultivation of auspicious signs in the *Fanwang jing*). In *Chūgoku Bukkyō shisōshi* 中国仏教思想史 (Intellectual history of Chinese Buddhism), edited by Aramaki Noritoshi 荒牧典俊, 205–269. Kyoto: Hōzōkan.

Yan Yaozhong 嚴耀中. 1999. *Han chuan mijiao* 漢傳密教 (The Chinese transmission of esoteric teachings). Shanghai: Xuelin chubanshe.

Yoshikawa Tadao 吉川忠夫. 1992. "Nicchū muei—shikai sen kō 日中無影―尸解仙考" (Throwing no shadow at noon: Immortals delivered from the corpse). In his *Chūgoku ko dōkyō shi kenkyū* 日中国古道教史研究 (Studies on ancient Chinese Taoism). Kyoto: Dōhōsha.

Yu Jiaxi 余嘉錫. 1977 (1963). *Yu Jiaxi lunxue zazhu* 余嘉錫論學雜著 (Collected essays of Yu Jiaxi). 2 vols. Beijing: Zhonghua shuju.

Yu Lingbo 于凌波. 1995. *Zhongguo jin-xiandai fojiao renwu zhi* 中國近現代佛教人物

志 (Buddhist figures of modern and contemporary China). Beijing: Zongjiao wenhua chubanshe.

Zhang Yong 張勇. 2000. *Fu dashi yanjiu* 傅大士研究 (Research on Mahāsattva Fu).
Chengdu: Ba Shu shushe.

Zhang Zikai 張子開. 1999. "*Biquini zhuan* suojian Shu di niseng zhuanji ji yuyan-
xue jiazhi《比丘尼傳》所見蜀地尼僧傳記及其語言學價值 (Accounts of
nuns from Shu in *Biographies of Bhikṣuṇī* and their linguistic value). *Zongjiao yanjiu* 宗教研究 2: 69–75.

Zheng Yuqing 鄭郁卿. 1986. Gaoseng zhuan *yanjiu* 高僧傳研究 (Research on the
Gaoseng zhuan). Taipei: Wenjin chubanshe.

Secondary Studies in European Languages

Abbott, Terry Rae. 1986. "Vasubandhu's Commentary to the "Saddharma-
puṇḍarīka-sūtra": A Study of Its History and Significance." PhD diss., University of California, Berkeley.

App, Urs. 1994. *Master Yunmen: From the Record of the Chan Teacher "Gate of the
Clouds."* New York: Kodansha International.

Bapat, P. V., and A. Hirakawa. 1970. *Shan-chien-p'i-p'o-sha; a Chinese version by
Saṅghabhadra of Samantapāsādikā.* Poona: Bhandarkar Oriental Research
Institute.

Bareau, André. 1963. *Recherches sur la biographie du Buddha dans les Sūtrapiṭaka et
les Vinayapiṭaka anciens.* Paris: École Française d'Extrême-Orient.

———. 1975. "Les récits canoniques des funérailles du Buddha et leurs anomalies: Nouvel essai d'interprétation." *Bulletin de l'École Française d'Extrême-
Orient* 62: 151–190.

Barrett, T. H. 1990a. "Exploratory Observations on Some Weeping Pilgrims." In
The Buddhist Forum, edited by Tadeusz Skorupski, 99–110. London: School
of Oriental and African Studies.

———. 1990b. "Kill the Patriarchs!" In *The Buddhist Forum,* edited by Tadeusz
Skorupski, 87–97. London: School of Oriental and African Studies.

———. 1996. *Taoism under the T'ang: Religion and Empire during the Golden Age of
Chinese History.* London: Wellsweep.

———. 1998. "Did I-ching go to India? Problems in Using I-ching as a Source
on South Asian Buddhism." *Buddhist Studies Review* 15, no. 2: 142–156.

———. 2000. "Edwardian Theatre and the Lost Shape of Asia: Some Remarks
on Behalf of a Cinderella Subject." *East Asian History* 19: 87–102.

———. 2001. *The Rise and Spread of Printing: A New Account of Religious Factors.*
SOAS Working Papers in the Study of Religions. London: School of Oriental and African Studies, University of London.

———. 2004. "The Madness of Emperor Wuzong." *Cahiers d'Extrême-Asie* 14: 173–186.

———. 2005. "Buddhist Precepts in a Lawless World. Some Observations on the Linhuai Ordination Scandal." In *Going Forth: Visions of Buddhist Vinaya*, edited by William M. Bodiford, 101–123. Honolulu: University of Hawai'i Press.

BBC News. 1998. "New light on human torch mystery." http://news.bbc.co.uk/1/hi/uk/158853.stm.

Beal, Samuel. 1969 (1884). *Si-yu-ki: Buddhist Records of the Western World*. Delhi: Low Price Publications.

Benn, James A. 1998. "Where Text Meets Flesh: Burning the Body as an 'Apocryphal Practice' in Chinese Buddhism." *History of Religions* 37, no. 4: 295–322.

———. 2000. "Self-cultivation and Self-immolation: Preparing the Body for Auto-cremation in Chinese Buddhism." Paper read at annual meeting of the Association for Asian Studies, San Diego, March 9, 2000.

———. 2006. "Written in Flames: Self-immolation in Sixth-century Sichuan." *T'oung Pao*, 92, nos. 4–5, 117–172.

———. Forthcoming. "Another Look at the pseudo-Śūraṃgama sutra." In *Études d'apocryphes bouddhiques: Mélanges en l'honneur de Monsieur Makita Tairyō*, edited by Kuo Li-ying. Paris: École française d'Extrême-Orient.

Best, Jonathan W. 1991. "Tales of Three Paekche Monks Who Traveled Afar in Search of the Law." *Harvard Journal of Asiatic Studies* 51, no.1: 139–197.

Birnbaum, Raoul. 1979. *The Healing Buddha*. Boulder, Colo.: Shambala Press.

———. 1983. *Studies on the Mysteries of Mañjuśrī: A Group of East Asian Maṇḍalas and Their Traditional Symbolism*. N.p: Society for the Study of Chinese Religion.

———. 1984. "Thoughts on T'ang Buddhist Mountain Traditions and Their Context." *T'ang Studies* 2: 5–23.

———. 1986. "The Manifestation of a Monastery: Shen-ying's Experiences on Mount Wu-t'ai in T'ang Context." *Journal of the American Oriental Society* 106, no.1: 119–137.

———. 1989–1990. "Secret Halls of the Mountain Lords: The Caves of Wu-t'ai Shan." *Cahiers d'Extrême-Asie* 5: 115–140.

———. 2004. "Light in the Wutai Mountains." In *The Presence of Light: Divine Radiance and Religious Experience*, edited by Matthew T. Kapstein, 195–226. Chicago: University of Chicago Press.

Boltz, Judith Magee. 1993. "Not by the Seal of Office Alone: New Weapons in Battles with the Supernatural." In *Religion and Society in T'ang and Sung China*, edited by Patricia Buckley Ebrey and Peter N. Gregory, 241–305. Honolulu: University of Hawai'i Press.

Boodberg, Peter A. 1939. "Marginalia to the Histories of the Northern Dynasties." *Harvard Journal of Asiatic Studies* 4, nos. 3–4: 230–283.

Bray, Francesca, and Joseph Needham. 1984. *Science and Civilisation in China*. Vol. 6, *Biology and Biological Technology*, pt. 2, *Agriculture*. Cambridge: Cambridge University Press.

Brook, Timothy. 1993. *Praying for Power: Buddhism and the Formation of Gentry Society in Late-Ming China*. Cambridge, Mass.: Harvard University Press.

Brown, Peter Robert Lamont. 1981. *The Cult of the Saints: Its Rise and Function in Latin Christianity*. Chicago: University of Chicago Press.

Buswell, Robert E. 1992. *The Zen Monastic Experience: Buddhist Practice in Contemporary Korea*. Princeton: Princeton University Press.

———, and Robert M. Gimello, eds. 1992. *Paths to Liberation: The Mārga and Its Transformations in Buddhist Thought*. Honolulu: University of Hawai'i Press.

Bynum, Caroline Walker. 1987. *Holy Feast and Holy Fast: The Religious Significance of Food to Medieval Women*. Berkeley: University of California Press.

Campany, Robert Ford. 1991. "Notes on the Devotional Uses and Symbolic Functions of Sutra Texts as Depicted in Early Chinese Buddhist Miracle Tales and Hagiographies." *Journal of the International Association of Buddhist Studies* 14: 28–72.

———. 1993. "The Real Presence." *History of Religions* 32: 233–272.

———. 1996. *Strange Writing: Anomaly Accounts in Early Medieval China*. Albany, N.Y.: State University of New York Press.

———. 2002. *To Live as Long as Heaven and Earth: A Translation and Study of Ge Hong's Traditions of Divine Transcendents*. Berkeley: University of California Press.

———. 2005. "The Meanings of Cuisines of Transcendence in Late Classical and Early Medieval China." *T'oung Pao* 91, nos. 1–3: 1–57.

Camporesi, Piero. 1988. *The Incorruptible Flesh: Bodily Mutation and Mortification in Religion and Folklore*. Cambridge: Cambridge University Press.

Chang, Chung-Yuan. 1982. *Original Teachings of Ch'an Buddhism: Selected from The Transmission of the Lamp*. New York: Grove Press.

Chavannes, Édouard. 1910. *Cinq cents contes et apologues extrait du tripiṭaka Chinois*. Paris: Société Asiatique.

———. 1916. "Le royaume de Wu et de Yue." *T'oung Pao* 17: 129–264.

Chen Jinhua. 1998a. "The Construction of Early Tendai Esoteric Buddhism: The Japanese Provenance of Saichō's Transmission Documents and Three Esoteric Buddhist Apocrypha Attributed to Śubhākarasiṃha." *Journal of the International Association for Buddhist Studies* 21, no.1: 21–76.

———. 1998b. "The Stories from the Life of Chi-tsang and Their Use in T'ient'ai Sectarian Historiography." *Asia Major,* 3rd ser., 11, no.1: 53–98.

———. 1999a. *Making and Remaking History: A Study of Tiantai Sectarian Historiography*. Tokyo: The International Institute for Buddhist Studies.

———. 1999b. "One Name, Three Monks: Two Northern Chan Masters Emerge from the Shadow of Their Contemporary, the Tiantai Master Zhanran (711–782)." *Journal of the International Association of Buddhist Studies* 22, no.1: 1–91.

———. 2002a. *Monks and Monarchs, Kinship and Kingship: Tanqian in Sui Buddhism and Politics*. Kyoto: Italian School of East Asian Studies.

———. 2002b. "An Alternative View of the Meditation Tradition in China: Meditation in the Life and Works of Daoxuan (596–667)." *T'oung Pao* 88, nos. 4–5: 332–395.

———. 2002c. "Family Ties and Buddhist Nuns in Tang China." *Asia Major* 15, no. 2: 51–85.

———. 2002d. "Śarīra and Scepter: Empress Wu's Political Use of Buddhist Relics." *Journal of the International Association of Buddhist Studies* 25, nos. 1–2: 33–150.

———. 2004. "The Indian Buddhist Missionary Dharmakṣema (385–433): A New Dating of His Arrival in Guzang and of His Translations." *T'oung Pao* 90, nos. 4–5: 215–263.

———. 2006. "Buddhist Establishments within Liang Wudi's (r. 502–549) Imperial Park." In *Engaged Buddhism, Its History, Doctrines and Practices: Essays in Memory of Master Yinshun (1906–2005)*, edited by Chen Jinhua, Hsu Mu-chu, and Lori Meeks. Hua-lien: Ciji Daxue chubanshe.

———. Forthcoming. "*Pañcavārṣika* Assemblies in Liang Wudi's Buddhist Palace Chapel." *Harvard Journal of Asiatic Studies* 66, no. 1.

———. In preparation. Early Chinese Meditation and Vinaya Traditions (5th–7th Century): A Study of the Chandingsi, a Forgotten Buddhist Center from the Turn of the Sui and Tang Dynasties.

Ch'en, Kenneth. 1964. *Buddhism in China*. Princeton: Princeton University Press.

Chong, Key Ray. 1990. *Cannibalism in China*. Wakefield, N.H.: Longwood Academic.

Chou, Yi-liang. 1945. "Tantrism in China." *Harvard Journal of Asiatic Studies* 8, nos. 3–4: 241–332.

Cohen, Paul A. 1997. *History in Three Keys: The Boxers as Event, Experience, and Myth*. New York: Columbia University Press.

Cole, Alan. 1996. "Upside-down, Right side-up: A Revisionist History of Buddhist Funerals in China." *History of Religions* 35, no. 4: 307–338.

———. 1998. *Mothers and Sons in Chinese Buddhism*. Stanford: Stanford University Press.

———. 1999. "Homestyle Vinaya and Docile Boys in Chinese Buddhism." *Positions* 7, no. 1: 5–50.

Cooper, W. C., and Nathan Sivin. 1973. "Man as a Medicine: Pharmacological and Ritual Aspects of Traditional Therapy Using Drugs Derived from the Human Body." In *Chinese Science,* edited by Nakayama Shigeru and Nathan Sivin, 203–272. Cambridge, Mass.: The MIT Press.

Dalia, Albert. 1987. "The 'Political Career' of the Buddhist Historian Tsan-ning." In *Buddhist and Taoist Practice in Medieval Chinese Society,* edited by David W. Chappell, 146–180. Honolulu: University of Hawai'i Press.

Declercq, Dominik. 1998. *Writing Against the State: Political Rhetorics in Third and Fourth Century China.* Leiden: E. J. Brill.

de Groot, J. J. M. 1892–1910. *The Religious System of China, Its Ancient Forms, Evolution, History and Present Aspect, Manners, Customs and Social Institutions Connected Therewith.* Leiden: E. J. Brill.

———. 1893. *Le code du Mahāyāna en Chine: Son influence sur la vie monacale et sur le monde laïque.* Amsterdam: Johannes Müller.

———. 1903. *Sectarianism and Religious Persecution in China, a Page in the History of Religions.* Amsterdam: Johannes Müller.

Demiéville, Paul. 1973. "Momies d'Extrême-Orient." In his *Choix d'Études Sinologiques (1921–1970),* 407–432. Leiden: E. J. Brill.

———. 1984. *Poèmes Chinois d'Avant la Mort.* Paris: L'Asiathèque.

des Rotours, Robert. 1963. "Quelques notes sur l'anthropophagie en Chine." *T'oung Pao* 50, nos. 4–5: 386–427.

———. 1968. "Encore quelques notes sur l'anthropophagie en Chine." *T'oung Pao* 54, nos. 1–3: 1–49.

DeWoskin, Kenneth J. 1983. *Doctors, Diviners, and Magicians of Ancient China: Biographies of Fang-shih.* New York: Columbia University Press.

Dubs, Homer H. 1946. "Han Yü and the Buddha's Relic: An Episode in Medieval Chinese Religion." *The Review of Religion* 11: 5–17.

Dudbridge, Glen. 1995. *Religious Experience and Lay Society in T'ang China: A Reading of Tai Fu's Kuang-i chi.* Cambridge: Cambridge University Press.

———. 1998. "Buddhist Images in Action: Five Stories from the Tang." *Cahiers d'Extrême-Asie* 10: 377–391.

Durt, Hubert. 1994. *Problems of Chronology and Eschatology: Four Lectures on the Essay on Buddhism by Tominaga Nakamoto (1715–1746).* Kyoto: Scuola di Studi sull'Asia Orientale.

———. 1998. "Two Interpretations of Human-flesh Offering: Misdeed or Supreme Sacrifice." *Journal of the International College for Advanced Buddhist Studies* (*Kokusai Bukkyōgaku daigakuin daigaku kenkyū kiyō* 国際仏教学大学院大学研究紀要) 1: 236–210 (reverse pagination).

———. 1999. "The Offering of the Children of Prince Viśvantara/Sudāna in the Chinese Tradition." *Journal of the International College for Advanced Buddhist Studies* (*Kokusai Bukkyōgaku daigakuin daigaku kenkyū kiyō* 国際仏教学大学院大学研究紀要) 2: 147–82 (reverse pagination).

Eberhard, Wolfram. 1968. *The Local Cultures of South and East China.* Leiden: E. J. Brill.

Ebrey, Patricia Buckley. 1990. "Cremation in Sung China." *American Historical Review* 95, no. 2: 406–428.

Farmer, David Hugh. 1992. *The Oxford Dictionary of Saints.* Oxford: Oxford University Press.

Faure, Bernard. 1986. "Bodhidharma as Textual and Religious Paradigm." *History of Religions* 25, no. 3: 187–198.

———. 1991. *The Rhetoric of Immediacy: A Cultural Critique of Chan/Zen Buddhism.* Princeton: Princeton University Press.

———. 1993. *Chan Insights and Oversights: An Epistemological Critique of the Chan Tradition.* Princeton: Princeton University Press.

———. 1995. "Quand l'habit fait le moine: The symbolism of the *kāṣāya* in Chan/Zen Buddhism." *Cahiers d'Extrême Asie* 8: 335–369.

———. 1998. *The Red Thread: Buddhist Approaches to Sexuality.* Princeton: Princeton University Press.

Filliozat, Jean. 1963. "La mort voluntaire par le feu et la tradition Bouddhique Indienne." *Journal Asiatique* 251, no. 1: 21–51.

Fitzgerald, C. P. 1968. *The Empress Wu.* London: Cresset.

Fong, Wen. 1958. *The Lohans and a Bridge to Heaven.* Washington, D.C.: Smithsonian Institution.

Forte, Antonino. 1976. *Political Propaganda and Ideology in China at the End of the Seventh Century: Inquiry into the Nature, Authors and Function of the Tunhuang Document S. 6502, Followed by an Annotated Translation.* Napoli: Istituto Universitario Orientale.

———. 1995. *The Hostage An Shigao and His Offspring: An Iranian Family in China.* Kyoto: Istituto Italiano di Cultura, Scuola di Studi sull'Asia Orientale.

———. 2003. "On the Origin of the Purple Kāṣāya in China." In *Buddhist Asia 1: Papers from the First Conference of Buddhist Studies in Naples in May 2001,* edited by Giovanni Verardi and Silvio Vita, 145–166. Kyoto: Italian School of East Asian Studies.

Foulk, T. Griffith, and Robert H. Sharf. 1994. "On the Ritual Use of Ch'an Portraiture in Medieval China." *Cahiers d'Extrême-Asie* 7: 149–210.

Fujita, Kōtatsu. 1990. "The Textual Origins of the *Kuan Wu-Liang-shou ching:* A Canonical Scripture of Pure Land Buddhism." In *Chinese Buddhist Apocrypha,* edited by Robert E. Buswell, Jr., 149–173. Honolulu: University of Hawai'i Press.

Georgieva, Valentina. 1996. "Representation of Buddhist Nuns in Chinese Edifying Miracle Tales during the Six Dynasties and the Tang." *Journal of Chinese Religions* 24: 47–76.

Gernet, Jacques. 1960. "Les suicides par le feu chez les bouddhistes chinois de Ve au Xe siècle." *Mélanges Publiés par l'Institute des Hautes Études Chinoises* 2: 527–558.

———. 1995. *Buddhism in Chinese Society: An Economic History from the Fifth to the Tenth Centuries,* translated by Franciscus Verellen. New York: Columbia University Press.

———. 1996. *A History of Chinese Civilization.* Cambridge: Cambridge University Press.

Gjertson, Donald E. 1981. "The Early Chinese Buddhist Miracle Tale: A Preliminary Survey." *Journal of the American Oriental Society* 101, no. 3: 287–300.

———. 1989. *Miraculous Retribution: A Study and Translation of T'ang Lin's Ming-pao chi.* Berkeley: Centers for South and Southeast Asia Studies, University of California, Berkeley.

Goossaert, Vincent. 2002. "Starved of Resources: Clerical Hunger and Enclosures in Nineteenth-century China." *Harvard Journal of Asiatic Studies* 62, no. 1: 77–133.

Graham, A. C. 1989. *Chuang-tzu: The Inner Chapters.* London: Unwin.

Granoff, Phyllis. 1992. "The Violence of Non-violence: Jain Responses to Buddhist Vinaya Rules on Murder." *Journal of the International Association of Buddhist Studies* 15: 1–43.

Gregory, Peter N. 1983. "The Teaching of Men and Gods: The Doctrinal and Social Basis of Lay Buddhist Practice in the Hua-yen Tradition." In *Studies in Ch'an and Hua-yen,* edited by Robert M. Gimello and Peter N. Gregory, 253–319. Honolulu: University of Hawai'i Press.

———. 1991. *Tsung-mi and the Sinification of Buddhism.* Princeton: Princeton University Press.

Groner, Paul. 1984. *Saichō: The Establishment of the Japanese Tendai School.* Berkeley: Centers for South and Southeast Asian Studies, University of California, Berkeley.

———. 1990. "The *Fan-wang ching* and Monastic Discipline in Japanese Tendai: A Study of Annen's 'Futsū jubosatsukai kōshaku.'" In *Chinese Buddhist Apocrypha,* edited by Robert E. Buswell, Jr., 251–290. Honolulu: University of Hawai'i Press.

Guisso, Richard. 1979. "The Reigns of the Empress Wu, Chung-tsung and Jui-tsung (684-712)." In *The Cambridge History of China,* vol. 3, pt. 1, *Sui and T'ang China, 589–906,* edited by Denis Twitchett, 290–332. Cambridge: Cambridge University Press.

Hammond, Charles E. 1991. "An Excursion in Tiger Lore." *Asia Major*, 3rd ser., 4, no.1: 87–100.

Hartman, Charles. 1986. *Han Yü and the T'ang Search for Unity*. Princeton: Princeton University Press.

Hawkes, David, trans. 1985. *The Songs of the South: An Anthology of Ancient Chinese Poems by Qu Yuan and Other Poets*. Harmondsworth: Penguin Books.

Hirakawa, Akira, and Paul Groner. 1990. *A History of Indian Buddhism: From Śākyamuni to Early Mahāyāna*. Honolulu: University of Hawai'i Press.

Horner, I. B. 1938. *The Book of Discipline (Vinaya-pitaka)*. London: Oxford University Press.

Hou, Ching-lang. 1979. "The Chinese Belief in Baleful Stars." In *Facets of Taoism,* edited by Holmes Welch and Anna Seidel, 193–228 New Haven: Yale University Press.

Howard, Angela Falco. 2001. *Summit of Treasures: Buddhist Cave Art of Dazu, China*. Trumbull, Conn.: Weatherhill.

Hsiao, Bea-hui. 1995. "Two Images of Maitreya: Fu Hsi and Pu-tai Ho-shang." PhD diss., School of Oriental and African Studies, University of London.

Huang Chi-chiang. 1994. "Imperial Rulership and Buddhism in the Early Northern Sung." In *Imperial Rulership and Cultural Change in Traditional China,* edited by Frederick P. Brandauer and Chün-chieh Huang, 144–187. Seattle: University of Washington Press.

———. 1998. "Consecrating the Buddha: Legend, Lore, and History of the Imperial Relic-Veneration Ritual in the T'ang Dynasty." *Zhonghua foxue xuebao* 11: 483–533.

Huang, Yi-hsun. 2001. "A Study of Yongming Yanshou's *Profound Pivot of the Contemplation of the Mind*." PhD diss., University of Virginia, Charlottesville.

Hubbard, Jamie. 2001. *Absolute Delusion, Perfect Buddhahood: The Rise and Fall of a Chinese Heresy*. Honolulu: University of Hawai'i Press.

Huber, Édouard. 1908. *Aśvaghoṣa Sūtralaṃkāra*. Paris: Ernest Leroux.

Hucker, Charles O. 1985. *A Dictionary of Official Titles in Imperial China*. Stanford: Stanford University Press.

Hurvitz, Leon. 1956. "Wei Shou. Treatise on Buddhism and Taoism. An English Translation of the Original Chinese Text of Wei-shu CXIV and the Japanese Annotation of Tsukamoto Zenryū." In Vol. 16, *Unkō sekkutsu. Seireki go-seiki ni okeru Chūgoku hokubu Bukkyō kutsu-in no kōkogaku-teki chōsa hōkoku. Tōyō bunka kenkyū-sho chōsa Shōwa jūsan-nen Shōwa nijūnen* 雲崗石窟．西暦五世紀における中國北部佛教窟院の考古學的調査報告 ― 東方文化研究所調査昭和十三年 ― 昭和二十年 *(Yun-kang, the Buddhist Cave-Temples of the Fifth Century A.D. in North China. Detailed Report of the Archaeological Survey Carried Out by the Mission of the Tōyō bunka kenkyū-sho, 1938–*

1945), suppl., Mizuno Seiichi 水野清一 and Nagahiro Toshio 長廣敏雄, comps., 25–103. Kyoto: Jinbunkagaku kenkyū-sho, Kyoto University.

———. 1962. *Chih-i (538–597): An Introduction to the Life and Ideas of a Chinese Buddhist Monk.* Vol. 12, *Mélanges Chinois et Bouddhiques.* Brussels: Institut Belge des Hautes Etudes Chinoises.

———. 1976. *Scripture of the Lotus Blossom of the Fine Dharma.* New York: Columbia University Press.

Jan, Yün-hua. 1965. "Buddhist Self-Immolation in Medieval China." *History of Religions* 4: 243–265.

———. 1977. "The Power of Recitation: An Unstudied Aspect of Chinese Buddhism." *Studi Storico-religiosi* 1, no.2: 289–299.

———. 1988. "Portrait and Self-portrait: A Case Study of Biographical and Autobiographical Records of Tsung-mi." In *Monks and Magicians: Religious Biography in Asia,* edited by Phyllis Granoff and Koichi Shinohara, 229–245. Oakville, N.Y.: Mosaic Press.

Janousch, Andreas. 1999. "The Emperor as Bodhisattva: The Bodhisattva Ordination and Ritual Assemblies of Emperor Wu of the Liang Dynasty." In *State and Court Ritual in China,* edited by Joseph P. McDermott, 112–149. Cambridge: Cambridge University Press.

Kaltenmark, Max. 1987 (1953). *Le lie-sien tchouan (Biographies légendaires des immortels Taoïstes de l'antiquité).* Paris: Collège de France.

Kamata, Shigeo. 1996. "Buddhism during Koryŏ." In *Buddhism in Koryŏ: A Royal Religion,* edited by Lewis R. Lancaster, Kikun Suh, and Chai-shin Yu, 35–66. Berkeley: Center for Korean Studies, University of California, Berkeley.

Kanno, Hiroshi. 1994. "An Overview of Research on Chinese Commentaries of the *Lotus Sūtra.*" *Acta Asiatica, Bulletin of the Institute of Eastern Culture* 66: 87–103.

Karetzky, Patricia Eichenbaum. 2000. *Early Buddhist Narrative Art: Illustrations of the Life of the Buddha from Central Asia to China, Korea, and Japan.* Lanham, Md.: University Press of America.

Keys, David. 1999. *Catastrophe: An Investigation into the Origins of the Modern World.* London: Century.

Kieschnick, John. 1997. *The Eminent Monk: Buddhist Ideals in Medieval Chinese Hagiography.* Honolulu: University of Hawai'i Press.

———. 1999. "The Symbolism of the Monk's Robe in China." *Asia Major,* 3rd ser., 12, no. 1: 9–32.

———. 2000. "Blood Writing in China." *Journal of the International Association of Buddhist Studies* 23, no. 2: 177–194.

Kim, Young-ho. 1990. *Tao-sheng's Commentary on the* Lotus Sūtra: *A Study and Translation.* Albany: State University of New York Press.

King, Sallie. 2000. "They Who Burned Themselves for Peace: Quaker and Buddhist Self-Immolators during the Vietnam War." *Buddhist-Christian Studies* 20: 127–149.

Kleeman, Terry F. 1994. "Licentious Cults and Bloody Victuals: Sacrifice, Reciprocity, and Violence in Traditional China." *Asia Major,* 3rd ser., 7, no. 1: 185–211.

Kleine, Christoph. 1998. "Portraits of Pious Women in East Asian Buddhist Hagiography: A Study of Accounts of Women Who Attained Birth in Amida's Pure Land." *Bulletin de l'École Française d'Exrême-Orient* 85: 325–361.

Knapp, Keith. 2004. "Reverent Caring: The Parent-Son Relationship in Early Medieval Tales of Filial Offspring." In *Filial Piety in Chinese Thought and History,* edited by Alan K. L. Chan and Sor-hoon Tan, 44–70. London: RoutledgeCurzon Press.

Knechtges, David R. 1982. *Wen xuan, or, Selections of Refined Literature.* Vol. 1, *Rhapsodies on Metropolises and Capitals.* Princeton: Princeton University Press.

Kohn, Livia. 1993. *The Taoist Experience.* Albany: State University of New York Press.

———. 1995. *Laughing at the Tao: Debates among Buddhists and Taoists in Medieval China.* Princeton: Princeton University Press.

———, ed. 2000. *Daoism Handbook.* Leiden: Brill.

———, in cooperation with Yoshinobu Sakade, eds. 1989. *Taoist Meditation and Longevity Techniques.* Ann Arbor: Center for Chinese Studies, University of Michigan.

Kolb, Raimund. 1996. "Kannibalismus im vormodernen China." Review of *Cannibalism in China,* by Key Ray Chong. *Monumenta Serica* 44: 393–403.

Kuo, Liying. 1995. "La récitation des noms de *Buddha* en Chine et au Japon." *T'oung Pao* 81: 230–268.

Lamotte, Étienne. 1944–1981. *Le traité de la grande vertu de sagesse de Nāgārjuna (Mahāprajñāpāramitāśāstra).* 5 vols. Louvain-La-Neuve: Institut Orientaliste, Université de Louvain.

———. 1965. "Le suicide religieux dans le Bouddhisme ancien." *Academie Royale de Belgique, Bulletin de la Classe des Lettres et des Sciences Morales et Politiques* 51: 156–168.

———. 1975. "Mañjuśrī." *T'oung Pao* 48: 1–96.

———. 1987. "Religious Suicide in Early Buddhism." *Buddhist Studies Review* 4: 105–126.

La Vallée Poussin, Louis de. 1919. "Quelques observations sur le suicide dans le bouddhisme ancien." *Bulletin de la Classe des Lettres et Sciences Morales et Politiques, Academie de Belgique:* 683–693.

———. 1922. "Suicide (Buddhist)." In Vol. 12, *The Encyclopedia of Religion and Ethics,* edited by James Hastings, 24–26. Edinburgh: Clark.

————. 1929. "Les neuf kalpas qu'a franchis Sakyamuni pour devancer Maitreya." *T'oung Pao* 26: 17–25.

Legge, James. 1899. *The Sacred Books of China. The Texts of Confucianism, Part One: The Shu King, The Religious Portions of the Shih King, The Hsiao King.* Oxford: Clarendon Press.

————. 1970. *The Works of Mencius.* New York: Dover.

————. 1991 (1935). *The Chinese Classics: With a Translation, Critical and Exegetical Notes, Prolegomena, and Copious Indexes.* 5 vols. Taipei: SMC Publishing.

Lévi, Jean. 1983. "L'abstinence des céréales chez les Taoïstes." *Études Chinoises* 1: 3–47.

Levy, Howard S. 1955. *Biography of Huang Ch'ao: Translated and Annotated.* Berkeley: Institute of East Asiatic Studies, University of California.

Lingat, Robert. 1965. "Les suicides religieux au Siam." In Vol. 1 of *Felicitation Volume of Southeast Asian Studies Presented to His Highness Prince Dhanninivat Kromanmany Bidyalabh Bridhyakorn,* 71–75. Bangkok: Siam Society.

Link, Arthur. 1958. "Biography of Shih Tao-an." *T'oung Pao* 46: 1–48.

Lippiello, Tiziana. 2001. *Auspicious Omens and Miracles in Ancient China: Han, Three Kingdoms and Six Dynasties.* Sankt Augustin; Nettetal: Steyler Verlag: Monumenta Serica Institute.

Liu, Hsin-ju (Xinru). 1988. *Ancient India and Ancient China: Trade and Religious Exchanges, A.D. 1–600.* Delhi: Oxford University Press.

Liu, Shufen. 2000. "Death and the Degeneration of Life: Exposure of the Corpse in Medieval Chinese Buddhism." *Journal of Chinese Religions* 28: 1–30.

Lopez, Donald S., Jr. 2005. "Buddha." In *Critical Terms for the Study of Buddhism,* edited by Donald S. Lopez, Jr., 13–36. Chicago: University of Chicago Press.

Luk, Charles (Lu Kuan Yü). 1966. *The Surangama Sutra (Leng Yen Ching).* London: Rider.

MacGowan, Daniel Jerome. 1889. *Papers on Self-Immolation by Fire, and on the Avenging Habits of the Cobra.* Shanghai: Kelly and Walsh; San Francisco: Bancroft.

Magnin, Paul. 1979. *La vie et l'œuvre de Huisi (515–577): Les origines de la secte Bouddhique Chinoise du Tiantai.* Paris: École Française d'Extrême-Orient (Dépositaire: Adrien-Maisonneuve).

Mair, Victor H. 1994. *The Columbia Anthology of Traditional Chinese Literature.* New York: Columbia University Press.

McCutcheon, Russell T. 1997. *Manufacturing Religion: The Discourse on Sui Generis Religion and the Politics of Nostalgia.* Oxford: Oxford University Press.

Molè, Gabriella. 1970. *The T'u-yü-hun from the Northern Wei to the Time of the Five Dynasties.* Edited by Giuseppe Tucci. Rome: Instituto Italiano per il Medio ad Estremo Oriente.

Morrell, Robert E. 1985. *Sand and Pebbles (Shasekishū): The Tales of Mujū Ichien, a*

Voice for Pluralism in Kamakura Buddhism. Albany: State University of New York Press.

Nakamura, Hajime. 1980. *Indian Buddhism: A Survey with Bibliographical Notes.* Hirakata: Kansai University of Foreign Studies.

Needham, Joseph, with Kenneth Girdwood Robinson and Wang Ling. 1962. *Science and Civilisation in China.* Vol. 4, *Physics,* pt. 1, *Physics and Physical Technology.* Cambridge: Cambridge University Press.

———, with Lu Gwei-Djen and Huang Hsing-Tsung (Huang Xingzong). 1986. *Science and Civilisation in China.* Vol. 6, *Biology and Biological Technology,* pt. 1, *Botany.* Cambridge: Cambridge University Press.

———, with Christian Daniels and Nicholas K. Menzies. 1996. *Science and Civilisation in China.* Vol. 6, *Biology and Biological Technology,* pt. 3, *Agro-Industries and Forestry.* Cambridge: Cambridge University Press.

Ohnuma, Reiko. 1997. "Dehadāna: The 'Gift of the Body' in Indian Buddhist Narrative Literature." PhD diss., University of Michigan, Ann Arbor.

———. 1998. "The Gift of the Body and the Gift of the Dharma." *History of Religions* 37, no. 4: 323–359.

Orzech, Charles D. 1994. "Provoked Suicide and the Victim's Behavior." In *Curing Violence,* edited by Mark I. Wallace and Theophus H. Smith, 137–160. Sonoma, Calif.: Polebridge Press.

Parlier, Edith. 1991. "La légende du roi des Śibi: Du sacrifice Brahmanique au don du corps Bouddhique." *Bulletin d'Études Indiennes* 9: 133–160.

Pas, Julian. 1987. "Dimensions in the Life and Thought of Shan-tao (613–681)." In *Buddhist and Taoist Practice in Medieval Chinese Society: Buddhist and Taoist Studies II,* edited by David W. Chappell, 65–84. Honolulu: University of Hawai'i Press.

Pearce, Scott. 2000. "Who, and What, Was Hou Jing?" *Early Medieval China* 6: 49–73.

Pelliot, Paul. 1912. Review of *Jade,* by Berthold Laufer. *T'oung Pao* 13: 433–446.

Penkower, Linda. 2000. "In the Beginning . . . Guanding 灌頂 (561–632) and the Creation of Early Tiantai." *Journal of the International Association of Buddhist Studies* 23, no. 2: 245–296.

Penny, Benjamin. 2000. "Immortality and Transcendence." In *Daoism Handbook,* edited by Livia Kohn, 109–133. Leiden: Brill.

Poo, Mu-chou. 1995. "The Images of Immortals and Eminent Monks: Religious Mentality in Early Medieval China." *Numen* 42: 225–248.

Prip-Møller, Johannes. 1967. *Chinese Buddhist Monasteries: Their Plan and Its Function as a Setting for Buddhist Monastic Life.* Hong Kong: Hong Kong University Press.

Pulleyblank, E. G. 1960. "Neo-Confucianism and Neo-legalism in T'ang Intellectual Life, 755–805." In *The Confucian Persuasion,* edited by Arthur F. Wright, 77–114. Stanford: Stanford University Press.

Raveri, Massimo. 1992. *Il corpo e il paradiso.* Venezia: Marsilio.

Ray, Reginald. 1994. *Buddhist Saints in India: A Study in Buddhist Values and Orientations.* Oxford: Oxford University Press.

Rhie, Marylin M. 1977. *The Fo-kuang ssu: Literary Evidences and Buddhist Images.* New York: Garland Publishing.

———. 1999. *Early Buddhist Art of China and Central Asia.* Leiden: Brill.

Robinet, Isabelle. 1979. "Metamorphosis and Deliverance from the Corpse in Taoism." *History of Religions* 19: 37–70.

———. 1997. *Taoism: Growth of a Religion.* Translated by Phyllis Brooks. Stanford: Stanford University Press.

Rockhill, William Woodville, Ernst Leumann, and Bunyiu Nanjio. 1972. *The Life of the Buddha and the Early History of His Order, Derived from Tibetan Works in the Bkah-hgyur and Bstan-hgyur, Followed by Notices on the Early History of Tibet and Khoten.* Varanasi: Orientalia Indica.

Saddhatissa, H. 1975. *The Birth-stories of the Ten Bodhisattas and the Dasabodhisattuppattikathā: Being a Translation and Edition of the Dasabodhisattuppattikathā.* London: Pali Text Society.

Sakade, Yoshinobu. 1992. "Sun Simiao et le Bouddhisme." *Kansai Daigaku bungaku ronshū* 関西大学文学論集 42, no. 1: 81–98.

Salazar, Christine. 2000. *The Treatment of War Wounds in Graeco-Roman Antiquity.* Leiden: Brill.

Schafer, Edward. 1963. *The Golden Peaches of Samarkand: A Study of T'ang Exotics.* Berkeley: University of California Press.

Schober, Juliane, ed. 1997. *Sacred Biographies in the Buddhist Traditions of South and Southeast Asia.* Honolulu: University of Hawai'i Press.

Schopen, Gregory. 1987. "Burial *Ad Sanctos* and the Physical Presence of the Buddha in Early Indian Buddhism: A Study in the Archeology of Religions." *Religion* 17: 193–225.

———. 1997. *Bones, Stones, and Buddhist Monks: Collected Papers on the Archaeology, Epigraphy, and Texts of Monastic Buddhism in India.* Honolulu: University of Hawai'i Press.

Shaffer, Lynda Norene. 1997. "A Concrete Panoply of Intercultural Exchange: Asia in World History." In *Asia in Western and World History,* edited by Ainslee T. Embree and Carol Gluck, 810–866. Armonk, N.Y.: M. E. Sharpe.

Sharf, Robert H. 1992. "The Idolization of Enlightenment: On the Mummification of Ch'an Masters in Medieval China." *History of Religions* 32, no. 1: 1–31.

———. 2002. *Coming to Terms with Chinese Buddhism: A Reading of the* Treasure

Store Treatise. Kuroda Studies in East Asian Buddhism, no. 14. Honolulu: University of Hawai'i Press.

Shih, Heng-ching. 1992. *The Syncretism of Ch'an and Pure Land Buddhism.* New York: Peter Lang.

Shih, Robert. 1968. *Biographies des moines éminentes (Kao seng tchouan) de Houei-kiao.* Louvain: Institut Orientaliste, Université de Louvain.

Shinohara, Koichi. 1988. "Two Sources of Chinese Buddhist Biographies: Stupa Inscriptions and Miracle Stories." In *Monks and Magicians: Religious Biographies in Asia,* edited by Phyllis Granoff and Koichi Shinohara, 119–228. Oakville, N.Y.: Mosaic Press.

———. 1990. "Dao-xuan's Collection of Miracle Stories about 'Supernatural Monks' (Shen-seng gan-tong lu): An Analysis of Its Sources." *Zhonghua foxue xuebao* 中華佛學學報 3: 319–376.

———. 1991. "The Maitreya Image in Shicheng and Guanding's Biography of Zhiyi." In *From Benares to Beijing: Essays on Buddhism and Chinese Religion in Honour of Prof. Jan Yün-Hua,* edited by Koichi Shinohara and Gregory Schopen, 203–228. Oakville, ON.: Mosaic Press.

———. 1992. "Guanding's Biography of Zhiyi, the Fourth Chinese Patriarch of the Tiantai Tradition." In *Speaking of Monks,* edited by Koichi Shinohara and Phyllis Granoff, 97–232. Oakville, ON.: Mosaic Press.

———. 1994. "'Biographies of Eminent Monks' in Comparative Perspective: The Function of the Holy in Medieval Chinese Buddhism." *Zhonghua foxue xuebao* 7: 477–498.

———. 1998a. "Dynastic Politics and Miraculous Images: The Example of Zhuli of the Changlesi Temple in Yangzhou." In *Images, Miracles and Authority in Asian Religious Traditions,* edited by Richard H. Davis, 189–206. Boulder, Colo.: Westview Press.

———. 1998b. "Evolution of Chan Biographies of Eminent Monks." *Bulletin de l'École Française d'Extrême-Orient* 85: 305–324.

Somers, Robert M. 1979. "The End of the T'ang." In *The Cambridge History of China,* vol. 3, pt. 1, *Sui and T'ang China, 589–906,* edited by Denis Twitchett, 682–789. Cambridge: Cambridge University Press.

Soper, Alexander C. 1960. "A Vacation Glimpse of the T'ang Temples of Ch'ang-an: The *Ssu-t'a chi* by Tuan Ch'eng-shih." *Artibus Asiae* 23: 15–40.

———, and Seigai Ōmura. 1959. *Literary Evidence for Early Buddhist Art in China.* Ascona: Artibus Asiae.

Sørensen, Henrik H. 1988. "The Life and Times of the Ch'an Master Yun-men Wen-yen." *Acta Orientalia* 49: 105–131.

Soymié, Michel. 1961. "Sources et sourciers en Chine." *Bulletin de la Maison Franco-Japonaise,* n.s., 7, no. 1: 1–56.

Stein, R. A. 1990. *The World in Miniature: Container Gardens and Dwellings in Far Eastern Religious Thought.* Translated by Phyllis Brooks. Stanford: Stanford University Press.

Stevenson, Daniel. 1995. "Tales of the *Lotus Sutra.*" In *Buddhism in Practice,* edited by Donald S. Lopez, 427–451. Princeton: Princeton University Press.

Strickmann, Michel. 1996. *Mantras et mandarins: Le Bouddhisme tantrique en Chine.* Paris: Gallimard.

Strong, John. 1983. *The Legend of King Aśoka: A Study and Translation of the Aśokāvadāna.* Princeton: Princeton University Press.

———. 1992. *The Legend and Cult of Upagupta: Sanskrit Buddhism in North India and Southeast Asia.* Princeton: Princeton University Press.

———. 2004. *Relics of the Buddha.* Princeton: Princeton University Press.

Takakusu, Junjiro. 1896. *Record of the Buddhist Religion as Practised in India and the Malay Archipelago (A.D. 671–695) by I-tsing.* London: Clarendon Press.

Tanabe, George J., and Willa Jane Tanabe, eds. 1989. *The Lotus Sutra in Japanese Culture.* Honolulu: University of Hawai'i Press.

Teiser, Stephen F. 1988a. *The Ghost Festival in Medieval China.* Princeton: Princeton University Press.

———. 1988b. "'Having once died and returned to life': Representations of Hell in Medieval China." *Harvard Journal of Asiatic Studies* 48, no. 2: 433–464.

ter Haar, Barend J. 1999. *The White Lotus Teachings in Chinese Religious History.* Honolulu: University of Hawai'i Press.

T'ien, Ju-K'ang. 1990. "The Decadence of Buddhist Temples in Fu-chien in Late Ming and Early Ch'ing." In *Development and Decline of Fukien Province in the 17th and 18th Centuries,* edited by E. B. Vermeer, 83–100. Leiden: Brill.

Tonami, Mamoru. 1990. *The Shaolin Monastery Stele on Mount Song.* Translated by P. A. Herbert, edited by Antonino Forte. Kyoto: Instituto Italiano di Cultura Scuola di Studi sull'Asia Orientale.

Tsai, Kathryn Ann. 1994. *Lives of the Nuns: Biographies of Chinese Buddhist Nuns from the Fourth to Sixth Centuries: A Translation of the* Pi-ch'iu-ni chuan *Compiled by Shih Pao-ch'ang.* Honolulu: University of Hawai'i Press.

Tsukamoto Zenryū. 1985. *A History of Early Chinese Buddhism: From Its Introduction to the Death of Hui-yüan.* Translated by Leon Hurvitz. Tokyo: Kodansha International.

Twitchett, Denis Crispin. 1992. *The Writing of Official History under the T'ang.* Cambridge: Cambridge University Press.

———. 1994. "The T'ang Imperial Family." *Asia Major,* 3rd ser., 7, no. 2: 1–61.

Verellen, Franciscus. 1989. "Liturgy and Sovereignty: The Role of Taoist Ritual in the Foundation of the Shu Kingdom (907–925)." *Asia Major,* 3rd ser., 2, no. 1: 59–78.

von Falkenhausen, Lothar. 1998. "Archaeology and the Study of Chinese Local Religion: A Discussant's Remarks." *Cahiers d'Extrême-Asie* 10: 411–425.

Wang, Eugene Yuejin. 2005. *Shaping the Lotus Sutra: Buddhist Visual Culture in Medieval China.* Seattle: University of Washington Press.

Ware, James R. 1966. *Alchemy, Medicine and Religion in the China of A.D. 320: The Nei P'ien of Ko Hung.* Cambridge, Mass.: The MIT Press.

Watson, Burton. 1961. *Records of the Grand Historian of China: Translated from the Shih chi of Ssu-ma Ch'ien.* Vol. 1, *Early Years of the Han Dynasty 209–141 B.C.* New York: Columbia University Press.

Wechsler, Howard J. 1976. "The Founding of the T'ang Dynasty: Kao-tsu (reign 618-26)." In *The Cambridge History of China,* vol. 3, pt.1, *Sui and T'ang China, 589–906,* edited by Denis Twitchett, 150–187. Cambridge: Cambridge University Press.

Weidner, Marsha Smith, ed. 1994. *Latter Days of the Law: Images of Chinese Buddhism, 850–1850.* Lawrence, Kans.: Spencer Museum of Art, University of Kansas, and Honolulu: University of Hawai'i Press.

Weinberger-Thomas, Catherine. 1999. *Ashes of Immortality: Widow-Burning in India.* Translated by Jeffrey Mehlman and David Gordon White. Chicago: University of Chicago Press.

Weinstein, Stanley. 1987. *Buddhism under the T'ang.* Cambridge: Cambridge University Press.

Welch, Holmes. 1967. *The Practice of Chinese Buddhism.* Cambridge, Mass.: Harvard University Press.

Welter, Albert. 1988. "The Contextual Study of Chinese Buddhist Biographies: The Example of Yung-ming Yen-shou (904–975)." In *Monks and Magicians: Religious Biographies in Asia,* edited by Phyllis Granoff and Koichi Shinohara, 247–268. Oakville, ON.: Mosaic Press.

———. 1993. *The Meaning of Myriad Good Deeds: A Study of Yung-ming Yen-shou and the* Wan-shan t'ung-kuei chi. New York: P. Lang.

———. 1995. "Zanning and Chan: The Changing Nature of Buddhism in Early Song China." *Journal of Chinese Religions* 23: 105–140.

———. 1999. "A Buddhist Response to the Confucian Revival: Tsan-ning and the Debate over *Wen* in the Early Sung." In *Buddhism in the Sung,* edited by Peter N. Gregory and Daniel A. Getz, 21–61. Honolulu: University of Hawai'i Press.

Willemen, Charles, trans. 1994. *The Storehouse of Sundry Valuables.* Berkeley: Numata Center for Buddhist Translation and Research.

Wilson, Liz. 1996. *Charming Cadavers: Horrific Figurations of the Feminine in Indian Buddhist Hagiographic Literature.* Chicago: University of Chicago Press.

———. 2003. "Human Torches of Enlightenment: Autocremation and Spontaneous Combustion as Marks of Sanctity in South Asian Buddhism." In *The Living and the Dead: Social Dimensions of Death in South Asian Religions,* edited by Liz Wilson, 29–50. Albany: State University of New York Press.

Worthy, Edmund H. 1983. "Diplomacy for Survival: Domestic and Foreign Relations of Wu Yüeh, 907–978." In *China Among Equals,* edited by Morris Rossabi, 17–44. Berkeley: University of California Press.

Wright, Arthur. 1954. "Biography and Hagiography: Hui-chiao's *Lives of Eminent Monks.*" In *Silver Jubilee Volume of the Zinbun-Kagaku-Kenkyusyo, Kyoto University,* 383–432. Kyoto: Kyoto University and Jimbun kagaku kenkyū-sho.

———. 1973. "T'ang T'ai-tsung and Buddhism." In *Perspectives on the T'ang,* edited by Denis Twitchett and Arthur F. Wright, 239–263. New Haven: Yale University Press.

———. 1976. "The Sui Dynasty (581–617)." In *The Cambridge History of China,* vol. 3, pt. 1, *Sui and T'ang China, 589–906,* edited by Denis Twitchett, 49–149. Cambridge: Cambridge University Press.

Wu, Fusheng. 2003. "Composed at Execution: A Look at Three 'Poems Composed upon Confronting the End (*Linzhong shi*).'" *Early Medieval China* 9: 105–126.

Wu Hung. 1989. *The Wu Liang Shrine: The Ideology of Early Chinese Pictorial Art.* Stanford: Stanford University Press.

Xiong, Victor Cunrui. 2000. *Sui-Tang Chang'an: A Study in the Urban History of Medieval China.* Ann Arbor: Center for Chinese Studies, University of Michigan.

Xu, Pingfang. 1998. "Les découvertes récentes de statues de Sengqie et le culte de Sengqie." *Cahiers d'Extrême-Asie* 10: 393–410.

Yamabe, Nobuyoshi. 2005. "Visionary Repentence and Visionary Ordination in the Brahmā Net Sūtra." In *Going Forth: Visions of Buddhist Vinaya,* edited by William M. Bodiford, 17–39. Honolulu: University of Hawai'i Press.

Yamada, Isshi. 1989 (1968). *Karuṇāpuṇḍarīka: The White Lotus of Compassion.* New Delhi: Heritage Publishers.

Yamada, Toshiaki. 1989. "Longevity Techniques and the Compilation of the *Lingbao Wufuxu.*" In *Taoist Meditation and Longevity Techniques,* edited by Livia Kohn, 99–124. Ann Arbor: Center for Chinese Studies, University of Michigan.

Yampolsky, Philip B. 1967. *The Platform Sutra of the Sixth Patriarch.* New York: Columbia University Press.

Young, Stuart Hawley. 2000. "The Dragon Tree, the Middle Way, and the Middle Kingdom: Images of the Indian Patriarch Nāgārjuna in Chinese Buddhism." Master's thesis, School of Oriental and African Studies, University of London.

Yü, Chün-fang. 1981. *The Renewal of Buddhism in China: Chu-hung and the Late Ming Synthesis*. New York: Columbia University Press.

———. 1998. "Buddhism in the Ming." In Vol. 8 of *The Cambridge History of China*, edited by Frederick Mote and Dennis Twitchett, 893–952. Cambridge: Cambridge University Press.

———. 2001. *Kuan-yin: The Chinese Transformation of Avalokiteśvara*. New York: Columbia University Press.

Zürcher, Erik. 1959. *The Buddhist Conquest of China: The Spread and Adaptation of Buddhism in Early Medieval China*. Leiden: Brill.

———. 1980. "Buddhist Influence on Early Taoism." *T'oung Pao* 66, nos. 1–3: 84–147.

———. 1982a. "Perspectives in the Study of Chinese Buddhism." *Journal of the Royal Asiatic Society* 2: 161–176.

———. 1982b. "'Prince Moonlight.' Messianism and Eschatology in Early Medieval Chinese Buddhism." *T'oung Pao* 68, nos. 1–3: 1–75.

Index

abandoning the body, 7, 57, 100, 135, 150, 193; as category for monastic biographies, 21–22, 25; Chapter on, 34, 206; defined, 9; Eulogy on, 83. *See also* self-immolation; *sheshen; wangshen; yishen*

Adhimukta, 301n. 97

*Āgama*s, 161, 253, 258

Alexander the Great (356–323 BCE), 263n. 29

Ambara, King, 95

Amitābha, 98, 137, 157, 174, 182, 188, 216, 217, 230, 309n. 11

Amituo jing (*Sukhāvatī[amṛta] vyūha*), 98, 216

Ānanda, 51, 130

An Shigao (d. late second or early third century), 65, 143–144, 292n. 51

Anthony of Padua (ca. 1193–1231), 70

anuttarasamyaksambodhi, 60–61, 122

apocryphal *sūtra*s, 8, 11, 112

arhats, 99, 159, 166, 180, 183–184, 248, 250, 274n. 135

arms, burning of, 9, 63, 65–67, 85–87, 113, 117, 124, 130, 139, 154, 160, 165, 174, 175, 176, 198, 213, 218, 229, 250, 264n. 45; in the *Lotus Sūtra*, 60–61, 115, 146

ascetic practice, 33, 140, 192, 213, 272n. 100, 310n. 32; of non-Buddhists, 11, 118, 128, 197, 263n. 31, 286n. 58; self-immolation as, 81, 113, 130, 169, 196

ascetics, 84–85, 92–93, 97, 101, 129, 209, 217, 233

Aśoka, King, 67, 68, 75, 161, 244, 258, 276n. 44

Aśvaghoṣa, 93

auto-cremation: definition of, 8–10; early cases of, 33–45; faked, 16–17; and female pollution, 181, 299n. 53; and images, 75, 242, 272n. 98; by non-Buddhists, 196; by nuns, 42–45, 52, 166, 169–170; objections to, 197–198; preparations for, 36–40, 59; scholarship on, 8, 269n. 63; as Sinitic Buddhist creation, 11; as transformation of the body, 47–48

*avadāna*s, 69, 81, 95, 108, 200, 268n. 46, 310n. 25

Avalokiteśvara, 63, 69. *See also* Guanyin

Bakkula, 152, 294n. 89

Ban Gu (32–92), 265n. 14

Baochang (463–after 514), 19–25, 45, 52, 53, 78, 202, 264–265, 282n. 17

Baogui (d. after 597), 106, 284n. 8

Baohai (474–after 559), 123, 211, 304n. 38

Baopuzi (The Master Who Embraces Simplicity), 32

Baotuan (512–561), 210

Beflowered by the King of Constellations (Xiuwanghua, Nakṣatrarāja-samkusumitābhijña), 58, 61

Bhadra (Fotuo, d.u.), 3, 261n. 6

Bhaiṣajyagururāja. *See* Medicine King, Bodhisattva

Biographies of Eminent Monks. See *Gaoseng zhuan*

Biqiuni zhuan (Biographies of Bhikṣunīs), 19, 22, 203–205, 264n. 3, 275n. 24

Birnbaum, Raoul, 263n. 37, 295n. 110

blood, 15, 26, 81, 108, 137–138, 142,

347

About the Author

JAMES A. BENN received his doctorate in Chinese Buddhism from the University of California, Los Angeles. He has written a number of articles on aspects of medieval Chinese Buddhism, such as self-immolation, apocryphal literature, and tea. He is currently assistant professor in the Department of Religious Studies at McMaster University. Previously he taught at Arizona State University. *Burning for the Buddha* is his first book.

Production Notes for Benn / *Burning for the Buddha*

Jacket design by Santos Barbasa Jr.

Text design by University of Hawai'i press production staff with text in New Baskerville and display in Papryus

Composition by inari information services

Printing and binding by the Maple-Vail Book Manufacturing Group

Printed on 60 lb. Glatfelter Offset B18, 420 ppi